1973

DISCARD

What's What
in
SPORTS

™

What's What™
in
SPORTS

The Visual Glossary of the Sports World

Reginald Bragonier Jr.
and
David Fisher

HAMMOND®
INCORPORATED
MAPLEWOOD, NEW JERSEY   07040-1396

Printed in the United States of America

Library of Congress Cataloging in Publication Data

Fisher, David, 1946-
   What's what in sports.

   Includes index.
   1. Sports—Dictionaries. I. Bragonier, Reginald.
II. Title.
GV567.F58   1984   796'.03   84-9032
ISBN 8-8437-3528-7 hardcover
ISBN 0-8437-3529-5 softcover

WHO'S WHO IN WHAT'S WHAT ™

EDITORS
Reginald Bragonier Jr., David Fisher

MANAGING EDITOR
Sandra Roemer Dorfman

SENIOR RESEARCH EDITOR
Glenn Deutsch

ASSOCIATE RESEARCH EDITORS
Stephanie Bernardo, Deborah Friedman, Robert Henry,
Dana Keeler, Marion Ratner, Shane Mitchell

DESIGN & PRODUCTION
Barnett Design Group

PROJECT MANAGER
Dennis Peter Barnett

DESIGN DIRECTOR
David Barnett

DESIGNER
Donna Moll

ASSOCIATE DESIGNERS
Jan Cain, Derek Fox, Patrick Weisel

ILLUSTRATOR
Claire Seiffert

NAUTICAL ILLUSTRATOR
Steven Davis

CONTRIBUTING PHOTOGRAPHERS
Nancie Battaglia, Steve Borowski, Rich Clarkson,
Joe DiMaggio/JoAnne Kalish, Guy Gurney,
Walter Iooss, Al Messerschmidt, Brent Nicastro,
Eduardo Patino, Phillip Stark, Strobe Studio

SEQUENTIAL PHOTOGRAPHY
Globus Brothers Studio

MOTION PHOTOGRAPHY
Ben Rose and Globus Brothers Studio

TYPOGRAPHY
Expertype, Inc.

851802

TABLE OF CONTENTS

Aerial Sports	1
Aerobatics	1
Air Racing	4
Ballooning	5
Gliding/Hang Gliding	6
Sky Diving	7
Angling	8
Basic Fishing Equipment	9
Flycasting	10
Spin Casting	12
Trolling	13
Surf Fishing	14
Deep Sea Fishing	15
*Archery	16
Automobile Racing	17
Indy Car/Formula Car	17
Drag Racing	20
Stock and Sports Car	22
Badminton	23
Baseball	24
Field/Diamond	25
Equipment	26
Batting	27
Pitching	28
*Basketball	30
*Bobsledding	34
Bocce	35
Bodybuilding/Physique	36
Bowling	38
*Boxing/Prize Fighting	40
Strategies and Fouls	43
*Canoeing and Kayaking	44
Canoeing	44
Kayaking	45
Whitewater Slalom	46
Cricket	47
Croquet	49
Curling	50
*Cycling	51
Darts	53

*Diving	54
Pool/Tank	54
Components of a Dive	55
Basic Dives	56
Diving/Spear Fishing	58
Dog Racing	59
*Equestrian Sports	61
Show Jumping	61
Dressage	63
Eventing	64
*Fencing	65
*Field Hockey	68
*Figure Skating	70
Compulsory Figures	71
Freestyle	72
Ice Dancing	74
Football	75
Field	76
Plays and Areas	77
Passing	78
Equipment	79
Officials	80
Gaelic Football	81
Golf	82
Swing	83
Equipment	84
Clubs	85
Putting and Scoring	86
*Gymnastics	87
Basic Movements/Tumbling	88
Floor Exercises and Rhythmic Exercises	90
Vaulting	92
Pommel Horse/Side Horse	93
Rings/Still Rings	94
Horizontal Bar/High Bar	95
Parallel Bars	96
Uneven Parallel Bars/Asymmetrical Bars	97
Balance Beam	98

Handball/Court Handball	99
*Handball/Team Handball	100
Horse Racing	101
Thoroughbred and Quarter Horse Racing	102
Harness Racing	103
Horseshoes/Horseshoe Pitching	105
Hurling	106
Iceboating	107
*Ice Hockey	108
Equipment and Positions	110
Officials' Signals	111
Jai Alai/Pelota	112
Karting	114
Lacrosse	115
Lawn Bowling	117
*Luge	118
Martial Arts	119
Karate	120
*Judo	123
Aikido	124
Kung Fu	125
Striking Points	126
Kendo	128
Motorcycling	129
Roadracing Bike	130
Motocross	131
Orienteering	132
Platform Tennis	133
Polo	134
Racquetball	136
Rodeo	137
Roller Skating	139
Artistic	139
Speed Skating and Roller Hockey	140
*Rowing	141
Sculling	141
Sweep Rowing	142

Rugby **143**
*Shooting **144**
   Rifle Shooting **144**
   Pistol Shooting **145**
   Trap and Skeet Shooting... **146**
Shuffleboard **148**
Skateboarding **149**
*Skiing..................... **150**
   Alpine Skiing **150**
   Nordic Skiing **153**
   Biathlon................. **154**
*Soccer/Association Football .. **155**
   Field and Positions........ **156**
   Officials' Signals **157**
Softball **158**
*Speed Skating **159**
Squash Racquets/Squash..... **160**
Surfing.................... **161**
*Swimming.................. **162**
   Synchronized Swimming ... **162**
   Racing **163**
   Basic Strokes **164**
Table Tennis/Ping Pong....... **166**
Tennis **168**
   Court and Equipment...... **168**
*Track and Field **173**
   Track **173**
   Sprints/Dashes........... **174**
   Relays/Relay Races........ **175**
   Hurdles **176**
   Steeplechase............. **177**
   Distance Running and Race
   Walking **178**
   Javelin **180**
   Shot Put................. **181**
   Discus **182**
   Hammer Throw **183**
   Long Jump/Broad Jump.... **184**
   Triple Jump/Hop, Step and
   Jump **184**

High Jump **185**
Pole Vault **186**
Decathlon and Heptathlon .. **188**
Officials' Equipment........ **189**
*Volleyball................... **190**
*Water Polo.................. **192**
Water Skiing **193**
*Weightlifting............... **194**
*Wrestling.................. **196**
   Starting Positions **196**
   Holds **197**
   Movements **198**
*Yachting **199**
   Yacht Racing............. **199**
   Sail Plan **200**
   Sailboarding............. **201**
   Basic Terminology **202**
   Nautical Nomenclature..... **203**
   Powerboat Racing **204**
   Motoryacht.............. **205**
   Competition Fishing Boat .. **206**
   Cruising Sailboat **208**
Trophies and Medals **209**
Index **211**

*Olympic Sport

FOREWORD

WHAT IT IS

WHAT'S WHAT™ IN SPORTS presents the world of competitive athletics in a way that has never been attempted before. It is a book that celebrates the beauty and grace of sport, while also serving as the first visual reference book for this special world. Through the use of photography and detailed illustration, it tells—and shows—the reader the object of most major sports, how games are played, and what equipment is used. It also identifies parts of playing fields, courts and arenas, as well as illustrating essential moves, maneuvers and plays.

WHAT'S WHAT™ IN SPORTS is not intended to be a substitute for engaging in or witnessing sports events. Rather, it is a valuable adjunct to the sports world, enabling anyone to better understand what happens, what to look for and how to score or judge contests. It prepares viewers beforehand for what will take place and afterwards helps them appreciate what has happened. When a gymnast performs a perfect maneuver, a "10," for example, it happens so quickly that it is virtually impossible to understand what was attempted and how well the feat was executed. WHAT'S WHAT™ IN SPORTS will bridge that gap, and in the process enhance the reader's appreciation for the glorious moments in sports.

HOW IT WORKS

We have extracted from each sport the elements and information that are essential for an understanding of how it is played. In team sports and sports whose outcome is determined by strictly defined scoring rules, this information includes the playing field, its dimensions, the positioning of players, and examples of team movements. In sports whose outcome is determined by a judging system, we have illustrated the basic movements that must be performed and the general criteria by which they will be judged, usually shown sequentially.

A typical page begins with a textblock that provides overall information about the sport or event, as well as additional background information. Lines running directly to illustrations clearly identify objects and their individual parts. Dotted lines are used to indicate pieces of equipment which are not readily visible. Brackets have been used to indicate areas.

To locate any sport, begin with the table of contents which lists all sports alphabetically. Individual events, which comprise the sport, are listed under the general heading. Pole vaulting, for example, is listed under Track and Field. The comprehensive index lists every sport, event, piece of equipment and playing field alphabetically.

AND WHY

This book's predecessor, *WHAT'S WHAT™: A Visual Glossary of the Physical World,* has been hailed by critics as either the most entertaining reference book or the most informative general book published in decades.

We have tried to bring the same combination of entertainment and information to this book by carefully selecting photographs and illustrations that will enable the reader to not only understand how a sport is played but also how to better appreciate the fine points.

We have been aided in our task by many well-known players and coaches, as well as experts in various fields of graphic endeavor. Use of this book, it is hoped, will enable every reader to gain a fuller understanding of the skill and effort that goes into every sport, and to come away informed and entertained.

In championship aerobatics, teams of pilots compete by performing spectacular flying feats and maneuvers in three programs: a known compulsory program, composed of figures in both normal and inverted flight (seven minutes); an unknown compulsory program, consisting of at least 15 figures chosen the day before by heads of delegations (seven minutes); and a free program, in which contestants may fly up to 30 figures of their own choosing in nine minutes.

Contestants must fly within an *aerobatic box*, a zone of 880 by 1,100 yards which is clearly marked on the ground. Additionally, they may fly no higher than 1,100 yards or lower than 110, or they risk being penalized.

Men and women's teams of at least three and not more than five pilots each compete in 150- to 350-hp piston-engined aircraft. They are judged for each figure performed and given between zero and 10 points. To arrive at the final score, the two highest and lowest scores are eliminated. The remaining scores are averaged and multiplied by each figure's *difficulty coefficient*, between one and 35. The pilot or team with the highest number of points in all programs wins.

Aerobatic maneuvers number in the thousands. Most, however, are composed of combinations of *rolls, loops, spins, climbs* and *dives*.

In addition to the figures shown below, *fliers* may perform the following maneuvers: *Wingover*, a

SPIN

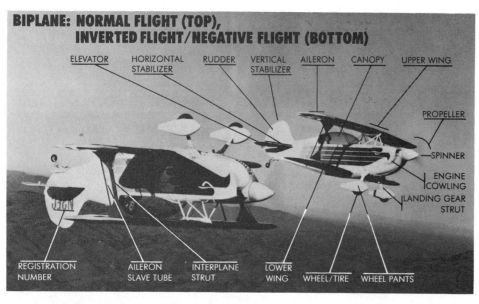

**BIPLANE: NORMAL FLIGHT (TOP),
INVERTED FLIGHT/NEGATIVE FLIGHT (BOTTOM)**

ELEVATOR — HORIZONTAL STABILIZER — RUDDER — VERTICAL STABILIZER — AILERON — CANOPY — UPPER WING — PROPELLER — SPINNER — ENGINE COWLING — LANDING GEAR STRUT — REGISTRATION NUMBER — AILERON SLAVE TUBE — INTERPLANE STRUT — LOWER WING — WHEEL/TIRE — WHEEL PANTS

BASIC COMPETITIVE FIGURES & MANEUVERS

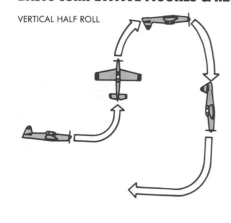

VERTICAL HALF ROLL

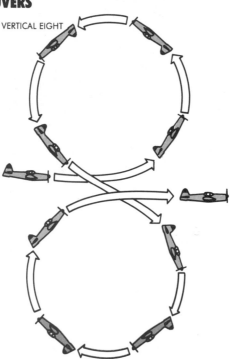

VERTICAL EIGHT

reversing maneuver in which the aircraft changes heading by 180 degrees; *Chandelle*, a coordinated turn-reversing maneuver during which the maximum amount of altitude is gained; *Immelmann*, a half loop immediately followed by a half roll; *Cuban Eight*, a combination of partial loops, 45-degree dives and half rolls; *Avalanche*, a snap roll on top of a loop; and *Humpty Bumps*, a family of maneuvers characterized by a vertical line with climbing half rolls, a half loop over to a diving vertical line, followed by recovery to horizontal flight at the same altitude as the entry.

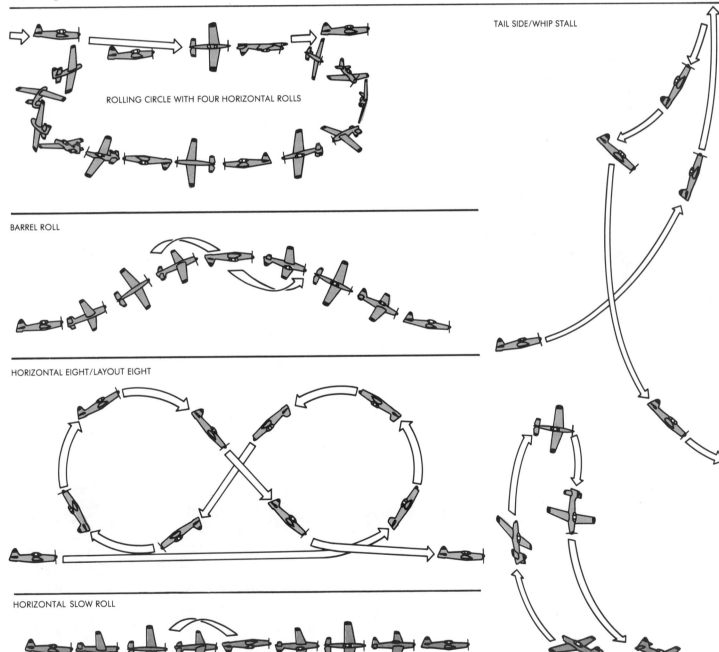

ROLLING CIRCLE WITH FOUR HORIZONTAL ROLLS

BARREL ROLL

HORIZONTAL EIGHT/LAYOUT EIGHT

HORIZONTAL SLOW ROLL

TAIL SIDE/WHIP STALL

STALL TURN/HAMMERHEAD

In *closed course air racing*, aircraft in five classes, from homebuilt planes powered by 60-hp engines to modified World War II fighters with 3,000-hp engines, race over fixed distances marked by turning pylons.

In International Formula One, the most popular class, aircraft approximately 16 feet long, with a similar *wingspan*, reach speeds of 240-mph powered by 100-hp engines.

In *air starts*, racers, already airborne, form up on a *pace plane* that dives across the starting line and pulls away. In *racehorse starts*, aircraft line up on the runway and start when a flag is dropped.

Handicap races, for stock aircraft, are flown cross country.

COCKPIT

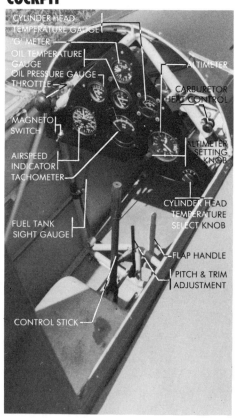

CYLINDER HEAD TEMPERATURE GAUGE
'G' METER
OIL TEMPERATURE GAUGE
OIL PRESSURE GAUGE
THROTTLE
ALTIMETER
CARBURETOR HEAT CONTROL
MAGNETO SWITCH
ALTIMETER SETTING KNOB
AIRSPEED INDICATOR
TACHOMETER
CYLINDER HEAD TEMPERATURE SELECT KNOB
FUEL TANK SIGHT GAUGE
FLAP HANDLE
PITCH & TRIM ADJUSTMENT
CONTROL STICK

FORMULA ONE RACECOURSE

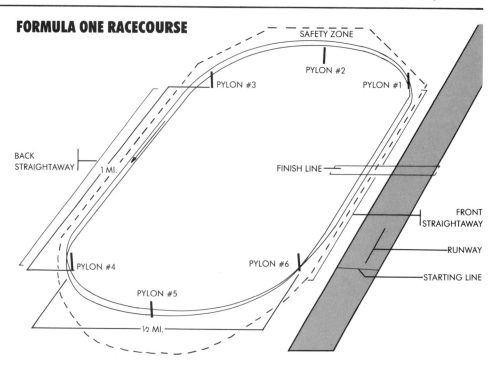

SAFETY ZONE
PYLON #2
PYLON #3
PYLON #1
BACK STRAIGHTAWAY
1 MI.
FINISH LINE
FRONT STRAIGHTAWAY
RUNWAY
STARTING LINE
PYLON #4
PYLON #6
PYLON #5
½ MI.

FORMULA ONE AIRCRAFT

DECAL
ACCESS DOOR
RACE NUMBER
REGISTRATION NUMBER
FUSELAGE
N711HM
41
ENGINE COWLING
RUNWAY MARKINGS

The ascent of a hot air balloon, or *montgolfier*, is controlled by regulating the temperature of the air inside the nylon envelope and by the amount of *ballast*, usually water or sandbags, carried in the gondola. At higher altitudes cooler air slows a balloon's ascent. Its lateral movement is determined by wind speed and direction. A *drag rope*, or *trail rope*, hangs from the wicker basket to provide stability in flight and to slow the balloon down on landing.

A *rip panel* near the top, or *apex*, of the envelope is opened to deflate the balloon.

Ballooners compete for flight duration, navigational skills and altitude achieved.

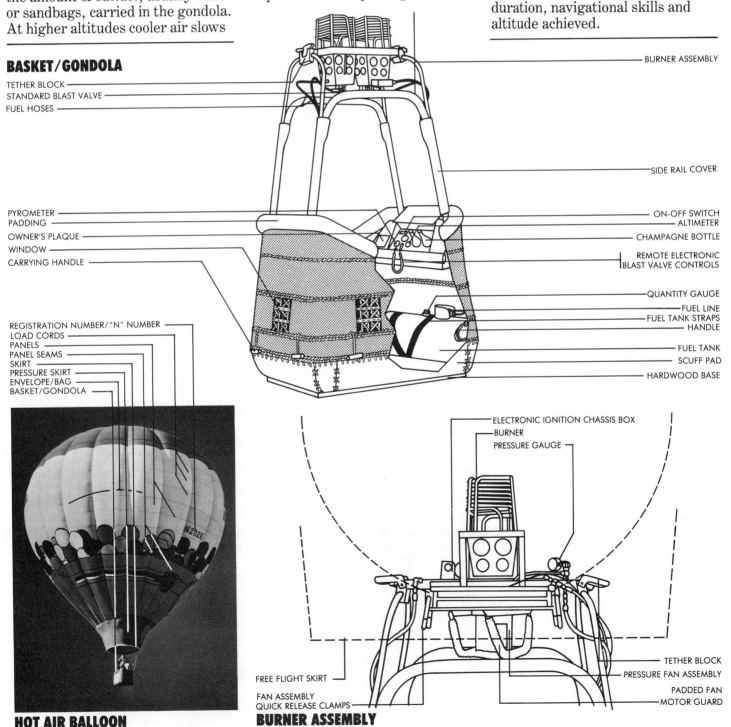

BASKET/GONDOLA

TETHER BLOCK
STANDARD BLAST VALVE
FUEL HOSES

PYROMETER
PADDING
OWNER'S PLAQUE
WINDOW
CARRYING HANDLE

REGISTRATION NUMBER/"N" NUMBER
LOAD CORDS
PANELS
PANEL SEAMS
SKIRT
PRESSURE SKIRT
ENVELOPE/BAG
BASKET/GONDOLA

BURNER ASSEMBLY

SIDE RAIL COVER

ON-OFF SWITCH
ALTIMETER
CHAMPAGNE BOTTLE
REMOTE ELECTRONIC BLAST VALVE CONTROLS
QUANTITY GAUGE
FUEL LINE
FUEL TANK STRAPS
HANDLE
FUEL TANK
SCUFF PAD
HARDWOOD BASE

ELECTRONIC IGNITION CHASSIS BOX
BURNER
PRESSURE GAUGE

TETHER BLOCK
PRESSURE FAN ASSEMBLY
PADDED FAN
MOTOR GUARD

FREE FLIGHT SKIRT

FAN ASSEMBLY
QUICK RELEASE CLAMPS

HOT AIR BALLOON

BURNER ASSEMBLY

Gliders are either towed to a suitable height by an airplane, called a *tug*, or launched from the ground by auto towing or winch towing. Like *sailplanes*, which engage in *soaring* and are piloted by *sailplaners*, gliders gain altitude and remain aloft by riding rising currents of warm air, or *thermals*. Competitors are judged on altitude gained, distance covered and speed on a closed course.

In hang gliding, also known as *self soaring* and *sky surfing*, contestants compete in *self launch open class*, in which the pilot must carry his craft to the *launch site* and *foot launch* it himself, and *open class*, in which any hang glider may be used and launched with the assistance of one person.

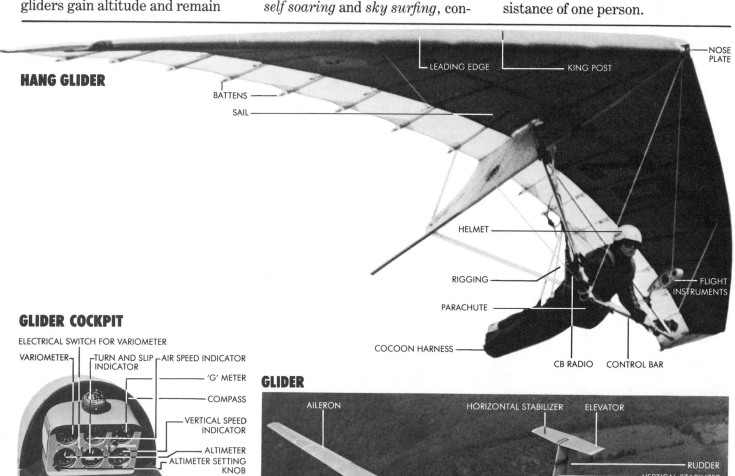

HANG GLIDER

LEADING EDGE — KING POST — NOSE PLATE — BATTENS — SAIL — HELMET — RIGGING — PARACHUTE — FLIGHT INSTRUMENTS — COCOON HARNESS — CB RADIO — CONTROL BAR

GLIDER COCKPIT

ELECTRICAL SWITCH FOR VARIOMETER
VARIOMETER — TURN AND SLIP INDICATOR — AIR SPEED INDICATOR — 'G' METER — COMPASS — VERTICAL SPEED INDICATOR — ALTIMETER — ALTIMETER SETTING KNOB — TOW RELEASE KNOB — CONTROL STICK — STATIC PORT TUBE — TOW HOOK RELEASE SPRING — RUDDER CABLE — FLAP CONTROL KNOB — FLAP CONTROL MECHANISM

GLIDER

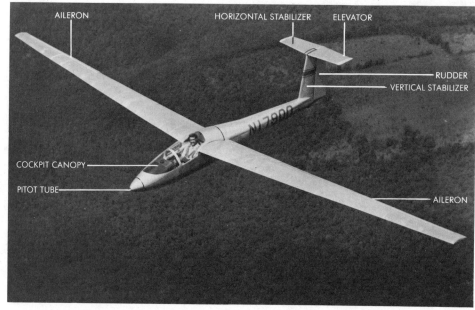

AILERON — HORIZONTAL STABILIZER — ELEVATOR — RUDDER — VERTICAL STABILIZER — COCKPIT CANOPY — PITOT TUBE — AILERON

There are three events in competitive sky diving. In style competition, *sky divers* perform stunts, such as spirals and loops, during *free fall*, the period between jumping from the airplane and opening their chutes. In accuracy competition, divers are judged on how close they land to a small disk in the target area. In *relative work*, four-, eight- and 10- man teams pass a baton to one another or attempt hook ups in order to form different patterns. All competitive *sport parachuting* is conducted over a hazard-free *dropping zone*, or *DZ*. The ground surrounding it is called the *overshoot area*.

Jumpmasters are in charge of all jumps from aircraft.

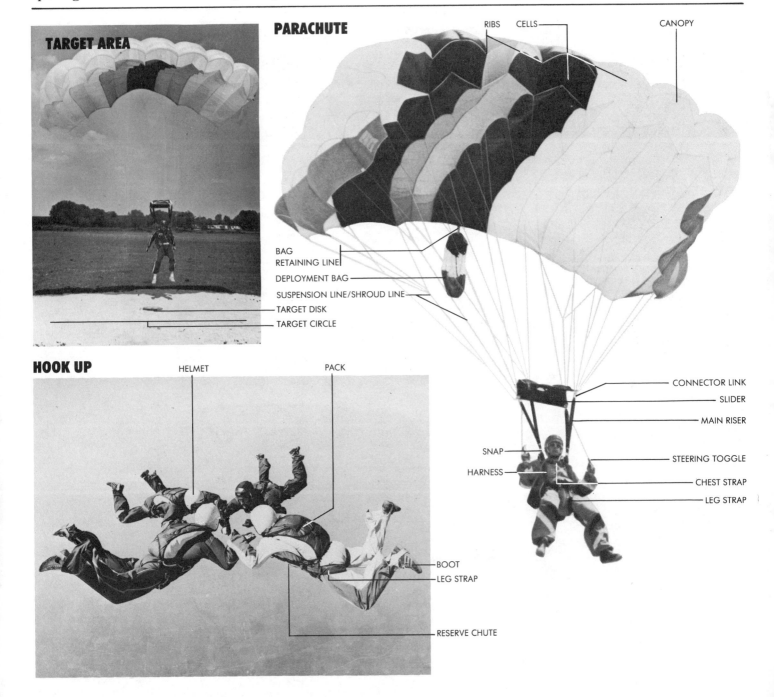

TARGET AREA

BAG RETAINING LINE
DEPLOYMENT BAG
SUSPENSION LINE/SHROUD LINE
TARGET DISK
TARGET CIRCLE

PARACHUTE

RIBS CELLS CANOPY

CONNECTOR LINK
SLIDER
MAIN RISER
SNAP
STEERING TOGGLE
HARNESS
CHEST STRAP
LEG STRAP

HOOK UP

HELMET PACK

BOOT
LEG STRAP

RESERVE CHUTE

Anyone who fishes for sport is called an *angler, fisherman, sportfisherman,* or *Izaak Walton.* He or she uses *freshwater* or *saltwater tackle* and *live* or *artificial bait,* depending on the fish's *feeding pattern* or habits.

When a fish *takes the bait,* or lure, the fisherman puts tension on the line to *set the hook* and drive the barb home, called *striking the fish,* and plays it until it is *landed, taken, boated,* or *tagged* and *released.*

Fishing tournaments and *world record catches* are governed by specific limitations on tackle.

The fish on page 9, *piscatoris bassasailus,* is a whimsical combination of a freshwater and saltwater *game fish.*

BASIC FISHING RIG

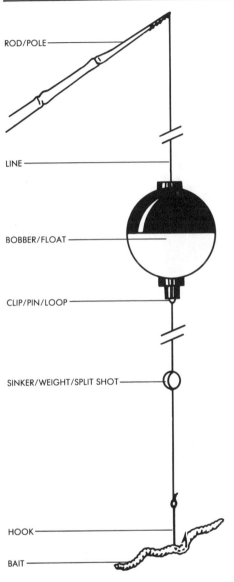

- ROD/POLE
- LINE
- BOBBER/FLOAT
- CLIP/PIN/LOOP
- SINKER/WEIGHT/SPLIT SHOT
- HOOK
- BAIT

FISH

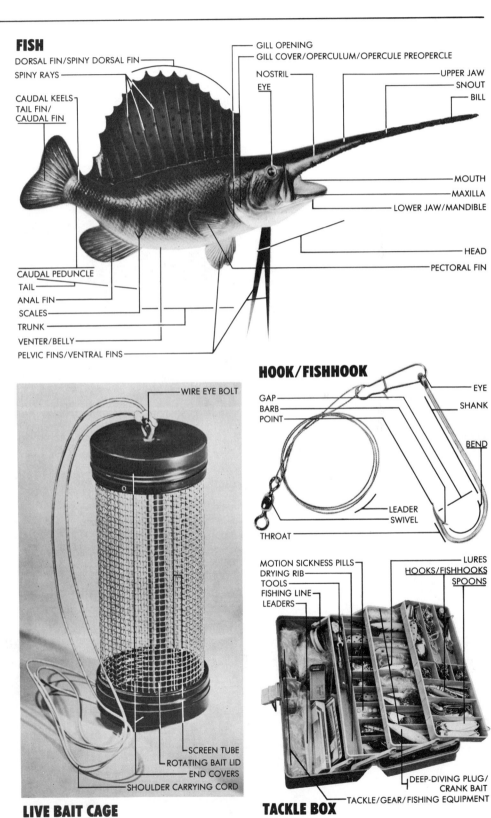

- DORSAL FIN/SPINY DORSAL FIN
- SPINY RAYS
- CAUDAL KEELS
- TAIL FIN/ CAUDAL FIN
- GILL OPENING
- GILL COVER/OPERCULUM/OPERCULE PREOPERCLE
- NOSTRIL
- EYE
- UPPER JAW
- SNOUT
- BILL
- MOUTH
- MAXILLA
- LOWER JAW/MANDIBLE
- HEAD
- PECTORAL FIN
- CAUDAL PEDUNCLE
- TAIL
- ANAL FIN
- SCALES
- TRUNK
- VENTER/BELLY
- PELVIC FINS/VENTRAL FINS

HOOK/FISHHOOK

- GAP
- BARB
- POINT
- EYE
- SHANK
- BEND
- LEADER
- SWIVEL
- THROAT

LIVE BAIT CAGE

- WIRE EYE BOLT
- SCREEN TUBE
- ROTATING BAIT LID
- END COVERS
- SHOULDER CARRYING CORD

TACKLE BOX

- MOTION SICKNESS PILLS
- DRYING RIB
- TOOLS
- FISHING LINE
- LEADERS
- LURES
- HOOKS/FISHHOOKS
- SPOONS
- DEEP-DIVING PLUG/ CRANK BAIT
- TACKLE/GEAR/FISHING EQUIPMENT

Artificial flies are tiny hooks, dressed with hair, yarn, feathers fur, or other material meant to suggest insects, small swimmers or crustaceans on which fish feed.

The fly is attached to a tippet, a short section of fine line at the end of a tapered leader.

Flies may be used in different ways, depending on their design and the bait they are meant to imitate. Dry flies are worked on the surface. Streamers, *nymphs* and *bucktails* are used at various depths.

A rod's *'action'* is its degree of bend, dependent on its *taper*, and the manner in which it affects casting and playing a fish.

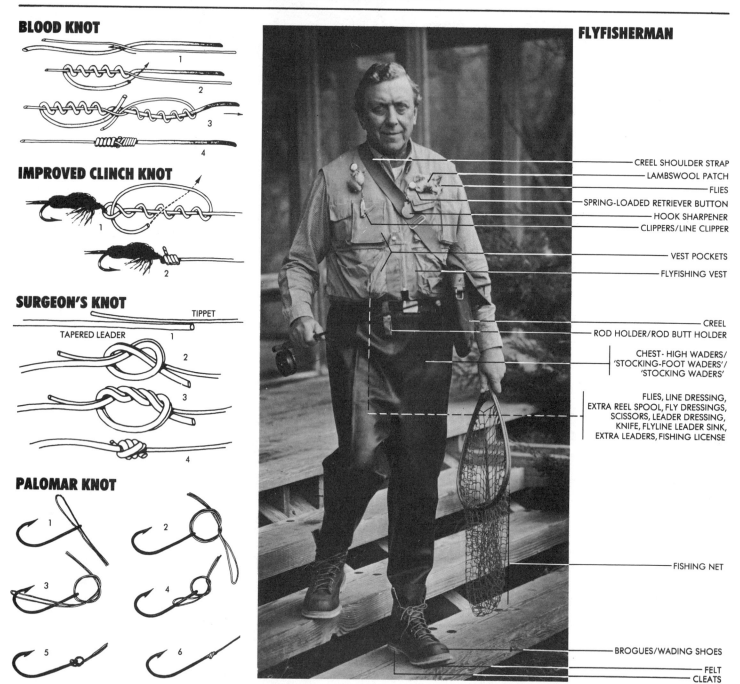

BLOOD KNOT

IMPROVED CLINCH KNOT

SURGEON'S KNOT

TIPPET

TAPERED LEADER

PALOMAR KNOT

FLYFISHERMAN

CREEL SHOULDER STRAP
LAMBSWOOL PATCH
FLIES
SPRING-LOADED RETRIEVER BUTTON
HOOK SHARPENER
CLIPPERS/LINE CLIPPER

VEST POCKETS
FLYFISHING VEST

CREEL
ROD HOLDER/ROD BUTT HOLDER

CHEST- HIGH WADERS/
'STOCKING-FOOT WADERS'/
'STOCKING WADERS'

FLIES, LINE DRESSING,
EXTRA REEL SPOOL, FLY DRESSINGS,
SCISSORS, LEADER DRESSING,
KNIFE, FLYLINE LEADER SINK,
EXTRA LEADERS, FISHING LICENSE

FISHING NET

BROGUES/WADING SHOES
FELT
CLEATS

FLY ROD

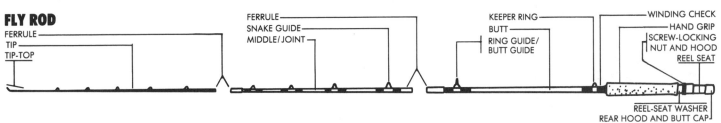

FERRULE
TIP
TIP-TOP

FERRULE
SNAKE GUIDE
MIDDLE/JOINT

KEEPER RING
BUTT
RING GUIDE/
BUTT GUIDE

WINDING CHECK
HAND GRIP
SCREW-LOCKING
NUT AND HOOD
REEL SEAT

REEL-SEAT WASHER
REAR HOOD AND BUTT CAP

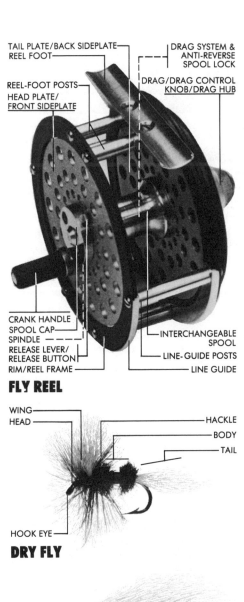

TAIL PLATE/BACK SIDEPLATE
REEL FOOT

DRAG SYSTEM &
ANTI-REVERSE
SPOOL LOCK

REEL-FOOT POSTS
HEAD PLATE/
FRONT SIDEPLATE

DRAG/DRAG CONTROL
KNOB/DRAG HUB

CRANK HANDLE
SPOOL CAP
SPINDLE
RELEASE LEVER/
RELEASE BUTTON
RIM/REEL FRAME

INTERCHANGEABLE
SPOOL
LINE-GUIDE POSTS
LINE GUIDE

FLY REEL

WING
HEAD

HACKLE
BODY
TAIL

HOOK EYE

DRY FLY

TINSEL BODY/TAG

WET FLY/STREAMER

FLYCASTING TECHNIQUE

REACH
1

PULL
2

LIFT
3

4

STOP 5

6
REACH

7
PULL

8

CAST

9

SHOOT
10

In spin casting or *bait casting*, the weight of the lure or bait uncoils the line from the spool.

Fishermen using *open-faced spinning reels* control the length of the cast with their index finger, *feathering* the unrolling line to prevent overshooting the target.

In bait casting, the reel's spool is not stationary. It revolves and can therefore overrun, or *backlash*. Since a plug is the most common lure used in bait casting, the technique is often called '*plug casting*.'

Spinners rotate and vibrate when drawn through the water. *Spoons* wobble and flash. Plugs and jigs imitate live bait when cast and *retrieved*.

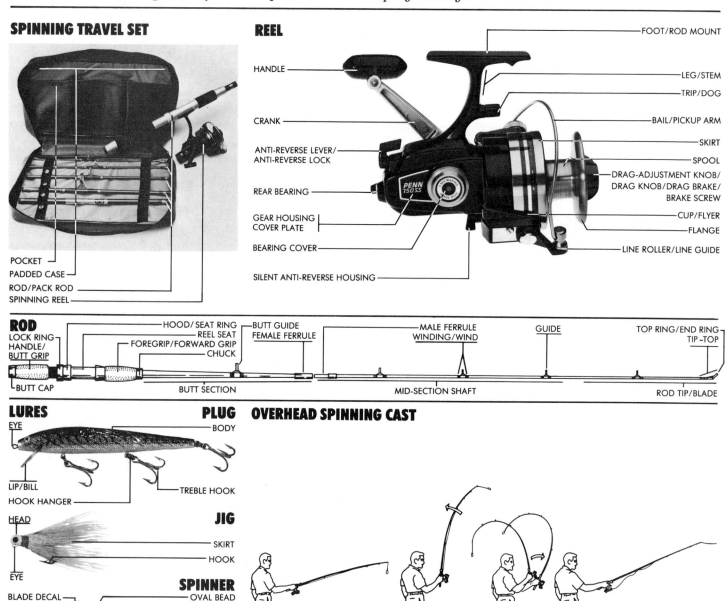

SPINNING TRAVEL SET

POCKET
PADDED CASE
ROD/PACK ROD
SPINNING REEL

REEL

HANDLE

CRANK

ANTI-REVERSE LEVER/
ANTI-REVERSE LOCK

REAR BEARING

GEAR HOUSING
COVER PLATE

BEARING COVER

SILENT ANTI-REVERSE HOUSING

FOOT/ROD MOUNT
LEG/STEM
TRIP/DOG
BAIL/PICKUP ARM
SKIRT
SPOOL
DRAG-ADJUSTMENT KNOB/
DRAG KNOB/DRAG BRAKE/
BRAKE SCREW
CUP/FLYER
FLANGE
LINE ROLLER/LINE GUIDE

PENN 150SS

ROD

LOCK RING
HANDLE/
BUTT GRIP
BUTT CAP

HOOD/ SEAT RING
REEL SEAT
FOREGRIP/FORWARD GRIP
CHUCK

BUTT GUIDE
FEMALE FERRULE

BUTT SECTION

MALE FERRULE
WINDING/WIND

GUIDE

MID-SECTION SHAFT

TOP RING/END RING
TIP -TOP

ROD TIP/BLADE

LURES   PLUG

EYE
BODY

LIP/BILL
HOOK HANGER
TREBLE HOOK

JIG

HEAD
SKIRT
HOOK
EYE

SPINNER

BLADE DECAL
BLADE
CLEVIS
EYE

OVAL BEAD
BELL BEAD
SPACER BEAD
WEIGHT
HOOK
TAIL/SKIRT

WIRE SHAFT

OVERHEAD SPINNING CAST

1. AIM
2. STOP
3. CAST
4. RELEASE

Trolling consists of pulling baits or lures behind a boat. *Surface trolling* and *deep* or *bottom trolling* require different methods.

In deep trolling, for example, *lead-core* or *wire line* is used. In *depth-control fishing* where a down-rigger is used, a heavy weight is attached to wire line wound on a large wheel. The lure and leader are fastened by a *breakaway coupling* to the weight and lowered to the desired depth, measured by turns on the downrigger wheel or a meter.

Vessels used for trolling may be large and motorized or small and manually operated. Quiet electric trolling motors are favored by anglers stalking fish they don't want to 'spook' or scare away.

BASS BOAT/BASS RIG

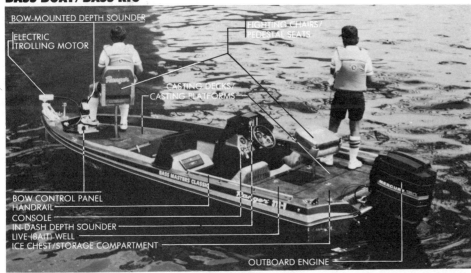

BOW-MOUNTED DEPTH SOUNDER
ELECTRIC TROLLING MOTOR
FIGHTING CHAIRS/PEDESTAL SEATS
CASTING DECKS/CASTING PLATFORMS
BOW CONTROL PANEL
HANDRAIL
CONSOLE
IN-DASH DEPTH SOUNDER
LIVE (BAIT) WELL
ICE CHEST/STORAGE COMPARTMENT
OUTBOARD ENGINE

DEEP TROLLING RIGS

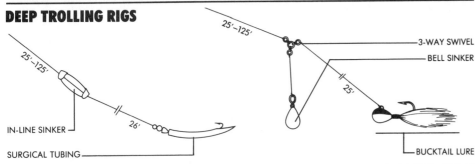

25'–125'
25'–125'
3-WAY SWIVEL
BELL SINKER
25'
IN-LINE SINKER
26'
SURGICAL TUBING
BUCKTAIL LURE

DOWNRIGGER

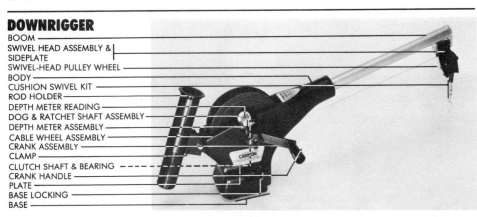

BOOM
SWIVEL HEAD ASSEMBLY & SIDEPLATE
SWIVEL-HEAD PULLEY WHEEL
BODY
CUSHION SWIVEL KIT
ROD HOLDER
DEPTH METER READING
DOG & RATCHET SHAFT ASSEMBLY
DEPTH METER ASSEMBLY
CABLE WHEEL ASSEMBLY
CRANK ASSEMBLY
CLAMP
CLUTCH SHAFT & BEARING
CRANK HANDLE
PLATE
BASE LOCKING
BASE

UMBRELLA RIG

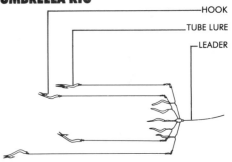

HOOK
TUBE LURE
LEADER

TROLLING REEL

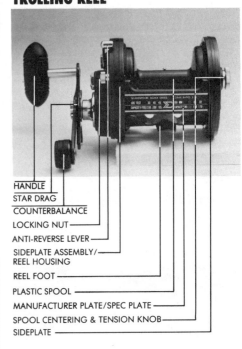

HANDLE
STAR DRAG
COUNTERBALANCE
LOCKING NUT
ANTI-REVERSE LEVER
SIDEPLATE ASSEMBLY/REEL HOUSING
REEL FOOT
PLASTIC SPOOL
MANUFACTURER PLATE/SPEC PLATE
SPOOL CENTERING & TENSION KNOB
SIDEPLATE

In surf fishing, oversized gear and a two-handed technique are generally required to reach fish in the *striking zone*.

Surfcasters may offer bait to 'bottom feeders' and game fish alike with a double-level fishfinder rig, or use only lures that imitate *bait fish* if they are interested in game fish alone.

Anglers who *bottom fish* use *dead, cut,* or *strip bait,* or live bait. Their *terminal tackle*, the equipment at the end of the line, is held fast on the bottom by heavy sinkers.

Surfcasters may *net* or *gaff* fish as they near shore, or they may *beach* their catch by dragging it out of the water and up the beach.

SURFCASTING TECHNIQUE

DOUBLE-LEVEL FISHFINDER RIG

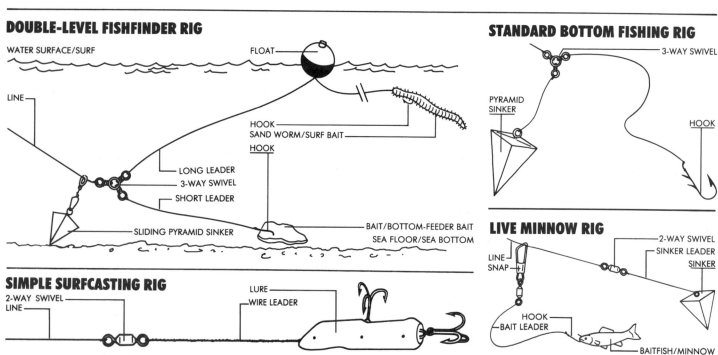

WATER SURFACE/SURF

LINE

FLOAT

HOOK
SAND WORM/SURF BAIT

HOOK

LONG LEADER
3-WAY SWIVEL
SHORT LEADER

SLIDING PYRAMID SINKER

BAIT/BOTTOM-FEEDER BAIT
SEA FLOOR/SEA BOTTOM

STANDARD BOTTOM FISHING RIG

3-WAY SWIVEL

PYRAMID
SINKER

HOOK

LIVE MINNOW RIG

2-WAY SWIVEL
SINKER LEADER
SINKER

LINE
SNAP

HOOK
BAIT LEADER

BAITFISH/MINNOW

SIMPLE SURFCASTING RIG

2-WAY SWIVEL
LINE

LURE
WIRE LEADER

Anglers troll for *big game fish* with oversized lures or baits. When a fish '*feeds*' the angler strikes it to set the hook, then reduces the drag on the reel as the fish makes its first *run*.

The main purpose of the fighting chair is to allow the angler to use his or her back and leg muscles against the fish.

With the rod butt resting in the chair's gimballed socket, the angler then begins pumping the rod between vertical and horizontal, taking in *slack line* on each drop.

When the fish is alongside and the *mate* has the angler's leader in hand, the fish is said to be *brought to wire*. Prior to *boating*, a fish's tail is immobilized with a gaff or *flying gaff*.

USING THE FIGHTING CHAIR

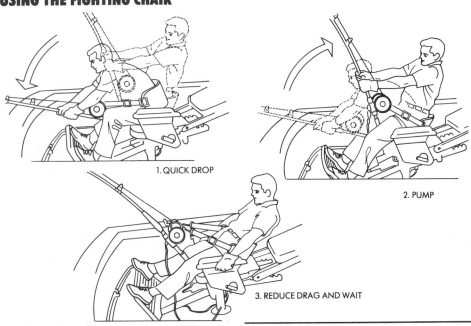

1. QUICK DROP

2. PUMP

3. REDUCE DRAG AND WAIT

FIGHTING CHAIR HARNESS

ROPE CONNECTOR/REEL CONNECTOR
BUCKET HARNESS/SEA HARNESS

GROMMETS
SAFETY SNAP
NYLON WEBBING/
ANTI-ROPE CHAFE STRIP
O-RING

FIGHTING CHAIR

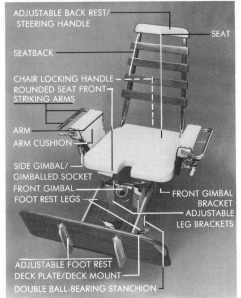

ADJUSTABLE BACK REST/
STEERING HANDLE
SEAT
SEATBACK
CHAIR LOCKING HANDLE
ROUNDED SEAT FRONT
STRIKING ARMS
ARM
ARM CUSHION
SIDE GIMBAL/
GIMBALLED SOCKET
FRONT GIMBAL
FOOT REST LEGS
FRONT GIMBAL
BRACKET
ADJUSTABLE
LEG BRACKETS
ADJUSTABLE FOOT REST
DECK PLATE/DECK MOUNT
DOUBLE BALL-BEARING STANCHION

BIG GAME ROD

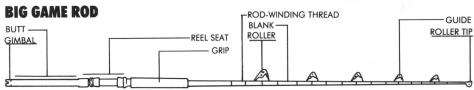

BUTT
GIMBAL
REEL SEAT
GRIP
ROD-WINDING THREAD
BLANK
ROLLER
GUIDE
ROLLER TIP

BIG GAME REEL

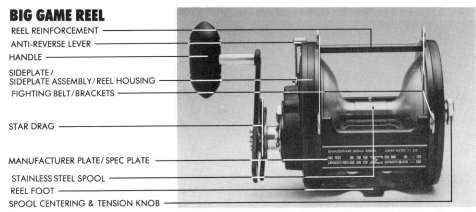

REEL REINFORCEMENT
ANTI-REVERSE LEVER
HANDLE
SIDEPLATE/
SIDEPLATE ASSEMBLY/REEL HOUSING
FIGHTING BELT/BRACKETS
STAR DRAG
MANUFACTURER PLATE/SPEC PLATE
STAINLESS STEEL SPOOL
REEL FOOT
SPOOL CENTERING & TENSION KNOB

In *target archery*, archers shoot *rounds*, or a specific number of arrows from various fixed distances. After shooting three arrows within 2½ minutes, which constitutes an *end*, archers total their points and are replaced at the shooting line by the next competitor. Each arrow landing in the target, or leaving a mark discernible by the *scorer*, is worth the value of the scoring zone in which it struck. The archer with the most points wins.

Target archery competitions may consist of numerous rounds and last as many as four days.

Field archers move about a forest-like terrain shooting at animal-shaped targets.

The *upshot* is the final arrow shot in a competition.

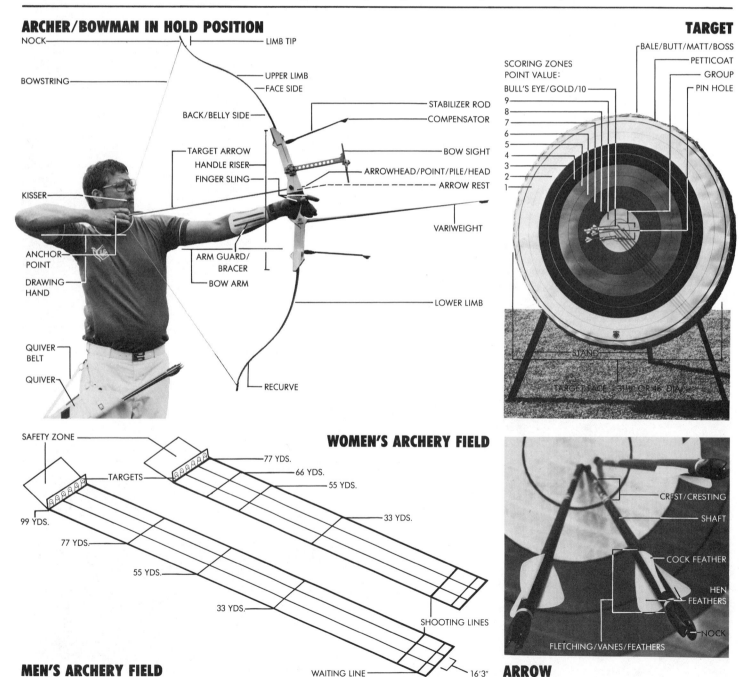

ARCHER/BOWMAN IN HOLD POSITION

NOCK — LIMB TIP

BOWSTRING

UPPER LIMB
FACE SIDE

BACK/BELLY SIDE

STABILIZER ROD
COMPENSATOR

TARGET ARROW
HANDLE RISER
FINGER SLING

BOW SIGHT
ARROWHEAD/POINT/PILE/HEAD
ARROW REST

KISSER

VARIWEIGHT

ANCHOR POINT

ARM GUARD/BRACER

DRAWING HAND

BOW ARM

QUIVER BELT

QUIVER

LOWER LIMB

RECURVE

TARGET

BALE/BUTT/MATT/BOSS
PETTICOAT
GROUP
PIN HOLE

SCORING ZONES POINT VALUE:
BULL'S EYE/GOLD/10
9
8
7
6
5
4
3
2
1

STAND

TARGET FACE — 31IN. OR 48 DIA.

WOMEN'S ARCHERY FIELD

SAFETY ZONE

TARGETS

77 YDS.
66 YDS.
55 YDS.

33 YDS.

99 YDS.

77 YDS.

55 YDS.

33 YDS.

SHOOTING LINES

MEN'S ARCHERY FIELD

WAITING LINE — 16'3"

ARROW

CREST/CRESTING

SHAFT

COCK FEATHER

HEN FEATHERS

NOCK

FLETCHING/VANES/FEATHERS

Indianapolis-type and *Formula* cars are *open-wheel, single-seat, open-cockpit racing cars*, differing mostly in weight and engine size. *'Indy cars'* race on a banked, oval *speedway* where *drivers 'put down rubber'* to stay in the *'groove,'* but sometimes fall *'in the marbles,'* the *slick* part of the track. In *closed-circuit road racing*, Formula drivers take *Esses*, continuous left-right turns, and *chicanes*, turns formed by temporary barriers. A *pace car* leads the *starting field* to a *safe start*. A race lasts a certain number of *miles, laps* or *hours*. During the race a *green* flag indicates go, *yellow* means caution, *red* means stop racing and a black-and-white *checkered* flag is waved at the finish line.

INDY CAR

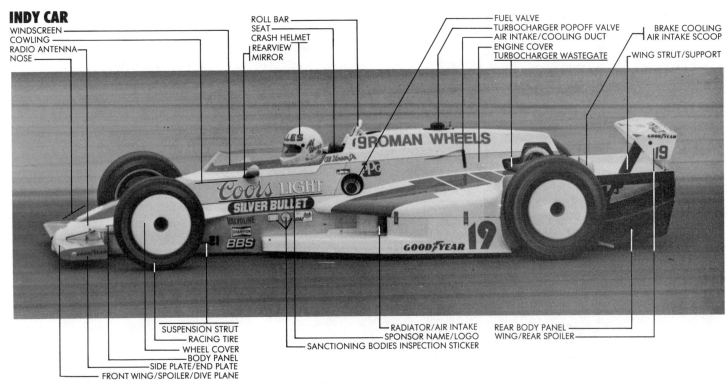

WINDSCREEN
COWLING
RADIO ANTENNA
NOSE
ROLL BAR
SEAT
CRASH HELMET
REARVIEW
MIRROR
FUEL VALVE
TURBOCHARGER POPOFF VALVE
AIR INTAKE/COOLING DUCT
ENGINE COVER
TURBOCHARGER WASTEGATE
BRAKE COOLING
AIR INTAKE SCOOP
WING STRUT/SUPPORT

SUSPENSION STRUT
RACING TIRE
WHEEL COVER
BODY PANEL
SIDE PLATE/END PLATE
FRONT WING/SPOILER/DIVE PLANE
RADIATOR/AIR INTAKE
SPONSOR NAME/LOGO
SANCTIONING BODIES INSPECTION STICKER
REAR BODY PANEL
WING/REAR SPOILER

INDY CAR CUTAWAY

TURBOCHARGER
REAR SUSPENSION SYSTEM
POPOFF VALVE
ENGINE
CYLINDER HEADS
FUSELAGE
FUEL INTAKE VALVE
EXHAUST SYSTEM

SIDEPOD

OIL COOLER

DISC BRAKE
RACK & PINION STEERING AND SUSPENSION SYSTEMS
FORWARD BULKHEAD
BRAKE FLUID RESERVOIR

RELIEF VALVE
SHOULDER HARNESS

TRACK

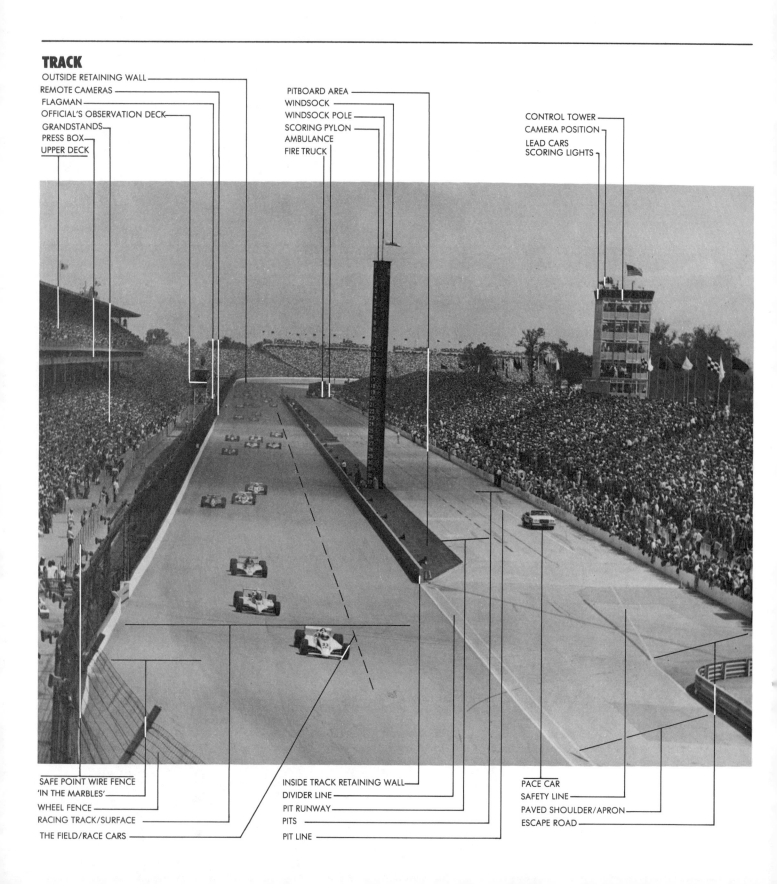

OUTSIDE RETAINING WALL
REMOTE CAMERAS
FLAGMAN
OFFICIAL'S OBSERVATION DECK
GRANDSTANDS
PRESS BOX
UPPER DECK

PITBOARD AREA
WINDSOCK
WINDSOCK POLE
SCORING PYLON
AMBULANCE
FIRE TRUCK

CONTROL TOWER
CAMERA POSITION
LEAD CARS
SCORING LIGHTS

SAFE POINT WIRE FENCE
'IN THE MARBLES'
WHEEL FENCE
RACING TRACK/SURFACE
THE FIELD/RACE CARS

INSIDE TRACK RETAINING WALL
DIVIDER LINE
PIT RUNWAY
PITS
PIT LINE

PACE CAR
SAFETY LINE
PAVED SHOULDER/APRON
ESCAPE ROAD

PIT CREW

FIRE CREWMAN
FUEL OVERFLOW MAN
PIT STEWARD/SANCTIONING-BODY OFFICIAL
PIT HEADSET
FUEL HOSE
REFUELER

FULLFACE HELMET
RIGHT SIDE TIRECHANGER/WHEELCHANGER
FIREPROOF GLOVES
QUICK-DISCONNECT REFUELING SAFETY VALVE

AIR CHUCK

LEFT SIDE TIRECHANGER/WHEELCHANGER

JACKING AIR HOSE
FIRE EXTINGUISHER
FIREPROOF UNIFORM
FUEL OVERFLOW HOSE

MANIFOLD PRESSURE GAUGE

COCKPIT FIRE EXTINGUISHER ACTIVATOR BUTTON

FIRE EXTINGUISHER ON-OFF SWITCH
TACHOMETER

STEERING WHEEL

WATER TEMPERATURE GAUGE

HAND STOP
OIL PRESSURE GAUGE
DUMMY BUTTON

ELECTRICAL SYSTEM KILL SWITCH

STEERING HUB/WHEEL HUB

RADIO PUSH-TO-TALK SWITCH
RADIO WIRING

DRIVER'S COMPARTMENT/COCKPIT/INSTRUMENT PANEL/DASH

Each drag racing *event, accelera-tion contest,* or *run,* involves two-car *heats,* the winner of which is deemed the *eliminator.* Vehicles include *slingshot dragsters* and *funny cars* whose mismatched *hulls* and *chassis* give them an unusual appearance. The *Christmas tree* is situated in the middle of a divided, two-lane *straight-line course, drag strip,* or *dragway. Elapsed time,* '*ET,'* is computed from the moment a car breaks a *light beam* at the *starting line* until it breaks a simi-lar beam at the *finish.* Most drivers try to leave between the flashes of the fifth amber *starting light* and green *GO-light.* A car leaving pre-maturely makes a *foul start,* and is said to be *red-lighting.*

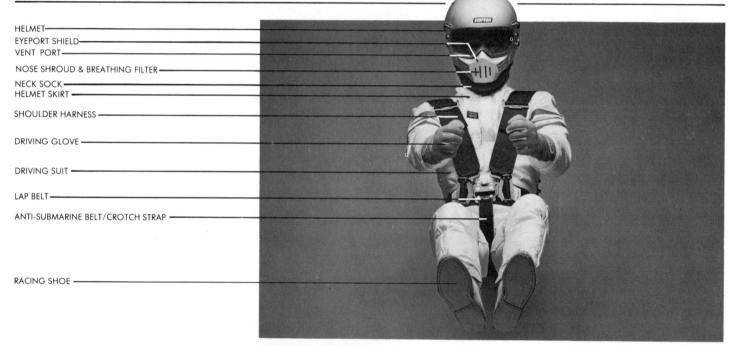

HELMET
EYEPORT SHIELD
VENT PORT
NOSE SHROUD & BREATHING FILTER
NECK SOCK
HELMET SKIRT
SHOULDER HARNESS
DRIVING GLOVE
DRIVING SUIT
LAP BELT
ANTI-SUBMARINE BELT/CROTCH STRAP
RACING SHOE

DRIVER'S FIRE SUIT

ELECTRONIC STARTING SYSTEM
SCOREBOARD
ELAPSED TIME IN SECONDS
SPEED AT FINISH
STANDS
CHRISTMAS TREE/STARTING LIGHTS
QUARTER-MILE/440 YARD COURSE
WATER BARREL
STARTER
BURNOUT DIRECTOR
CENTERLINE DIVIDER
LANE 1
LANE 2

TRACK/DRAG STRIP/DRAGWAY

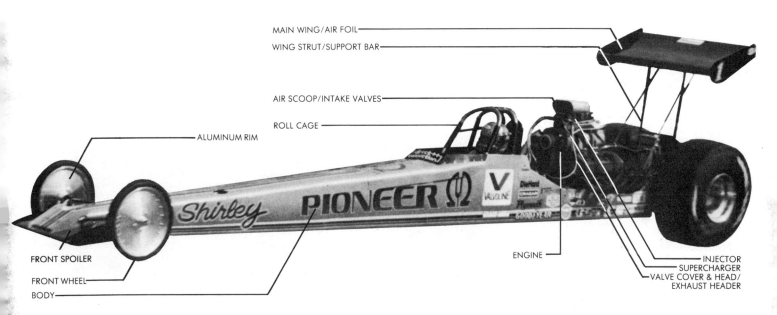

MAIN WING/AIR FOIL

WING STRUT/SUPPORT BAR

AIR SCOOP/INTAKE VALVES

ROLL CAGE

ALUMINUM RIM

FRONT SPOILER

FRONT WHEEL

BODY

ENGINE

INJECTOR
SUPERCHARGER
VALVE COVER & HEAD/
EXHAUST HEADER

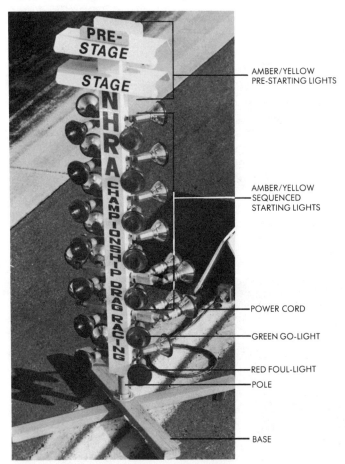

PRE-STAGE

STAGE

NHRA CHAMPIONSHIP DRAG RACING

AMBER/YELLOW
PRE-STARTING LIGHTS

AMBER/YELLOW
SEQUENCED
STARTING LIGHTS

POWER CORD

GREEN GO-LIGHT

RED FOUL-LIGHT

POLE

BASE

CHRISTMAS TREE/STARTING LIGHTS

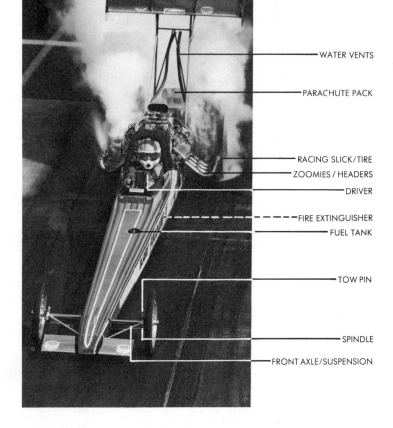

WATER VENTS

PARACHUTE PACK

RACING SLICK/TIRE
ZOOMIES / HEADERS
DRIVER

FIRE EXTINGUISHER
FUEL TANK

TOW PIN

SPINDLE

FRONT AXLE/SUSPENSION

Sports cars are comprised of many different types of race cars. They compete in a *Group* or *Class* determined by performance, design or engine size, (including *Sedan, Production, Grand Touring (GT)* and single-seat *Formulas*) on both open road and twisting track courses. In endurance events known as *factory* or *team challenges*, two to five drivers alternate in one car.

Stock cars are modified factory production vehicles. Their interiors have been stripped and safety rollcages have been installed. *Heavy-duty suspensions* are adjusted for the way dirt or asphalt track corners are inclined, or *banked*. Short, oval tracks are called *'bullpens.'* The first car to cover the race distance wins.

SPORTS CAR

- CATCH FENCING
- CONCRETE RETAINING WALL
- FOOTING
- STALL GATE
- ADJUSTABLE SECONDARY WING PART
- SIDE PLATE
- ADJUSTABLE PRIMARY WING PART
- ADJUSTABLE REAR WING/SPOILER/TAIL
- FLOW ROOF OVERLAY
- PRODUCTION ROOF
- REAR DECK OVERLAY
- ROLLCAGE
- OIL FILLER
- SIDE SKIRT/AEROFOIL
- SIDE MIRROR
- FUEL FILLER
- HOOD PIN
- BRAKE COOLING DUCT
- HEADLIGHT BOX
- OIL COOLER
- SPLITTER

STOCK CAR

- ANTENNA
- REAR SPOILER
- GLASSLESS WINDOW
- DRIVER'S SAFETY NET
- ROLLCAGE
- HOOD PINS
- FIREWALL
- SCREEN-WIRE COVER
- JACK-POINT INDICATOR
- FRONT SPOILER

Badminton is usually played indoors by individuals or two-player teams. The object is to hit the 'bird' over the net, in bounds, so the opposition cannot return it. The serving team continues to serve until losing a *rally* or committing a *fault*, a rules violation such as serving overhand, touching the net, moving before the server strikes the bird, or not serving diagonally across court. Points may only be scored by the serving team. In doubles, both players serve each *inning*, or change of serve.

All doubles and men's singles games are played to 15 or 21 points, while women play to 11. Tie games may be *set* to an additional 2, 3 or 5 points, depending on the number of points in the game being played.

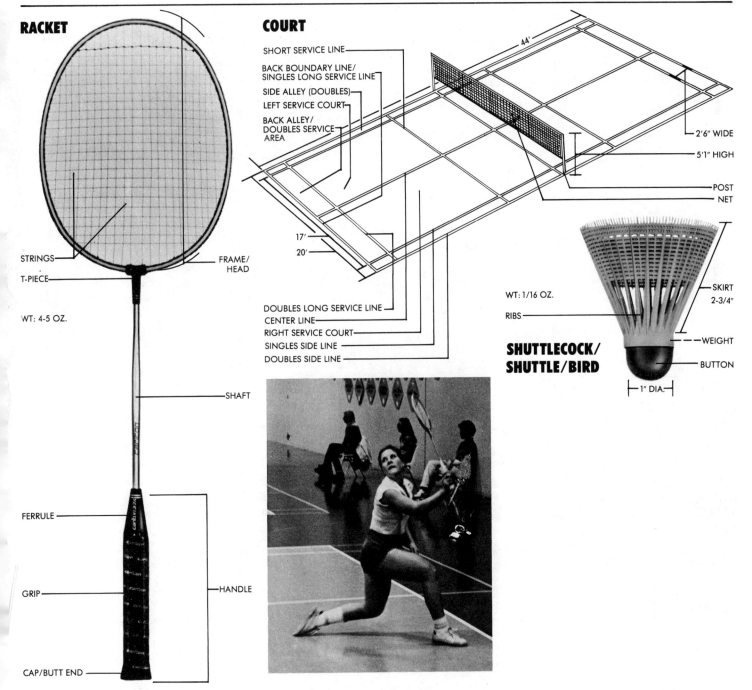

RACKET

STRINGS

T-PIECE

FRAME/HEAD

WT: 4-5 OZ.

SHAFT

FERRULE

GRIP

HANDLE

CAP/BUTT END

COURT

SHORT SERVICE LINE

BACK BOUNDARY LINE/ SINGLES LONG SERVICE LINE

SIDE ALLEY (DOUBLES)

LEFT SERVICE COURT

BACK ALLEY/ DOUBLES SERVICE AREA

44'

2'6" WIDE

5'1" HIGH

POST

NET

17'

20'

DOUBLES LONG SERVICE LINE

CENTER LINE

RIGHT SERVICE COURT

SINGLES SIDE LINE

DOUBLES SIDE LINE

WT: 1/16 OZ.

RIBS

SKIRT 2-3/4"

WEIGHT

BUTTON

1" DIA.

SHUTTLECOCK/ SHUTTLE/BIRD

Baseball is played by two nine-man teams. The object of players on the batting team is to advance from home plate around the bases, in order, returning home. This is a *run*. The team scoring the most runs wins.

A game consists of nine innings. *Extra innings* are played to break a tie. Each team gets three outs in an inning. The team not at bat is on defense in the field. The visiting team bats first, at *the top* of each inning.

The pitcher throws to the batter. If the batter swings and misses, hits the pitch into foul territory or does not swing at a pitch in the strike zone, it is called a *strike*. Three strikes is an out. (Fouled third strikes are replayed). A batter

may also be put out by hitting a ball caught on the fly, or hitting the ball on the ground so that a fielder holding the ball touches first base before the batter steps on the base.

If the batter does not swing and the pitch is outside the strike zone, it is a ball. Four balls is a *walk, free pass* or *base on balls*, entitling the batter to go to first base, where he becomes a *runner*. A batted ball landing in fair territory so that the defense cannot put out the runner is a hit. If the batter reaches second on a hit it is a *double*, reaching third is a *triple*, circling the bases on one hit is a *home run*. Balls hit over the fence in fair territory on the fly are also home runs, entitling all runners on base to score.

PLAYER POSITIONS AND DIMENSIONS

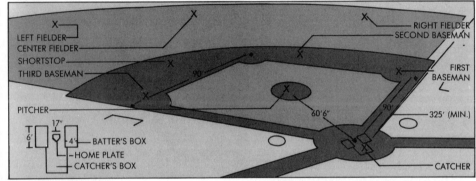

BASEBALL SLANG

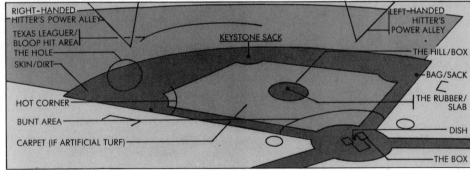

BASEBALL FIELD

Base runners are *safe* while touching a base and cannot be put out. Runners can be put out while off base if touched by a fielder holding the ball.

Runners may hold their base unless forced. *A force* occurs when all bases behind a runner are occupied and the runners on those bases are attempting to advance. (A runner on first is forced by the batter.) If a fielder holding the ball touches a base before a forced runner gets there, the runner is out.

A runner not forced can advance at his own risk on a batted ball. He may also *steal*, or run while the defense has the ball, advance on defensive misplays, or *errors*, on minor rules violations, or when forced by a walk.

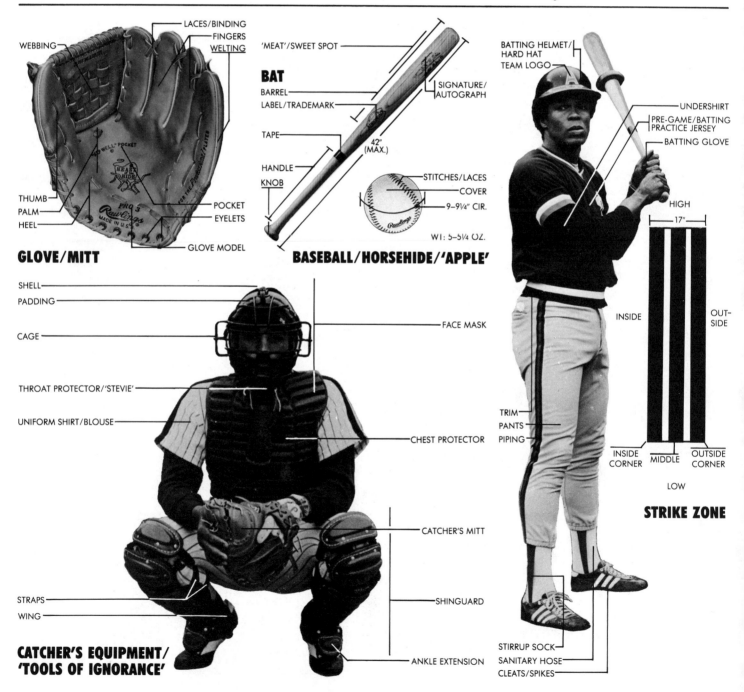

LACES/BINDING
FINGERS
WELTING
WEBBING
THUMB
PALM
HEEL
POCKET
EYELETS
GLOVE MODEL

GLOVE/MITT

'MEAT'/SWEET SPOT

BAT
BARREL
LABEL/TRADEMARK
SIGNATURE/AUTOGRAPH
TAPE
42" (MAX.)
HANDLE
KNOB

STITCHES/LACES
COVER
9–9¼" CIR.
WT: 5–5¼ OZ.

BASEBALL/HORSEHIDE/'APPLE'

BATTING HELMET/HARD HAT
TEAM LOGO
UNDERSHIRT
PRE-GAME/BATTING PRACTICE JERSEY
BATTING GLOVE
HIGH
17"
INSIDE
OUT-SIDE
TRIM
PANTS
PIPING
INSIDE CORNER
MIDDLE
OUTSIDE CORNER
LOW

STRIKE ZONE

SHELL
PADDING
CAGE
FACE MASK
THROAT PROTECTOR/'STEVIE'
UNIFORM SHIRT/BLOUSE
CHEST PROTECTOR
CATCHER'S MITT
STRAPS
WING
SHINGUARD
STIRRUP SOCK
SANITARY HOSE
CLEATS/SPIKES
ANKLE EXTENSION

**CATCHER'S EQUIPMENT/
'TOOLS OF IGNORANCE'**

BATTING/HITTING/SWINGING

| BATTING STANCE | BACKSWING AND STRIDE | SWING | CONTACT | FOLLOW-THROUGH |

SCOREBOARD

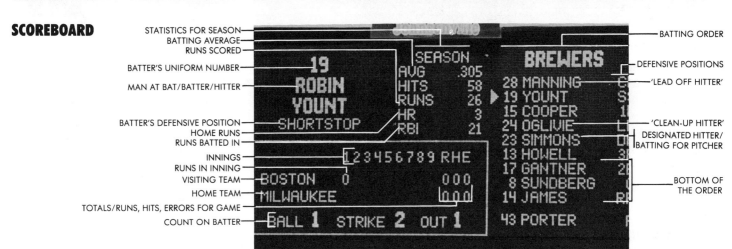

STATISTICS FOR SEASON
BATTING AVERAGE
RUNS SCORED
BATTER'S UNIFORM NUMBER
MAN AT BAT/BATTER/HITTER
BATTER'S DEFENSIVE POSITION
HOME RUNS
RUNS BATTED IN
INNINGS
RUNS IN INNING
VISITING TEAM
HOME TEAM
TOTALS/RUNS, HITS, ERRORS FOR GAME
COUNT ON BATTER

BATTING ORDER
DEFENSIVE POSITIONS
'LEAD OFF HITTER'
'CLEAN-UP HITTER'
DESIGNATED HITTER/
BATTING FOR PITCHER
BOTTOM OF
THE ORDER

19
ROBIN
YOUNT
SHORTSTOP

SEASON
AVG .305
HITS 58
RUNS 26
HR 3
RBI 21

1 2 3 4 5 6 7 8 9 RHE
BOSTON 0 0 0 0
MILWAUKEE 0 0 0

BALL 1 STRIKE 2 OUT 1

BREWERS
28 MANNING C
19 YOUNT S
15 COOPER 1
24 OGLIVIE L
23 SIMMONS D
13 HOWELL 3
17 GANTNER 2
8 SUNDBERG C
14 JAMES R
43 PORTER P

Unlimited substituting is permitted, but replaced players cannot re-enter the game. Batters are often replaced by *pinch-hitters* and starting pitchers by *relief pitchers*.

Pitchers throw from a stretch, or set position with runners on base.

They use a variety of pitches and change speeds in an effort to prevent the batter from hitting.

There may be as few as one or as many as six umpires. The home plate umpire calls balls and strikes and runs the game. Base umpires call safes and outs, fair and foul.

Some games for young players take place on down-sized fields. (Little League bases are 60' apart). Some amateur and minor league games are shorter than nine innings.

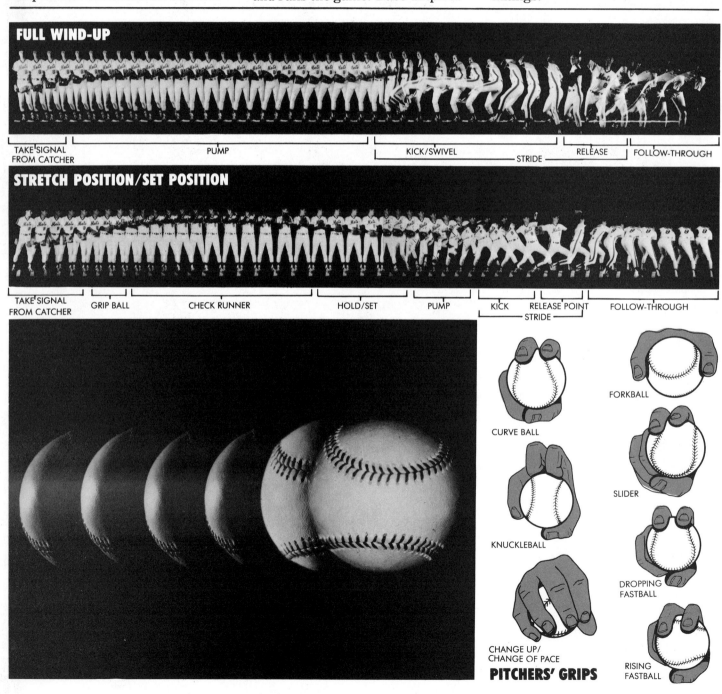

FULL WIND-UP

TAKE SIGNAL FROM CATCHER — PUMP — KICK/SWIVEL — STRIDE — RELEASE — FOLLOW-THROUGH

STRETCH POSITION/SET POSITION

TAKE SIGNAL FROM CATCHER — GRIP BALL — CHECK RUNNER — HOLD/SET — PUMP — KICK — RELEASE POINT — STRIDE — FOLLOW-THROUGH

CURVE BALL

KNUCKLEBALL

CHANGE UP/ CHANGE OF PACE

FORKBALL

SLIDER

DROPPING FASTBALL

RISING FASTBALL

PITCHERS' GRIPS

UMPIRE'S SIGNALS

OUT/STRIKE

FOUL/TIME OUT

SAFE

SPECTATOR INTERFERENCE

FAIR BALL

FOUL TIP

MOVEMENT OF PITCHES

In this overhead view a rising ball gets larger, a sinking ball diminishes.

Ron Luciano

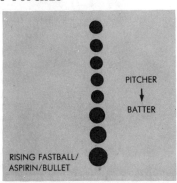

RISING FASTBALL/ ASPIRIN/BULLET

PITCHER ↓ BATTER

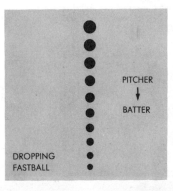

DROPPING FASTBALL

PITCHER ↓ BATTER

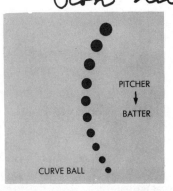

CURVE BALL

PITCHER ↓ BATTER

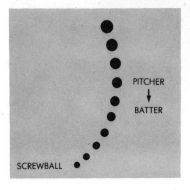

SCREWBALL

PITCHER ↓ BATTER

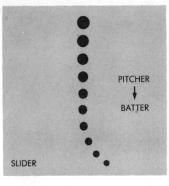

SLIDER

PITCHER ↓ BATTER

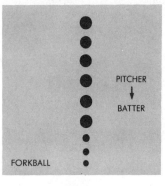

FORKBALL

PITCHER ↓ BATTER

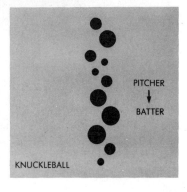

KNUCKLEBALL

PITCHER ↓ BATTER

Basketball is played indoors by two 5-player teams. Unlimited substitutions are permitted. American college and international games are played in two 20-minute halves. Professional games consist of four 12-minute quarters.

The object is to shoot an inflated rubber ball through the opponent's basket while preventing the other team from scoring at the opposite end. A *basket*, or *field goal*, scored from the floor is worth two points. In 'pro ball,' baskets made from beyond the 3-point line are worth three points.

Free throws, or *foul shots*, are awarded by referees when a *foul*, usually illegal contact, is committed. The fouled player is given one or two uncontested throws from

COURT

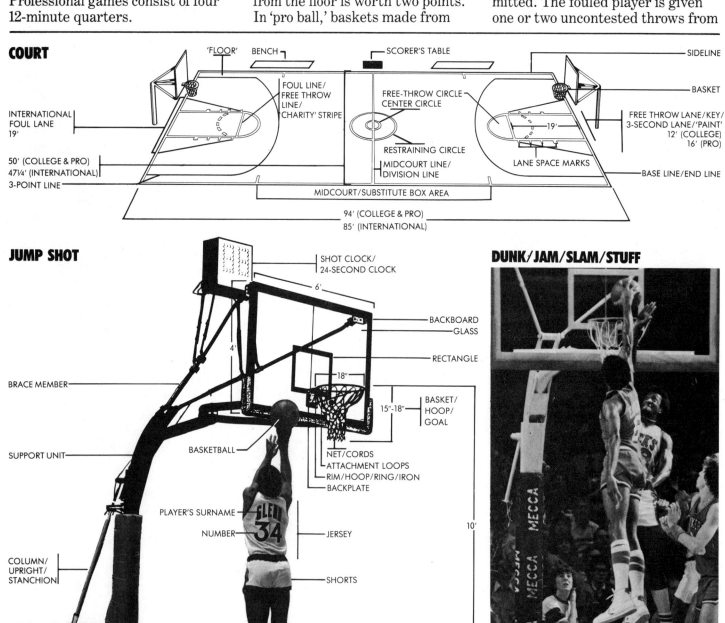

'FLOOR' BENCH SCORER'S TABLE SIDELINE

FOUL LINE/
FREE THROW LINE/
'CHARITY' STRIPE

FREE-THROW CIRCLE
CENTER CIRCLE

BASKET

INTERNATIONAL FOUL LANE 19'

RESTRAINING CIRCLE

19'

FREE THROW LANE/KEY/
3-SECOND LANE/'PAINT'
12' (COLLEGE)
16' (PRO)

50' (COLLEGE & PRO)
47¼' (INTERNATIONAL)

MIDCOURT LINE/
DIVISION LINE

LANE SPACE MARKS

3-POINT LINE

BASE LINE/END LINE

MIDCOURT/SUBSTITUTE BOX AREA

94' (COLLEGE & PRO)
85' (INTERNATIONAL)

JUMP SHOT

SHOT CLOCK/
24-SECOND CLOCK

6'

BACKBOARD
GLASS

RECTANGLE

4'

18"

BRACE MEMBER

15"-18"

BASKET/
HOOP/
GOAL

SUPPORT UNIT

BASKETBALL

NET/CORDS
ATTACHMENT LOOPS
RIM/HOOP/RING/IRON
BACKPLATE

PLAYER'S SURNAME

GLENN
34

NUMBER

JERSEY

10'

COLUMN/
UPRIGHT/
STANCHION

SHORTS

PADDED BASE

SOCKS

SNEAKERS

DUNK/JAM/SLAM/STUFF

the foul line, worth one point if made.

The ball may be thrown, passed or dribbled. Players may take only one-and-a-half steps without dribbling, or bouncing the ball.

When a shot is missed, players vie for the ball as it bounds off the rim, or rebounds. The offensive team tries to slap it through the basket, a *tip in*, or regain control (*offensive rebound*) and maneuver for another shot. If the opposition gets the *defensive rebound*, it at-tempts to bring the ball upcourt to shoot at the other basket.

If a basket is scored, the defense inbounds from beneath its own basket. After a score or rebound, college and pro teams have 10 seconds to cross the midcourt line.

9½" DIA.
WT: 20-22 OZ.
30" CIR.

BALL

DRIBBLING

REBOUNDING

In pro basketball and some college leagues, a team has 24 seconds (30 in international play) from the time it gains possession to attempt a shot or it loses the ball.

Depending on the league, players may commit five or six *personal* *fouls*, for example, blocking, charging or pushing, before *fouling out*, before having to leave the game.

The basic shots are the dunk, in which a player leaps over the basket and slams the ball through it, the lay up, a shot bounced off the back-board from very close, the jump shot, attempted from long range, and the hook, in which a player pivots on one foot and hooks the ball over his head.

Two or three on-court *referees* or *umpires* officiate.

OFFICIALS' SIGNALS

NO BASKET/PLAY DOES NOT COUNT

3-PT. FIELD GOAL ATTEMPT

3-PT. ATTEMPT GOOD

PLAYER NUMBER COMMITTING FOUL

TIME OUT

OFFENSIVE FOUL/CHARGING

TRAVELING

HOLDING

ILLEGAL DRIBBLE/DOUBLE DRIBBLE

TECHNICAL FOUL

PUSHING

PERSONAL FOUL

BLOCKING

GOAL TENDING

HACKING/ ILLEGAL USE OF HANDS

DIRECTION OF PLAY

SCORE COUNTS & NUMBER OF FREE THROWS

OUT OF BOUNDS

LAY UP

ZONE DEFENSES

Defensive players are responsible for protecting an area. The zone rotates as the ball is passed.

MAN-TO-MAN DEFENSES

Defensive players stay with their offensive counterpart wherever he or she goes.

John Wooden
JOHN WOODEN
FORMER HEAD COACH UCLA

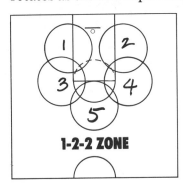

1-2-2 ZONE

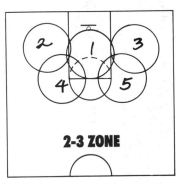

2-3 ZONE

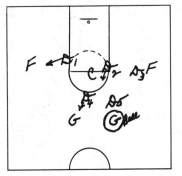

Bobsledders race two-man or four-man *bobs*, or *sleds*, down a curving, narrow *chute* of solid ice through a minimum of 15 banked turns.

Events consist of four runs, or *heats*, over two or more days. The team with the lowest total time for all runs wins.

In both two-man '*boblets*' and four-man sleds, the crew's seats may be no more than 8″ off the ice.

Lead or iron *ballast* is often carried in sleds to bring them up to maximum weight.

Brakes are only used to stop at the completion of a run. Braking on the course results in automatic disqualification.

BOBRUN/COURSE

4-MAN BOBSLED

START

- BOBSLED SUIT
- ELBOW PAD
- GLOVES
- SIDE PUSH HANDLE
- PUSH BAR RETRACTION ASSEMBLY
- SPIKED SHOE ARTICULATION
- RETRACTABLE LIFTING HANDLE
- STARTING GROOVES

- DRIVER
- NUMBER 2 MAN
- NUMBER 3 MAN
- BRAKEMAN
- WALL
- 2'2¼" WIDE (MAX.)
- 12'2" LONG (MAX.)
- ICE
- GOGGLES
- HELMET

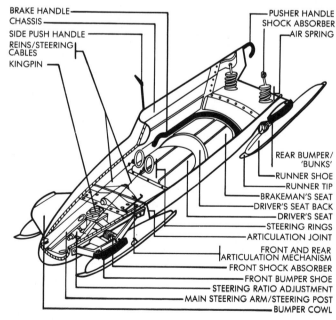

- BRAKE HANDLE
- CHASSIS
- SIDE PUSH HANDLE
- REINS/STEERING CABLES
- KINGPIN
- PUSHER HANDLE
- SHOCK ABSORBER
- AIR SPRING
- REAR BUMPER/ 'BUNKS'
- RUNNER SHOE
- RUNNER TIP
- BRAKEMAN'S SEAT
- DRIVER'S SEAT BACK
- DRIVER'S SEAT
- STEERING RINGS
- ARTICULATION JOINT
- FRONT AND REAR ARTICULATION MECHANISM
- FRONT SHOCK ABSORBER
- FRONT BUMPER SHOE
- STEERING RATIO ADJUSTMENT
- MAIN STEERING ARM/STEERING POST
- BUMPER COWL

BOBSLED CUTAWAY

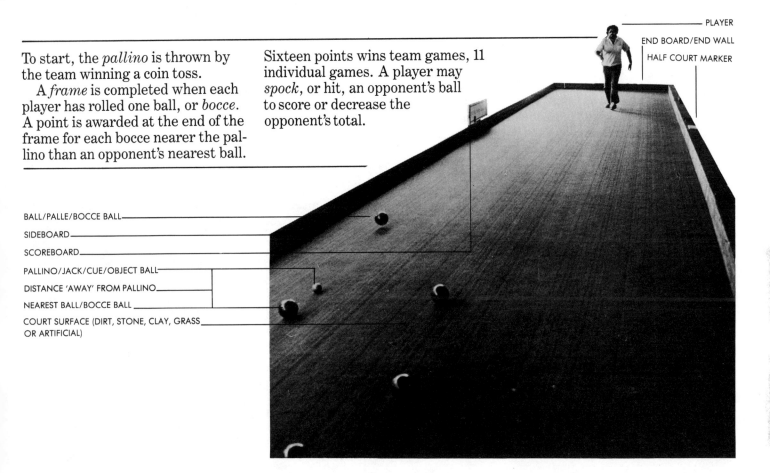

To start, the *pallino* is thrown by the team winning a coin toss.

A *frame* is completed when each player has rolled one ball, or *bocce*. A point is awarded at the end of the frame for each bocce nearer the pallino than an opponent's nearest ball.

Sixteen points wins team games, 11 individual games. A player may *spock*, or hit, an opponent's ball to score or decrease the opponent's total.

PLAYER
END BOARD/END WALL
HALF COURT MARKER

BALL/PALLE/BOCCE BALL
SIDEBOARD
SCOREBOARD
PALLINO/JACK/CUE/OBJECT BALL
DISTANCE 'AWAY' FROM PALLINO
NEAREST BALL/BOCCE BALL
COURT SURFACE (DIRT, STONE, CLAY, GRASS OR ARTIFICIAL)

COURT/PIT/CAMPO

SIDE WALL (MIN. HT. 4½")
IN-BOUNDS LINES FOR 1ST THROW OF PALLINO
END WALL/END BOARD
FOUL LINE FOR POINTING/'ROLL LINE'
FOUL LINE FOR SPOCKING OR HITTING/SPOCK LINE
HALF COURT MARKER

1'
12'

—3'—
—4'—
—9'—
—30'—

BALLS/EQUIPMENT

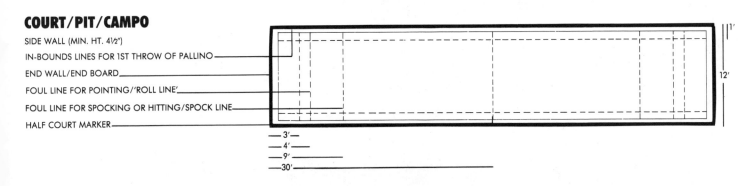

FULL TEAM'S BOCCE BALLS
DIA: 4⅜"-4½"

PALLINO/JACK/CUE/OBJECT BALL
DIA: 2⅛"-2½"

When judging a *physique contest*, the five to seven *judges* evaluate the *symmetry*, *muscularity* and *presentation* of the competitors.

Symmetry includes overall *balance* of body parts and muscle groups. Muscles must show rela- tively equal development and be in *harmony* with other body parts.

Muscularity includes *muscle size*, *development*, *definition* and *hardness*.

Presentation encompasses *grooming*, *posture*, *carriage*, *projection* and *posing ability*.

In female contests, judges also score *choreography* and *grace*. Prior to appearing before judges on a *posing platform*, *'builders'* apply light oil to their bodies and work out to *'pump up'* their muscles in a

MANDATORY POSES JUDGING POINTS

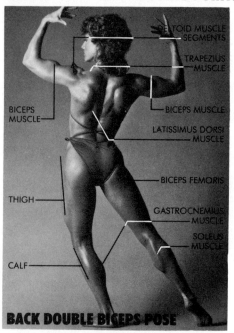

BACK DOUBLE BICEPS POSE

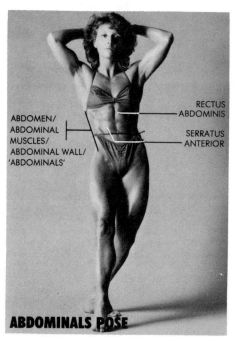

ABDOMINALS POSE

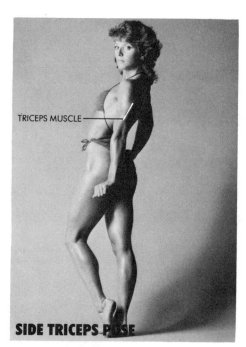

SIDE TRICEPS POSE

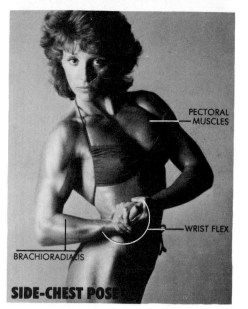

SIDE-CHEST POSE

FREESTYLE ROUTINE/FREE POSING

warm-up room.

Competition begins with a *group facing* in which all entries in a class stand in a line and execute a series of *quarter-turns*. That is followed by *individual posing*, or *freestyle*, in which builders pose alone and perform a timed *full-posing routine*, including mandatory poses, to music. Last is *comparison posing*, in which all contestants are on stage and may be moved for easy comparison. The *meet winner* is chosen in a *posedown* of height or weight class winners.

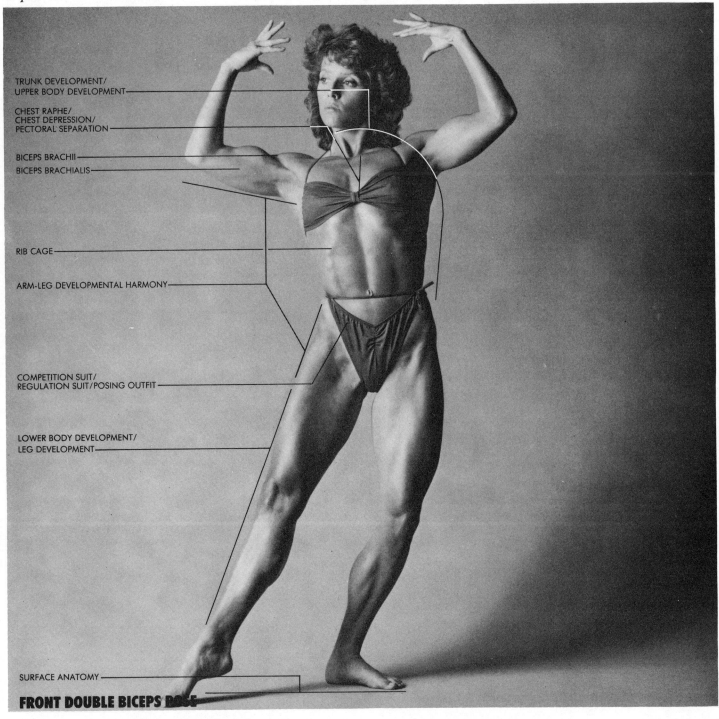

TRUNK DEVELOPMENT/
UPPER BODY DEVELOPMENT

CHEST RAPHE/
CHEST DEPRESSION/
PECTORAL SEPARATION

BICEPS BRACHII

BICEPS BRACHIALIS

RIB CAGE

ARM-LEG DEVELOPMENTAL HARMONY

COMPETITION SUIT/
REGULATION SUIT/POSING OUTFIT

LOWER BODY DEVELOPMENT/
LEG DEVELOPMENT

SURFACE ANATOMY

FRONT DOUBLE BICEPS POSE

A *game*, or *line*, consists of ten *frames*. A *bowler*, or *kegler*, gets two *rolls* in each frame. If all pins are knocked down on the first *shot* a *strike* (X), worth 10 plus the total pins knocked down on the next two balls, is scored. Knocking down all pins with two balls is a spare (/), worth 10 plus all pins knocked down on the next shot.

Candlepins and *duckpins* are forms of bowling with a lighter ball and smaller pins.

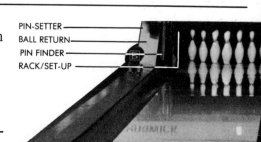

PIN-SETTER
BALL RETURN
PIN FINDER
RACK/SET-UP

LANES/ALLEYS

BALL RETURN CAPPING/'SUBWAY BALL RETURN'
SPOTS/TARGET ARROWS/MARKERS
BOARDS

GUIDES
CHANNEL/GUTTER

FOUL LINE
FOUL LIGHT/FOUL DETECTOR
APPROACH/RUNWAY

THUMB HOLE
SPAN
FINGER HOLE
BRIDGE
WEIGHT
WT: 10-16 LB.

BALL **MOVEMENT OF BALL**

STRAIGHT BALL

CURVE BALL

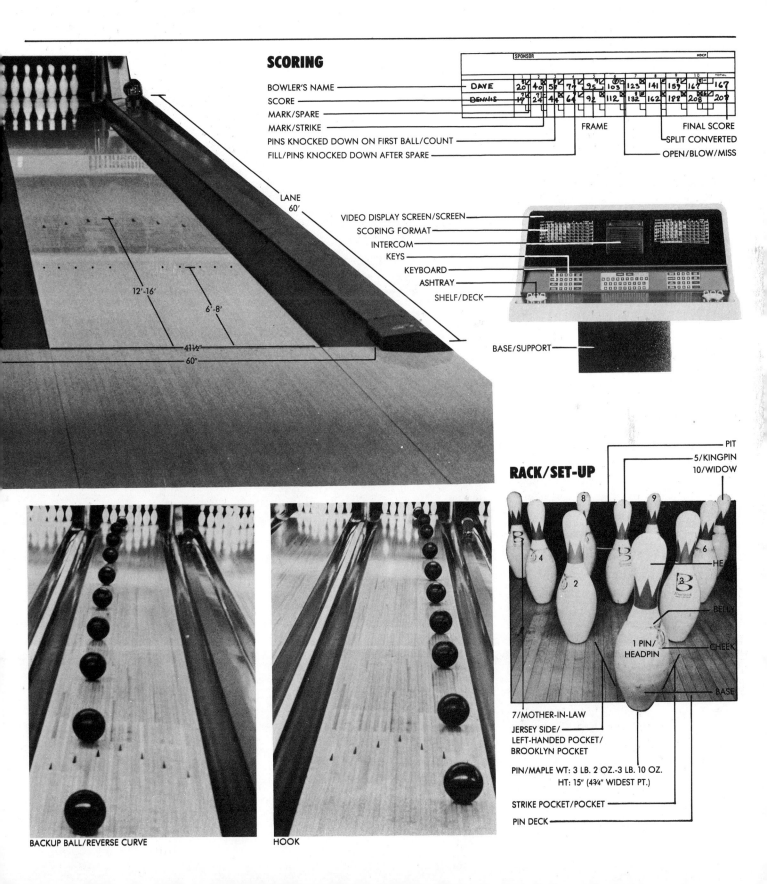

SCORING

			SPONSOR								HDCP	
	1	2	3	4	5	6	7	8	9	10		TOTAL
DAVE	20	40	57	77	95	103	123	141	157	167		167
DENNIS	17	24	44	64	92	112	132	162	188	208		208

BOWLER'S NAME
SCORE
MARK/SPARE
MARK/STRIKE
PINS KNOCKED DOWN ON FIRST BALL/COUNT
FILL/PINS KNOCKED DOWN AFTER SPARE
FRAME
FINAL SCORE
SPLIT CONVERTED
OPEN/BLOW/MISS

LANE
60'

12'-16'
6'-8'
41½"
60"

VIDEO DISPLAY SCREEN/SCREEN
SCORING FORMAT
INTERCOM
KEYS
KEYBOARD
ASHTRAY
SHELF/DECK

BASE/SUPPORT

RACK/SET-UP

PIT
5/KINGPIN
10/WIDOW
8
9
4
6
2
3
HEEL
BELLY
1 PIN/
HEADPIN
CHEEK
BASE
7/MOTHER-IN-LAW
JERSEY SIDE/
LEFT-HANDED POCKET/
BROOKLYN POCKET

PIN/MAPLE WT: 3 LB. 2 OZ.-3 LB. 10 OZ.
HT: 15" (4¾" WIDEST PT.)

STRIKE POCKET/POCKET
PIN DECK

BACKUP BALL/REVERSE CURVE

HOOK

A boxing *match*, *bout* or *fight* is contested in three-minute *rounds*. The predetermined number of rounds, based on the level of competition, varies between three for amateur bouts and 15 for professional championships, or *title bouts*. A *timekeeper* sounds a *bell* to indicate the beginning and end of rounds. Between rounds boxers return to their corners for one-minute rests.

Boxers may only punch above the waistline and the front of the body.

Fights are decided by the judges' *decision*, by *retirement* (if a boxer concedes, or *'throws in the towel'*), by *disqualification* for fouling, by *knock out*, or by having the referee stop the fight, a *technical knock out*.

SCORECARD/CARD

BOXER/FIGHTER
COLOR OF TRUNKS
WINNER OF ROUND

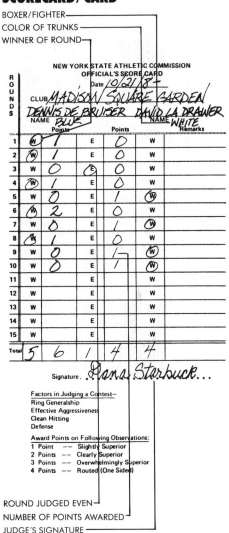

ROUND JUDGED EVEN
NUMBER OF POINTS AWARDED
JUDGE'S SIGNATURE

BOXING RING/PRIZE RING

CORNER
CORNER CUSHION/
TURNBUCKLE PADDING

ROPES
NEUTRAL CORNER
TURNBUCKLE
RINGSIDE

CANVAS

REFEREE/REF
RING POST
LACING ROPES
APRON

AMATEUR BOXERS

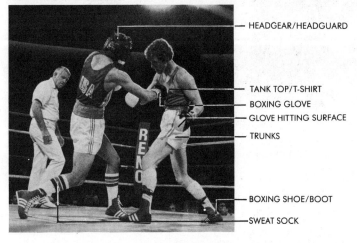

HEADGEAR/HEADGUARD

TANK TOP/T-SHIRT
BOXING GLOVE
GLOVE HITTING SURFACE
TRUNKS

BOXING SHOE/BOOT
SWEAT SOCK

In pro boxing the judges' decision may be based on the number of rounds awarded to a fighter or the total number of points the fighter has won in a bout. When all judges vote for the same boxer it is called a *unanimous decision*. A fighter win-ning by majority vote wins a *split decision*.

A knockout, or *KO*, occurs when a fighter is beaten to the canvas and cannot rise before the referee counts to 10. A technical knockout, or *TKO*, occurs when the ref stops the fight.

Most amateur fights are judged on a *20-point must system*. The winner of a round is given 20 points, the loser receives fewer, depending on performance. The fighter with the most points wins.

BOXING SLANG

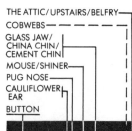
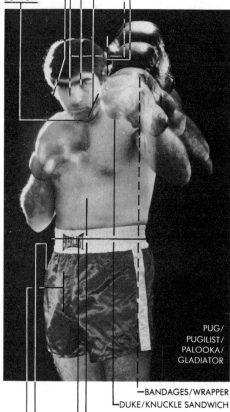

THE ATTIC/UPSTAIRS/BELFRY
COBWEBS
GLASS JAW/ CHINA CHIN/ CEMENT CHIN
MOUSE/SHINER
PUG NOSE
CAULIFLOWER EAR
BUTTON

PUG/ PUGILIST/ PALOOKA/ GLADIATOR

BANDAGES/WRAPPER
DUKE/KNUCKLE SANDWICH
BREADBASKET/LABONZA/ LUNCH BOX
BELT
SOUTH OF THE BORDER/ DOWNSTAIRS
GROIN

FIGHTER'S CORNER

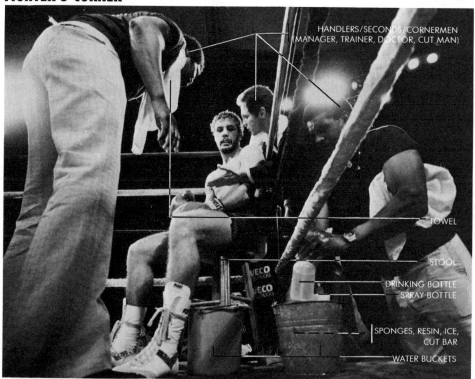

HANDLERS/SECONDS/CORNERMEN (MANAGER, TRAINER, DOCTOR, CUT MAN)

TOWEL
STOOL
DRINKING BOTTLE
SPRAY BOTTLE
SPONGES, RESIN, ICE, CUT BAR
WATER BUCKETS

SPARRING EQUIPMENT

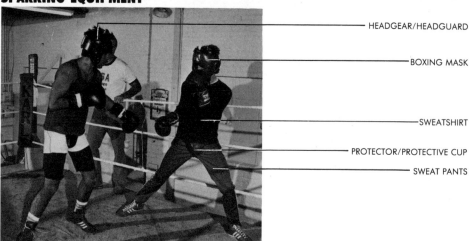

HEADGEAR/HEADGUARD
BOXING MASK
SWEATSHIRT
PROTECTOR/PROTECTIVE CUP
SWEAT PANTS

Amateur boxing places greater emphasis on boxing skills than does pro fighting. The hitting surface of the glove is painted to help judges determine how many *scoring blows* are landed. A *knockdown* is credited as an effective blow, only worth a certain number of points.

Fouls in pro and amateur bouts result in points being deducted, as well as disqualification.

There are between two and five voting judges.

Fighters compete in one of 14 *weight divisions* or *classes*. Among them are *flyweights* (below 112 lb.), *bantamweights* (112-118), *lightweights* (126-135), *welterweights* (135-147), *middleweights* (147-160), *light-heavyweights* (160-175) and *heavyweights* (unlimited).

PUNCHES & STRATEGIES

STRAIGHT LEFT

ROUNDHOUSE/ OVERHAND RIGHT

LEFT JAB/DEFENSE 'SLIPS' THE PUNCH

LEFT HOOK

UPPERCUT

RIGHT CROSS

CLINCH/TIE UP

FOULS

HITTING ON BACK OF NECK/RABBIT PUNCH

HITTING BELOW THE BELT

HITTING ON THE BACK/KIDNEY PUNCH

HITTING WITH OPEN GLOVE

HITTING A MAN WHO IS DOWN

BUTTING

HITTING ON BACK OF HEAD OR SHOULDER, OR WRESTLING

International competition is conducted in one-man, two-man and seven-man Canadian canoes, and in one-man, two-man and four-man kayaks. *Canoeists* and *kayakers*, also known as *kayakists*, compete on *flat water courses* in *sprint races* (500 and 1,000 meters) and *distance races* (5,000 and 10,000 meters).

In championship starts, officials hold the boats so that their sterns are touching the starting pontoons. An *aligner* raises a white flag when all boats are level and stationary. A start then takes place.

In sprints, boats race straight and must remain in their lanes from start to finish. In distance races, boats may leave their lanes but must return to them for the last 1,000 meters. During distance

CANOE/ CANADIAN CANOE/ ALASKAN CANOE

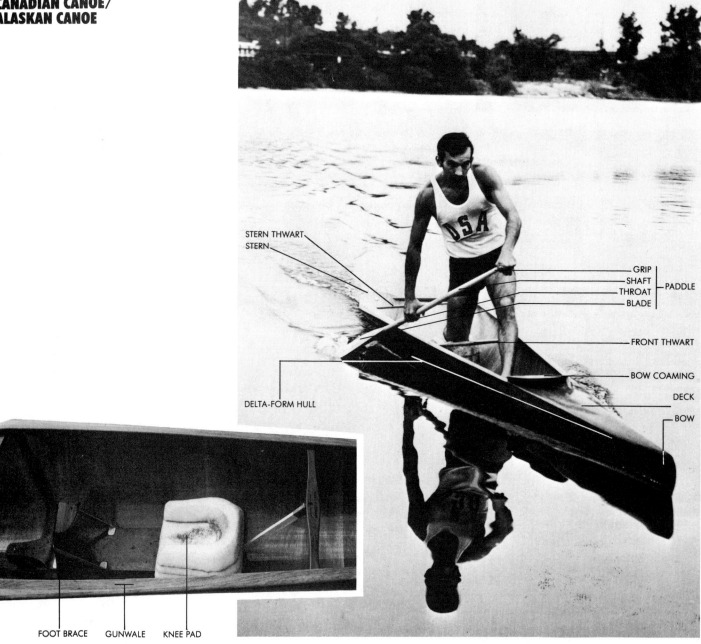

STERN THWART
STERN
DELTA-FORM HULL

GRIP
SHAFT
THROAT — PADDLE
BLADE

FRONT THWART
BOW COAMING
DECK
BOW

FOOT BRACE   GUNWALE   KNEE PAD

races, one canoe may position itself so that it rides on an opponent's bow wave, a maneuver called *wash hanging*.

In Canadian canoes *paddlers* kneel in the open boats and *J stroke* with a single-bladed paddle. The twisting stroke maneuvers the boat in a straight line. Kayakers propel their craft with a *double-bladed paddle* and guide them with a *foot-controlled rudder*.

All boats must meet maximum and minimum requirements. The one-man canoe, for example, may be no longer than 17'7" and weigh no more than 35 pounds.

Competitors may be disqualified for a variety of infractions, but a capsize always results in elimination.

KAYAK

STERN AFT DECK SHAFT BLADES PADDLE FOREDECK BOW

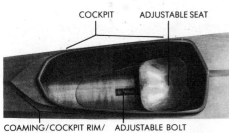

COCKPIT ADJUSTABLE SEAT

COAMING/COCKPIT RIM/ SPLASH GUARD ADJUSTABLE BOLT

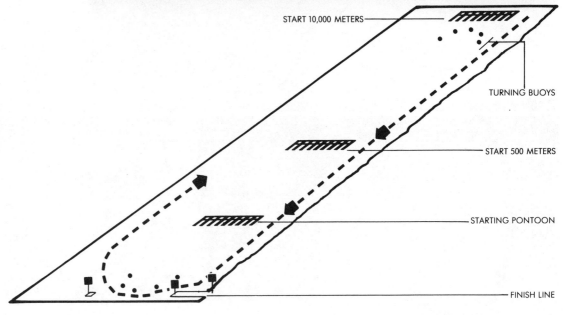

START 10,000 METERS TURNING BUOYS START 500 METERS STARTING PONTOON FINISH LINE

OLYMPIC RACE COURSE

In *whitewater canoe races*, one- and two-man kayaks, two-man canoes (decked over with individual *cockpits*) and open canoes, paddled solo or by two-man teams, compete on rapid river courses.

Contestants must navigate 25 to 30 *control gates*, pairs of poles suspended just above the water, in the correct order and direction, sometimes by reversing, paddling back through an *eddy*, or driving through a series of large standing waves, called *haystacks.*

Penalty points, in the form of seconds subtracted from elapsed time, are imposed for touching gates, failure to negotiate them in the proper direction, or for missing them entirely.

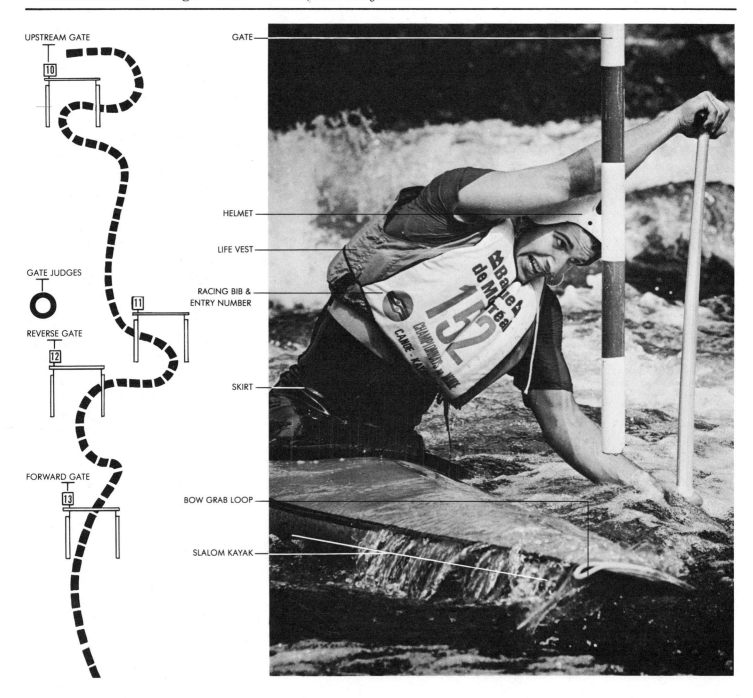

UPSTREAM GATE

10

GATE JUDGES

REVERSE GATE

12

11

FORWARD GATE

13

GATE

HELMET

LIFE VEST

RACING BIB & ENTRY NUMBER

SKIRT

BOW GRAB LOOP

SLALOM KAYAK

Cricket is played by two teams of 11 *cricketers* each, with one team in the field, the other at bat. The bowler, at one wicket, throws, or *bowls*, to the batsman at the other in such a way that the ball bounces in front of the wicket. If the ball knocks the bails off the wicket, or if it hits the batsman standing directly in front of the wicket, the batsman is out. The batsman, or *striker*, tries to hit the ball away from *fieldsmen* so that he and a batsman stationed at the other wicket, the *non-striker*, may exchange places. Each exchange is one *run*. Once a bowler has bowled six balls at one wicket, called an *over*, a teammate bowls to the batsman at the opposite wicket.

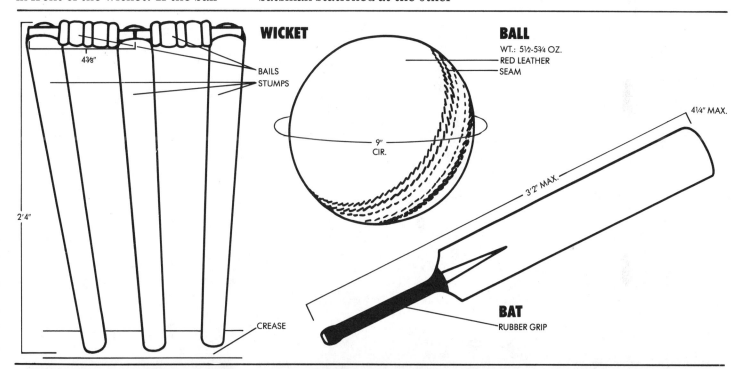

WICKET
4⅜"
BAILS
STUMPS
2'4"
CREASE

BALL
WT.: 5½-5¾ OZ.
RED LEATHER
SEAM
9"
CIR.

4¼" MAX.
3'2" MAX.
BAT
RUBBER GRIP

BOWLER

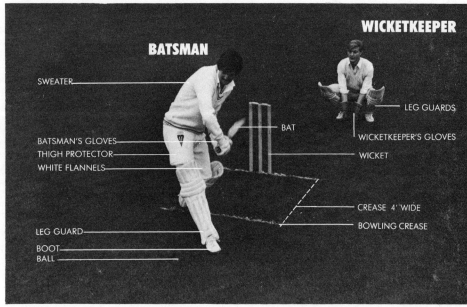

BATSMAN

WICKETKEEPER

SWEATER

BATSMAN'S GLOVES
THIGH PROTECTOR
WHITE FLANNELS

BAT

LEG GUARDS
WICKETKEEPER'S GLOVES
WICKET

LEG GUARD
BOOT
BALL

CREASE 4' WIDE
BOWLING CREASE

A batsman may be put out by having a hit ball caught in the air, by allowing a bowled ball to knock the bails off the wicket behind him, or having a fieldsman similarly 'break' the wicket behind him with the ball while he is running between wickets. Batsmen do not have to run on hit balls.

As each batsman is put out a new man takes his place until 10 of a team's players have been put out. That ends a team's *inning*. Major matches usually consist of two innings, played over two or three days, with breaks for lunch and tea.

The captain of the fielding team, and the bowler, decide in which, of many field positions, to place the fieldsmen.

CRICKET GROUND & FIELDING POSITIONS

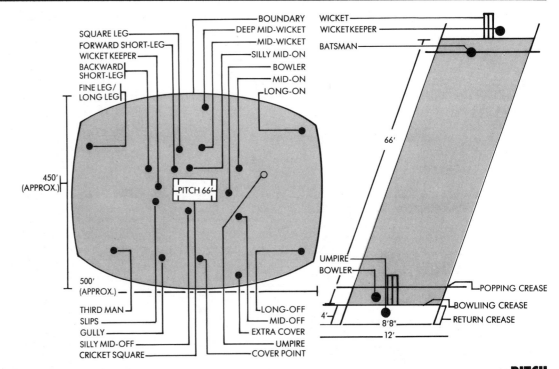

PITCH

UMPIRE SIGNALS

OUT   **NO BALL**   **ONE SHORT**   **LEG BYE**   **SIX RUNS**   **FOUR RUNS**

A toss determines the allocation of the four colors. These colors are painted on the stake, or peg, and control the order of play. Players use balls of the color allocated to them. The first *striker* hits the ball with his mallet at the balkline. Sub-sequent strikers do likewise. The course leads through the wickets, or hoops, toward the stake, with strikers alternating turns. A striker makes a *roquet* by knocking his ball into an opponent's. A ball through the proper wicket in the proper direction scores a point. Winners are decided by total points or by order of course completion. There are two courses: nine wickets and two stakes, or six wickets and one stake.

COURT

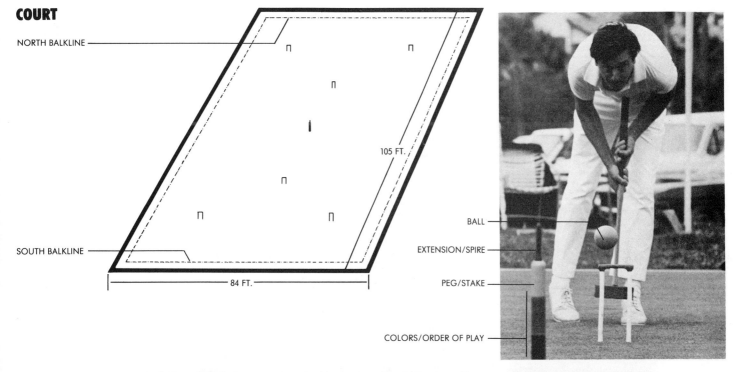

NORTH BALKLINE

105 FT.

SOUTH BALKLINE

84 FT.

BALL

EXTENSION/SPIRE

PEG/STAKE

COLORS/ORDER OF PLAY

MALLET

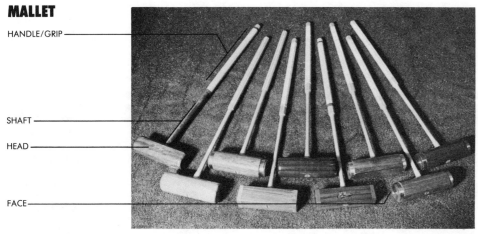

HANDLE/GRIP

SHAFT

HEAD

FACE

CROWN

CLIP/MARKER

UPRIGHT

JAWS

WICKET/HOOP

A curling team, or *rink*, consists of four players, led by a captain, or *skip*. The game is played on a lane of ice called a rink, or *sheet*. A player slides his stone, or rock, toward a *tee* at the center of the house, also called a *head* or *goal*.

Sweepers use brooms to alter the speed, or *weight*, of the stone and its direction, *curl* or *bend*.

Teams alternate, with each player *delivering* two stones. The 16 deliveries make up one *end*, or *inning*. A point is awarded for each of a team's stones that is closer to the tee than the opponents' nearest stone. A game consists of any prearranged number of ends, usually 10 or 12. The team with the most points wins.

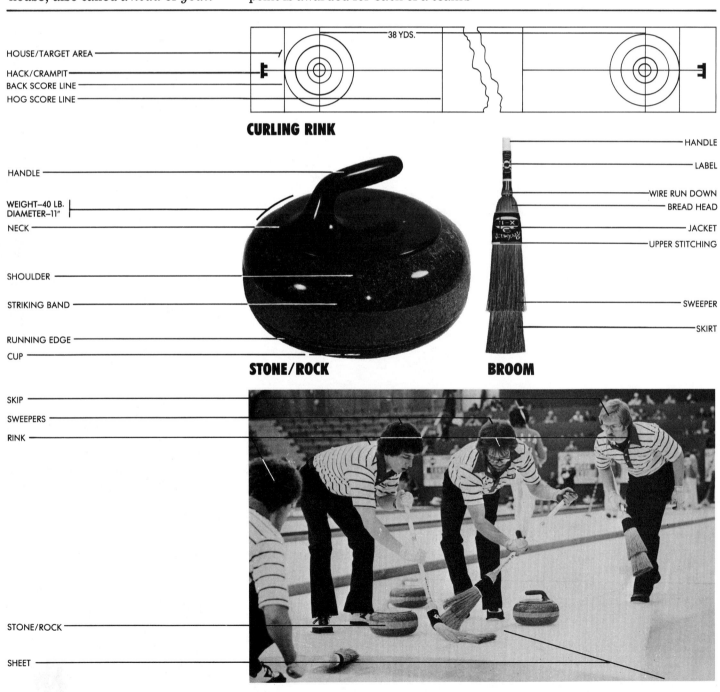

HOUSE/TARGET AREA

HACK/CRAMPIT

BACK SCORE LINE

HOG SCORE LINE

38 YDS.

CURLING RINK

HANDLE

WEIGHT–40 LB.
DIAMETER–11"

NECK

SHOULDER

STRIKING BAND

RUNNING EDGE

CUP

STONE/ROCK

HANDLE

LABEL

WIRE RUN DOWN

BREAD HEAD

JACKET

UPPER STITCHING

SWEEPER

SKIRT

BROOM

SKIP

SWEEPERS

RINK

STONE/ROCK

SHEET

Cycle racing is divided into track and road events. Track racers compete at various distances in *pursuits*, in which racers start at opposite sides of the track and try to overtake each other (if racers are not caught, the *rider* covering a specified distance first wins), *time trials*, one rider against the clock, and *sprints*, in which two or three cyclists race over one or more laps. Timing is over the last 200 meters, so earlier laps are used to gain the inside position.

Track bikes have lightweight *frames*, one gear and no brakes.

Road races may take place over hundreds of miles and many days. They are often raced in *stages*, in which competitors cover a specified number of miles per day.

ROAD RACING BIKE

PADDED HELMET
CHIN STRAP
SLEEVED JERSEY
DARK-COLORED RACING SHORTS
STEM
BRAKE LEVER
DROPPED HANDLEBAR
FRONT BRAKE CABLE
REAR BRAKE CABLE
SHIFTERS
REAR BRAKE
FRONT BRAKE
FORK/FORK BLADE
WATER BOTTLE HOLDER
CHAIN RING
FRONT HUB
FRONT WHEEL QUICK RELEASE
CHAIN STAY
TOE CLIP
TOE STRAP
PEDAL
DRIVE CHAIN
REAR DERAILLEUR

RACING SHOE

EYELET FACING
MESH TOP
SOLE
CLEAT
VENTILATION HOLES

VELODROME/RACING TRACK

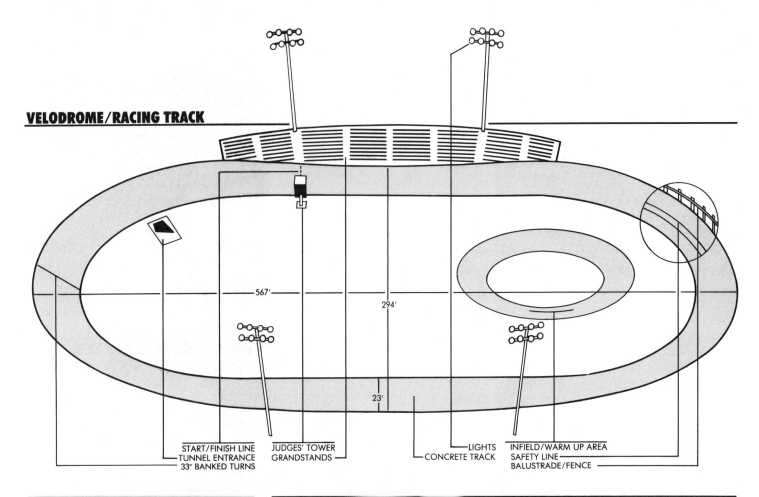

567'

294'

23'

START/FINISH LINE
TUNNEL ENTRANCE
33° BANKED TURNS

JUDGES' TOWER
GRANDSTANDS

LIGHTS
CONCRETE TRACK

INFIELD/WARM UP AREA
SAFETY LINE
BALUSTRADE/FENCE

INDIVIDUAL PURSUIT & TIME TRIAL FLAT

TRACK BIKE

TIRE
RIM
SPOKES
UPRIGHT HANDLEBARS
FORK
HEAD TUBE

BOLT-ON PEDAL
DOWNTUBE
CROSS BAR/TOP TUBE
SEAT TUBE
SEAT
SEAT STAY
HELMET/SHELL

Darts, or *darting*, is played by individuals, pairs or teams of any number. In *tournament darts*, the most universally played game, individuals start with 301 points. In team play, the *opening score* may be increased to 501 or 1,001. Sides take turns throwing three darts. The score from each *throw* is subtracted from the remaining total. The first side to reduce its score to exactly zero wins. Each game is called a *leg*. Three legs win a match.

Other *clockface games* include *round-the-clock*, *all fives*, *scrubbers* (also called *cricket*), *baseball*, *high score*, *killer*, *Mulligan*, *sudden death*, and *Shanghai*.

DART

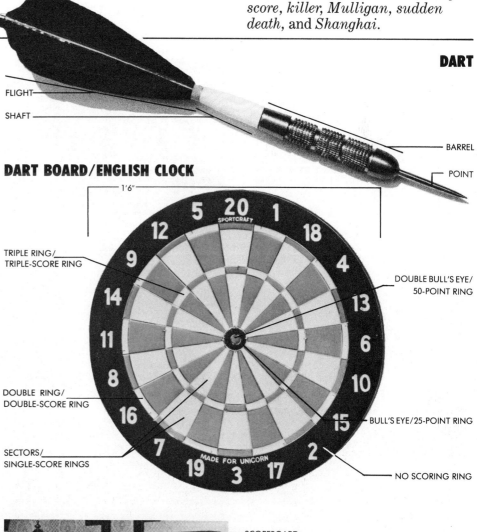

FLIGHT

SHAFT

BARREL

POINT

DART BOARD/ENGLISH CLOCK

1'6"

TRIPLE RING/
TRIPLE-SCORE RING

DOUBLE BULL'S EYE/
50-POINT RING

DOUBLE RING/
DOUBLE-SCORE RING

BULL'S EYE/25-POINT RING

SECTORS/
SINGLE-SCORE RINGS

NO SCORING RING

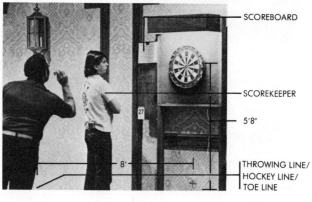

SCOREBOARD

SCOREKEEPER

5'8"

8'

THROWING LINE/
HOCKEY LINE/
TOE LINE

Fancy diving, the formal name for the sport of diving, consists of intricate in-air maneuvers culminating with a graceful entry into the water. There are four events: platform and springboard competitions for men and women.

Men are judged on 11 dives, women on 10. *Preliminary contests* are held when there are more than 16 divers. The eight divers with the most points advance to the final round where they perform the same dives they executed in the preliminary.

Each dive has a preassigned *degree of difficulty* coefficient, or *DD*. Thus, dives range in numerical value from 1.2, for a simple forward dive, to 3.5 for a highly difficult *forward 4 1/2 somersault*.

DIVING POOL/TANK

- 10-METER PLATFORM/HIGHBOARD (33')
- DIVERS' ELEVATOR
- 7.5-METER PLATFORM (24'5")
- 5-METER PLATFORM (16'3")
- 3-METER PLATFORM (9'9")
- —THE TOWER
- 3-METER SPRINGBOARD (9'9")
- 1-METER SPRINGBOARD (3'3")
- MECHANICAL SURFACE AGITATION
- JUDGES
- DIVING TANK (17' DEEP)
- PRACTICE BOARDS/WARM-UP BOARDS

A panel of seven judges awards points for each dive, as follows: failed dive—0; unsatisfactory—½-2; deficient—2½-4½; satisfactory—5-6; good—6½-8; very good—8½-10. The highest and lowest scores are discarded and the remaining five are multiplied first by ⅗, then by the dive's degree of difficulty to determine the final score for the dive. The winner of each event is the diver with the greatest number of points.

Divers lose points for restarting a running dive, touching the end of the board, diving to the side of the direct line of flight, or entering the water 'short' or 'over' (less than or beyond the 90-degree entry angle).

COMPONENTS OF A DIVE & JUDGING POINTS

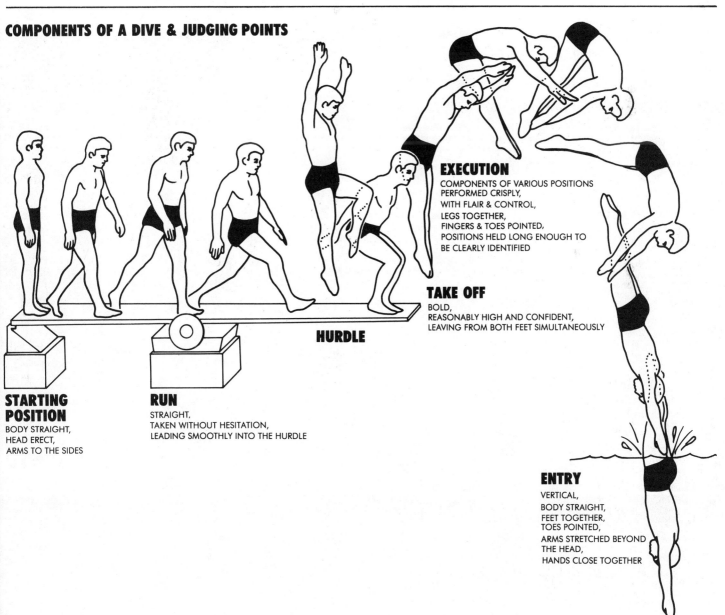

EXECUTION
COMPONENTS OF VARIOUS POSITIONS
PERFORMED CRISPLY,
WITH FLAIR & CONTROL,
LEGS TOGETHER,
FINGERS & TOES POINTED,
POSITIONS HELD LONG ENOUGH TO
BE CLEARLY IDENTIFIED

TAKE OFF
BOLD,
REASONABLY HIGH AND CONFIDENT,
LEAVING FROM BOTH FEET SIMULTANEOUSLY

HURDLE

STARTING POSITION
BODY STRAIGHT,
HEAD ERECT,
ARMS TO THE SIDES

RUN
STRAIGHT,
TAKEN WITHOUT HESITATION,
LEADING SMOOTHLY INTO THE HURDLE

ENTRY
VERTICAL,
BODY STRAIGHT,
FEET TOGETHER,
TOES POINTED,
ARMS STRETCHED BEYOND
THE HEAD,
HANDS CLOSE TOGETHER

Dives are divided into the six *groups* illustrated below. The first five dive groups are practiced on the springboard. All six are contested in platform diving. A twist dive is a forward, backward, reverse or inward dive, combined with a twist.

Dives in each group may be performed in one of many *positions*— straight, with no bends at waist, hips or knees; pike, bent at the waist only; tuck, with body bent at the knees, hips and waist; free, a combination of straight, pike or

tuck, also used in certain twisting dives.

Running dives begin when the diver takes the first step of his *run*. *Standing dives* begin at the front end of the platform.

A forward dive in the pike posi-

FORWARD DIVE

STRAIGHT POSITION

INWARD DIVE
(INWARD 1½ SOMERSAULT)

TUCK POSITION

BACKWARD DIVE
(FLYING BACK SOMERSAULT)

STRAIGHT POSITION

FREE POSITION

TUCK POSITION

tion is also called a *jackknife*, just as a forward dive in a straight, or *layout*, position is often referred to as a *swan dive*. A somersault is a *flip*, a reverse dive is a *gainer*, or *Mohlberg*, and an improper form of landing is a *bellyflop*.

Entering the water with virtually no splash is a *rip entry*, accomplished by landing on the palms of the hands and opening the water with them. In addition, the diver may perform a breaststroke motion with his arms underwater, thereby

creating pockets of air on either side and vanishing through the vacuum between them, leaving only puddles of foam on the surface.

REVERSE DIVE

PIKE POSITION

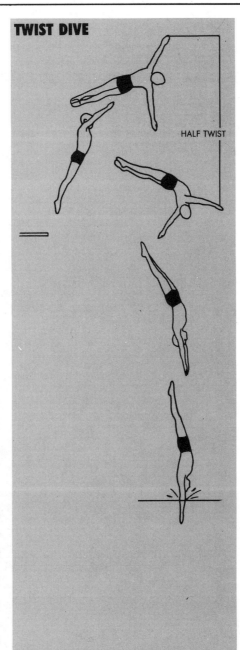

TWIST DIVE

HALF TWIST

ARMSTAND DIVE

CUT THROUGH

Although much recreational diving is done with *scuba*, an acronym for *self-contained underwater breathing apparatus*, competitive events usually involve *breathhold diving*, or *free diving*, without equipment.

In spearfishing tournaments, contested by men and women, pairs, mixed pairs and juniors, points are accrued by *spearfishermen*, or *spearfishers*, for the number of fish species taken and their size. In *underwater*

hockey, breathhold divers compete with sticks and balls, in much the same way as field hockey players.

Navigation contests, in which individual skills are tested underwater, are conducted with scuba equipment.

SCUBA DIVER

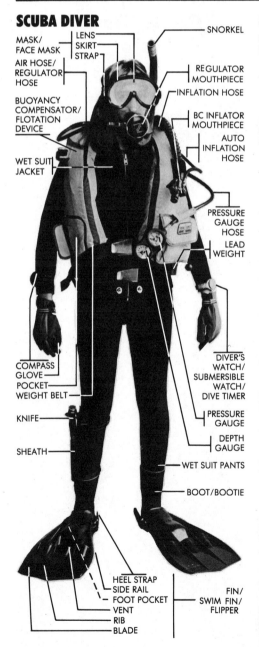

MASK/FACE MASK
LENS
SKIRT
STRAP
SNORKEL
AIR HOSE/REGULATOR HOSE
REGULATOR MOUTHPIECE
INFLATION HOSE
BUOYANCY COMPENSATOR/FLOTATION DEVICE
BC INFLATOR MOUTHPIECE
AUTO INFLATION HOSE
WET SUIT JACKET
PRESSURE GAUGE HOSE
LEAD WEIGHT
COMPASS
GLOVE
POCKET
WEIGHT BELT
DIVER'S WATCH/SUBMERSIBLE WATCH/DIVE TIMER
KNIFE
PRESSURE GAUGE
SHEATH
DEPTH GAUGE
WET SUIT PANTS
BOOT/BOOTIE
HEEL STRAP
SIDE RAIL
FOOT POCKET
VENT
RIB
BLADE
FIN/SWIM FIN/FLIPPER

SPEAR GUN

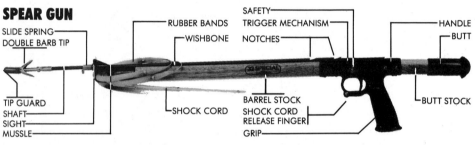

SLIDE SPRING
DOUBLE BARB TIP
RUBBER BANDS
WISHBONE
SAFETY
TRIGGER MECHANISM
NOTCHES
HANDLE
BUTT
TIP GUARD
SHAFT
SIGHT
MUSSLE
SHOCK CORD
BARREL STOCK
SHOCK CORD RELEASE FINGER
GRIP
BUTT STOCK

A greyhound race begins when an *electrically operated lure* passes *starting boxes* holding seven to nine greyhounds. The male *dogs* and female *bitches* are released to chase the *'rabbit'* around an oval course.

Coursing greyhounds are registered in a *stud book* and identified on a *bertillion card*, which is used by *Paddock Judges* to prevent illegal substitution. Greyhounds are rated by performance on the track into six categories, *A,B,C,D,E*, and *M* (Maiden.) A *Maiden* is a greyhound who has never won a race. Greyhounds race in category and are raised or lowered depending on finish over a few consecutive races.

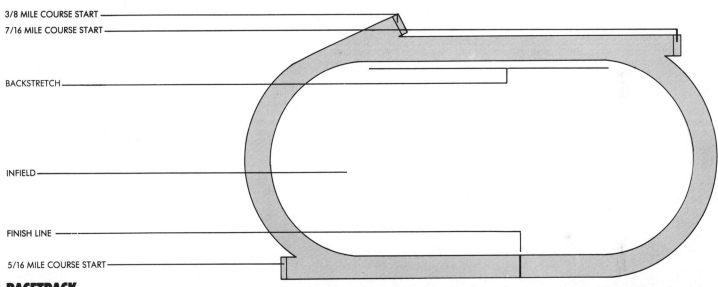

3/8 MILE COURSE START
7/16 MILE COURSE START
BACKSTRETCH
INFIELD
FINISH LINE
5/16 MILE COURSE START

RACETRACK

THE START

GREYHOUND
MUZZLE
TRAP NUMBER
BLANKET/JACKET
STARTING TRAPS/BOXES

TRACK/COURSE
INSIDE LURE TRACK

RABBIT/LURE/
MECHANICAL LURE

TRACK
MOUNT
WHEELED CARRIAGE

BERTILLION CARD/IDENTITY CARD

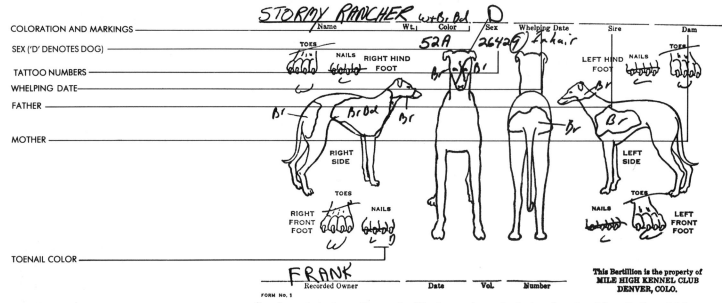

COLORATION AND MARKINGS

SEX ('D' DENOTES DOG)

TATTOO NUMBERS

WHELPING DATE

FATHER

MOTHER

TOENAIL COLOR

FORM NO. 1

Greyhounds look pretty much alike to most people, but each animal has distinguishing markings. Every hound on a racing list, then, has its own bertillion card. This identity card includes the greyhound's name, coloration and markings, sex ('Dog' denotes a male), owner, and tattoo numbers. Coloration and all markings are drawn in detail, even to include the color of the toenails.

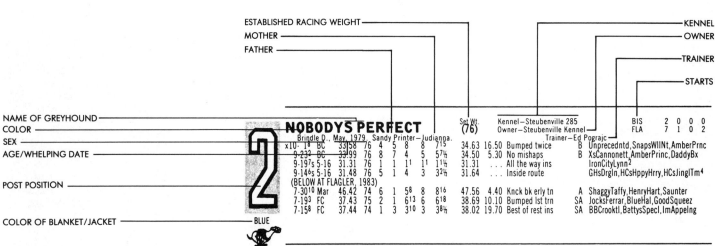

ESTABLISHED RACING WEIGHT — — — KENNEL

MOTHER — — — OWNER

FATHER — — — TRAINER

— — — STARTS

NAME OF GREYHOUND

COLOR

SEX

AGE/WHELPING DATE

POST POSITION

COLOR OF BLANKET/JACKET — BLUE

NOBODYS PERFECT

Brindle D., May, 1979. Sandy Printer—Judianna.

x10- 1⁸	BC	33⁵⁸	76	4	5	8	8	7¹⁵	34.63	16.50	Bumped twice	B	Unprecedntd, SnapsWilNt, AmberPrnc
9-23²	BC	33⁹⁹	76	8	7	4	5	5⁷½	34.50	5.30	No mishaps	B	XsCannonett, AmberPrinc, DaddyBx
9-19⁷s	5-16	31.31	76	1	1	1¹	1¹	1¹½	31.31	. . .	All the way ins		IronCityLynn²
9-14⁶s	5-16	31.48	76	5	1	4	3	3²½	31.64	. . .	Inside route		GHsDrgln, HCsHppyHrry, HCsJinglTm⁴
(BELOW AT FLAGLER, 1983)													
7-30¹⁰	Mar	46.42	74	6	1	5⁸	8	8¹⁶	47.56	4.40	Knck bk erly tn	A	ShaggyTaffy, HenryHart, Saunter
7-19³	FC	37.43	75	2	1	6¹³	6	6¹⁸	38.69	10.10	Bumped lst trn	SA	JocksFerrar, BlueHal, GoodSqueez
7-15⁸	FC	37.44	74	1	3	3¹⁰	3	3⁸½	38.02	19.70	Best of rest ins	SA	BBCrooktl, BattysSpecl, ImAppelng

Set Wt: (76)

Kennel—Steubenville 285
Owner—Steubenville Kennel
Trainer—Ed Pograjc

	BIS	2	0	0	0
	FLA	7	1	0	2

RACING PROGRAM

RACING FORM

Howard Haley's Light Brindle D.
January 19, 1981. Detroit City*—Daddy's Date.

Little Howard	12.00	4.20	4.20	
Neka Jones		3.00	2.60	Trif. 1-4-7—$287.60
IV's Captain			3.80	Quin. 1-4—$20.40

2nd RACE—5-16 MILE   GRADE BB   TIME: 31.48

2-1¹¹	Unwindable	67	6 6 4	2	1¹½	31.48	5.50		
1-31¹¹	Four Stroke	69	3 3 1³	1¹	2¹½	31.57	2.50		
2-1⁴	River Moss	68	2 7 6	4	3¹½	31.60	11.70		
1-31⁴	Pat C Streaker	66	8 1 2	3	4²½	31.64	2.50		
1-31¹⁰	Fire In The Hole	70	1 4 5	5	5⁵½	31.87	16.80		
2-1⁴	Dutch D West	66	4 8 7	7	6⁸½	32.06	14.20		
2-1⁴	Another Dollar	59	5 5 8	8	7¹⁰	32.18	3.10		
1-31¹⁰	Dane Hunter	73	7 2 3	6	8¹²	32.34	15.60		

PAST PERFORMANCE CHART

Date and Race Previous Event	Distance	Track Condition	Time of Winner	Weight at Post Time	Post Position	Start	One-Eighth Lengths Back	Stretch Call	Finish—Lengths From Winner	Actual Running Time	Odds	Comment	Grade	Order of Finish	
4-21¹¹	5/16 mi	F	30⁸⁴	71	4	8	8	4	4⁸	31⁵³	4.50	Blkd 1st, closed	[A]	ProudBeauty ChfDan George DQ'sTurry	8
4-16⁸	5/16 mi	F	31³³	71½	3	8	5	5	3⁸	31⁸⁸	10.40	Blkd early, rcvrd	[A]	JR'sMelissa PrideEckert DaleMRector	8
x4-13⁸	5/16 mi	F	31⁹³	71	8	4	1⁸	1¹⁰	1¹³	31⁹³	1.50*	In full command	[B]	WorldFree RenoGMC LadyJontue	8
4- 8¹³	5/16 mi	F	32⁶³	71	4	7	5	3¹²	32⁹³		1.60*	Much trble, rcvrd	[B]	KASlumber ElectronicPwr BogusCash	8
4- 3⁴	5/16 mi	F	31¹⁶	70	1	1	1²	1⁴²	31¹⁰		7.40	Backstretch drive	[C]	JR'sWineta LC'sLadyAnn SlickJocker	8
x3-30¹	5/16 mi	F	30⁸⁵	71	7	6	1³	1³	1⁵½	30⁸⁵	6.00	Cleared, 1st turn	[D]	SpotOfMusic ColorSargeant PowerTrip	8

Equestrianism, the training of horses for specific tasks, is contested in show jumping, dressage, and eventing, also called *horse trials* of the *three-day event.*

Show jumping takes place in an arena. *Riders* direct their *mounts* over 12-15 *obstacles* which range in height from 2'6" to 7'2" and are placed on a course 763 to 981 yards long.

Hunter class horses are judged primarily on style, grace and the compatibility of horse and rider.

Open Jumpers are judged solely on their ability to clear fences. The horse with the fewest *faults* over a prescribed number of runs wins.

Faults include refusing to jump, knocking down a rail and exceeding the time limit for a run.

COURSE

HARD HAT/
HUNT CAP
RIDING SHIRT/
'RAT CATCHER'
BRIDLE

COAT
BREECHES
BOOTS
SPURS

ENGLISH SADDLE
SADDLE PAD

SHOW JUMPING

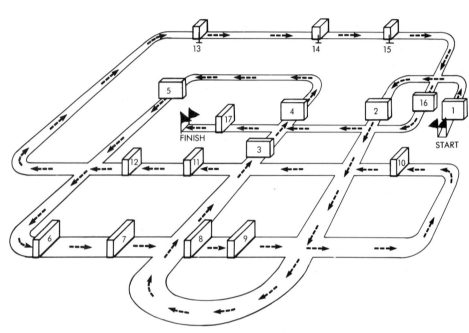

SHOW JUMPING FENCES

UPRIGHT/GATE

UPRIGHT/STONE WALL

COMBINATION JUMP/IN AND OUT

WATER JUMP

WATER JUMP

SPREAD/CROSS BARS

SPREAD/OXER

SPREAD/PARALLEL POLES

SPREAD/PARALLEL POLES

TRIPLE BARS/STAIRCASE

Dressage, or *schooling*, tests the ability of the horse and rider to perform a variety of specific movements which demonstrate control, *pace*, *seat* (rider's posture), fluidity and ease of movement.

Five judges around the arena score each movement from zero to 10.

Competitors have 10-12 minutes to complete a 30-movement *test*. These include command of the *natural gaits* (walk, trot, canter) and numerous variations (including the *piaffe*, an elegant trot in place, and *passage*, the same trot but with forward movement), *transitions* between paces, *halts* and *pirouettes* (turns done with the horse's hind legs remaining in place.)

There is both individual and team competition.

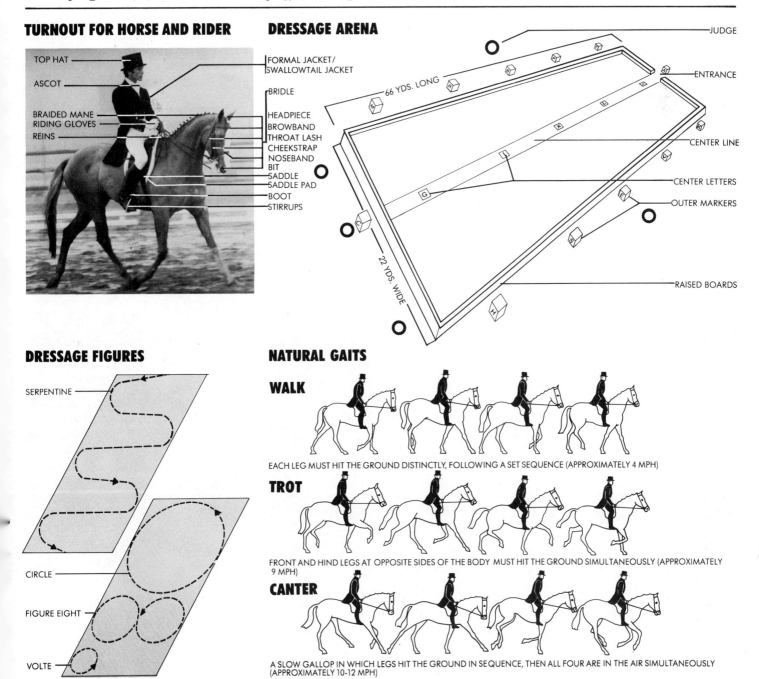

TURNOUT FOR HORSE AND RIDER

TOP HAT
ASCOT
BRAIDED MANE
RIDING GLOVES
REINS
FORMAL JACKET/
SWALLOWTAIL JACKET
BRIDLE
HEADPIECE
BROWBAND
THROAT LASH
CHEEKSTRAP
NOSEBAND
BIT
SADDLE
SADDLE PAD
BOOT
STIRRUPS

DRESSAGE ARENA

JUDGE
ENTRANCE
66 YDS. LONG
CENTER LINE
CENTER LETTERS
OUTER MARKERS
22 YDS. WIDE
RAISED BOARDS

DRESSAGE FIGURES

SERPENTINE
CIRCLE
FIGURE EIGHT
VOLTE

NATURAL GAITS

WALK

EACH LEG MUST HIT THE GROUND DISTINCTLY, FOLLOWING A SET SEQUENCE (APPROXIMATELY 4 MPH)

TROT

FRONT AND HIND LEGS AT OPPOSITE SIDES OF THE BODY MUST HIT THE GROUND SIMULTANEOUSLY (APPROXIMATELY 9 MPH)

CANTER

A SLOW GALLOP IN WHICH LEGS HIT THE GROUND IN SEQUENCE, THEN ALL FOUR ARE IN THE AIR SIMULTANEOUSLY (APPROXIMATELY 10-12 MPH)

During a three-day event, horse and rider compete in dressage, *speed and endurance*, and stadium jumping, on consecutive days.

Dressage is worth three points in the total score, speed and endurance 12 and jumping one.

In eventing dressage, the ability of the horse to shorten and lengthen gait is of primary importance.

Speed and endurance is tested over a 4-mile *road and track* run, a 2½-mile *steeplechase* (including 10 obstacles), a longer road and track run and a 5-mile *cross country* run over uneven terrain with numerous obstacles to be jumped.

Stadium jumping includes 10-15 obstacles. Penalty points in each phase are added together and the lowest total score wins.

CROSS COUNTRY

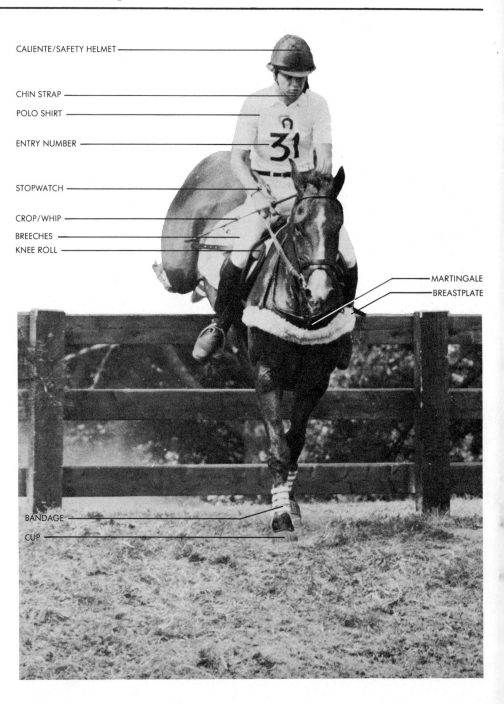

CALIENTE/SAFETY HELMET

CHIN STRAP

POLO SHIRT

ENTRY NUMBER

STOPWATCH

CROP/WHIP

BREECHES

KNEE ROLL

MARTINGALE

BREASTPLATE

BANDAGE

CUP

Two fencers participate in a *match*, *bout* or *assault*, on a narrow mat, strip or piste. They fence with foils, épées or sabres, flexible blunted swords that differ slightly in weight and design.

Before the bout, fencers salute each other, their spectators and a *jury*. The jury director or president orders opponents 'On Guard', asks if they are 'Ready' and commands them to 'Play' or 'Fence.'

Each fencer must wear a chest-protecting plastron under his padded fencing jacket. Women must also wear a breast protector.

EQUIPMENT

SALUTE

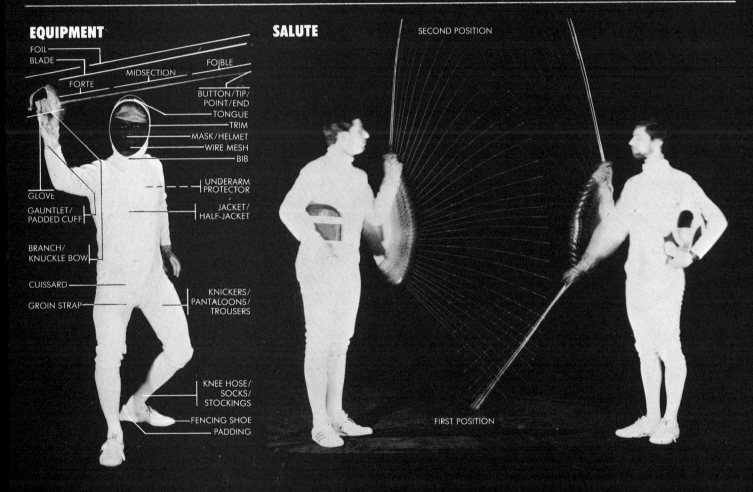

FOIL
BLADE
MIDSECTION
FOIBLE
FORTE
BUTTON/TIP/
POINT/END
TONGUE
TRIM
MASK/HELMET
WIRE MESH
BIB
UNDERARM
PROTECTOR
GLOVE
GAUNTLET/
PADDED CUFF
JACKET/
HALF-JACKET
BRANCH/
KNUCKLE BOW
CUISSARD
GROIN STRAP
KNICKERS/
PANTALOONS/
TROUSERS
KNEE HOSE/
SOCKS/
STOCKINGS
FENCING SHOE
PADDING

SECOND POSITION

FIRST POSITION

In foil and saber, fencers who seize the initiative with an *arm extension* or attack receive *fencing precedence* or *right of way* to score. By *deflecting,* or parrying the blade, a defender gets the right of way to *riposte,* or counterattack.

A blade-contacting *engagement* is sought by a fencer who wants to know where the opponent's blade is and how loosely or tightly it is being held. No contact is *absence of blade.*

French is the official judging language of fencing.

STRIP/PISTE/MAT

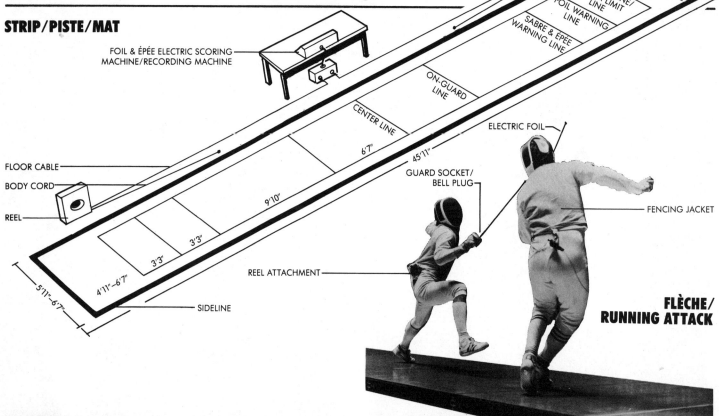

FOIL & ÉPÉE ELECTRIC SCORING MACHINE/RECORDING MACHINE

SAFETY ZONE/END ZONE/RETREAT ZONE

END LINE/ REAR LIMIT LINE

FOIL WARNING LINE

SABRE & ÉPÉE WARNING LINE

ON-GUARD LINE

CENTER LINE

ELECTRIC FOIL

6'7"

45'11"

GUARD SOCKET/ BELL PLUG

FLOOR CABLE

9'10"

BODY CORD

FENCING JACKET

REEL

3'3"

3'3"

REEL ATTACHMENT

4'11"–6'7"

5'11"–6'7"

SIDELINE

FLÈCHE/ RUNNING ATTACK

ON-GUARD

QUARTE POSITION

PARRY 4

HIGH INSIDE LINE

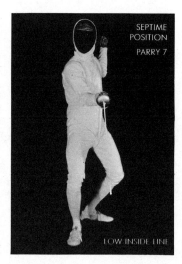

SEPTIME POSITION

PARRY 7

LOW INSIDE LINE

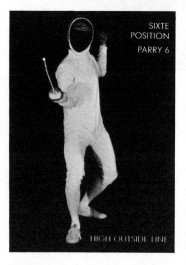

SIXTE POSITION

PARRY 6

HIGH OUTSIDE LINE

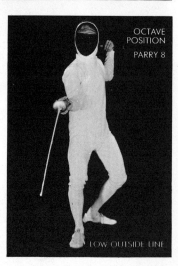

OCTAVE POSITION

PARRY 8

LOW OUTSIDE LINE

Swords are thrust into an opponent's *valid hits*, or valid target areas. Four judges determine the *materiality* of hits in *dry* or *non-electric* matches. The president calls 'Halt' so the jury can reconstruct the *phrase d'armes*, or exchange of blade action. Hits that *land and stick on-target* score points and are called *touches*. Two ground judges referee *electrically scored* matches.

The *bouting* ends when one fencer scores a prescribed number of touches or when a time limit expires: generally five touches or six minutes for men; four touches or five minutes for women. A deciding bout, or *barrage*, is a *fence-off* that settles a tie in foil and sabre. A tie in épée is a defeat for both fencers.

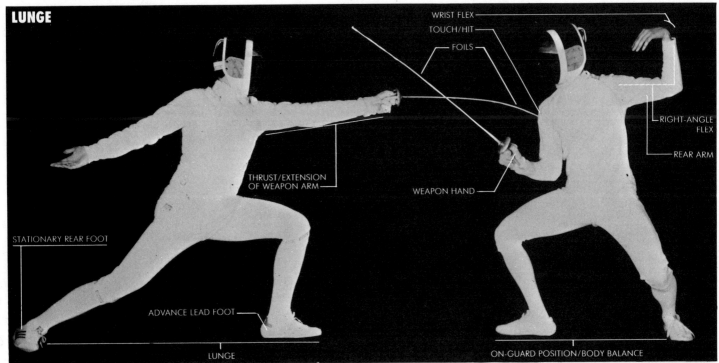

LUNGE

WRIST FLEX
TOUCH/HIT
FOILS
RIGHT-ANGLE FLEX
REAR ARM
THRUST/EXTENSION OF WEAPON ARM
WEAPON HAND
STATIONARY REAR FOOT
ADVANCE LEAD FOOT
LUNGE
ON-GUARD POSITION/BODY BALANCE

FOIL   SABRE   ÉPÉE

TARGET AREAS/VALID HITS AREAS

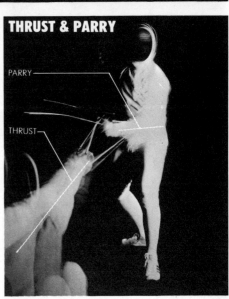

THRUST & PARRY

PARRY

THRUST

Field hockey is played by two teams of 11 men or women. The object of the game is to use a curved stick to hit a hard leather-covered ball into the opponent's goal. *Goals* may only be scored from within the shooting circle. The team scoring the most goals wins.

The ball may be hit forward, passed, or dribbled, but only with the flat side of the stick. The goalie, except in some penalty situations, may stop the ball with any part of his body, or kick it.

The game is played in two 30-minute halves, with no time-outs except for injury. Play is begun and resumed after a goal, with a two-player face-off called a *'bully,'* at the center of the field.

Violations committed outside the

BALL

CHINGFORD
RED SEAL
MADE IN ENGLAND

CIR: 9-9¼"   WT: 5½-5¾ OZ.

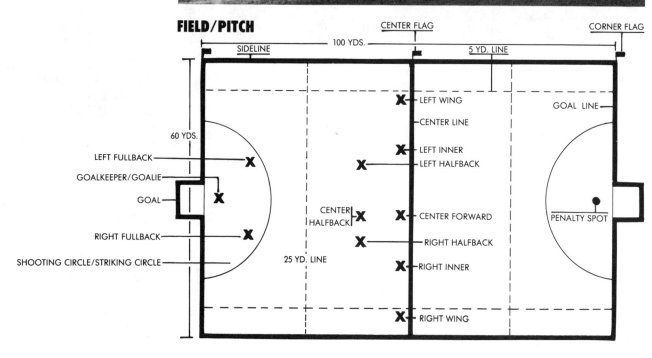

FIELD/PITCH

CENTER FLAG   CORNER FLAG

SIDELINE   100 YDS.   5 YD. LINE

LEFT WING
CENTER LINE
GOAL LINE
60 YDS.
LEFT INNER
LEFT FULLBACK
LEFT HALFBACK
GOALKEEPER/GOALIE
GOAL
CENTER
HALFBACK
CENTER FORWARD
PENALTY SPOT
RIGHT FULLBACK
RIGHT HALFBACK
SHOOTING CIRCLE/STRIKING CIRCLE
25 YD. LINE
RIGHT INNER

RIGHT WING

shooting circle are penalized by a *free hit*. The defense also receives a free hit if the offense commits a foul inside the circle. If the defense commits an unintentional foul there, the offense receives a *penalty corner*, or free hit from the goal line. Inten-

tional fouls within the circle, or unintentional fouls that prevent a sure goal, are penalized by a *penalty stroke* (called a *penalty bully* in women's hockey), taken from the penalty spot.

Violations include '*stick*,' or rais-

ing any part of the stick above the shoulder, *obstruction*, *dangerous hitting* (hitting the ball into the air towards a player), *tripping* or *pushing*, or using the rounded side of the stick.

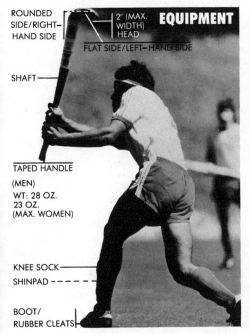

EQUIPMENT

ROUNDED SIDE/RIGHT-HAND SIDE
2" (MAX. WIDTH) HEAD
FLAT SIDE/LEFT-HAND SIDE
SHAFT
TAPED HANDLE
(MEN)
WT: 28 OZ.
23 OZ.
(MAX. WOMEN)
KNEE SOCK
SHINPAD
BOOT/
RUBBER CLEATS

GOALIE EQUIPMENT

FACE MASK
STEEL TOE
KICKING BOOT/KICKER
ATHLETIC SHOE
CANE FENCING
GLOVE
LEG GUARD

GOAL

NET
CROSSBAR
4 YDS.
GOAL POST
BACKBOARD
SIDEBOARD
(18" HIGH)
GOAL LINE
SKIRT/KILT
STICK

FIGURE SKATING
COMPULSORY FIGURES

Compulsory, or *school figures,* are worth 30% of total score. All figures are started from a *rest position* and traced three times, one on top of the others. Diameter of the figure should be three times the skater's height. *Loops* must be oval, ⅓-size of circle.

Skaters are judged on distance between *tracings* and other imperfections *(bulge, flatting)* as well as *control, posture, position of hands, fingers* and *non-skating foot, balance* and overall *grace* and *smoothness.*

All figures are skated on *either forward outside edge* of blade, *backward outside edge, forward inside edge, backward inside edge.*

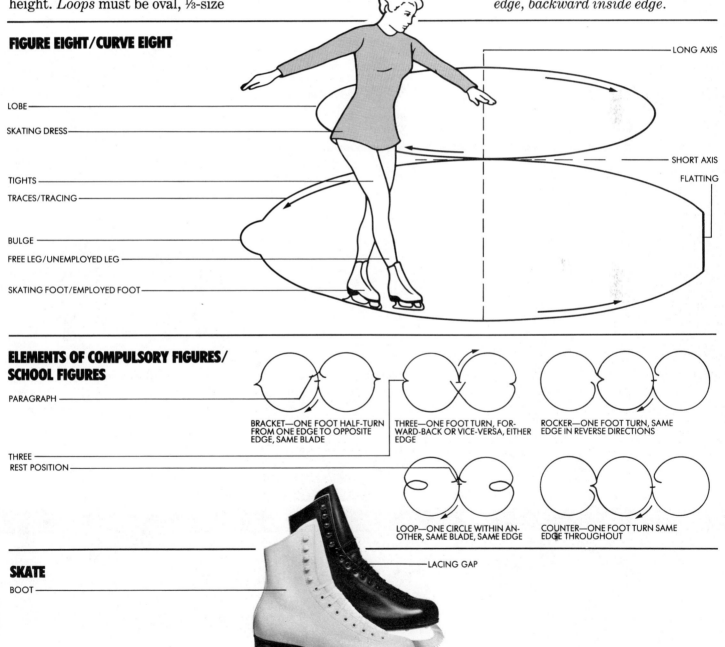

FIGURE EIGHT/CURVE EIGHT

LOBE

SKATING DRESS

TIGHTS

TRACES/TRACING

BULGE

FREE LEG/UNEMPLOYED LEG

SKATING FOOT/EMPLOYED FOOT

LONG AXIS

SHORT AXIS

FLATTING

ELEMENTS OF COMPULSORY FIGURES/ SCHOOL FIGURES

PARAGRAPH

THREE

REST POSITION

BRACKET—ONE FOOT HALF-TURN FROM ONE EDGE TO OPPOSITE EDGE, SAME BLADE

THREE—ONE FOOT TURN, FORWARD-BACK OR VICE-VERSA, EITHER EDGE

ROCKER—ONE FOOT TURN, SAME EDGE IN REVERSE DIRECTIONS

LOOP—ONE CIRCLE WITHIN ANOTHER, SAME BLADE, SAME EDGE

COUNTER—ONE FOOT TURN SAME EDGE THROUGHOUT

SKATE

BOOT

LACING GAP

HEEL PLATE

STANCHION/BRACE

TOEPICKS/TEETH/NOTCHES

Freestyle, or *free skating*, in both *singles* and *pairs* competition, requires combinations of *spins* and *jumps*, connected by forward and backward *turns*, *spirals*, *lifts* and other maneuvers. Free skating is comprised of a two-minute *short* program and a four-or five-minute *long program*, skated to music. The short program includes compulsory moves pre-selected by the judges, while the long program is choreographed by the skater. Both are judged on content, or *artistic impression*, and skill, or *technical merit*. A perfect score is *6.0*.

Pairs may skate in a *shadowed*, or parallel fashion, or in a *mirror*, or symmetrical manner, but all movements must be synchronized with the music.

AXEL LIFT

IN PAIRS SKATING, LIFTS REQUIRE THE MAN TO PICK HIS FEMALE PARTNER OFF THE ICE. HE MAY NOT USE ANY PART OF HIS BODY EXCEPT HIS HANDS DURING THE LIFT, AND MAY NOT CARRY HER FOR MORE THAN THREE ROTATIONS. A LIFTED SKATER MAY NOT BE TURNED IN A HORIZONTAL POSITION.

**DEATH SPIRAL/
BACK OUTSIDE SPIN**

IN SINGLES COMPETITION, A SPIRAL IS A SUSTAINED GLIDING MOVEMENT, EITHER FORWARD OR BACKWARDS, USUALLY USED WITH STEPS TO CONNECT JUMPS AND SPINS. IT IS PERFORMED WITH ONE FOOT IN THE AIR. IN PAIRS SKATING, THE DEATH SPIRAL REQUIRES THE MAN TO SPIN IN PLACE WHILE LOWERING HIS PARTNER SO THAT HER HEAD IS INCHES OFF THE ICE.

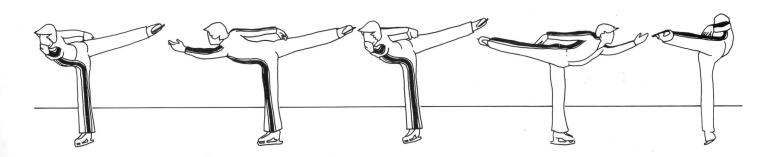

PARALLEL SPIN/
CAMEL SPIN/
ARABESQUE SPIN

SPINS MUST BE PERFORMED ON ONE SPOT WITHOUT 'DRIFTING.' THEY REQUIRE A MINIMUM OF SIX ROTATIONS OR, IF THERE

IS A FOOT CHANGE, FIVE ON EACH SKATE. IN A GRAB SPIN THE SKATER GRASPS THE FREE SKATE. A SIT SPIN BEGINS AS AN

UPRIGHT SPIN, BUT THE SKATER LOWERS INTO A SITTING POSITION, WITH HIS LEG EXTENDED.

AXEL JUMP

JUMPS ARE DIFFERENTIATED BY THE SKATE EDGE AND BLADE USED TO TAKE OFF AND LAND. SKATERS MAY LEAP OFF EITHER

FOOT, FROM THE EDGE OR TOE OF THE BLADE. ALL JUMPS REQUIRE ONE MID-AIR ROTATION, EXCEPT THE AXEL, WHICH

CONSISTS OF ONE-AND-A-HALF. JUMPS, (EXCEPT THE LUTZ) ARE PERFORMED COUNTER-CLOCKWISE.

Movements and steps in ice dancing are similar to those of ballroom dancing. In competition, couples skate three *compulsory dances*, an original *set dance* and a 4-minute *free skating* program.

Compulsory dances are chosen by lot. Steps, timing and movements must be in accordance with descriptions and diagrams in the international rule book.

Couples may select their own music, tempo, steps and composition for the set dance, but it must be performed to a rhythm named by the international committee.

All steps, turns, changes of position and sequences are permitted in free dancing. Nine judges score each dance, with 6.0 being the highest possible total.

WALTZ HOLD

TANGO HOLD

FOXTROT HOLD

KILIAN HOLD

A football team consists of 11 players. A *game* consists of four 15-minute *quarters*, with a 15-minute break, or *halftime*, between the second and third quarters. A coin toss determines which team *kicks off* to begin play.

The team in possession of the ball, the *offense*, advances it by *running* or *passing*. Action is not continuous. Between *plays* the offense *huddles* to plan the next play. Each attempt to advance the ball is a *down*. If the *defense* prevents the offense from gaining ten yards in four downs it takes control of the ball. If the offense does gain ten yards, it gets a *first down* and an additional four downs to make ten more yards.

**LINEMAN'S STANCE/
3-POINT STANCE**

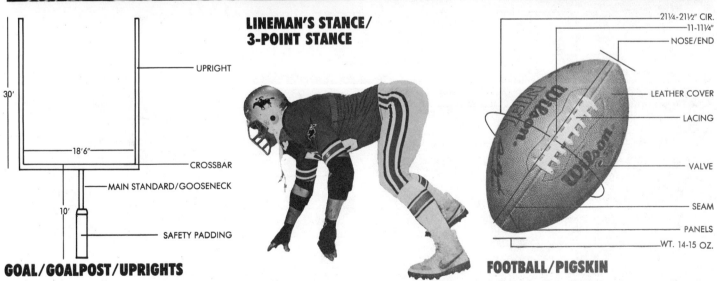

UPRIGHT

30'

18'6"

CROSSBAR

MAIN STANDARD/GOOSENECK

10'

SAFETY PADDING

GOAL/GOALPOST/UPRIGHTS

21¼-21½" CIR.

11-11¼"

NOSE/END

LEATHER COVER

LACING

VALVE

SEAM

PANELS

WT. 14-15 OZ.

FOOTBALL/PIGSKIN

If the offense fails to gain ten yards in three downs it usually elects to *punt*, or kick, the ball on *fourth down*, forcing the defense to take control further downfield. When punting, the offense brings in a *special team* called the *punting* team.

Other special teams include the *field-goal team*, *kick-off team*, *punt return team*, *goal-line defensive team*, and *kick-off return team*. Players may be part of special teams as well as *first string* on regular offensive or defensive teams.

Kickoff and punting teams are known as *suicide squads* because of the high degree of injury.

Teams employ numerous offensive and defensive formations based on their skills and the game situation.

FOOTBALL FIELD/GRIDIRON

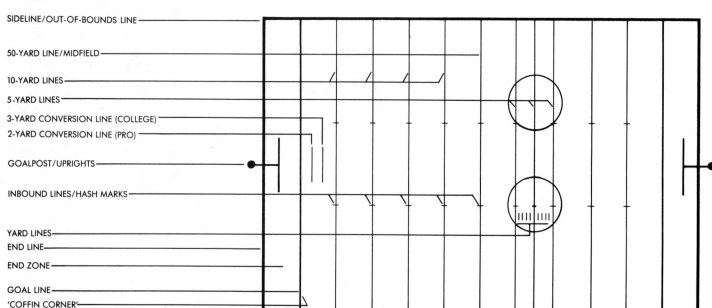

SIDELINE/OUT-OF-BOUNDS LINE

50-YARD LINE/MIDFIELD

10-YARD LINES

5-YARD LINES

3-YARD CONVERSION LINE (COLLEGE)

2-YARD CONVERSION LINE (PRO)

GOALPOST/UPRIGHTS

INBOUND LINES/HASH MARKS

YARD LINES

END LINE

END ZONE

GOAL LINE

'COFFIN CORNER'

DEFENSIVE FORMATION/'4-3-4'

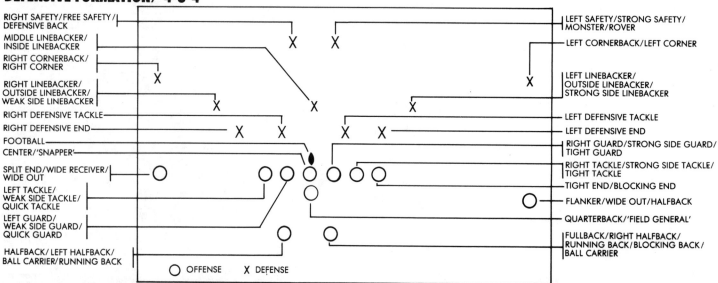

RIGHT SAFETY/FREE SAFETY/DEFENSIVE BACK

MIDDLE LINEBACKER/INSIDE LINEBACKER

RIGHT CORNERBACK/RIGHT CORNER

RIGHT LINEBACKER/OUTSIDE LINEBACKER/WEAK SIDE LINEBACKER

RIGHT DEFENSIVE TACKLE

RIGHT DEFENSIVE END

FOOTBALL

CENTER/'SNAPPER'

SPLIT END/WIDE RECEIVER/WIDE OUT

LEFT TACKLE/WEAK SIDE TACKLE/QUICK TACKLE

LEFT GUARD/WEAK SIDE GUARD/QUICK GUARD

HALFBACK/LEFT HALFBACK/BALL CARRIER/RUNNING BACK

LEFT SAFETY/STRONG SAFETY/MONSTER/ROVER

LEFT CORNERBACK/LEFT CORNER

LEFT LINEBACKER/OUTSIDE LINEBACKER/STRONG SIDE LINEBACKER

LEFT DEFENSIVE TACKLE

LEFT DEFENSIVE END

RIGHT GUARD/STRONG SIDE GUARD/TIGHT GUARD

RIGHT TACKLE/STRONG SIDE TACKLE/TIGHT TACKLE

TIGHT END/BLOCKING END

FLANKER/WIDE OUT/HALFBACK

QUARTERBACK/'FIELD GENERAL'

FULLBACK/RIGHT HALFBACK/RUNNING BACK/BLOCKING BACK/BALL CARRIER

○ OFFENSE   X DEFENSE

OFFENSIVE FORMATION/T FORMATION

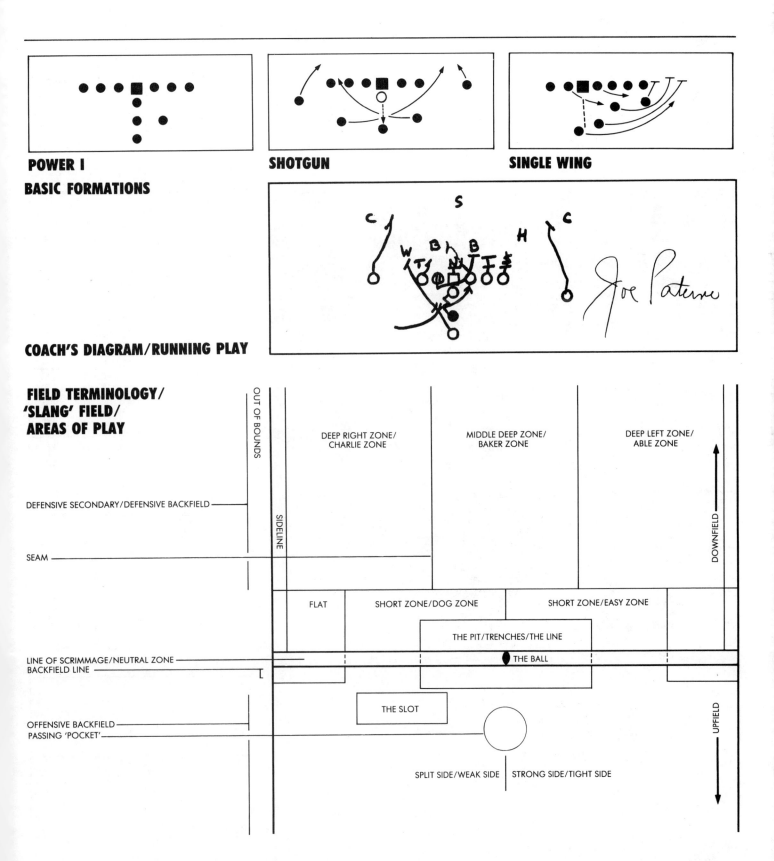

POWER I
BASIC FORMATIONS

SHOTGUN

SINGLE WING

COACH'S DIAGRAM/RUNNING PLAY

**FIELD TERMINOLOGY/
'SLANG' FIELD/
AREAS OF PLAY**

OUT OF BOUNDS

DEEP RIGHT ZONE/
CHARLIE ZONE

MIDDLE DEEP ZONE/
BAKER ZONE

DEEP LEFT ZONE/
ABLE ZONE

DOWNFIELD

DEFENSIVE SECONDARY/DEFENSIVE BACKFIELD

SIDELINE

SEAM

FLAT

SHORT ZONE/DOG ZONE

SHORT ZONE/EASY ZONE

THE PIT/TRENCHES/THE LINE

LINE OF SCRIMMAGE/NEUTRAL ZONE
BACKFIELD LINE

THE BALL

THE SLOT

OFFENSIVE BACKFIELD
PASSING 'POCKET'

UPFIELD

SPLIT SIDE/WEAK SIDE | STRONG SIDE/TIGHT SIDE

A *touchdown*, or *TD*, worth six points, is scored by getting the ball across goal line in an offensive player's possession. The scoring team then attempts a *point-after-touchdown*, or *PAT*, by kicking the ball above the crossbar between the uprights. In some leagues the scoring team may attempt to run or pass the ball over the goal line for a *two-point conversion*.

The offense may also elect to placekick the ball through the goalposts from anyplace on the field. This *field goal* is worth three points.

The defense can score a two-point *safety* by tackling an offensive player with the ball in his own end zone. The team scoring the most points wins.

PASSING FROM THE POCKET

PASS PATTERNS/PASS ROUTES

POST

HITCH AND GO

THE BOMB /FLY

SQUARE-IN   SQUARE-OUT

BUTTONHOOK/CURL-IN

SLANT/SLANT-IN

HALFBACK FLARE

SPRINT DRAW PASS

Frank Broyles

COACHES DIAGRAM/PASSING PLAY

PROTECTIVE PADDING

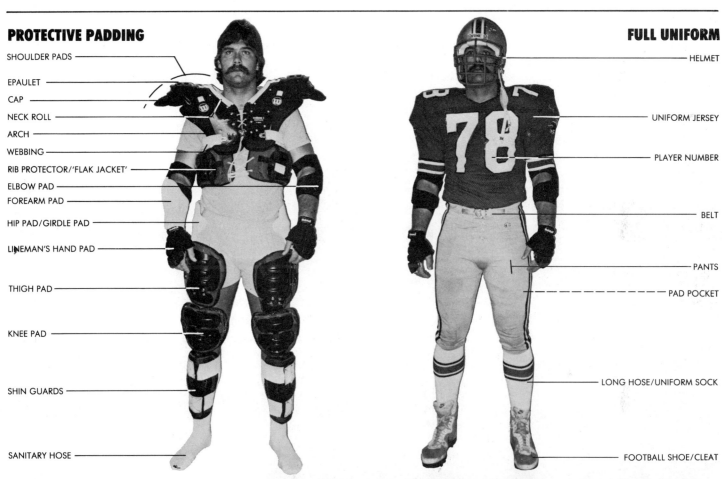

- SHOULDER PADS
- EPAULET
- CAP
- NECK ROLL
- ARCH
- WEBBING
- RIB PROTECTOR/'FLAK JACKET'
- ELBOW PAD
- FOREARM PAD
- HIP PAD/GIRDLE PAD
- LINEMAN'S HAND PAD
- THIGH PAD
- KNEE PAD
- SHIN GUARDS
- SANITARY HOSE

FULL UNIFORM

- HELMET
- UNIFORM JERSEY
- PLAYER NUMBER
- BELT
- PANTS
- PAD POCKET
- LONG HOSE/UNIFORM SOCK
- FOOTBALL SHOE/CLEAT

HELMET

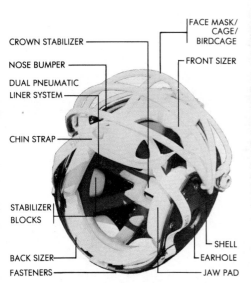

- CROWN STABILIZER
- NOSE BUMPER
- DUAL PNEUMATIC LINER SYSTEM
- CHIN STRAP
- STABILIZER BLOCKS
- BACK SIZER
- FASTENERS
- FACE MASK/ CAGE/ BIRDCAGE
- FRONT SIZER
- SHELL
- EARHOLE
- JAW PAD

BLOCKING

Officials signal *penalties*, or violations of the rules, by dropping a handkerchief, or *flag*. An *infraction* may be penalized by loss of yards or loss of down, depending on the severity.

In most cases, the unoffending team has the option of accepting the penalty, in which case the official moves the football, or rejecting it and taking the result of the play. Penalty yardage is either added to or subtracted from the *necessary yards*, the yardage needed to gain a first down.

Penalties range from crossing the scrimmage line before the ball is *hiked*, or *snapped*, called *offside*, to more serious penalties such as blocking from behind, or *clipping*.

OFFICIALS' SIGNALS

OFFICIALS' POSITIONING

FIELD JUDGE
UMPIRE
ROD MAN
ALTERNATE
BOX MAN
ROD MAN
CHAIN GANG

SIDE JUDGE
REFEREE
(PUT BALL IN PLAY/
SUPERVISE PENALTIES)
HEAD LINESMAN
(CHAIN GANG SUPERVISOR)
LINE JUDGE/OFFICIAL TIMER
(MARK OUT-OF-BOUNDS)
BACK JUDGE

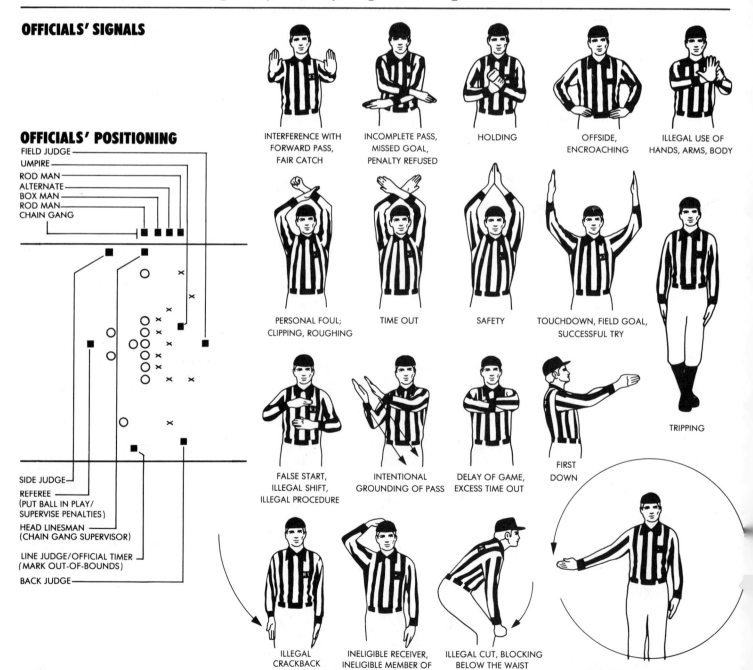

INTERFERENCE WITH
FORWARD PASS,
FAIR CATCH

INCOMPLETE PASS,
MISSED GOAL,
PENALTY REFUSED

HOLDING

OFFSIDE,
ENCROACHING

ILLEGAL USE OF
HANDS, ARMS, BODY

PERSONAL FOUL;
CLIPPING, ROUGHING

TIME OUT

SAFETY

TOUCHDOWN, FIELD GOAL,
SUCCESSFUL TRY

TRIPPING

FALSE START,
ILLEGAL SHIFT,
ILLEGAL PROCEDURE

INTENTIONAL
GROUNDING OF PASS

DELAY OF GAME,
EXCESS TIME OUT

FIRST
DOWN

ILLEGAL
CRACKBACK

INELIGIBLE RECEIVER,
INELIGIBLE MEMBER OF
KICKING TEAM DOWNFIELD

ILLEGAL CUT, BLOCKING
BELOW THE WAIST

NO TIME OUT, TIME IN WITH WHISTLE

A captain heads a team of 15 players who advance the ball by either kicking it, hitting it with a fist (called *fisting*), or by passing it from player to player. However, no player may carry the ball for more than three steps, and the opposition may tackle or shoulder the carrier.

A game, or *match*, usually lasts for two halves of 30 minutes each, although some championship games have 40-minute halves.

The object is to get the football into the opponent's goal, or *net*. This scores a *goal*, for three points. Getting the ball above the cross-bar and between the goalposts score a *point*, worth one point.

PLAYER

BALL/FOOTBALL
SLEEVE
COLLAR

SWEATER/JERSEY

UNIFORM

STRIPE/BAND
KNICKS/TOGS

SOCKS/STOCKINGS

PITCH/FIELD

GOAL
PARALLELOGRAM
LEFT FRONT FORWARD
CENTER FRONT FORWARD
RIGHT FRONT FORWARD

LEFT HALF FORWARD
CENTER HALF FORWARD
RIGHT HALF FORWARD

LEFT CENTER
RIGHT CENTER
RIGHT HALFBACK
CENTER HALFBACK
LEFT HALFBACK

RIGHT FULLBACK
CENTER FULLBACK
LEFT FULLBACK

GOALTENDER

160 YDS

50-YARD LINE

21-YARD LINE
14-YARD LINE
NET

100 YDS

BALL/FOOTBALL/GAELIC FOOTBALL

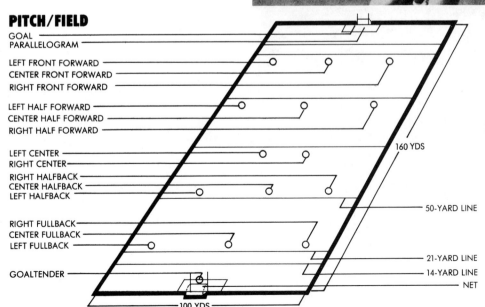

PANEL

VALVE

SEWING

WEIGHT: 13–15 OZ.
CIRCUMFERENCE: 27"–29"

A golf course generally consists of 18 holes of widely differing distances and design. The object of the game is for the *golfer*, or *player*, to hit the ball into a cup located on a smooth, grassy area called a green at the end of the hole. Most holes are protected by *hazards*, usually water or sand traps, to make this more difficult. To do this he may select from as many as 14 clubs, each of which has a different function.

Each swing at the ball is a *stroke*. In *medal play*, the golfer complet-ing the course with the lowest stroke total wins. In *match play*, the golfer who takes the fewest strokes on a hole wins that hole, and at the end of 18 holes, or a *round*, the golfer who has won the most holes wins the match.

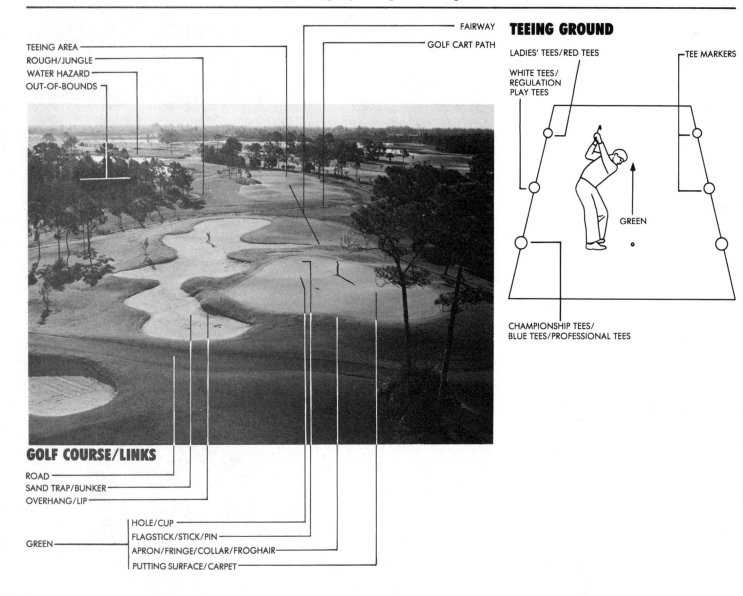

FAIRWAY
GOLF CART PATH

TEEING AREA
ROUGH/JUNGLE
WATER HAZARD
OUT-OF-BOUNDS

GOLF COURSE/LINKS

ROAD
SAND TRAP/BUNKER
OVERHANG/LIP

HOLE/CUP
FLAGSTICK/STICK/PIN
GREEN
APRON/FRINGE/COLLAR/FROGHAIR
PUTTING SURFACE/CARPET

TEEING GROUND

LADIES' TEES/RED TEES
TEE MARKERS
WHITE TEES/
REGULATION
PLAY TEES

GREEN

CHAMPIONSHIP TEES/
BLUE TEES/PROFESSIONAL TEES

BACKSWING

FOLLOW-THROUGH

DOWNSWING

GOLF SWING

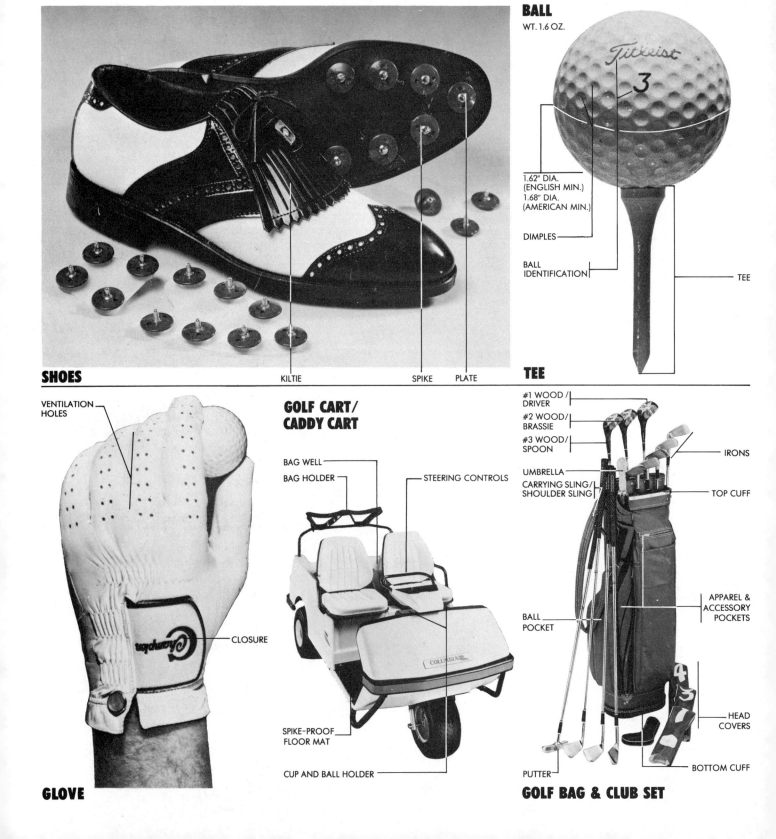

BALL

WT. 1.6 OZ.

1.62" DIA.
(ENGLISH MIN.)
1.68" DIA.
(AMERICAN MIN.)

DIMPLES

BALL
IDENTIFICATION

TEE

SHOES

KILTIE   SPIKE   PLATE

TEE

VENTILATION
HOLES

CLOSURE

GLOVE

**GOLF CART/
CADDY CART**

BAG WELL

BAG HOLDER

STEERING CONTROLS

SPIKE-PROOF
FLOOR MAT

CUP AND BALL HOLDER

#1 WOOD /
DRIVER

#2 WOOD/
BRASSIE

#3 WOOD/
SPOON

IRONS

UMBRELLA

CARRYING SLING/
SHOULDER SLING

TOP CUFF

BALL
POCKET

APPAREL &
ACCESSORY
POCKETS

HEAD
COVERS

PUTTER

BOTTOM CUFF

GOLF BAG & CLUB SET

Clubs are numbered in order of increasing loft, the angle of the club-face to the vertical. A basic club set consists of woods, or drivers, irons used mainly on the fairway, and a flat-faced putter to hit the ball on greens. Golfers may also use spe-cialized clubs, for example a *pitching wedge* or *sand wedge* in certain situations.

The place where a ball stops after being hit is its *lie*. The optimum path between the lie and the hole is called the *line*. Because some fair-ways abruptly change directions, or *dogleg*, and are bordered by *obstructions* and hazards, the line is usually the safest, rather than the shortest, distance from tee to hole.

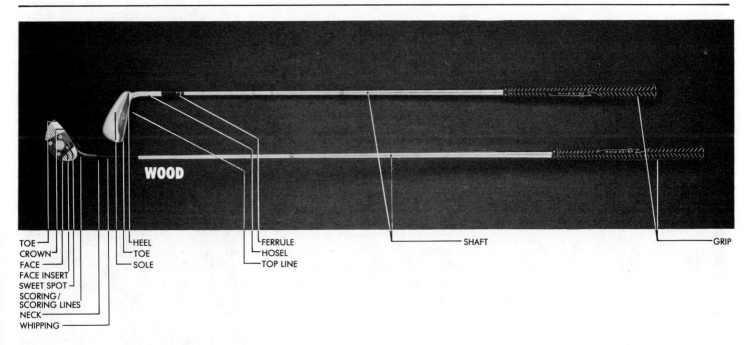

WOOD

TOE
CROWN
FACE
FACE INSERT
SWEET SPOT
SCORING/
SCORING LINES
NECK
WHIPPING

HEEL
TOE
SOLE

FERRULE
HOSEL
TOP LINE

SHAFT

GRIP

RANGE & LOFT OF CLUBS

MIS-HIT DRIVES

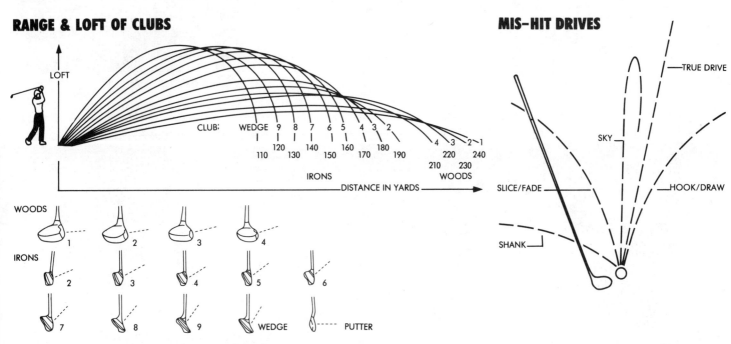

LOFT

CLUB: WEDGE 9 8 7 6 5 4 3 2 1
110 120 130 140 150 160 170 180 190 4 3 2 1
210 230 220 240

IRONS
WOODS

DISTANCE IN YARDS

WOODS   1   2   3   4

IRONS   2   3   4   5   6

7   8   9   WEDGE   PUTTER

TRUE DRIVE
SKY
SLICE/FADE
HOOK/DRAW
SHANK

Each hole is designed to be played by an expert golfer in a specific number of strokes, called *par*. Scoring two strokes less than par on a hole is an *eagle*, one stroke less is a *birdie*, one over is a *bogey*, two over is a *double bogey*, three over is a *triple bogey*. *Penalty strokes* are added to the score for rules violations such as kicking a ball.

Inexperienced golfers, known as *duffers* or *hackers*, will often pull their *shot* to their dominant hand causing the ball to hook or draw, or push the ball away from their dominant hand, a slice or fade. Some players even *whiff*, or miss the ball completely. In friendly games they are often given a *mulligan*, or a chance to hit again without penalty.

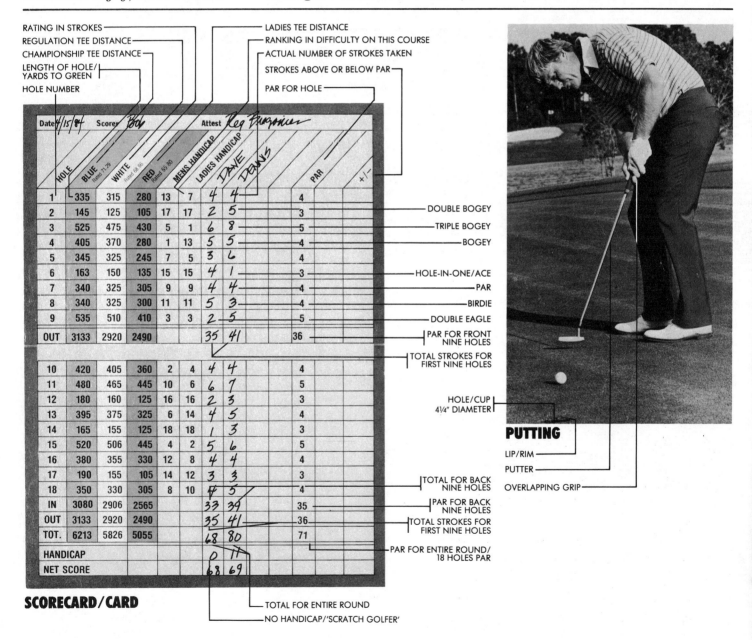

RATING IN STROKES
REGULATION TEE DISTANCE
CHAMPIONSHIP TEE DISTANCE
LENGTH OF HOLE/ YARDS TO GREEN
HOLE NUMBER

LADIES TEE DISTANCE
RANKING IN DIFFICULTY ON THIS COURSE
ACTUAL NUMBER OF STROKES TAKEN
STROKES ABOVE OR BELOW PAR
PAR FOR HOLE

Date 4/15/84   Scorer Bob   Attest Reg Burgomer

HOLE	BLUE Rated 71-79	WHITE Rated 68-95	RED Rated 55-80	MENS HANDICAP	LADIES HANDICAP	DAVE	DENNIS	PAR	+/−	
1	335	315	280	13	7	4	4	4		
2	145	125	105	17	17	2	5	3		DOUBLE BOGEY
3	525	475	430	5	1	6	8	5		TRIPLE BOGEY
4	405	370	280	1	13	5	5	4		BOGEY
5	345	325	245	7	5	3	6	4		
6	163	150	135	15	15	4	1	3		HOLE-IN-ONE/ACE
7	340	325	305	9	9	4	4	4		PAR
8	340	325	300	11	11	5	3	4		BIRDIE
9	535	510	410	3	3	2	5	5		DOUBLE EAGLE
OUT	3133	2920	2490			35	41	36		PAR FOR FRONT NINE HOLES
										TOTAL STROKES FOR FIRST NINE HOLES
10	420	405	360	2	4	4	4	4		
11	480	465	445	10	6	6	7	5		
12	180	160	125	16	16	2	3	3		
13	395	375	325	6	14	4	5	4		
14	165	155	125	18	18	1	3	3		
15	520	506	445	4	2	5	6	5		
16	380	355	330	12	8	4	4	4		
17	190	155	105	14	12	3	3	3		
18	350	330	305	8	10	4	5	4		
IN	3080	2906	2565			33	39	35		PAR FOR BACK NINE HOLES
OUT	3133	2920	2490			35	41	36		TOTAL STROKES FOR FIRST NINE HOLES
TOT.	6213	5826	5055			68	80	71		PAR FOR ENTIRE ROUND/ 18 HOLES PAR
HANDICAP						0	11			
NET SCORE						68	69			

TOTAL FOR BACK NINE HOLES

TOTAL FOR ENTIRE ROUND
NO HANDICAP/'SCRATCH GOLFER'

SCORECARD/CARD

PUTTING

HOLE/CUP 4¼" DIAMETER

LIP/RIM
PUTTER
OVERLAPPING GRIP

Gymnastics requires men and women to demonstrate strength, balance, body control and grace on the floor as well as on various pieces of equipment, called *apparatus*.

Men compete in floor exercises, on the vaulting horse, pommel horse, horizontal bars, parallel bars and still rings.

Women compete in floor exercises, the vaulting horse, balance beam, and uneven, or asymmetrical, bars.

In some *meets*, men's and women's trampolining and women's rhythmic events are contested.

Gymnasts may enter one or more events. An *all-around gymnast* competes in all events. *Compulsory* and *optional routines* are performed in each event.

Tumbling, acrobatic movements performed on mats, is the foundation of gymnastics. These movements, and their variations, are incorporated into floor exercises and routines on most pieces of apparatus.

Four judges score each event.

A gymnast's score is determined by eliminating highest and lowest scores and averaging middle ones.

In the compulsory phase, 4 points are given for content and 6 points for execution.

In the optional phase, 6 points are awarded for composition (4 for *difficulty*, 1.5 for *amplitude*, or extension and lift, and .5 for general impression), and four points are given for execution (1.5 amplitude, 1.5 for technical ability and 1 point for impression).

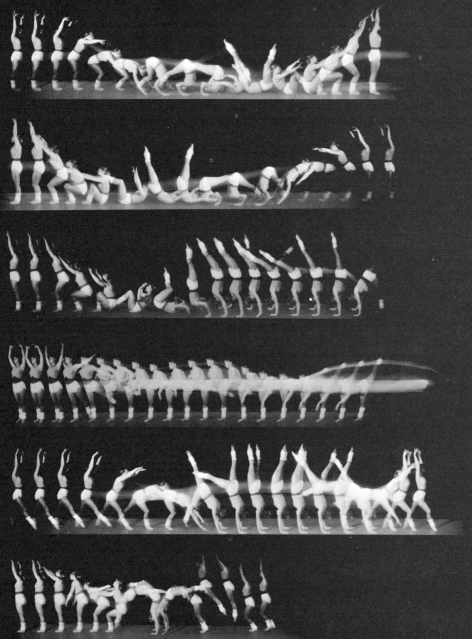

FORWARD ROLL/FRONT PIKE ROLL

BACKWARD ROLL

BACK EXTENSION ROLL

ARABESQUE

HANDSTAND

BACK HANDSPRING

Movements, or *tricks*, are given a difficulty rating by the Federation of International Gymnastics according to the effort required and the risk involved.

To receive the maximum score in this phase, the gymnast must include in his or her routine tricks rated *A parts*, or movements of lower difficulty, *B parts*, tricks of intermediate difficulty, and *C parts*, movements of superior difficulty. The precise number of each part to be included varies according to event.

More difficult parts may be substituted for movements rated less difficult. Gymnasts are penalized for not including the proper number of parts in their routines.

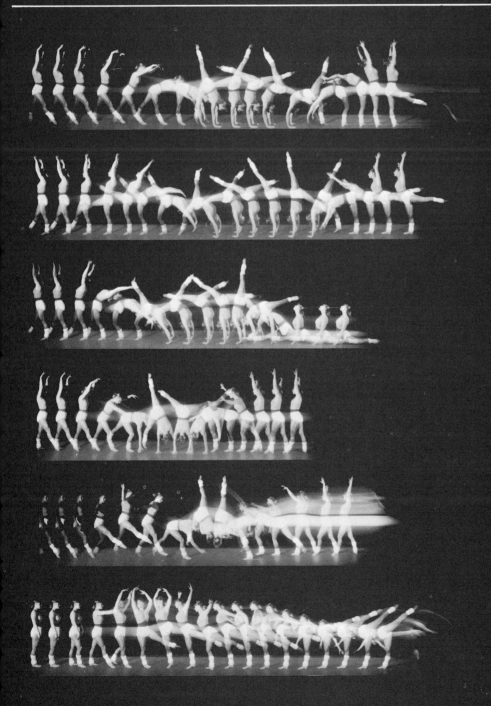

WALKOVER

BACK WALKOVER

BACK WALKOVER SPLIT

CARTWHEEL

SIDE AERIAL

KICKTURN ARABESQUE/SCALE

Floor exercises must be performed within the boundary line, and the gymnast must make use of the whole mat, working in all four corners.

Men have 50 to 70 seconds to complete a routine that emphasizes tumbling skills, but also includes demonstrations of flexibility, strength hold and balance.

Women's exercises last 60 to 90 seconds and are performed to music selected by the gymnast. Women are judged on grace, balance, rhythm, modern and classical dance skills as well as flexibility, tumbling ability, strength and personality.

Rhythmic gymnasts must perform variously with a bouncing ball, a flat, 10½ oz. hoop, two 5¼ oz. balanced *clubs*, a rope, and a flowing, colorful *ribbon*.

FLOOR EXERCISE

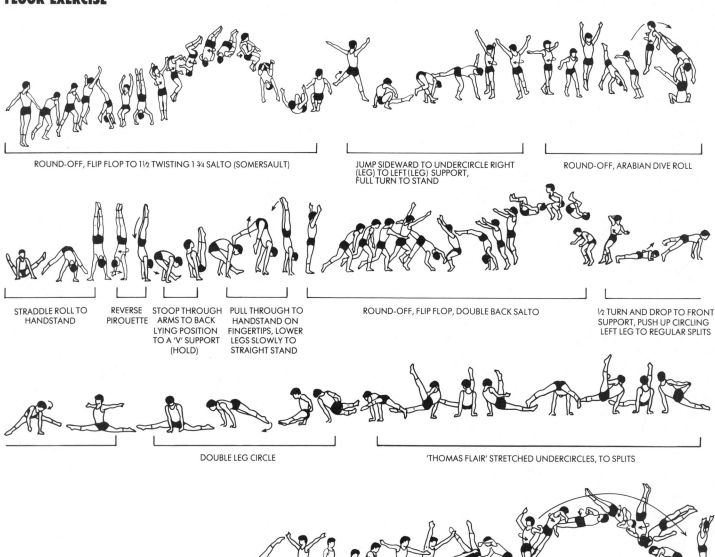

ROUND-OFF, FLIP FLOP TO 1½ TWISTING 1 ¾ SALTO (SOMERSAULT)

JUMP SIDEWARD TO UNDERCIRCLE RIGHT (LEG) TO LEFT (LEG) SUPPORT, FULL TURN TO STAND

ROUND-OFF, ARABIAN DIVE ROLL

STRADDLE ROLL TO HANDSTAND

REVERSE PIROUETTE

STOOP THROUGH ARMS TO BACK LYING POSITION TO A 'V' SUPPORT (HOLD)

PULL THROUGH TO HANDSTAND ON FINGERTIPS, LOWER LEGS SLOWLY TO STRAIGHT STAND

ROUND-OFF, FLIP FLOP, DOUBLE BACK SALTO

½ TURN AND DROP TO FRONT SUPPORT, PUSH UP CIRCLING LEFT LEG TO REGULAR SPLITS

DOUBLE LEG CIRCLE

'THOMAS FLAIR' STRETCHED UNDERCIRCLES, TO SPLITS

TURN LEFT TO FRONT SUPPORT, SINGLE LEG STOOP UP TO STRETCHED STAND

ROUND-OFF, DOUBLE TWISTING BACK SALTO TO FINAL POSE

MAT (1" THICK)
CARPET COVER
BOUNDARY LINE

NISSEN

COMPETITIVE AREA

40' x 40'

ROPE

BALL

HOOP

WOMEN'S RHYTHMIC EXERCISE

Men vault over the length of the horse, while women vault over its width. *Vaulters* are permitted two attempts, with only the highest scored vault counting.

There are three types of vaults; *handstand*, *horizontal* and *vaults with turns*. Gymnasts may only touch the horse with their hands. Vaults are judged on *difficulty* (prior to competition judges assign ratings), pre-flight, post-flight and *form and execution*.

During pre-flight, men must be a minimum of 20° above the horizontal top of the horse at repulsion.

Post-flight must be higher than pre-flight.

Women are permitted one step upon landing without penalty, if it is not caused by loss of balance.

SPRINGBOARD/RUETHER BOARD/BEAT BOARD

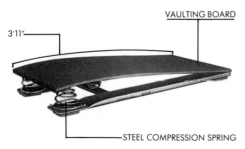

VAULTING BOARD

3'11"

STEEL COMPRESSION SPRING

MEN'S VAULT

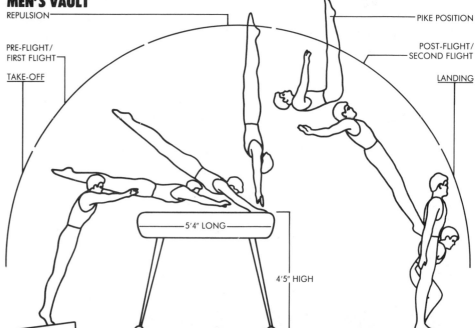

REPULSION

PRE-FLIGHT/FIRST FLIGHT

TAKE-OFF

PIKE POSITION

POST-FLIGHT/SECOND FLIGHT

LANDING

5'4" LONG

4'5" HIGH

WOMEN'S VAULT

13½" WIDE

3'7" HIGH

HORSE

PISTON

T-HANDLE/LOCK

UPRIGHT

SPRINGBOARD/RUETHER BOARD/BEAT BOARD

BASE

LANDING MAT

RUNWAY

Pommel horse routines require clean swings without stopping. A gymnast will be judged on how often he turns to face a different direction and the number of times he moves up and down the horse, or *travels*.

Basic exercises are undercuts (in which the gymnast releases one hand from the pommel and brings his leg around), circles and scissors. In the optional phase, double leg circles must predominate.

The gymnast is penalized for touching the horse with any part of his body except his hands, for lack of amplitude in double leg circles and for performing scissors below head height.

The gymnast must be *supported* by his hands and arms exclusively.

UNDERCUT/CUT

SLIPPERS

SUSPENDERS
STRETCH TROUSERS
STIRRUPS

POMMEL/HANDLE

CROUP
SADDLE 17"
NECK

3'6-7/8"

PROTECTIVE CONE

DOUBLE LEG CIRCLES

FRONT SCISSORS/LEG WORK

The rings are suspended 8'2" above the ground and are 19" apart. The rings must remain still throughout the routine. The gymnast must alternate between swinging parts (movements of his body), hold positions (which must be maintained for 2 seconds), and strength parts.

A routine must include two handstands, one showing strength, the other swung into from below the rings.

A gymnast is penalized for shaking the rings and for unintended movements of his body.

A *giant* is a trick in which the gymnast, starting from a handstand, does a complete circle to return to the handstand.

Somersaults are often used in *dismounting*, or releasing the rings.

STRAP

WRIST WRAP
RING, 7½" DIA.

HOLD POSITION/IRON CROSS

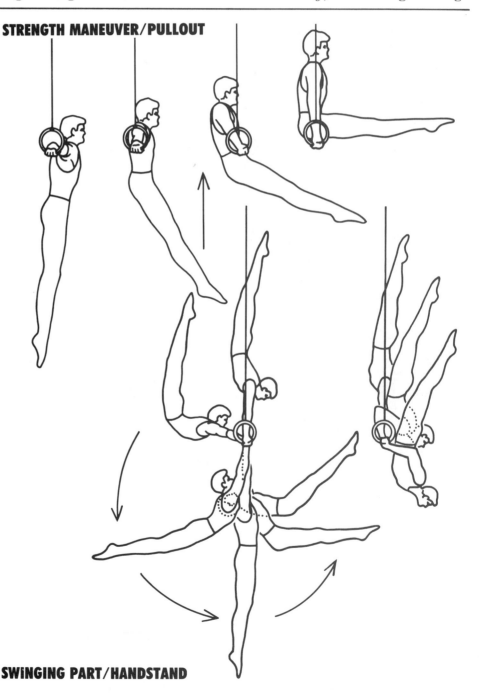

STRENGTH MANEUVER/PULLOUT

SWINGING PART/HANDSTAND

Routines on the high bar are composed of a *mount*, giant swings that allow the gymnast to make numerous changes in his grip and direction, and a dismount. The gymnast must swing throughout his entire routine without stopping. To gain maximum score, he must include at least one move in which he releases the bar with both hands simultaneously and regrasps it.

A competitor is penalized for hesitations or for holding a position.

Dismounts often reach heights above 12′ and include twists, flips and somersaults, but all must end with a controlled *landing*.

REVERSE GIANT

DISMOUNT

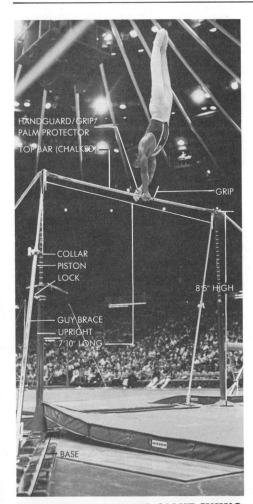

HANDGUARD/GRIP7
PALM PROTECTOR

TOP BAR (CHALKED)

GRIP

COLLAR
PISTON
LOCK

8′5″ HIGH

GUY BRACE
UPRIGHT
7′10″ LONG

BASE

GRIP CHANGE DURING GIANT SWING

RELEASE AND REGRASP OF BAR

Almost every gymnastic movement can be performed on the parallel bars since the gymnast may use one or both bars, perform between or outside them, or under and over the bars.

A routine on the parallel bars must include both swinging and hold parts. Strength parts are not required, but are allowed.

The gymnast must work smoothly. He is permitted only three pauses of 2 seconds, or *stops*. A move held longer than 3 seconds is penalized. He must release either one or both hands during almost every movement.

Parallel bars may be mounted at either end. A gymnast may use a springboard if a running approach is desired.

BARS (CHALKED)

PISTON

LOCK

UPRIGHT

STRENGTH PART/
PRESS TO A HANDSTAND

11'5" LONG

1'5" WIDE

5'6" HIGH

PARALLEL BARS

ROUTINE

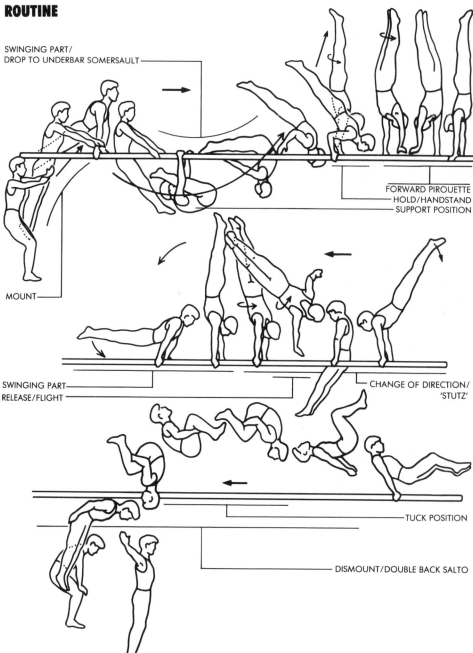

SWINGING PART/
DROP TO UNDERBAR SOMERSAULT

FORWARD PIROUETTE
HOLD/HANDSTAND
SUPPORT POSITION

MOUNT

SWINGING PART
RELEASE/FLIGHT

CHANGE OF DIRECTION/
'STUTZ'

TUCK POSITION

DISMOUNT/DOUBLE BACK SALTO

The uneven parallel bars are 1′5″ apart. A routine consists of a mount, for which a springboard may be used, free flowing swinging movements around both bars (which should include releases, re-grasps, changes of direction, kips and twists) and a dismount. Kips, moving from a hanging position below the bar to a support position above the bar, are necessary to maintain continuous motion.

Gymnasts are judged on the passage of the body between the bars, the different hand grips used on each bar, suspension and the composition of the routine.

The routine should be continuous. Two pauses are allowed, but the gymnast may only remain static for a brief period.

GLIDE KIP

CAST WRAP

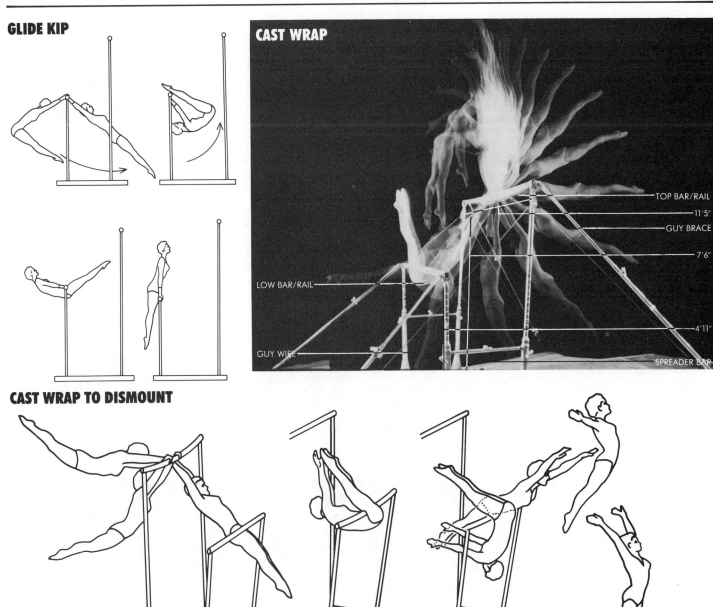

TOP BAR/RAIL
11′5″
GUY BRACE
7′6″
LOW BAR/RAIL
4′11″
GUY WIRE
SPREADER BAR

CAST WRAP TO DISMOUNT

A routine on the balance beam includes dance moves, acrobatic moves and tumbling moves, all demonstrating the gymnast's balance.

The exercise should be dominated by standing moves, but should include sitting, crouching and lying on the beam, tricks executed in both upright and vertical positions, left and right 180° turns on one foot, leaps and jumps showing good height and distance, and stepping movements, including running steps with dramatic arm configurations.

The gymnast has 70 to 90 seconds to complete her routine, which must continue without hesitation. Three brief *still positions* are permitted.

A gymnast falling off the beam has 10 seconds to resume her routine.

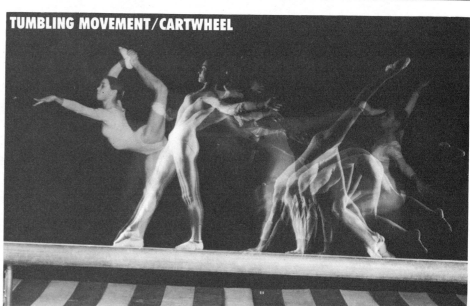

TUMBLING MOVEMENT/CARTWHEEL

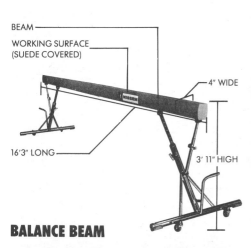

BEAM
WORKING SURFACE (SUEDE COVERED)
4" WIDE
16'3" LONG
3' 11" HIGH

BALANCE BEAM

INVERTED POSITION

UPRIGHT POSITION

ACROBATIC MOVEMENT/ LEAP OR JUMP

Court handball is played by individuals or doubles teams on one-, three- or four-walled courts. Players attempt to hit a *hard rubber* ball so that it bounds off the front wall in such a way that their opponent cannot return it to the front wall on the fly before it bounces twice. A good return, or *volley*, may hit other walls or the ceiling before hitting the front wall.

A game is 21 points. A *match* is two games, with an 11-point *tie-breaker* played if each side wins a game. Only the serving side may score points. A side continues serving until it loses a volley.

Players may hit the ball with any part of one hand. Intentionally blocking, pushing or obstructing is penalized by loss of the volley.

FOUR-WALL COURT

ONE-WALL COURT

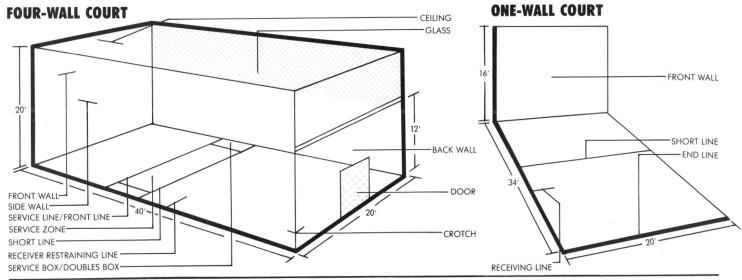

FOUR-WALL, SINGLES GAME

HANDBALL AND HANDBALL GLOVE

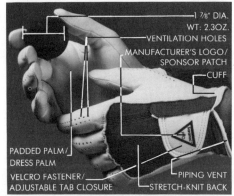

ONE-WALL, DOUBLES GAME

Team handball is a non-contact sport played indoors by seven-player teams (as in the Olympics) or outdoors with 11 players. The object is to throw the leather covered ball into the opposition's goal. A game is played in two 30-minute halves.

Players may stop, catch, throw, bounce or hit the ball with any part of their bodies above the knee. They may take only three steps with the ball, then must bounce, or *dribble* it, before taking additional steps. They may hold the ball for three

seconds, then must pass, dribble or shoot.

Action centers around the goal area. Only the goalie is allowed inside the area. Shooters can dive into the circle but must throw the ball before touching the ground.

COURT

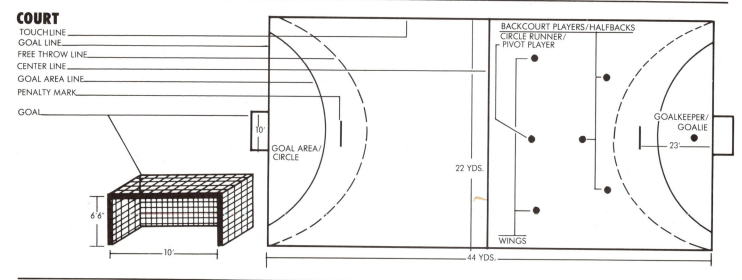

TOUCHLINE
GOAL LINE
FREE THROW LINE
CENTER LINE
GOAL AREA LINE
PENALTY MARK
GOAL

GOAL AREA/CIRCLE

10'

6'6"

10'

22 YDS.

44 YDS.

BACKCOURT PLAYERS/HALFBACKS
CIRCLE RUNNER/PIVOT PLAYER

WINGS

GOALKEEPER/GOALIE

23'

BASIC ATTACK FORMATION

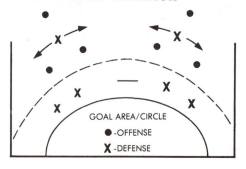

GOAL AREA/CIRCLE
● -OFFENSE
X -DEFENSE

PENALTY THROW

BALL

WT: 16 OZ. (MEN)
WT: 13 OZ. (WOMEN)

23" CIR. (MEN)
21½" CIR. (WOMEN)

Thoroughbred horse racing, or *flat racing*, takes place on a level, oval dirt or grass track having no obstacles. Races vary in distance, but are usually a mile or more. Quarter horse races are run on flat tracks over much shorter distances, often a quarter-mile. Both thoroughbred and quarter horses carry a rider, called a jockey.

Harness race horses must pull a driver riding a two-wheeled carriage called a sulky. Harness races are conducted in two gaits (the sequence in which a horse's legs hit the ground), called trotting and pacing.

The first horse and rider, or driver, to cover the race distance without fouling wins.

THOROUGHBRED RACING/FLAT RACING

THOROUGHBRED AND QUARTER HORSE STARTING GATE/'POST'

GATE
STARTING GATE CREWMAN
GATE NUMBER
POLE POSITION
STARTER'S STAND
STARTING GATE MOVER
Ruidoso Downs
TIRE
STARTER (WITH ELECTRONIC STARTER B.T. BUTTON)

RACETRACK/RACEWAY/RACECOURSE

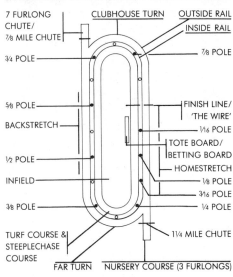

7 FURLONG CHUTE/ 7/8 MILE CHUTE
CLUBHOUSE TURN
OUTSIDE RAIL
INSIDE RAIL
3/4 POLE
7/8 POLE
5/8 POLE
FINISH LINE/ 'THE WIRE'
BACKSTRETCH
1/16 POLE
TOTE BOARD/ BETTING BOARD
1/2 POLE
HOMESTRETCH
INFIELD
1/8 POLE
3/16 POLE
3/8 POLE
1/4 POLE
TURF COURSE & STEEPLECHASE COURSE
1 1/4 MILE CHUTE
FAR TURN
NURSERY COURSE (3 FURLONGS)

There are many types of races. *Maiden races* are for horses that have never won. In *handicaps*, a *track secretary* assigns a total weight (consisting of jockey, saddle and *lead weights*), to be carried by a horse in an attempt to equalize a *field*. Handicaps are based on past performance. Weights are also assigned in *allowance races*, set according to formula.

All horses in a *claiming race* may be bought for the *claiming price* before a race starts. This prevents horses more valuable than the set price from entering.

Better horses run in *sweeps*, or *sweepstakes*, in which the winner's prize, or *purse*, is made up of owner's entry fees supplemented by money 'put up' by the track.

RACEHORSE/MOUNT & JOCKEY

WHIP/BAT/CROP/STICK
CRASH HELMET/"SKULL CAP"
GOGGLES
SILKS/COLORS
STARTING GATE NUMBER/ PROGRAM NUMBER
SADDLE
BLINKERS/BLINDERS/ BLINKER HOOD/ ROGUE'S BADGE
NUMBER CLOTH
SPUR
BOOT
SHADOW ROLL
CROWN PIECE
LEADWEIGHT (HANDICAP WEIGHT)
NECK PIECE — BRIDLE
STIRRUP IRON
HEAD PIECE
LEATHERS/WEBS
BIT
REIN
BANDAGES
BOOT
GIRTH & SURCINGLE
GIRTH PAD

TOTE BOARD/ODDS BOARD

MONEY BET ON RACE/BETTING POOL
ODDS ON WINNING
HORSE NUMBER/POST POSITION
MONEY BET ON HORSE TO WIN
MONEY BET ON HORSE TO PLACE
MONEY BET ON HORSE TO SHOW

	TOTAL		1	2	3	4	30	5	8	6	35	7		8	9
7			1	2	3	1				1445				
	66492	WIN	16237	13118	27036	1890	6056	1445				
1022	24753	PLC	6912	5583	7617	1045	2643	1033				
	9641	SHW	2326	1761	2512	610	1468	964				

Horse racing is a betting sport. *Bettors* wager money on their ability to predict which horses will finish first, second or third, called win, place and show. The *payoff*, the amount of money won, is determined by the *odds*. Odds are the amount of money bet on one horse in relation to the amount bet on the race as a whole.

In *parimutuel betting* the total amount bet is distributed to people holding winning tickets after track operating expenses and state taxes have been deducted.

Exotic bets include the *double*, in which winners of two races are picked, the *quinella*, in which the first two finishers are picked, and the *trifecta*, in which the three finishers are picked in order.

DRIVER IN SULKY/'BIKE' & PACER IN HARNESS

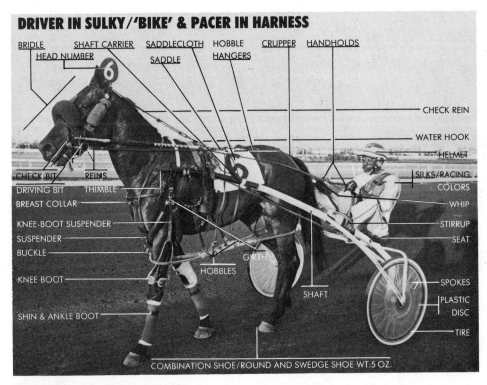

PARIMUTUEL TICKET/ BETTING TICKET

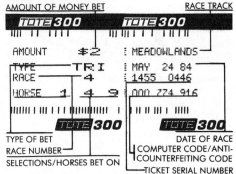

RACING PROGRAM ENTRY

PAST PERFORMANCE CHART

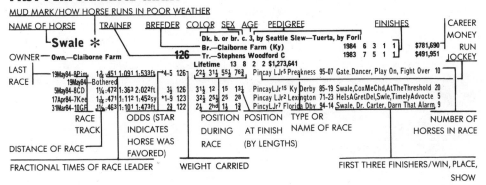

MOBILE STARTING GATE

TROTTING AND PACING GAITS

TROTTERS MOVE LEGS ON A DIAGONAL IN UNISON

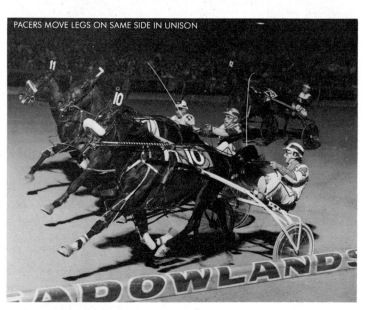

PACERS MOVE LEGS ON SAME SIDE IN UNISON

FINISH LINE PHOTO/PHOTO FINISH

The object of horseshoe pitching is to toss a shoe so that it rings, or encircles, the metal stake or comes closer to the stake than an opponent's toss. Each *ringer* is worth three points; each shoe closer than an opponent's shoe is worth one point. Shoes score when landing within 6″ of the stake. Singles matches are usually played to 50 points, doubles matches to 21. *Leaners*, or *hobbers*, and shoes actually touching the stake count only as close shoes. Shoes are tossed, or pitched, underhanded. Each pitcher is allotted two tosses in an *inning*.

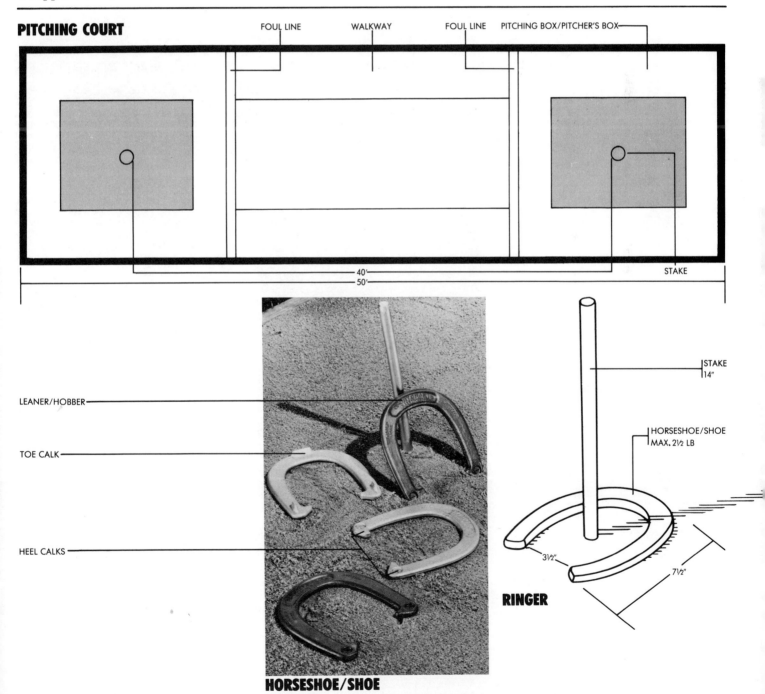

PITCHING COURT

FOUL LINE   WALKWAY   FOUL LINE   PITCHING BOX/PITCHER'S BOX

40′

50′

STAKE

LEANER/HOBBER

TOE CALK

HEEL CALKS

STAKE
14″

HORSESHOE/SHOE
MAX. 2½ LB

3½″

7½″

RINGER

HORSESHOE/SHOE

Captains head teams of 15 players each. They toss for choice of ends of field. Players move the ball down the field by hitting it with the hurley, by knocking it with their hands while the ball is in the air, or by kicking it.

A game consists of two 30-minute halves, with a maximum interval of 10 minutes between halves, called half time.

Sending the ball into the net is a *goal*, worth three points. Sending it over the crossbar and between the goal posts scores one *point*. The team scoring the most points wins.

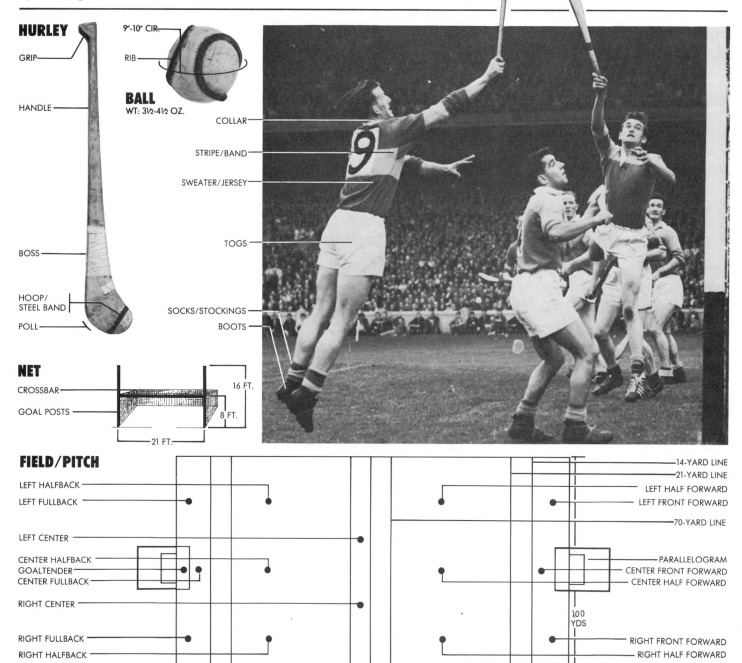

HURLEY

GRIP

HANDLE

BOSS

HOOP/STEEL BAND

POLL

BALL
WT: 3½-4½ OZ.
9"-10" CIR.
RIB

COLLAR

STRIPE/BAND

SWEATER/JERSEY

TOGS

SOCKS/STOCKINGS

BOOTS

NET

CROSSBAR

GOAL POSTS

16 FT.

8 FT.

21 FT.

FIELD/PITCH

LEFT HALFBACK

LEFT FULLBACK

LEFT CENTER

CENTER HALFBACK

GOALTENDER

CENTER FULLBACK

RIGHT CENTER

RIGHT FULLBACK

RIGHT HALFBACK

14-YARD LINE

21-YARD LINE

LEFT HALF FORWARD

LEFT FRONT FORWARD

70-YARD LINE

PARALLELOGRAM

CENTER FRONT FORWARD

CENTER HALF FORWARD

100 YDS

RIGHT FRONT FORWARD

RIGHT HALF FORWARD

160 YDS

Iceboating, or *hardwater sailing*, takes place in one- or two-man boats, in classes ranging from nine to 30 feet in length.

Most classes race *windward-leeward* courses which they complete three to five times, circling a pair of marks placed one mile apart.

Before a race, skippers draw for positions, either a *starboard tack position* or a *port tack position*, and wait for a dropped flag. At the start, skippers push their iceboats off and jump into the cockpit.

Most iceboats are made of steel, aluminum or wood, and travel at upwards of 100 miles per hour.

ICEBOAT

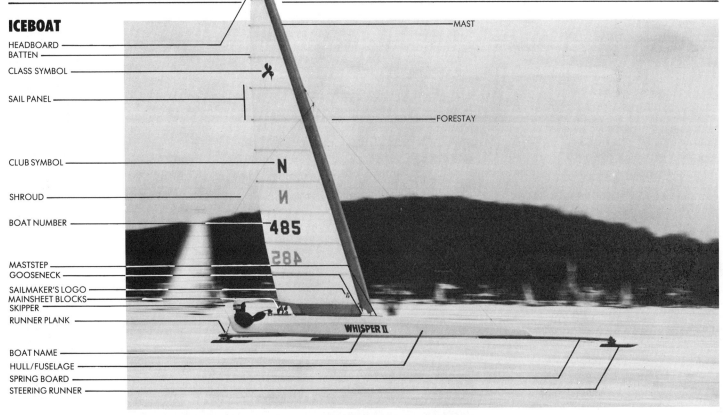

HEADBOARD
BATTEN
CLASS SYMBOL
SAIL PANEL
CLUB SYMBOL
SHROUD
BOAT NUMBER
MASTSTEP
GOOSENECK
SAILMAKER'S LOGO
MAINSHEET BLOCKS
SKIPPER
RUNNER PLANK
BOAT NAME
HULL/FUSELAGE
SPRING BOARD
STEERING RUNNER

MAST
FORESTAY

WHISPER II

SAIL
WINDOW
SAFETY HELMET/
CRASH HELMET
SAFETY GOGGLES
BOOM
FOUL WEATHER GEAR
SHROUD/SIDESTAY
RUNNER PLANK
RUNNER CHOCK
RUNNER
HULL
MAST
MAIN SHEET
SPIKES/CREEPERS
TILLER
MAINSHEET BLOCK

ICEBOATER

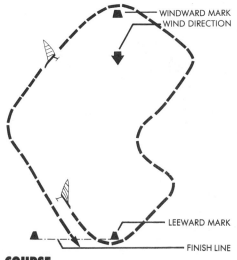

WINDWARD MARK
WIND DIRECTION

LEEWARD MARK
FINISH LINE

COURSE

An ice hockey game consists of three, twenty-minute *periods*.

Rules infractions, or *penalties*, result in the offending player being removed from play, for usually two or five minutes. His team plays *short-handed*, giving the opposition a *power play*.

An offensive player tries to block the goalie's view, or *screen* him. The goalie is credited with a *save* when he knocks a *shot* away. A blinking *red light* atop the goal judge's box is lit when a *goal* is scored.

The angle between the shaft of a stick and the blade is the *lie*. The puck is made of vulcanized rubber. In professional hockey a *sudden-death overtime* (first goal, wins) is sometimes used to decide a game tied at the end of *regulation play*.

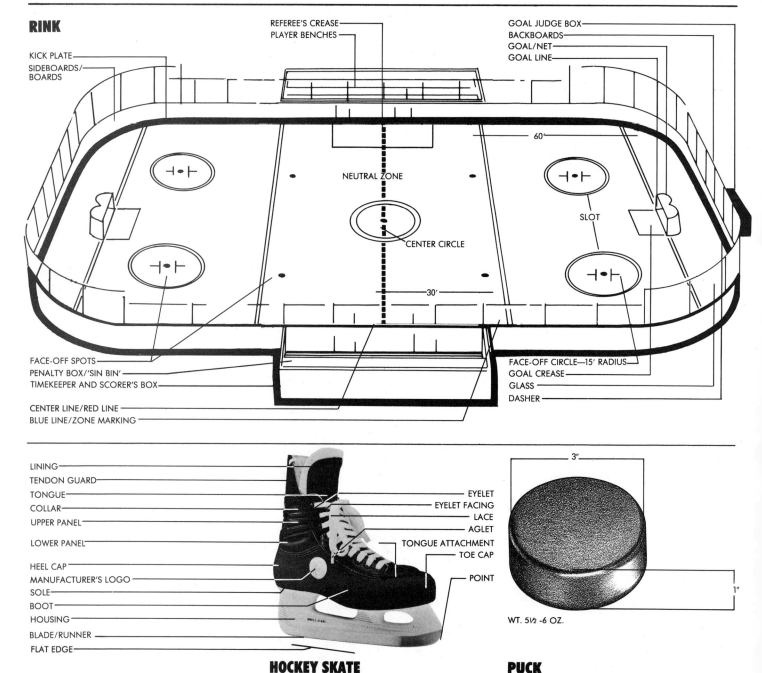

RINK

KICK PLATE
SIDEBOARDS/BOARDS

REFEREE'S CREASE
PLAYER BENCHES

GOAL JUDGE BOX
BACKBOARDS
GOAL/NET
GOAL LINE

60'

NEUTRAL ZONE

SLOT

CENTER CIRCLE

30'

FACE-OFF SPOTS
PENALTY BOX/'SIN BIN'
TIMEKEEPER AND SCORER'S BOX

FACE-OFF CIRCLE—15' RADIUS
GOAL CREASE
GLASS
DASHER

CENTER LINE/RED LINE
BLUE LINE/ZONE MARKING

LINING
TENDON GUARD
TONGUE
COLLAR
UPPER PANEL
LOWER PANEL
HEEL CAP
MANUFACTURER'S LOGO
SOLE
BOOT
HOUSING
BLADE/RUNNER
FLAT EDGE

EYELET
EYELET FACING
LACE
AGLET
TONGUE ATTACHMENT
TOE CAP
POINT

HOCKEY SKATE

3"

1"

WT. 5½ -6 OZ.

PUCK

Physical contact occurs when a player blocks his opponent with his body, or *bodychecks* him. A check may send a player crashing into the *boards*. Trying to steal the puck with a stick is *stick-checking*.

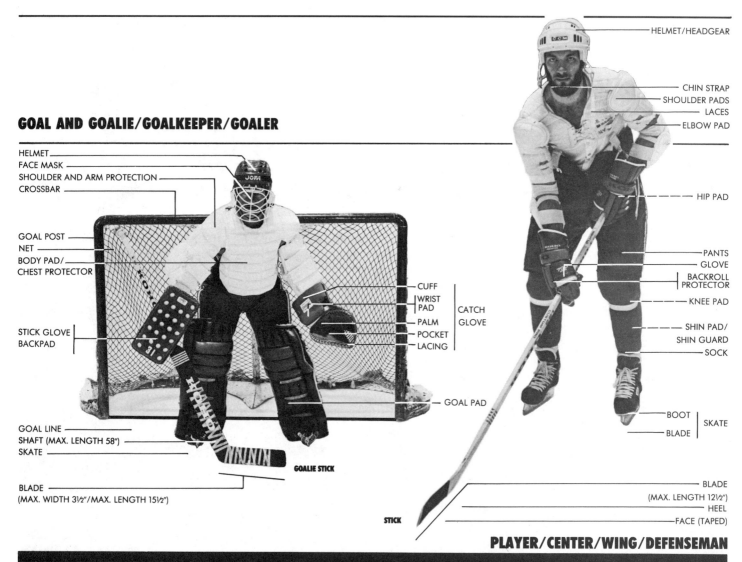

GOAL AND GOALIE/GOALKEEPER/GOALER

HELMET
FACE MASK
SHOULDER AND ARM PROTECTION
CROSSBAR

GOAL POST
NET
BODY PAD/
CHEST PROTECTOR

STICK GLOVE
BACKPAD

GOAL LINE
SHAFT (MAX. LENGTH 58″)
SKATE

BLADE
(MAX. WIDTH 3½″/MAX. LENGTH 15½″)

CUFF
WRIST PAD
PALM
POCKET
LACING

CATCH GLOVE

GOAL PAD

GOALIE STICK

HELMET/HEADGEAR

CHIN STRAP
SHOULDER PADS
LACES
ELBOW PAD

HIP PAD

PANTS
GLOVE
BACKROLL PROTECTOR
KNEE PAD

SHIN PAD/
SHIN GUARD
SOCK

BOOT
SKATE
BLADE

BLADE
(MAX. LENGTH 12½″)
HEEL
FACE (TAPED)

STICK

PLAYER/CENTER/WING/DEFENSEMAN

PLAYER POSITIONS

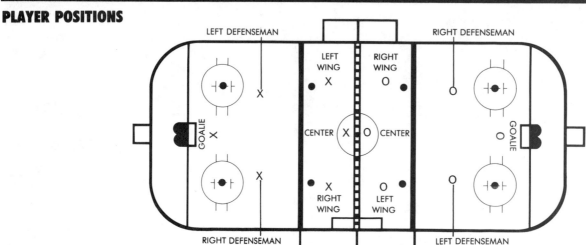

LEFT DEFENSEMAN
RIGHT DEFENSEMAN

LEFT WING
RIGHT WING

GOALIE

CENTER
CENTER

GOALIE

RIGHT WING
LEFT WING

RIGHT DEFENSEMAN
LEFT DEFENSEMAN

OFFICIALS SIGNALS

HIGH-STICKING   CROSS-CHECKING   DELAYED CALLING OF PENALTY   HOLDING   HOOKING   INTERFERENCE

WASH-OUT   UNSPORTSMANLIKE CONDUCT   BOARDING   CHARGING   ELBOWING

MISCONDUCT   ROUGHING   SLASHING   SPEARING   TRIPPING   ICING

BASIC PLAYS

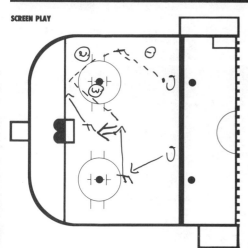

SCREEN PLAY

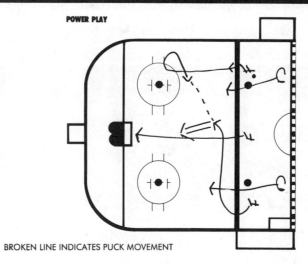

POWER PLAY

BROKEN LINE INDICATES PUCK MOVEMENT

Herb Brooks
US
Olympic
Team
1980

HERB BROOKS, 1980 GOLD MEDAL
WINNING U.S. OLYMPIC TEAM

Jai alai is played in a *fronton*, an auditorium that includes a court, tiered spectator seating area and *parimutuel betting* facilities. Spectators watch the game through a *mesh screen*.

Jai alai is played by individuals, or two- and three-man teams. The pelota is thrown off the frontis and must be caught in the cesta on the fly or after one bounce, then returned to the wall in a continuous motion.

Only the serving team can score.

The losing team returns to the bench and is replaced by another team. The game ends when a player or team scores enough points to win the match, usually between 6 (singles) and 40. Spectators wager on the results.

SCOREBOARD/ BETTING BOARD

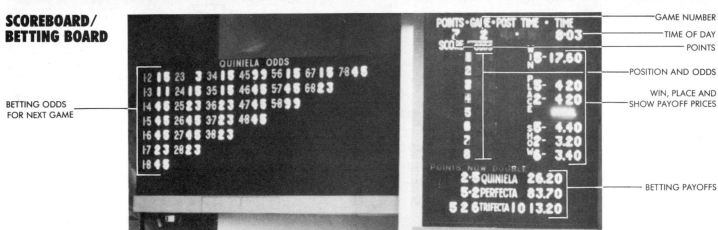

BETTING ODDS FOR NEXT GAME

GAME NUMBER

TIME OF DAY

POINTS

POSITION AND ODDS

WIN, PLACE AND SHOW PAYOFF PRICES

BETTING PAYOFFS

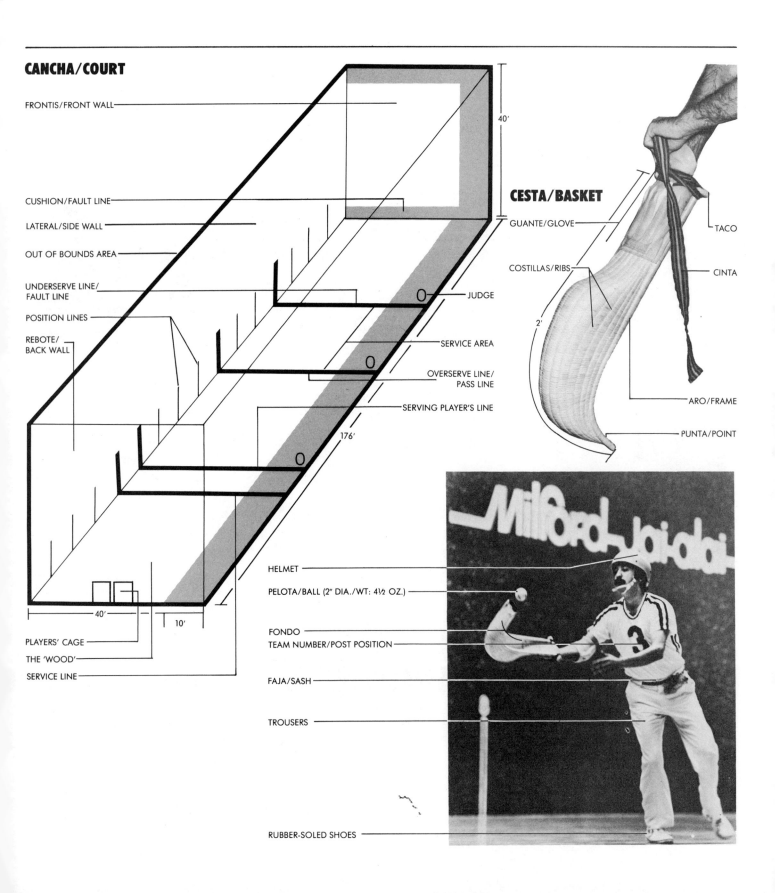

CANCHA/COURT

FRONTIS/FRONT WALL

40'

CUSHION/FAULT LINE

LATERAL/SIDE WALL

OUT OF BOUNDS AREA

UNDERSERVE LINE/
FAULT LINE

POSITION LINES

REBOTE/
BACK WALL

JUDGE

SERVICE AREA

OVERSERVE LINE/
PASS LINE

SERVING PLAYER'S LINE

176'

CESTA/BASKET

GUANTE/GLOVE

COSTILLAS/RIBS

2'

TACO

CINTA

ARO/FRAME

PUNTA/POINT

HELMET

PELOTA/BALL (2" DIA./WT: 4½ OZ.)

FONDO
TEAM NUMBER/POST POSITION

FAJA/SASH

TROUSERS

40'

10'

PLAYERS' CAGE

THE 'WOOD'

SERVICE LINE

RUBBER-SOLED SHOES

Karters race miniature race cars, or *karts*, in events conducted to scale with sports car and stock car racing. *Sprint* karters sit upright beside or in front of a 2- or 4-cycle motor and race on a twisting road course consisting of about nine *left-*, *right-* and *ess-turns*. *Speedway* karters, also using 2- or 4-cycle *engines*, run short lap races, or *heats*, around ⅛-mile oval dirt tracks, or *'bullrings.'*

Powerful *roadracing* karts are driven in a reclining, or *'laydown position'*, at speeds of up to 140-mph on full-sized road courses during hour-long *enduro* races. The aerodynamics of some of these *superkarts* are similar to full-sized race cars, enabling karters to create *drafts* and *slipstreams*.

RACEWAY

CRASH HELMET
FUEL TANK
ROADRACING KART/ENDURO KART

EXHAUST SYSTEM/PIPES

MOTOR
SEAT

DISC BRAKE
STEERING WHEEL

CHAIN DRIVE
CHAIN

STEERING SHAFT
MASTER BRAKE CYLINDER

SIDE NUMBER PANEL
NERF BAR
FUEL TANK

TIE ROD

BRAKE PEDAL
FRONT NUMBER PANEL

RACING SLICK/TIRE

GAS PEDAL/THROTTLE

WHEEL

FRONT PORCH & BUMPER

SPRINT KART

A men's team is made up of 10 players, and games consist of four 15-minute *quarters*, with two-minute rest intervals between the first and third quarters and a 10-minute break, or *half time*, after the second quarter.

Women's teams are made up of 12 players, and their games consist of two 25-minute halves, with a 10-minute half-time.

The two *center players* engage in a *face-off* at the center line to begin a game. All players must then stay in their assigned areas throughout play.

The ball is carried, thrown and caught with sticks. Each goal counts one point and the team scoring the most points wins the game.

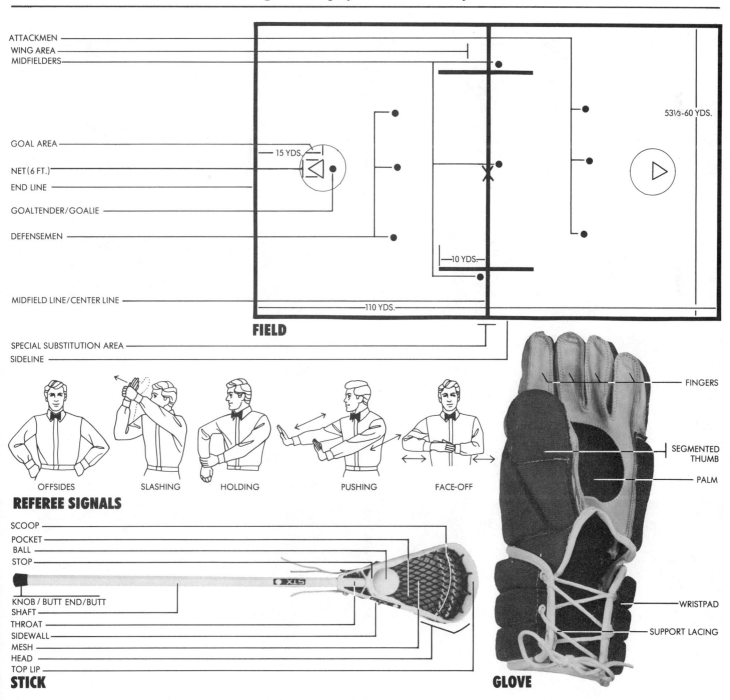

ATTACKMEN
WING AREA
MIDFIELDERS

GOAL AREA
NET (6 FT.)
END LINE
GOALTENDER/GOALIE
DEFENSEMEN
MIDFIELD LINE/CENTER LINE

15 YDS.
53⅓-60 YDS.
10 YDS.
110 YDS.

FIELD

SPECIAL SUBSTITUTION AREA
SIDELINE

OFFSIDES   SLASHING   HOLDING   PUSHING   FACE-OFF

REFEREE SIGNALS

SCOOP
POCKET
BALL
STOP
KNOB / BUTT END/BUTT
SHAFT
THROAT
SIDEWALL
MESH
HEAD
TOP LIP

STICK

FINGERS
SEGMENTED THUMB
PALM
WRISTPAD
SUPPORT LACING

GLOVE

NET

BIB

STICK

CHEST & STOMACH PAD

GOAL

BALL

HELMET

FACE MASK/MASK

CHIN STRAP

CHIN PAD

SHOULDER PAD

ELBOW PAD

FLOATING CUFF

GLOVE

JERSEY

SHORTS/TRUNKS/PANTS

Lawn bowling, also called *bowls* or *flat green bowls*, is played on a green which is divided into *rinks*. Matches are played by individuals or teams. A toss determines who bowls first. The mat, or footer, is placed and the jack is delivered.

While standing on the mat *bowlers* roll their bowls next to the jack, maybe even getting a *toucher*.

A point is awarded for each bowl closer to the jack than the opposition's nearest bowl. After all bowls are rolled, a new *end* is begun.

Matches may be played either for a certain number of ends or to a predetermined number of points.

RINK NUMBER

DITCH/WALL

MAT/FOOTER

CENTER OF RINK MARKER

GREEN/BOWLING GREEN

SCORER

CALIBRATED TAPE/TAPE

LOCATING SPIGOT

TAPE HANDLING

CALIPERS

MEASURE

JACK/KITTY

EMBLEM/ENGRAVING

BOWL/WOOD

BOWLS & JACK

International *lugers* race in iced *courses* having at least one *labyrinth, straightaway*, and *left-, right-, hairpin-*, and *S-curve*. The *starting line* is crossed in a *flying start*, usually from raised *starting blocks*. Racers '*flow in the ice groove*.' They find their *driving track*, the shortest path from start to finish. Lugers lean backward to reduce *air resistance;* stamp on *sled runners*, pull *reins* and shift weight to *steer;* and brake by pressing their soles against the ice while pulling the front of the *luge* into the air. *Double-seaters* have a *sunken seat* for the second rider who lies under the first while *luging*. Aggregate times from a series of *runs* determine winners. Courses are about 1000 meters long.

LUGER/LUGE TOBOGGANIST/LUGE RACER
PLASTIC-COATED RACING SUIT
KNEE PROTECTOR
PADDED GLOVE
GLOVE STUDS
START HANDLE
LUGE TOBOGGAN SLED/LUGE/RODEL

CRASH HELMET
FACE SHIELD/VISOR
ELBOW GUARD
MANUFACTURER'S LOGO
SUPPORT BELT/KIDNEY PROTECTION BELT
BOOTIES/BOOTS/SHOES
FRONT BRIDGE
RUNNER/BLADE/ 'STEELS'
RUNNER

THE START

LUGE TOBOGGAN SLED/ LUGE/RODEL

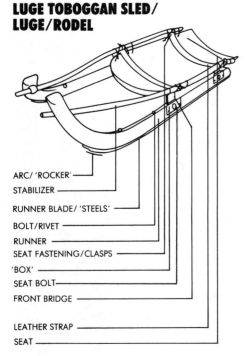

ARC/ 'ROCKER'
STABILIZER
RUNNER BLADE/ 'STEELS'
BOLT/RIVET
RUNNER
SEAT FASTENING/CLASPS
'BOX'
SEAT BOLT
FRONT BRIDGE
LEATHER STRAP
SEAT

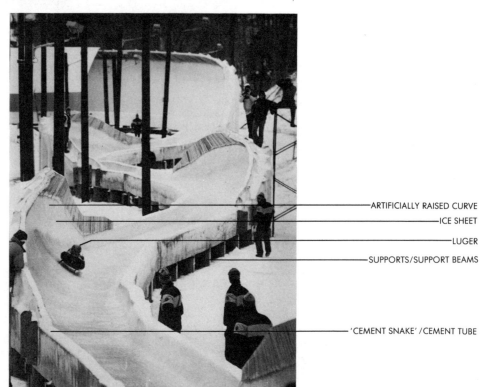

ARTIFICIALLY RAISED CURVE
ICE SHEET
LUGER
SUPPORTS/SUPPORT BEAMS
'CEMENT SNAKE' /CEMENT TUBE

LUGE/TRACK/COURSE/RUN

There are over 50 types of martial arts, with variations and individual styles within each type. Competitive tournaments, sanctioned by organizational bodies and international committees, exist for several of the martial arts. However, since many of the *fighting arts* develop spiritual skills as well as self-defense techniques, much of the sport is more concerned with private activity than with public competition.

Martial arts practitioners work out in a dojo, or school, run by a *sensei*, a master or teacher.

The *double middle quarter block in horse stance* shown below illustrates the fluid movement, strength and quickness typical of martial arts moves.

Karate, or *empty-handed fighting*, is characterized by crippling kicks and punches meant to disable an attacker or group of attackers. Participants, or *players*, engage in two types of sanctioned matches: *kata* (form) and *kumite* (sparring).

In kata, a formal exercise in which an individual performs various movements according to a prescribed pattern, contestants are judged on form, appropriate speed and strength, and on correct breathing and direction of movement. The action, which simulates simultaneous combat with a number of attackers from several directions, is judged on a scale of zero to ten. The player with the most points wins.

KATAS

BACK-STANCE KNIFE HAND

HEEL FRONT KICK

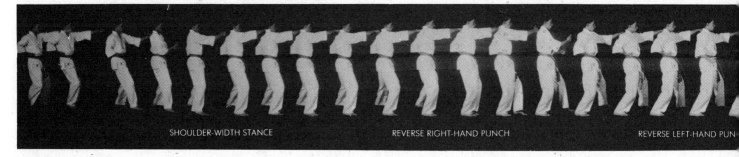

SHOULDER-WIDTH STANCE

REVERSE RIGHT-HAND PUNCH

REVERSE LEFT-HAND PUN

KUMITES

ATTACK BY MALE

AVOIDANCE BY FEMALE

ARM LOCK BY FEMALE

LUNGE PUNCH BY MALE

BLOCK DEFLECTED BY FEMALE

In kumite matches, a player directs kicks and punches at his opponent while also blocking his opponent's attacks. Physical contact is strictly limited, thus blows need not actually land to score and are pulled back at the last moment to avoid injuring an opponent.

A full point, or *ippon*, is awarded for a likely hit. A less effective blow is awarded a half-point, or *waza ari*.

Players accumulating a set number of points, or scoring a killing blow, win. A killing blow is one that would have landed in one of the 20 vital points of the body and would have killed the opponent if it had not been pulled back in time.

ROUNDHOUSE KICK   KNIFE HAND

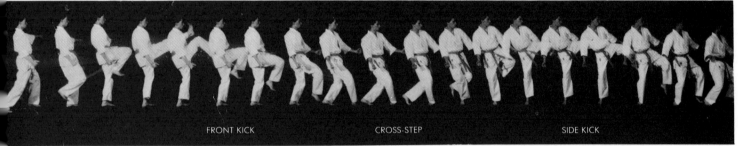

FRONT KICK   CROSS-STEP   SIDE KICK

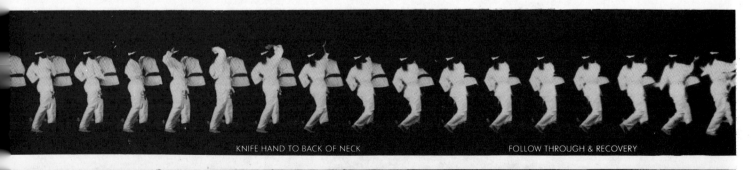

KNIFE HAND TO BACK OF NECK   FOLLOW THROUGH & RECOVERY

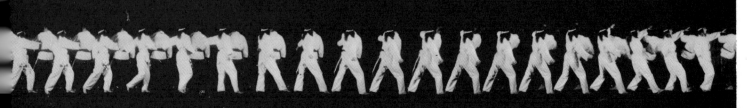

VERSE PUNCH BY FEMALE   STEP & RIDGE HAND TO THROAT   FOLLOW THROUGH

Points in kumite are awarded for blows struck with good form, good attitude, strong vigor, proper timing, an alert mind, or *zanshin*, and correct distancing, within two inches of the target area. A blow that is thwarted or falls short of the correct distance is awarded no score.

Certain karate techniques are not allowed in competition because of their lethal nature. Others, such as dangerous blows to the eyes or testicles, persistent attacks on the shins or direct attacks to the hips, knee joints or insteps, may result in fouls. A player may be disqualified due to repeated fouls after being warned, first privately, then publicly, by the match referee.

BLOCKING A KICK

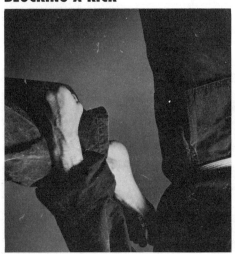

BLOCKING A PUNCH

FRONT KICK

SIDE KICK

SCORING AN IPPON

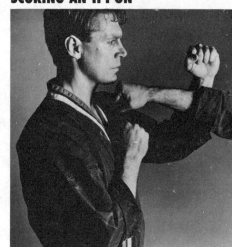

NO SCORE

Judo, an Oriental form of wrestling derived from *jujitsu*, or *jujutsu*, its medieval predecessor, combines balance and strength with holding and throwing techniques.

A judo player, or *judoka*, can win a match with an ippon by bodily dumping his opponent on his back, pinning him to the mat and keeping him there for 30 seconds, or by applying a submission hold (such as a twisting lock on the arm or elbow, or a choke hold) until his opponent signifies defeat by *tapping out*, hitting the mat or his attacker twice with the hand. A player is awarded a half-point waza-ari for an imperfect throw. Two waza-aris equal one ippon. A sanctioned match lasts from three to 10 minutes.

DOJO/SCHOOL

UNIFORM/
GI/JUDOGI
BELT/OBI
JACKET/UWAGI
PANTS/ZUBAN
MAT/TATAMI

STRANGLEHOLD

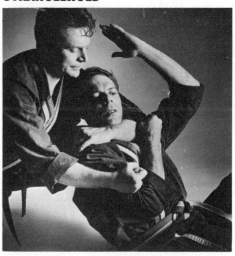

ONE-POINT SHOULDER THROW/IPPON SEOINAGE

JUDO MAT/COMPETITION MAT

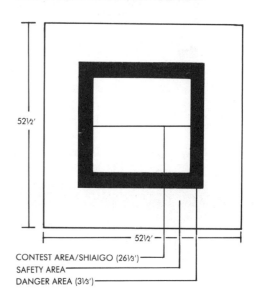

52½'

52½'

CONTEST AREA/SHIAIGO (26⅓')
SAFETY AREA
DANGER AREA (3⅓')

Aikido's method of self-defense is based on dodging an attacker while simultaneously using the force of his momentum against him.

Competitive fighting takes various forms. In kata, two participants, one designated attacker, or *uke*, the other defender, or *tori*, are judged on a set routine of attack and defense.

In three-round *ninin dori*, three *aikidoists* stage a spontaneous mock fight. *Tanto randori* consists of two one-minute rounds of free fighting between an unarmed defender and an attacker armed with a rubber knife. The attacker makes a point by striking the defender in the chest with the knife. The defender is awarded a point for disarming his opponent.

WRISTLOCK

WRIST & NECK LOCK

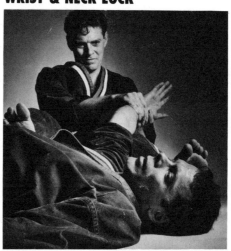

ELBOW LOCK

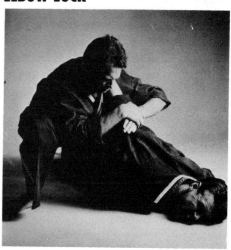

MAT

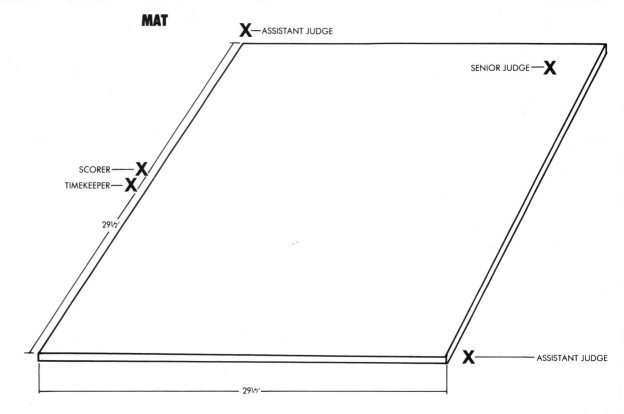

X—ASSISTANT JUDGE

SENIOR JUDGE—X

SCORER—X

TIMEKEEPER—X

29½'

X——ASSISTANT JUDGE

29½'

Kung fu, the Chinese art of self-defense from which karate was developed, is a broad term used to refer to any of a number of martially inspired systems for fighting, fitness and dance.

There are several hundred styles, many of which involve weapons. Other styles use animal postures as spiritual and physical models. Such stances and movements imitate those of a crane, tiger, snake, monkey, etc. The sport also involves free fighting, or *sparring*, in which a variety of styles are used.

Kung fu, called *kempo*, or *wu shu* in China, means "skill" or "ability." Today the emphasis of most forms of kung fu is on its use in combat.

FREE FIGHTING

MONKEY STANCE

CRANE STANCE

When the martial arts are used for fighting, there are certain parts of the body which are more vulnerable to blows than others.

When attacking the head and neck, for example, an open or closed fist, the elbow and the foot are most effective. The eyes, temples and throat are especially vulnerable.

On the other hand, when attacking the groin, body and internal organs, an open or closed fist, the elbow, knee and foot are used with

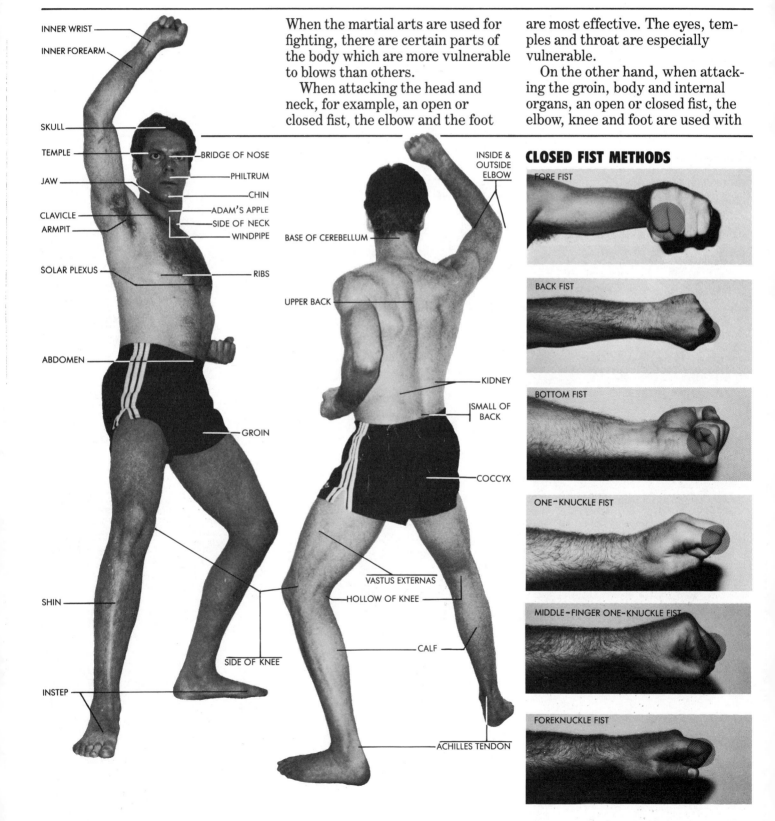

INNER WRIST
INNER FOREARM
SKULL
TEMPLE
JAW
CLAVICLE
ARMPIT
SOLAR PLEXUS
ABDOMEN
SHIN
INSTEP

BRIDGE OF NOSE
PHILTRUM
CHIN
ADAM'S APPLE
SIDE OF NECK
WINDPIPE
RIBS

GROIN

SIDE OF KNEE

INSIDE & OUTSIDE ELBOW
BASE OF CEREBELLUM
UPPER BACK
KIDNEY
SMALL OF BACK
COCCYX
VASTUS EXTERNAS
HOLLOW OF KNEE
CALF
ACHILLES TENDON

CLOSED FIST METHODS

FORE FIST

BACK FIST

BOTTOM FIST

ONE-KNUCKLE FIST

MIDDLE-FINGER ONE-KNUCKLE FIST

FOREKNUCKLE FIST

greatest effect. Most vulnerable areas are the groin, coccyx, solar plexus and kidney.

When attacking the legs and feet, the foot is used with particular effect against the knee, arch and achilles tendon.

OPEN HAND METHODS

RIDGE HAND

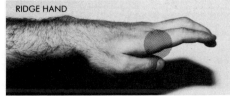

KNIFE HAND

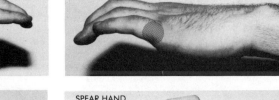

FOOT METHODS

HEEL

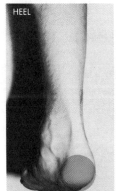

BALL OF FOOT

BACK HAND

SPEAR HAND

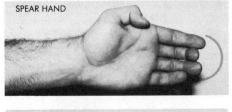

BEAR HAND

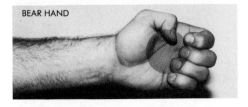

PALM HEEL

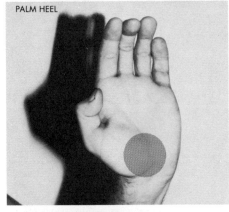

FOOT EDGE

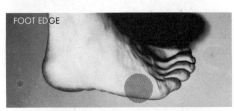

TIGER-MOUTH HAND

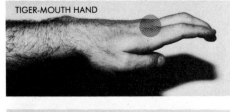

SOLE

TWO-FINGER SPEAR HAND

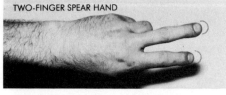

OX-JAW HAND

INSTEP

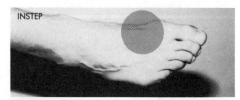

ONE-FINGER SPEAR HAND

ELBOW

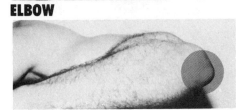

KNEE

The martial art of kendo, developed from *kenjutsu*, "the art of the sword," is the Japanese form of fencing with bamboo swords.

In competition, two *kendoka* "cut" with the forward third of their sword or "thrust" with its tip, scoring points by striking either the temples, wrists, breastplate or throat of their opponent. A strike counts as a point only if it is delivered with full spirit and correct form, and is accompanied by a forceful yell, or *kiai*. The first to score two points or the one with the higher score by the time limit, wins.

A kendo match is conducted within a 33- by 36-foot competition area and normally lasts three to five minutes.

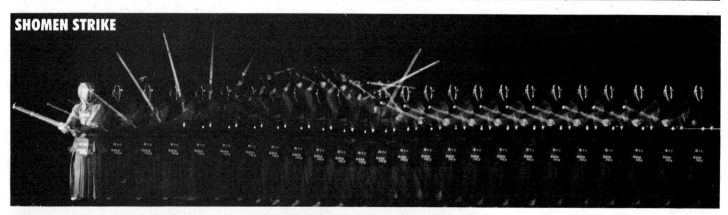

SHOMEN STRIKE

BAMBOO SWORD/SHINAI

MASK/MEN
HEADCLOTH/HACHIMAKI

SHIRT/KENDO JACKET/KEIKOGI

BREASTPLATE/DO

GAUNTLET/HANDGUARD/KOTE

APRON/TARE

DIVIDED SKIRT/HAKAMA

Motorcycles are raced on many different surfaces which test the *bike's* speed and durability, as well as the rider's skill and endurance. Events include roadracing on a specially built *circuit* or public road; motocross, or *MX*, or *scramble*, which takes place on natural terrain courses with hills, jumps, mud, and other obstacles that require gear changing; *hill climbing*, races against time or distance up a prepared steep hill; *dirt track* racing on an oval track with flat or banked

MOTOCROSS BIKE

THROTTLE CABLE

BRAKE

THROTTLE

FUEL TANK

AIR FILTER

NUMBER PLATE

EXHAUST PIPE

CLUTCH CABLE

AIR SCOOP

RADIATOR

FORK TUBE

CLUTCH

FENDER

BRAKE LINE

TENSION BAR

SPROCKET

SWING ARM

CHAIN

SUSPENSION AIR TANK

KICK STARTER

REAR BRAKE LEVER

CLUTCH COVER

CARBURETOR

MUFFLER

SPOKES

HUB

DISC BRAKE

NOBBY TIRE

OFFICIAL'S STAND

JUMP

SAND WHOOPS

surfaces; and *speedway* races (*handicap*, *scratch* or *match*), run on an ash or shale oval track. Dirt track racing requires a special riding technique since these *machines* do not have brakes.

Courses vary in distance and composition (from deserts to ice, on which bikers use steel-studded rear tires). Races are conducted in classes determined by the size of bike engines, measured in cubic centimeters (cc's), ranging from lightweight *50cc's* to *unlimited class* 750 + cc's.

Motocross races usually consist of two or three *motos*, or *heats*. They may be held over a set distance, ranging from one to two miles, include a specific number of laps, or simply be determined by distance

ROADRACING BIKE/STREET BIKE

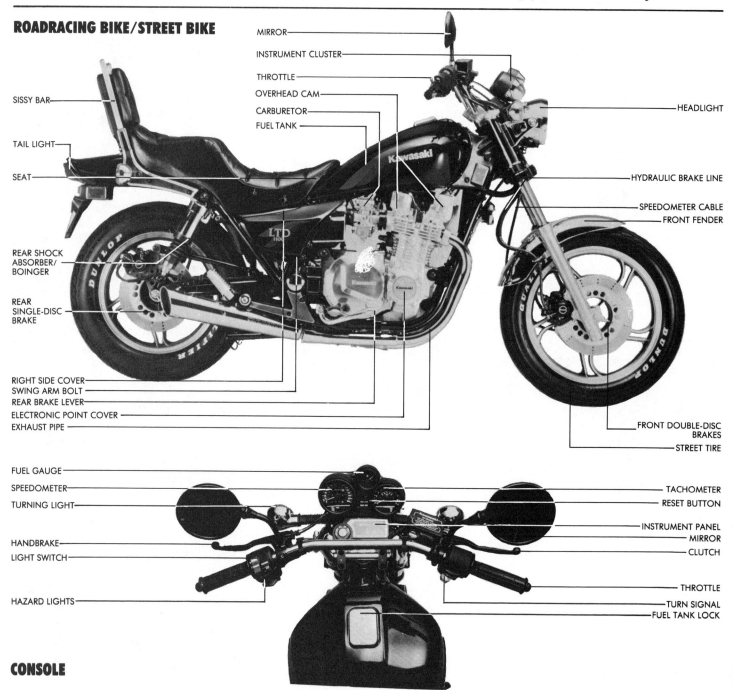

SISSY BAR

TAIL LIGHT

SEAT

REAR SHOCK ABSORBER/ BOINGER

REAR SINGLE-DISC BRAKE

RIGHT SIDE COVER
SWING ARM BOLT
REAR BRAKE LEVER
ELECTRONIC POINT COVER
EXHAUST PIPE

MIRROR
INSTRUMENT CLUSTER
THROTTLE
OVERHEAD CAM
CARBURETOR
FUEL TANK

HEADLIGHT

HYDRAULIC BRAKE LINE

SPEEDOMETER CABLE
FRONT FENDER

FRONT DOUBLE-DISC BRAKES
STREET TIRE

FUEL GAUGE
SPEEDOMETER
TURNING LIGHT

HANDBRAKE
LIGHT SWITCH

HAZARD LIGHTS

TACHOMETER
RESET BUTTON

INSTRUMENT PANEL
MIRROR
CLUTCH

THROTTLE
TURN SIGNAL
FUEL TANK LOCK

CONSOLE

covered in a set length of time. They are generally raced in single bikes, although races with *sidecars* are popular in Europe.

Riders win classification points toward a national championship, as well as prize money.

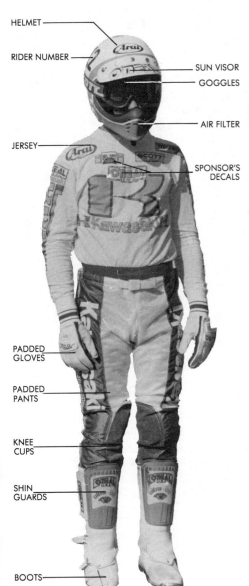

HELMET

RIDER NUMBER

SUN VISOR

GOGGLES

AIR FILTER

JERSEY

SPONSOR'S DECALS

PADDED GLOVES

PADDED PANTS

KNEE CUPS

SHIN GUARDS

BOOTS

MOTOCROSS RIDER

MOTOCROSS TRACK

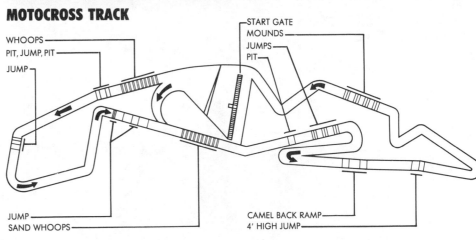

WHOOPS

PIT, JUMP, PIT

JUMP

START GATE

MOUNDS

JUMPS

PIT

JUMP

SAND WHOOPS

CAMEL BACK RAMP

4' HIGH JUMP

Cross-country *orienteers* use protractor compasses and topographic maps, or specially drawn orienteering maps in a race to reach the control points. In navigating between map and terrain, they *aim off*, *pace*, *check*, *contour*, find *attack points* and *catching features*. Each control point is marked with a control marker where the orienteer stops to stamp his or her control point card with a control clipper, to prove to officials at the finish that every control was reached. In *point*, *relay* or *line orienteering* control points must be reached in sequence. Courses are mapped by *course setters*, or *planners*, and reviewed for accuracy by course *vetters*.

CONTROL POINT/CHECK POINT/ CONTROL

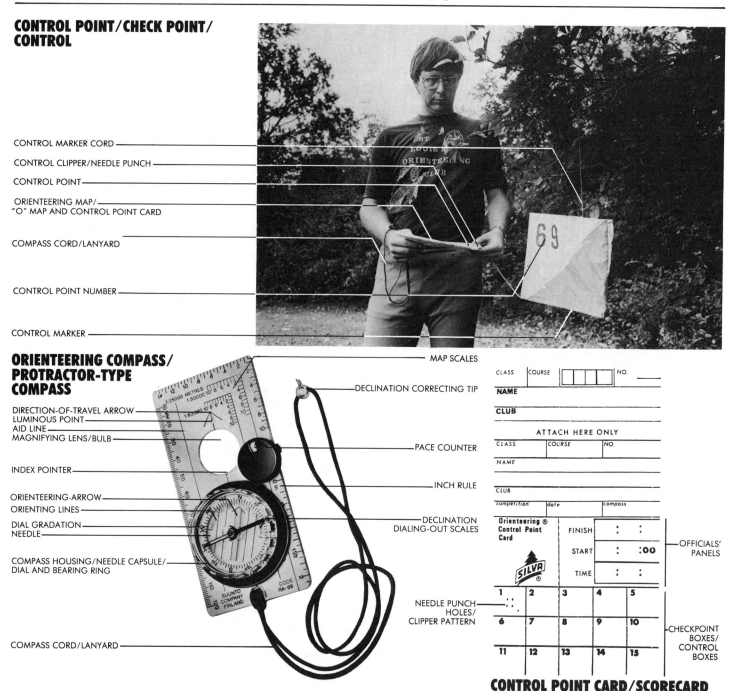

CONTROL MARKER CORD

CONTROL CLIPPER/NEEDLE PUNCH

CONTROL POINT

ORIENTEERING MAP/ "O" MAP AND CONTROL POINT CARD

COMPASS CORD/LANYARD

CONTROL POINT NUMBER

CONTROL MARKER

ORIENTEERING COMPASS/ PROTRACTOR-TYPE COMPASS

DIRECTION-OF-TRAVEL ARROW
LUMINOUS POINT
AID LINE
MAGNIFYING LENS/BULB

INDEX POINTER

ORIENTEERING-ARROW
ORIENTING LINES

DIAL GRADATION
NEEDLE

COMPASS HOUSING/NEEDLE CAPSULE/ DIAL AND BEARING RING

COMPASS CORD/LANYARD

MAP SCALES

DECLINATION CORRECTING TIP

PACE COUNTER

INCH RULE

DECLINATION DIALING-OUT SCALES

NEEDLE PUNCH HOLES/ CLIPPER PATTERN

CLASS | COURSE | NO.
NAME
CLUB

ATTACH HERE ONLY

CLASS | COURSE | NO.
NAME
CLUB

competition | date | compass

Orienteering ® Control Point Card

	FINISH	: :
SILVA ®	START	: :00
	TIME	: :

OFFICIALS' PANELS

1	2	3	4	5
6	7	8	9	10
11	12	13	14	15

CHECKPOINT BOXES/ CONTROL BOXES

CONTROL POINT CARD/SCORECARD

Platform tennis, or *'paddle,'* is an outdoor game, normally played in cold weather by *singles* players or by *doubles* teams. The rules are similar to tennis', except that only one service is allowed and the ball may be played off the side and back screens so long as it does not bounce on the deck a second time before being hit back, or *returned.* The clashing of partners' paddles in doubles does not make a return illegal, provided only one player strikes the ball.

Paddles are made of laminated wood or aluminum. The bright yellow ball is of firm sponge rubber.

Paddle tennis is played on a larger court with a punctured, or *'deadened,'* tennis ball.

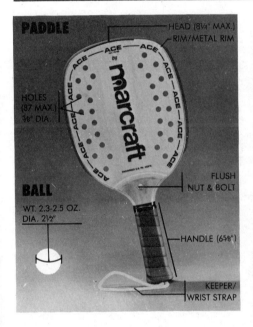

PADDLE
HEAD (8¼" MAX.)
RIM/METAL RIM
HOLES (87 MAX.) ⅜" DIA.
FLUSH NUT & BOLT
HANDLE (6⅝")
KEEPER/WRIST STRAP

BALL
WT. 2.3-2.5 OZ. DIA. 2½"

PLATFORM
EYE PROTECTOR
WIRE-MESH SCREEN
BACK SCREEN/BACK WALL
SNOW BOARD
PLATFORM/PLAYING SURFACE
COURT

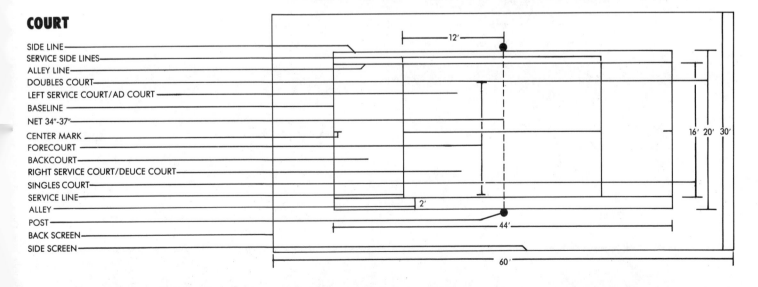

COURT
SIDE LINE
SERVICE SIDE LINES
ALLEY LINE
DOUBLES COURT
LEFT SERVICE COURT/AD COURT
BASELINE
NET 34"-37"
CENTER MARK
FORECOURT
BACKCOURT
RIGHT SERVICE COURT/DEUCE COURT
SINGLES COURT
SERVICE LINE
ALLEY
POST
BACK SCREEN
SIDE SCREEN

12'
16' 20' 30'
2'
44'
60'

Polo is played on horseback by two teams of four players each. Goals are scored by hitting the bamboo, ash, or plastic ball between the opponent's goal posts at any height. The mallet must be held in the right hand. The pony is controlled with the left hand.

A 7-minute period is a *chukker*. A game consists of eight such periods, known collectively as *chukkas*. Ties are broken in a *sudden-death chukker*, with the first score winning.

Players are numbered according to position. Forwards, numbered 1 and 2, play near the opposition's goal. Number 3 hits the ball upfield to the forwards. Number 4 protects the goal.

Two mounted *umpires* and a

ENGLISH SADDLE/POLO SADDLE

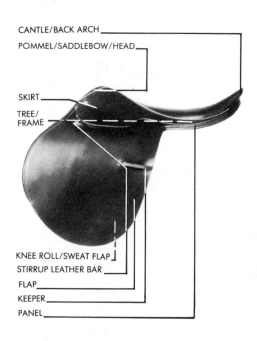

CANTLE/BACK ARCH
POMMEL/SADDLEBOW/HEAD
SKIRT
TREE/FRAME
KNEE ROLL/SWEAT FLAP
STIRRUP LEATHER BAR
FLAP
KEEPER
PANEL

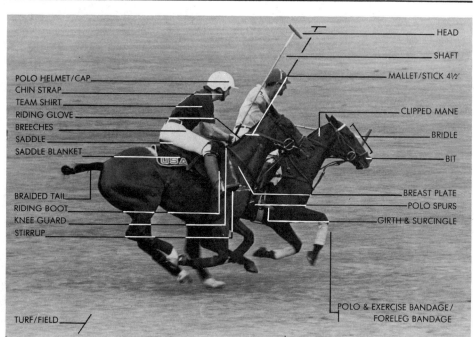

POLO HELMET/CAP
CHIN STRAP
TEAM SHIRT
RIDING GLOVE
BREECHES
SADDLE
SADDLE BLANKET
BRAIDED TAIL
RIDING BOOT
KNEE GUARD
STIRRUP
TURF/FIELD

HEAD
SHAFT
MALLET/STICK 4½'
CLIPPED MANE
BRIDLE
BIT
BREAST PLATE
POLO SPURS
GIRTH & SURCINGLE
POLO & EXERCISE BANDAGE/FORELEG BANDAGE

PLAYER/POLOIST AND MOUNT/PONY/HORSE

POLO GROUND

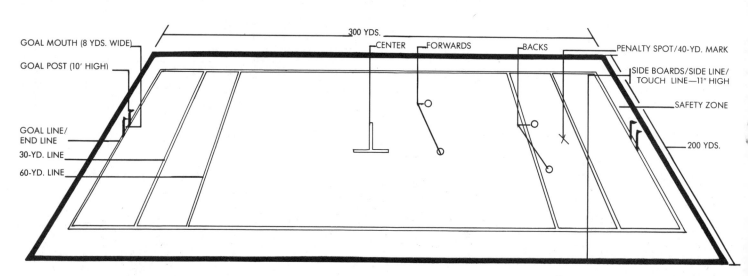

GOAL MOUTH (8 YDS. WIDE)
GOAL POST (10' HIGH)
GOAL LINE/END LINE
30-YD. LINE
60-YD. LINE
300 YDS.
CENTER
FORWARDS
BACKS
PENALTY SPOT/40-YD. MARK
SIDE BOARDS/SIDE LINE/TOUCH LINE—11" HIGH
SAFETY ZONE
200 YDS.

referee on the sideline officiate. Polo players often ride a group of ponies, called a *string*, during a game.

Each player has a *handicap*, or rating, based on his record. In tournaments, these ratings are added to produce a *team handicap*. Extra points are given to weaker teams to equalize games.

During play, a player following the exact line of the ball, or pursuing it on a smaller angle than any other player, has the *right of way*. Other players cannot interfere with him. But when players are riding after the ball in the same direction they may bump, or *ride off*, other players. Violations are penalized by the awarding of a goal or a free hit, depending on the foul.

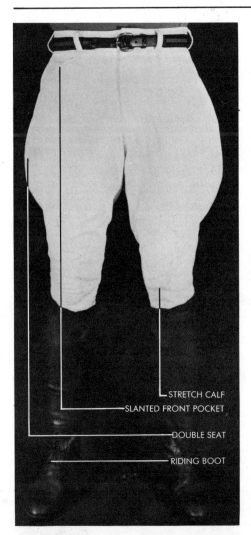

STRETCH CALF
SLANTED FRONT POCKET
DOUBLE SEAT
RIDING BOOT

BREECHES

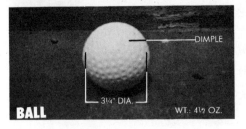

DIMPLE
3¼" DIA.
WT.: 4½ OZ.

BALL

UMPIRE
BACK'S STRIPE
POSITION NUMBER

Racquetball may be played by *singles* or two-person doubles teams. The object is to hit the ball off the front wall so that an opponent cannot return it before it bounces twice. A rally also ends when a *hinder* is called. *Avoidable hinders* are intentional interference and are penalized by loss of point or serve. *Unavoidable hinders* and *court hinders*, in which the ball is unintentionally obstructed, result in replays.

A ball may hit any wall or walls or the ceiling before hitting the front wall, but may not hit the floor.

A game is 21 points. Points may only be scored by the serving team. A serving team losing a rally loses the serve. A match is two out of three games.

RACQUET

COURT

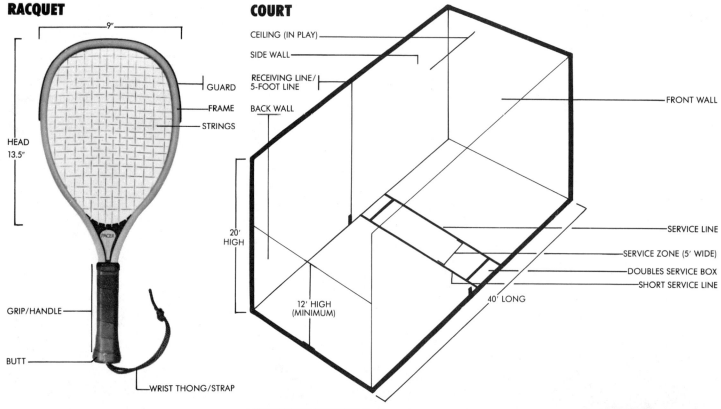

9"

GUARD
FRAME
STRINGS

HEAD
13.5"

GRIP/HANDLE

BUTT

WRIST THONG/STRAP

CEILING (IN PLAY)
SIDE WALL
RECEIVING LINE/
5-FOOT LINE
BACK WALL

FRONT WALL

20'
HIGH

12' HIGH
(MINIMUM)

40' LONG

SERVICE LINE
SERVICE ZONE (5' WIDE)
DOUBLES SERVICE BOX
SHORT SERVICE LINE

SWEATBAND/HEADBAND
RACQUETBALL GLOVE

GOGGLES

WRISTBAND

2¼" DIA

RACQUETBALL
WT: 1.4 OZ.

A rodeo is an exhibition of *cowboy skills* in which contestants, or *eventers*, demonstrate their ability to control livestock, or *stock*.

Judges score, or *mark*, an eventer's overall control of his animal, his *ride*, which requires both *spurring* and *reining*. The response of the stock to the rider, *stock performance*, is scored separately and is based on *kicks* and *jumps*.

Principal events are saddle bronc riding, bareback bronc riding, bull riding, calf roping and steer wrestling. Other competitions include barrel racing, *wild-horse racing* and *wild-cow milking*. Eventers are usually permitted two or more attempts in each event, the winner compiling the highest score or lowest time.

BAREBACK BRONC RIDING

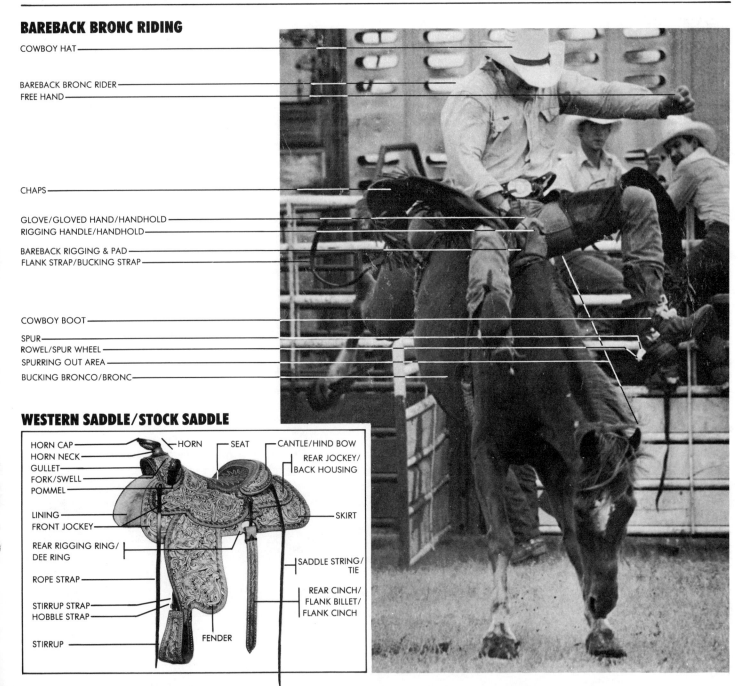

COWBOY HAT

BAREBACK BRONC RIDER
FREE HAND

CHAPS

GLOVE/GLOVED HAND/HANDHOLD
RIGGING HANDLE/HANDHOLD

BAREBACK RIGGING & PAD
FLANK STRAP/BUCKING STRAP

COWBOY BOOT

SPUR
ROWEL/SPUR WHEEL
SPURRING OUT AREA
BUCKING BRONCO/BRONC

WESTERN SADDLE/STOCK SADDLE

HORN CAP
HORN NECK
GULLET
FORK/SWELL
POMMEL

LINING
FRONT JOCKEY

REAR RIGGING RING/
DEE RING

ROPE STRAP

STIRRUP STRAP
HOBBLE STRAP

STIRRUP

HORN — SEAT — CANTLE/HIND BOW

REAR JOCKEY/
BACK HOUSING

SKIRT

SADDLE STRING/
TIE

REAR CINCH/
FLANK BILLET/
FLANK CINCH

FENDER

Bronc riders are allowed a *single handhold* on the reins. A rider who *'pulls leather,'* or touches the saddle with his free hand during his eight-second ride, is disqualified.

Bull riders also ride for eight seconds using a single handhold.

After a rider is thrown, *rodeo clowns* attract the bull from him.

A calf roper ropes the stock from horseback, dismounts, throws the calf to the ground and ties three of its legs together for a five-second count, timing to begin after he remounts.

Steer ropers slide off their *mounts* onto a steer and wrestle it to the ground.

Barrel racers lose five seconds for each barrel they knock over.

SADDLE BRONC RIDING

HALTER & HORSE'S CHAMPION TITLE
BUCKING REIN/BRONC REIN/BUCK REIN
SADDLE BRONC RIDER

BULL RIDING

BULL
BULL RIDER
FLANK STRAP/BUCKING STRAP
CHUTE/BUCKING CHUTE

COWGIRLS BARREL RACING

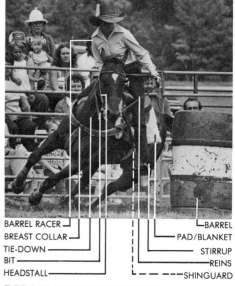

BARREL RACER
BREAST COLLAR
TIE-DOWN
BIT
HEADSTALL
BARREL
PAD/BLANKET
STIRRUP
REINS
SHINGUARD

BARREL RACING COURSES

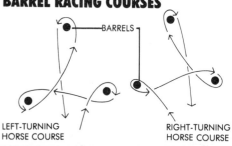

BARRELS

LEFT-TURNING HORSE COURSE

RIGHT-TURNING HORSE COURSE

STEER WRESTLING/'BULLDOGGING'

HAZER
RODEO PLANT/RODEO ARENA
STEER WRESTLER
STEER

TEAM ROPING

HIND-LEGS ROPER

HIND LEGS CATCH
HEAD CATCH/HORN CATCH
HEAD ROPER
TEAM-ROPING ROPE
QUARTER HORSES

CALF ROPING

PIGGIN' STRING
CALF-ROPING ROPE/LARIAT
QUARTER HORSE
CALF

Artistic roller skating consists of three separate competitive entities: figure, free and dance.

Figure skating, similar in nature to the *compulsory figures* in ice skating, requires mastery of standard edges and turns in executing prescribed patterns.

In dancing, all competing couples perform a prescribed set of steps to the same music. All movements must be performed in unison. They are judged by the accuracy of their steps and by their ability to interpret the rhythm of the music.

Movements and choice of music in free skating are left up to the skater. Performances are judged by the speed and height of *jumps*, the control and velocity of *spins*, and the individuality of *footwork*.

FREE SKATING
CAMEL SPIN

DANCE SKATING
LIFT/ONE-ARM REVERSE KENNEDY

LIFT BEGINS WITH MAN BENDING BOTH KNEES, KEEPING BACK STRAIGHT. THE WOMAN LOCKS BOTH ARMS.

KEEPING HEAD UP AND BACK ARCHED, THE MAN LIFTS THE WOMAN UP OVER THE CENTER OF HIS HEAD.

THE WOMAN KEEPS HER BODY RIGID AND HER HEAD DIRECTLY OVER THE MAN'S AS HER HAND IS RELEASED.

IN THE FINAL LIFT POSITION, THE MAN AND THE WOMAN EACH EXTEND THEIR FREE ARM DURING FOUR ROTATIONS.

Unlike ice hockey, roller hockey is a non-contact game whose rules are similar to soccer's. If the ball goes out of play, for example, it is put back into play with a *free hit*.

International speed skating involves *sprints* and *distance races* on either a 200-meter banked track or on an *'open'* or *'closed circuit' road race course*. In the U.S., indoor racing takes place on a 100-meter flat, oval track, with distances determined by age and sex. Outdoor road races, for skaters age fourteen and up, are conducted on a 300-meter flat, oval track made of asphalt.

ROLLER HOCKEY

SHIRT
SHORTS
KNEE PAD

PADDED GLOVE
SHIN GUARD
SOCK
HOCKEY BOOT
ROLLER SKATE
STICK (3–3¾' LONG)
BALL : CIRC. 9 IN.
WT. 5½ OZ.

RINK

GOAL
GOALIE
CREASE
GOALKEEPER'S PENALTY LINE
PENALTY AREA
DEFENSEMEN

BASE SPOT CIRCLE
BASE SPOT
PENALTY SPOT
RINK BARRIER (8" HIGH)
FORWARDS

CENTER CIRCLE
CENTER LINE

18 FT.

40½ FT.

SPEED SKATING TRACK

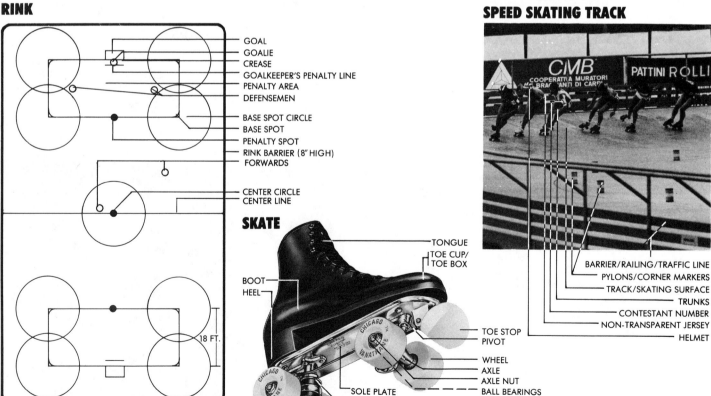

BARRIER/RAILING/TRAFFIC LINE
PYLONS/CORNER MARKERS
TRACK/SKATING SURFACE
TRUNKS
CONTESTANT NUMBER
NON-TRANSPARENT JERSEY
HELMET

SKATE

TONGUE
TOE CUP/
TOE BOX

BOOT
HEEL

TOE STOP
PIVOT

WHEEL
AXLE
AXLE NUT
BALL BEARINGS

SOLE PLATE

ACTION NUT/LOCK NUT
CUSHIONS
KING PIN/ACTION BOLT/TRUCK BOLT

TRUCK

International competition is comprised of sculling, in which one, two or four *scullers* propel *racing shells* called sculls by simultaneously pulling on two oars mounted on opposite sides of the boat, and rowing, in which two, four or eight *oarsmen* each use single oars.

A *regatta*, or *sprint*, is conducted in *heats* over a six-lane course laid out on a straight stretch of still water. Boats not placing high enough to qualify for the final heat are allowed to compete again in a second-chance heat called a *repechage*.

In *head of the river races*, competitors starting at intervals are timed over a course too narrow to accommodate all *crews*.

SCULLING HEAT

CATCH

DRIVE/PULL THROUGH

FINISH & RECOVERY

SCULLING TECHNIQUE

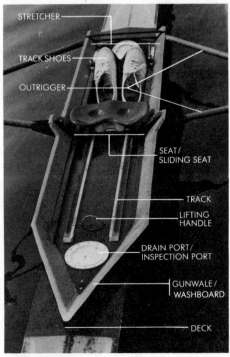

SCULL DETAIL

Rowing races are contested in coxless pairs and four-man boats, and coxed pairs, fours and eight-man boats. Many regattas have separate competition for heavyweight crews and *lightweights* (consisting of crews averaging no more than 150 pounds per person).

An eight-man shell may be up to 60 feet long. The sliding seat and the outrigger, which extends the *pivot point* of the oar outboard of the shell, allows the oarsman to use back and legs as well as arms in pulling the oar through a long, powerful arc, or *sweep*.

An oarsman is said to '*catch a crab*' if the feathered tip of his oar digs into the water during the recovery phase of a stroke.

The coxswain steers the shell.

SHELL

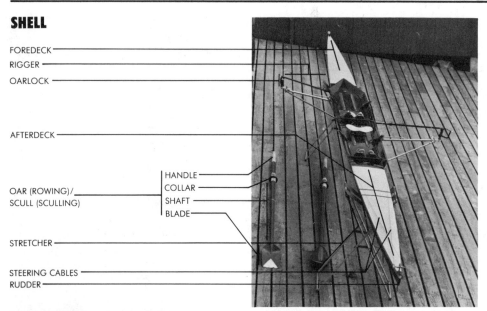

- FOREDECK
- RIGGER
- OARLOCK
- AFTERDECK
- OAR (ROWING)/SCULL (SCULLING)
  - HANDLE
  - COLLAR
  - SHAFT
  - BLADE
- STRETCHER
- STEERING CABLES
- RUDDER

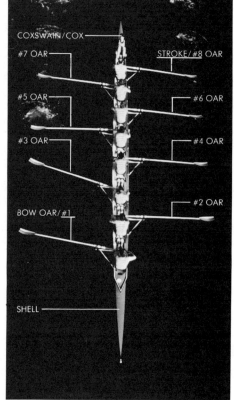

- COXSWAIN/COX
- #7 OAR
- STROKE/#8 OAR
- #5 OAR
- #6 OAR
- #3 OAR
- #4 OAR
- BOW OAR/#1
- #2 OAR
- SHELL

EIGHT-MAN CREW

SWEEP-ROWING TECHNIQUE

CATCH

DRIVE/PULL THROUGH

RELEASE AND FEATHER

RECOVERY

Amateur rugby, *rugby union*, is played by 15-man teams. Professional rugby, *rugby league*, is played by 13-man teams. The object of the game, generally played in two 40-minute *halves* with no time outs or substitutions, is to carry the ball into the opponent's 'in goal area' and touch it to the ground (called a *try*, worth 4 points), or *dropkick* or *placekick* the ball over the *crossbar* and between the *goal posts* (called a *goal*, or *dropped goal*, worth 3 points).

The ball may only be kicked or run forward, but may be passed laterally. When the ball carrier is *tackled*, he must release the ball. For common infractions, a scrum is formed and the ball put back into play.

SCRUM

JERSEY

13½–15½ OZ.
11″–11¼″ LONG ├─BALL
24″–25½″ CIR.

SHORTS

STOCKING/SOCK

BOOT

PITCH/FIELD

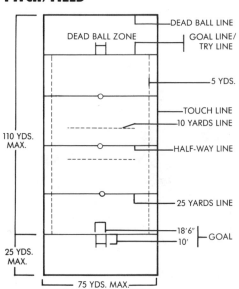

DEAD BALL LINE
DEAD BALL ZONE
GOAL LINE/
TRY LINE

5 YDS.

TOUCH LINE
10 YARDS LINE

110 YDS.
MAX.

HALF-WAY LINE

25 YARDS LINE

18'6" ┐
GOAL
10' ┘

25 YDS.
MAX.

75 YDS. MAX.

SCRUMMAGE FORMATION

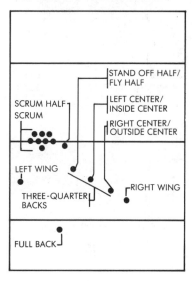

STAND OFF HALF/
FLY HALF

SCRUM HALF
SCRUM

LEFT CENTER/
INSIDE CENTER

RIGHT CENTER/
OUTSIDE CENTER

LEFT WING

RIGHT WING

THREE-QUARTER
BACKS

FULL BACK

SCRUM POSITIONS

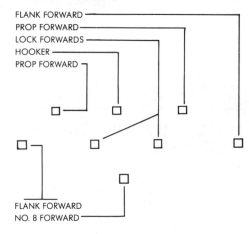

FLANK FORWARD
PROP FORWARD
LOCK FORWARDS
HOOKER
PROP FORWARD

FLANK FORWARD
NO. 8 FORWARD

Rifle events are divided into *small-bore* and *bigbore* rifles (the *bore* being measured in *calibers*, bore diameter in 100ths or 1000ths of an inch), and *air rifle*, powered by compressed air or CO_2 cartridge. Shooting positions include prone, bench rest, sitting, standing, and kneeling, in which a cylindrical *kneeling pad*, or *roll* may be used. In *running game target* shooting, 60 shots are fired at a simulated boar, moving on rails at slow speed for 30 shots and at high speed for the remaining 30. This is the only event in which *telescopic sights* are allowed.

The competitor with the highest score wins.

SHOOTING POSITIONS

BENCH REST

KNEELING

PRONE

SITTING

STANDING/OFF-HAND

RUNNING GAME TARGET SHOOTING/ RUNNING BOAR

Pistol shooting is comprised of *free pistol, rapid-fire pistol* and *smallbore sport pistol*. In each event the pistol may be held unsupported with only one hand and the competitor must stand.

In free pistol, competitors are allowed 2½ hours to take six *series* of 10 shots each at small targets with scoring rings valued from one to 10. A shot that hits one of the scoring ring boundaries scores the higher value.

In rapid-fire, or *silhouette* shooting, 60 shots are fired in groups of five, each at five different targets that pop up simultaneously when the competitor calls *"Ready."* Smallbore sport pistol is a combination of free-and rapid-fire, with 30 shots fired in each.

NATIONAL MATCH TARGET PISTOL

FRONT SIGHT — SLIDE — SLIDE STOP NOTCH — DISASSEMBLY NOTCH — EJECTION PORT — REAR SIGHT — FIRING PIN LOCK
BARREL
HAMMER
SLIDE LOCK SAFETY NOTCH
RECOIL SPRING PLUG
SLIDE STOP
TRIGGER
TRIGGER STOP
SLIDE LOCK SAFETY
GRIP SAFETY
MAGAZINE CATCH
STOCK

CARTRIDGE/BULLET

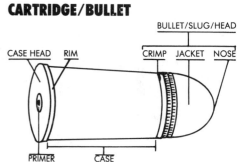

BULLET/SLUG/HEAD
CASE HEAD — RIM — CRIMP — JACKET — NOSE
PRIMER — CASE

TARGET

SCORING BOX
'BLACK'
BULLSEYE — POINT VALUE

PISTOL RANGE

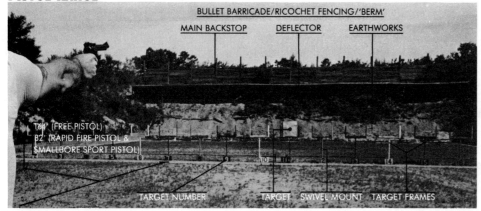

BULLET BARRICADE/RICOCHET FENCING/'BERM'
MAIN BACKSTOP — DEFLECTOR — EARTHWORKS
164' (FREE PISTOL)
82' (RAPID FIRE PISTOL & SMALLBORE SPORT PISTOL)
TARGET NUMBER — TARGET SWIVEL MOUNT — TARGET FRAMES

FIRING STATION

EAR MUFFS/SILENCERS — TARGET NUMBER
OVERHANG HEADER
TARGET TURNER — FIRING LINE

In trapshooting, also called *trench shooting*, a competitor shoots at five targets from each of five stations.

Targets are launched on command, whenever the gunner calls *'pull.'* The birds are thrown in varying directions by three traps located opposite each shooting station in the trap pit, or trench.

Competitors load two *cartridges* into their shotguns and may use both if the target is missed on the first shot. Three *misfires* are allowed each competitor in a round. If the target is launched before the shooter's call or not immediately thereafter, it is called *'no bird'* and a new target is allowed.

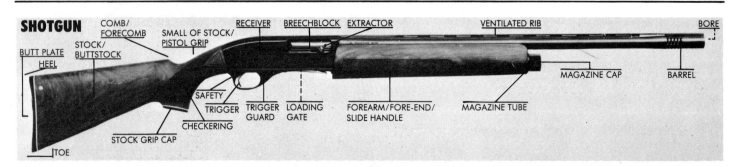

SHOTGUN — COMB/FORECOMB — SMALL OF STOCK/PISTOL GRIP — RECEIVER — BREECHBLOCK — EXTRACTOR — VENTILATED RIB — BORE — BUTT PLATE — HEEL — STOCK/BUTTSTOCK — SAFETY — TRIGGER — TRIGGER GUARD — LOADING GATE — FOREARM/FORE-END/SLIDE HANDLE — MAGAZINE TUBE — MAGAZINE CAP — BARREL — CHECKERING — STOCK GRIP CAP — TOE

SCORER & PULLER — TRAP HOUSE — POWER HOOK-UP — 49'3" — TRAP RELEASE/PULLING MECHANISM — FIRING STATION

TRAPSHOOTING RANGE

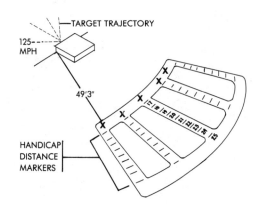

TARGET TRAJECTORY — 125 MPH — 49'3" — HANDICAP DISTANCE MARKERS

Shotguns are used in trap and skeet shooting events to down saucer-shaped targets called *clay pigeons*, *clays*, or *birds*. To score a hit, the *gunner* must break the target, which is flung into the air by a *trap* to simulate the take-off flight of a *game bird*.

In skeet shooting, targets thrown from the high house follow a horizontal trajectory, those from the low house are thrown on a rising path. In a *round*, which consists of 25 shots, a competitor fires from eight positions at 16 targets thrown alternately from the two houses, then fires from four of the positions at eight targets thrown by both houses simultaneously. The 25th shot is taken at any time in the round.

MARKSMAN

OVER & UNDER SHOTGUN

HIT PAIR/DEAD TARGETS

SKEET VEST/ TRAP VEST

EMPTY SHELLS/HULLS TO RELOAD

SHOTGUN SHELLS/CARTRIDGES/'AMMO'

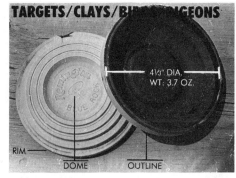

TARGETS/CLAYS/BIRDS/PIGEONS

4⅓" DIA.
WT: 3.7 OZ.

RIM

DOME

OUTLINE

SKEET RANGE

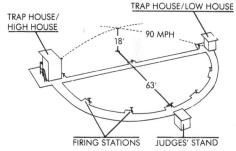

TRAP HOUSE/ LOW HOUSE

TRAP HOUSE/ HIGH HOUSE

90 MPH

18'

63'

FIRING STATIONS

JUDGES' STAND

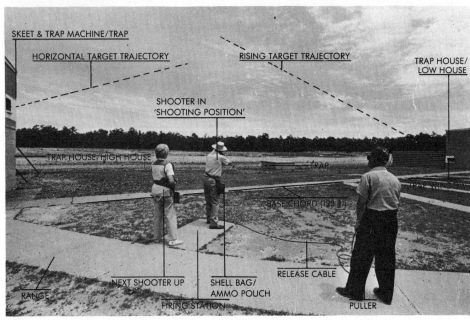

SKEET & TRAP MACHINE/TRAP

HORIZONTAL TARGET TRAJECTORY

RISING TARGET TRAJECTORY

TRAP HOUSE/ LOW HOUSE

SHOOTER IN 'SHOOTING POSITION'

TRAP HOUSE/HIGH HOUSE

TRAP

TRAP WINDOW

BASE CHORD (120'9")

NEXT SHOOTER UP

SHELL BAG/ AMMO POUCH

RELEASE CABLE

RANGE

FIRING STATION

PULLER

Shuffleboard players attempt to push wood or composition disks so that they stop within one of five *scoring areas* in the triangle. (Disks touching lines do not count.) Ten points are deducted for disks stopping in the 10-off area. Each player pushes four red or black disks, and may knock opponents' disks from one area to another, or out of play. Scores are tallied after each player has pushed his or her four disks. The area from which play begins is the *head* of the court, and disks are pushed toward the *foot*. In doubles, a member of each team plays from the baseline of either triangle.

Games may be 21, 50, 75 or 100 points, as desired. A *match* is the best two out of three games.

COURT

NEUTRAL ZONE

DEAD LINES

SCORING DIAGRAM/SCORING TRIANGLE

10-OFF SQUARE/MINUS SQUARE

SEPARATION TRIANGLE

BASE LINE

BACKSTOP

GUTTER

PLAYER

CUE

COURT NUMBER

DISK

6" DIAMETER
11½-15OZ.

RUNNER/GLIDE

FORK

SHAFT

CUE

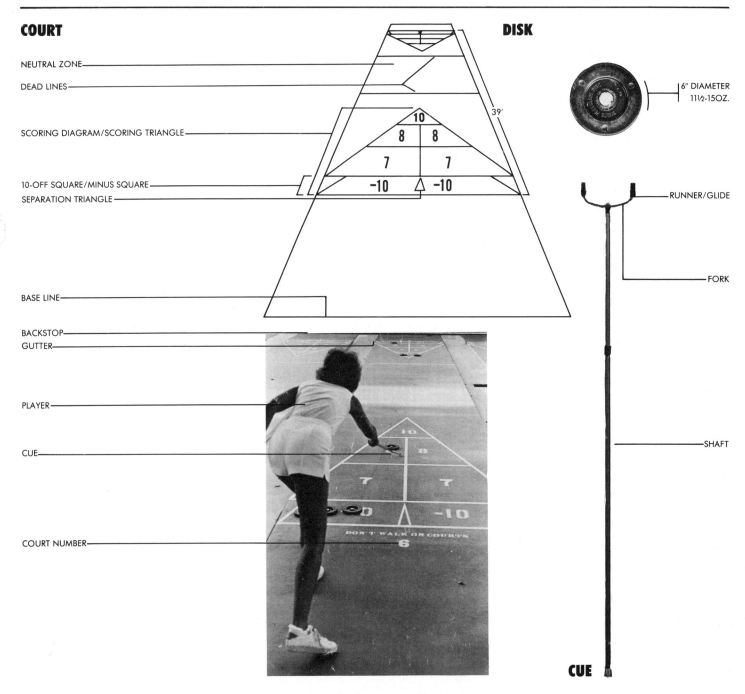

There is no standardized course or field on which competitive skateboarding is staged. Events are adapted to whatever space is available. *Vertical, full-pipe* or *half-pipe,* or *bowl riding* events take place in an area with banked or vertical sides, such as an empty swimming pool. Contestants are judged on the radicalness of their tricks, continuity and style. Judging in *flat freestyle* events is similar. In the *slalom,* skateboarders race against the clock over a designated course, weaving between cones. Speed on a skateboard is controlled by movement of the body forward and backwards.

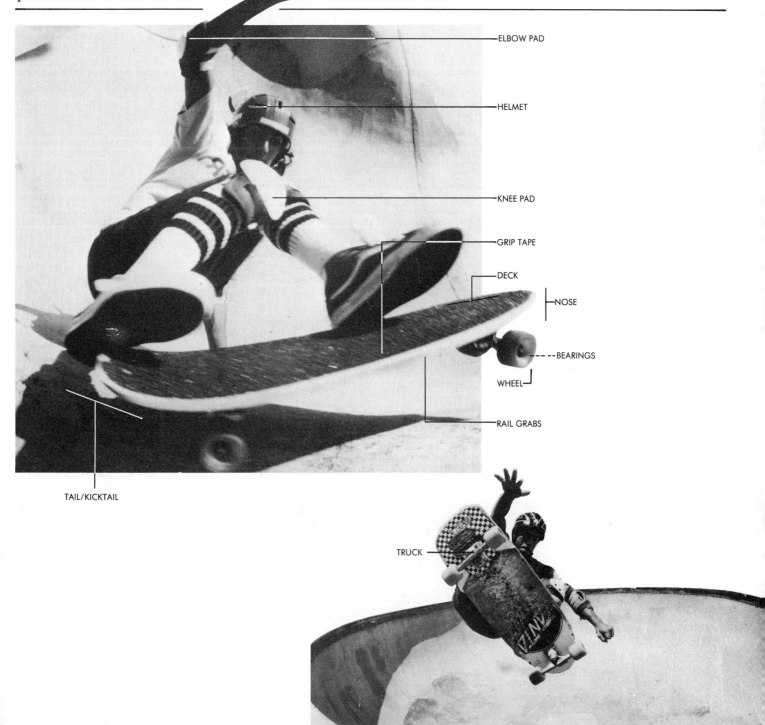

ELBOW PAD

HELMET

KNEE PAD

GRIP TAPE

DECK

NOSE

BEARINGS

WHEEL

RAIL GRABS

TAIL/KICKTAIL

TRUCK

Alpine skiing consists of *downhill*, *slalom* and *giant slalom*. The fastest event, in which skiers follow the *fall line* as closely as possible in the crouched, *egg position*, is the downhill. In slalom, competition is decided by the fastest aggregate time down two different, twisting *courses* containing *open* and *closed gates*. Giant slalom combines the speed of downhill with the turning skill of slalom. The event is similar to slalom except that the course is longer, with gates further apart.

The ideal *line* through gates is not necessarily the shortest distance between them. Racers approach gates from a *high position*, enabling them to make rounded turns that reduce the need for braking.

THE SKIER

GOGGLES
SLALOM SWEATER
ELASTIC BAND
GLOVE

SKI POLE
GRIP
SHAFT
BASKET/SNOW RING
TIP

STARTING GATE

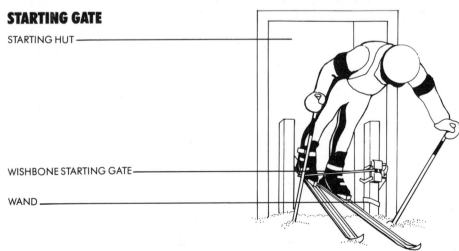

STARTING HUT

WISHBONE STARTING GATE

WAND

COURSE/PISTE

DOWNHILL **SLALOM** **GIANT SLALOM**

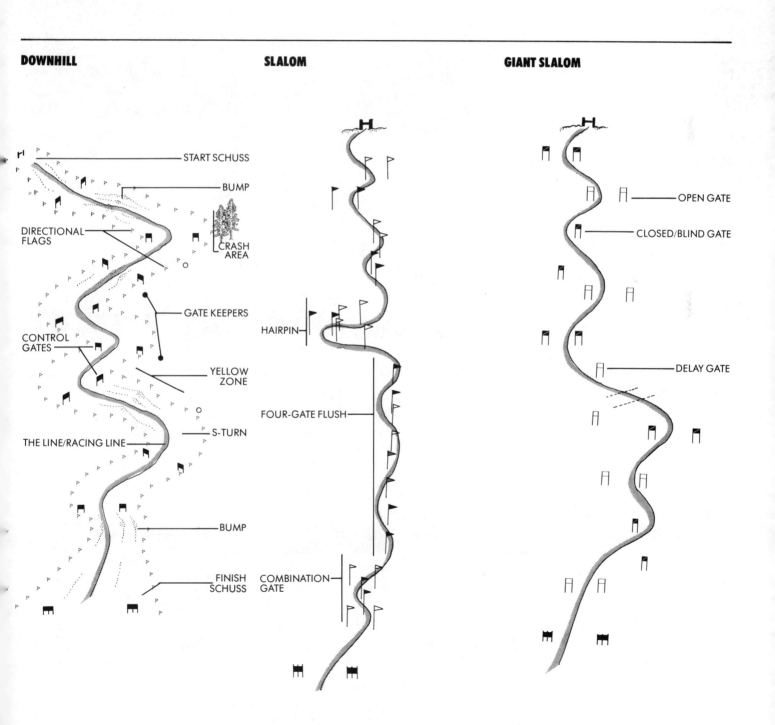

- START SCHUSS
- BUMP
- CRASH AREA
- DIRECTIONAL FLAGS
- GATE KEEPERS
- CONTROL GATES
- YELLOW ZONE
- S-TURN
- THE LINE/RACING LINE
- BUMP
- FINISH SCHUSS
- HAIRPIN
- FOUR-GATE FLUSH
- COMBINATION GATE
- OPEN GATE
- CLOSED/BLIND GATE
- DELAY GATE

EQUIPMENT

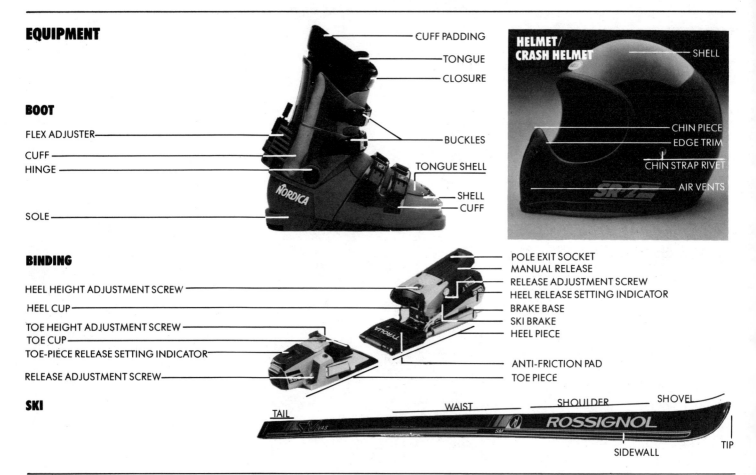

BOOT

CUFF PADDING

TONGUE

CLOSURE

FLEX ADJUSTER

CUFF

HINGE

BUCKLES

TONGUE SHELL

SHELL

CUFF

SOLE

HELMET/ CRASH HELMET

SHELL

CHIN PIECE

EDGE TRIM

CHIN STRAP RIVET

AIR VENTS

BINDING

HEEL HEIGHT ADJUSTMENT SCREW

HEEL CUP

TOE HEIGHT ADJUSTMENT SCREW

TOE CUP

TOE-PIECE RELEASE SETTING INDICATOR

RELEASE ADJUSTMENT SCREW

POLE EXIT SOCKET

MANUAL RELEASE

RELEASE ADJUSTMENT SCREW

HEEL RELEASE SETTING INDICATOR

BRAKE BASE

SKI BRAKE

HEEL PIECE

ANTI-FRICTION PAD

TOE PIECE

SKI

TAIL

WAIST

SHOULDER

SHOVEL

ROSSIGNOL

SIDEWALL

TIP

FINISH AREA

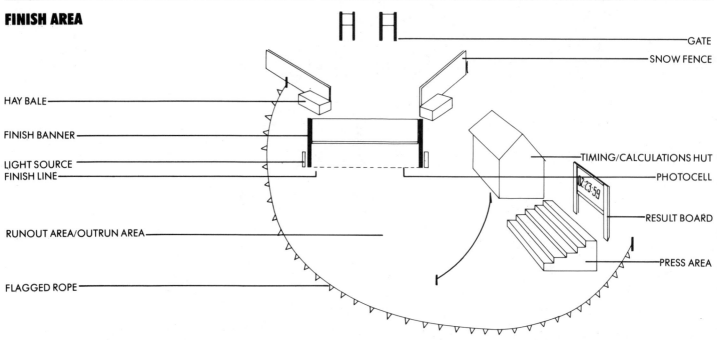

GATE

SNOW FENCE

HAY BALE

FINISH BANNER

LIGHT SOURCE

FINISH LINE

TIMING/CALCULATIONS HUT

PHOTOCELL

RESULT BOARD

RUNOUT AREA/OUTRUN AREA

PRESS AREA

FLAGGED ROPE

Nordic skiing encompasses cross country racing, ski jumping and *Nordic Combined*, which includes both events.

Ski jumpers are permitted two jumps in competition. They are scored on *distance* and *style*, or *form*. Five *style judges* may award as many as 20 points, but high and low scores are eliminated. These points are added to points for distance, which are awarded based on the number of meters jumped, for a total.

Jumping skis are longer, wider and heavier than alpine skis. They have no edges and may have built-in *air scoops*. Ski jumpers wear streamlined suits with no protective padding.

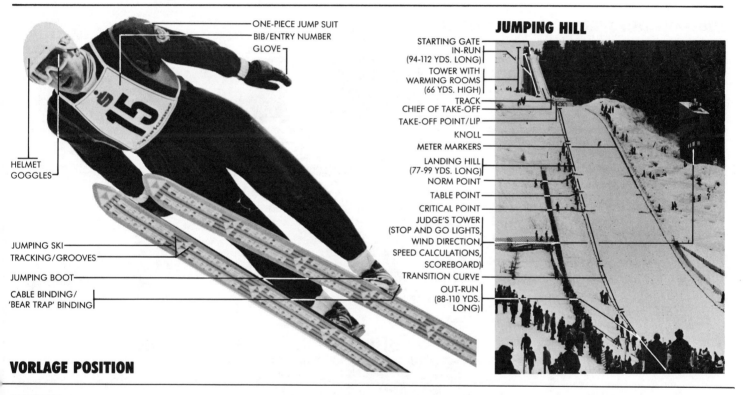

ONE-PIECE JUMP SUIT
BIB/ENTRY NUMBER
GLOVE

HELMET
GOGGLES

JUMPING SKI
TRACKING/GROOVES

JUMPING BOOT

CABLE BINDING/
'BEAR TRAP' BINDING

VORLAGE POSITION

JUMPING HILL

STARTING GATE
IN-RUN
(94-112 YDS. LONG)
TOWER WITH
WARMING ROOMS
(66 YDS. HIGH)
TRACK
CHIEF OF TAKE-OFF
TAKE-OFF POINT/LIP
KNOLL
METER MARKERS
LANDING HILL
(77-99 YDS. LONG)
NORM POINT
TABLE POINT
CRITICAL POINT
JUDGE'S TOWER
(STOP AND GO LIGHTS,
WIND DIRECTION,
SPEED CALCULATIONS,
SCOREBOARD)
TRANSITION CURVE
OUT-RUN
(88-110 YDS.
LONG)

JUMPER

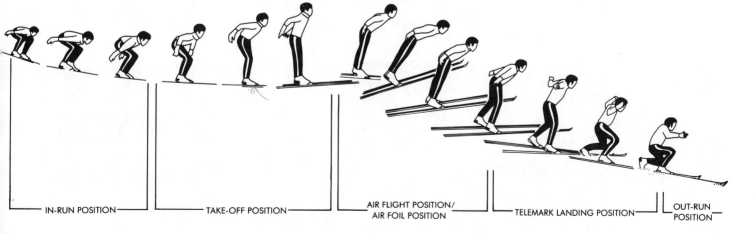

IN-RUN POSITION — TAKE-OFF POSITION — AIR FLIGHT POSITION/AIR FOIL POSITION — TELEMARK LANDING POSITION — OUT-RUN POSITION

Cross country racers start 30 seconds apart and race against the clock on a *trail* composed of uphill, flat and downhill sections. A second track alongside the main trail is used for passing, but skiers must give way upon request. There are individual and relay races for men and women, with distances ranging from about 3 miles to 9½ miles.

Biathlon contestants pause several times during their cross country ski run to shoot at targets. They shoot from both a prone and a standing position. Penalty minutes are added to a contestant's final time for each miss. In some events, laps must be skied on a penalty course for each miss. The contestant with the fastest adjusted time wins.

CROSS COUNTRY SKIER

HEADBAND
CONTESTANT BIB & NUMBER
MITTEN
SKI POLE
BASKET/SNOW RING
KNEE SOCK
CROSS COUNTRY SKI
KNICKERS
RACING BOOT
TOE CLAMP BINDING
TRACK/TRAIL

BIATHLON TARGETS

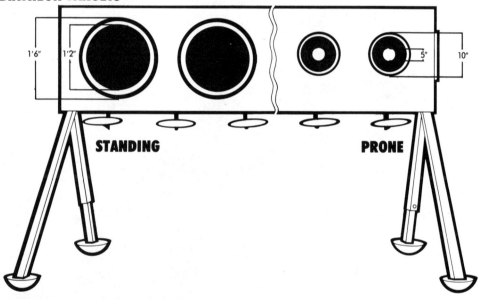

1'6" 1'2" 5" 10"

STANDING PRONE

TOE CLAMP BINDING

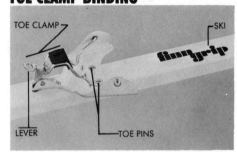

TOE CLAMP
SKI
LEVER
TOE PINS

RACING BOOT

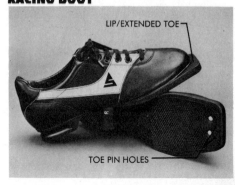

LIP/EXTENDED TOE
TOE PIN HOLES

STANDING POSITION

CHEEK PIECE
EYESHADE
.22 RIFLE
REAR SIGHT
FRONT SIGHT
PROTECTIVE CAP
HARNESS
SLING
MAGAZINE POUCH BELT
FIRING POINT NUMBER
CROSS COUNTRY SKI

PRONE POSITION

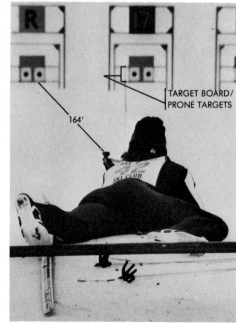

TARGET BOARD/ PRONE TARGETS
164'

Soccer is played by two 11-man teams on a field of grass or hard clay. The object is to drive the ball past the opposing goalkeeper into the goal for a score, worth one point. The team with the most *goals* at the end of two 45-minute periods of play, or halves, wins. In the event of a tie, or *draw*, regulation play is extended by a 15-minute, first goal wins, *sudden death* overtime, or by a series of *penalty kicks*, called a *shootout*.

The only *footballer* allowed to use his hands while the ball is in play is the goalkeeper. All others must use their feet, thighs, chests or heads to control, pass and to shoot the ball. Only two substitutions are allowed in a game, or *match*, and no time-outs.

At the start of play, each team must stay in its own half of the field, with defending players remaining at least 10 yards away from the ball until it has been kicked forward at least 27 inches by the opposition. When one team drives the ball out of bounds across a sideline, the other team puts it back in play with a *throw in*. If the attacking team drives it over the other's goal line, the defending team puts it back in play with a *goal kick*, from the goal area. If it was last touched by the defending team, a *corner kick* is awarded to the attackers.

Since no rules govern player positions, their makeup depends on game tactics and strategy.

FIELD/PITCH

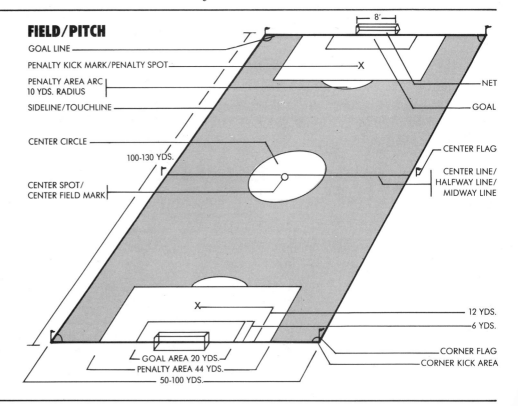

GOAL LINE
PENALTY KICK MARK/PENALTY SPOT
PENALTY AREA ARC 10 YDS. RADIUS
SIDELINE/TOUCHLINE
CENTER CIRCLE
CENTER SPOT/ CENTER FIELD MARK
100-130 YDS.
NET
GOAL
CENTER FLAG
CENTER LINE/ HALFWAY LINE/ MIDWAY LINE
12 YDS.
6 YDS.
CORNER FLAG
CORNER KICK AREA
GOAL AREA 20 YDS.
PENALTY AREA 44 YDS.
50-100 YDS.
8'

BASIC FORMATIONS

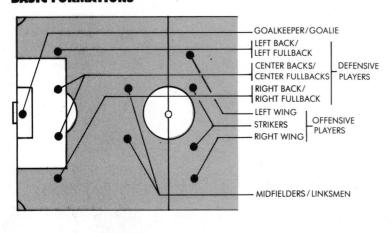

GOALKEEPER/GOALIE
LEFT BACK/ LEFT FULLBACK
CENTER BACKS/ CENTER FULLBACKS — DEFENSIVE PLAYERS
RIGHT BACK/ RIGHT FULLBACK
LEFT WING
STRIKERS — OFFENSIVE PLAYERS
RIGHT WING
MIDFIELDERS / LINKSMEN

4-2-4

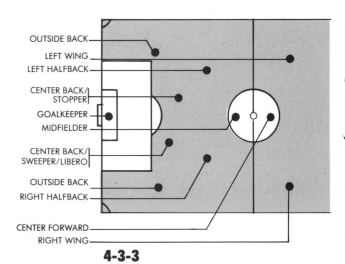

OUTSIDE BACK
LEFT WING
LEFT HALFBACK
CENTER BACK/ STOPPER
GOALKEEPER
MIDFIELDER
CENTER BACK/ SWEEPER/LIBERO
OUTSIDE BACK
RIGHT HALFBACK
CENTER FORWARD
RIGHT WING

4-3-3

Players are not permitted to hold, push or trip an opponent, but they may bump him with a shoulder charge and use their feet in an effort to *tackle*, or take the ball away from an opponent. For rules violations (such as touching the ball with a hand) or for fouls, the offending team is penalized by the awarding of a *direct* or *indirect free kick* to the opposition. In an indirect kick the attacker may not score a goal without a second player touching it first. The player taking the direct free kick may score directly. If a defending player commits a foul in his own penalty area, the opposition is awarded a penalty kick, taken from the penalty spot with only the goalkeeper allowed to defend.

PLAYING THE BALL

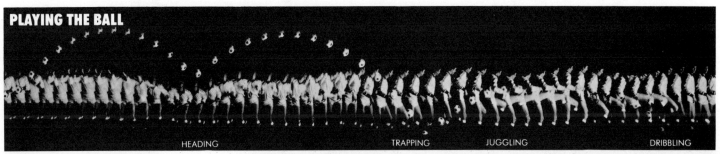

HEADING   TRAPPING   JUGGLING   DRIBBLING

FOULS

DANGEROUS PLAY

TRIPPING

CHARGING

HOLDING

OFFICIALS' SIGNALS

HANDBALL

PUSHING

SHOOTOUT

OFFSIDE

INDIRECT FREE KICK

UNFAIR TACKLE FROM BEHIND

FOUL THROW

Softball is popular as both a recreational and highly organized sport for men and women. The rules and terminology are similar to those of baseball, but pitchers must throw underhand, the dimensions of the field and the size of the ball differ, and games are only seven innings long.

Two distinct versions of softball are played. In *slow pitch*, the pitcher throws the ball in a three- to 10-foot arc at moderate speed. A 10th player, called a *short fielder*, or *rover*, usually plays between the infielders and outfielders. Bunting and base stealing are prohibited.

In *fast pitch*, the pitcher may throw as hard and as fast as he or she is able, so long as the ball is released from below hip level.

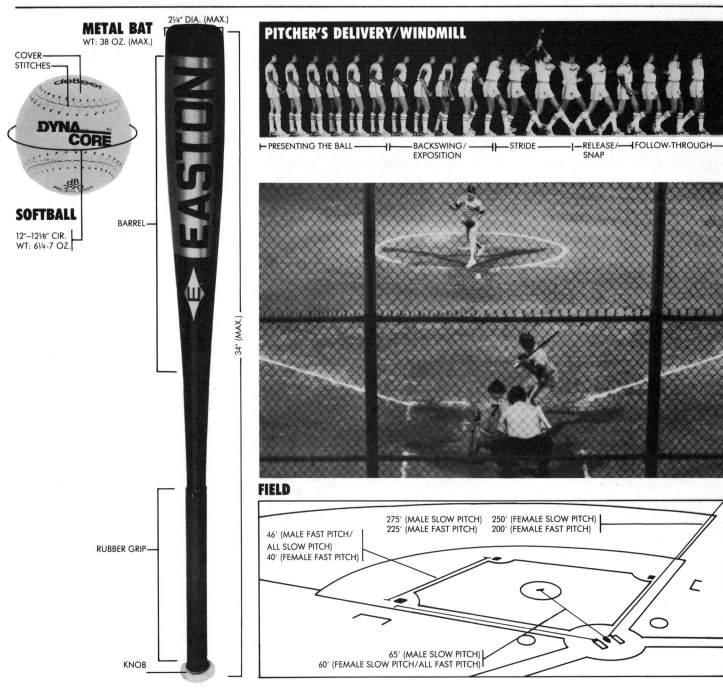

METAL BAT
2¼" DIA. (MAX.)
WT: 38 OZ. (MAX.)

COVER STITCHES

DYNA CORE

SOFTBALL
12"–12⅛" CIR.
WT: 6¼-7 OZ.

BARREL

34" (MAX.)

RUBBER GRIP

KNOB

EASTON

PITCHER'S DELIVERY/WINDMILL

├ PRESENTING THE BALL ──┤├─ BACKSWING/ ─┤├─ STRIDE ──┤├─ RELEASE/ ─┤├ FOLLOW-THROUGH ─┤
EXPOSITION   SNAP

FIELD

275' (MALE SLOW PITCH)   250' (FEMALE SLOW PITCH)
225' (MALE FAST PITCH)   200' (FEMALE FAST PITCH)

46' (MALE FAST PITCH/
ALL SLOW PITCH)
40' (FEMALE FAST PITCH)

65' (MALE SLOW PITCH)
60' (FEMALE SLOW PITCH/ALL FAST PITCH)

Olympic or metric style skating consists of two skaters competing at the same time on a 400-meter *track*, *rink*, or *oval*. A *staggered start* ensures that both skaters race the same distance. After the first *lap*, skaters cross over each time they make a full circle. Since skaters race against the clock, winning does not necessarily mean beating the other person.

In non-Olympic "pack" style meets, skaters race in crowded *heats*. *Short track speed skating* consists of *individual*, *team relay* and two-skater *pursuit races*.

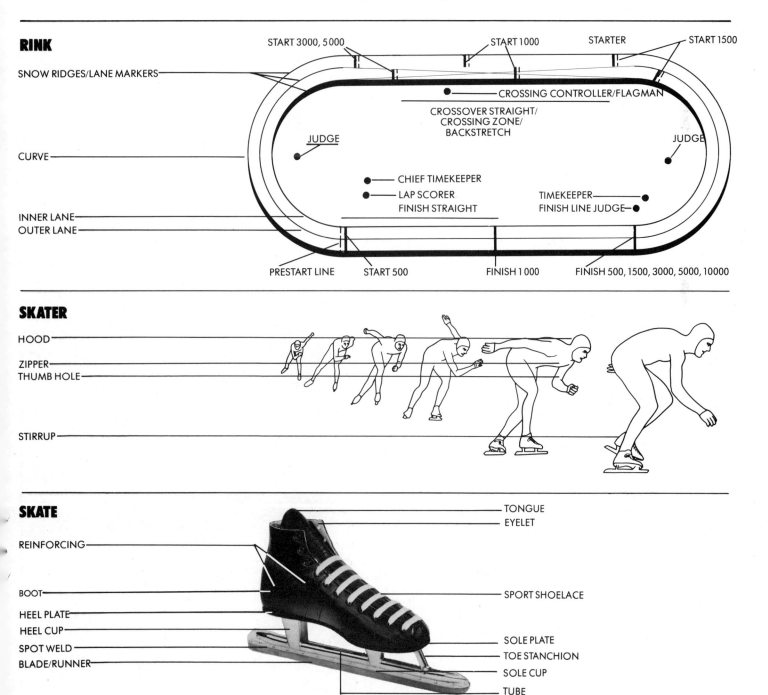

RINK

SNOW RIDGES/LANE MARKERS

START 3000, 5000
START 1000
STARTER
START 1500

CROSSING CONTROLLER/FLAGMAN

CROSSOVER STRAIGHT/
CROSSING ZONE/
BACKSTRETCH

CURVE

JUDGE

JUDGE

CHIEF TIMEKEEPER
LAP SCORER
FINISH STRAIGHT

TIMEKEEPER
FINISH LINE JUDGE

INNER LANE
OUTER LANE

PRESTART LINE   START 500   FINISH 1000   FINISH 500, 1500, 3000, 5000, 10000

SKATER

HOOD

ZIPPER
THUMB HOLE

STIRRUP

SKATE

REINFORCING

TONGUE
EYELET

BOOT

HEEL PLATE
HEEL CUP
SPOT WELD
BLADE/RUNNER

SPORT SHOELACE

SOLE PLATE
TOE STANCHION
SOLE CUP
TUBE

In squash, a singles or doubles game played in a four-walled court, the object is to hit the ball to the front wall in such a way that an opponent may not return it to the wall before it bounces twice.

Under international rules, games are played to 9 points and only the serving side may score. If the server fails to keep the ball in play, the serve passes to the opponent.

In the American version, played to 15 points, both server and receiver may score points.

Squash tennis, similar to squash racquets, is played with a larger, highly pressurized ball and a larger, heavier racquet, making it a faster game.

COURT

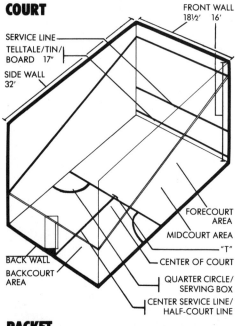

FRONT WALL
18½'   16'

SERVICE LINE
TELLTALE/TIN/
BOARD 17"

SIDE WALL
32'

BACK WALL
BACKCOURT
AREA

FORECOURT
AREA

MIDCOURT AREA

"T"

CENTER OF COURT

QUARTER CIRCLE/
SERVING BOX

CENTER SERVICE LINE/
HALF-COURT LINE

RACKET

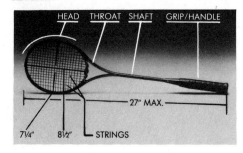

HEAD   THROAT SHAFT   GRIP/HANDLE

27" MAX.

7¼"   8½"   STRINGS

BALL

1.6" DIA.
WT. .68–.77 OZ.

CORNER

FRONT WALL

TELLTALE

Competitive surfing rules vary from beach to beach. Generally, however, surfers are required to ride a certain number of waves in specified time periods, called *heats*. The surfer who executes the most radical ma-neuvers in the most critical sections of the biggest waves for the longest distance is deemed the winner.

The area where surfers straddle their boards waiting for waves to begin curling is called *'the lineup.'*

Riding a board while completely enclosed by the pipeline is *'tubing.'* The object is to ride the tube before it *'closes out,'* or collapses. A *'regular foot'* stands with his left foot forward. *'Goofy foots'* take a reverse stance.

ANATOMY OF A WAVE

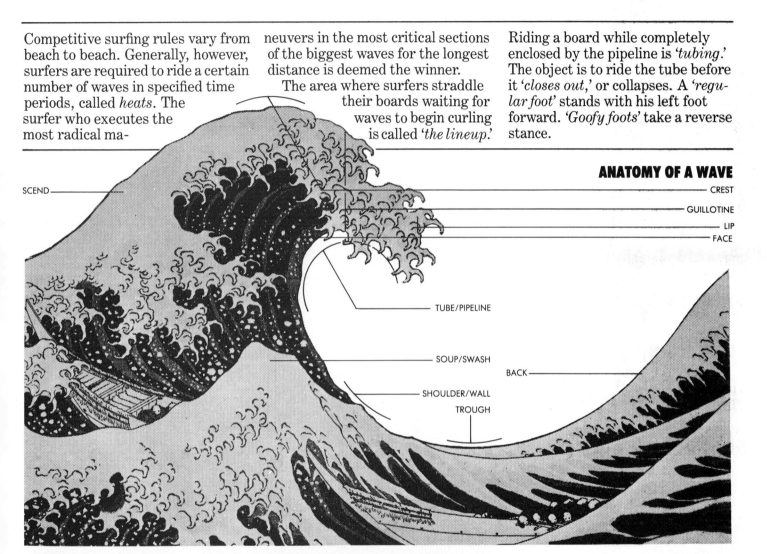

SCEND

CREST

GUILLOTINE

LIP

FACE

TUBE/PIPELINE

SOUP/SWASH

BACK

SHOULDER/WALL

TROUGH

SURFER

SURF LEASH/SHOCK CORD — WETSUIT

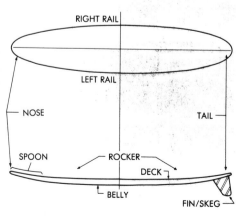

RIGHT RAIL

LEFT RAIL

NOSE

TAIL

SPOON

ROCKER

DECK

BELLY

FIN/SKEG

SURFBOARD/BOARD

Synchronized competition, or *synchro*, consists of two parts: *compulsory figures*, done without music and judged on skill and technique, and *routines*, performed to music and judged on presentation and showmanship. Seven judges award 0-10 points for each performance by solo, duet and eight-swimmer teams.

In compulsories, which count for about 50% of the total score, each contestant performs six figures chosen from a possible 46 by officials. In routines, a series of basic movements choreographed into a graceful balletic presentation, swimmers may spend half their time upside down in the water. Underwater speakers help keep them in synch with the music.

BASIC POSITIONS

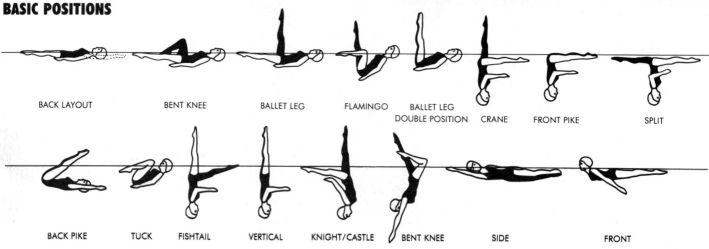

BACK LAYOUT   BENT KNEE   BALLET LEG   FLAMINGO   BALLET LEG DOUBLE POSITION   CRANE   FRONT PIKE   SPLIT

BACK PIKE   TUCK   FISHTAIL   VERTICAL   KNIGHT/CASTLE   BENT KNEE   SIDE   FRONT

Eight-lane Olympic pools, considered 'fast pools,' are designed to minimize two types of waves that check swimmers' speed. *Surface tension waves* are controlled by lane marker *discs* that spin and absorb kinetic energy and by overflow gutters that keep water from 'sloshing' back into competitors' lanes. *Gravity waves*, generated by the force of swimmers going through the water, bounce off the bottom and are reflected upwards. The depth of the pool allows the swimmer to get past the point where the gravity wave resurfaces.

The recall rope is for *false starts*. The individual responsible for the third false start is disqualified, or *DQ'd*.

POOL

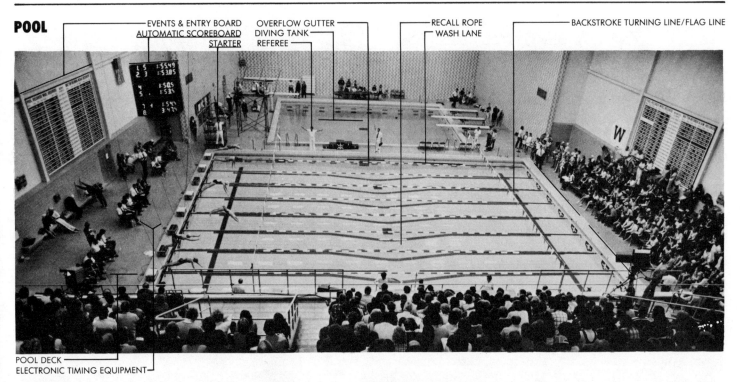

EVENTS & ENTRY BOARD
AUTOMATIC SCOREBOARD
STARTER
OVERFLOW GUTTER
DIVING TANK
REFEREE
RECALL ROPE
WASH LANE
BACKSTROKE TURNING LINE/FLAG LINE
POOL DECK
ELECTRONIC TIMING EQUIPMENT

TURN

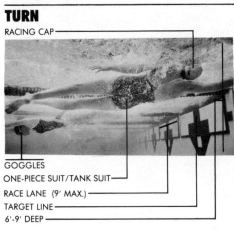

RACING CAP
GOGGLES
ONE-PIECE SUIT/TANK SUIT
RACE LANE (9' MAX.)
TARGET LINE
6'-9' DEEP

START

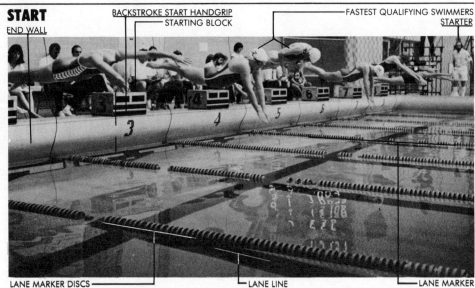

BACKSTROKE START HANDGRIP
STARTING BLOCK
FASTEST QUALIFYING SWIMMERS
STARTER
END WALL
LANE MARKER DISCS
LANE LINE
LANE MARKER

Individuals compete by sex in the following events: *freestyle, butterfly, backstroke, breaststroke* and *individual medley*, in which competitors swim equal distances in each of four strokes. Team events include *medley relay* and *freestyle*

medley.

In freestyle races, swimmers may choose any style or stroke. The crawl is preferred since it is fastest. At turns and at the finish the swimmer may touch the wall with any part of the body.

In butterfly, the second fastest stroke, arm and leg movements must be simultaneous, and shoulders must be parallel to the surface of the water at all times. At turns and finishes the swimmer must touch the wall with both hands

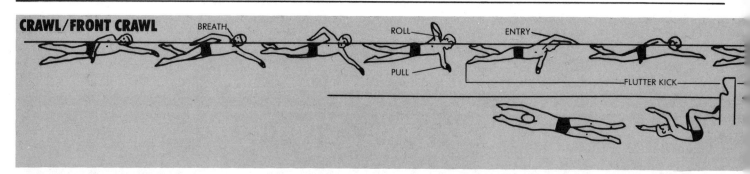

CRAWL/FRONT CRAWL — BREATH — ROLL — ENTRY — PULL — FLUTTER KICK

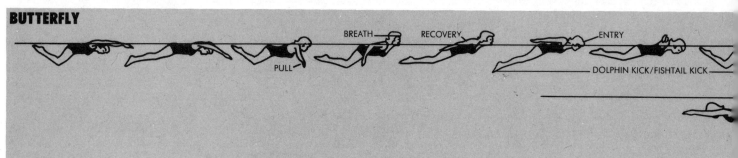

BUTTERFLY — BREATH — RECOVERY — ENTRY — PULL — DOLPHIN KICK/FISHTAIL KICK

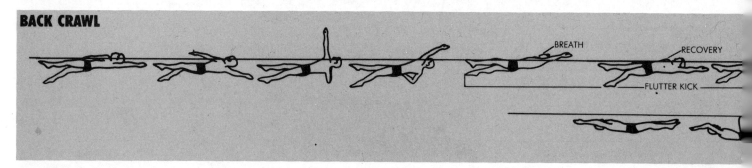

BACK CRAWL — BREATH — RECOVERY — FLUTTER KICK

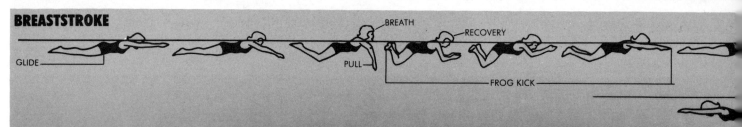

BREASTSTROKE — BREATH — RECOVERY — GLIDE — PULL — FROG KICK

at the same time and at the same level.

The third fastest event is the backstroke which is started in the water, with hands on the starting platform's grips and feet placed under the water against the end wall.

Although no particular style is required for the backstroke, except that it be performed on the back, most swimmers prefer the back crawl for its speed.

In breaststroke the body must be kept parallel to the surface of the

water, and arms and legs must be pushed and pulled simultaneously and symmetrically. Like butterfly, touches at turns and at the finish must be made at the same time and at the same level.

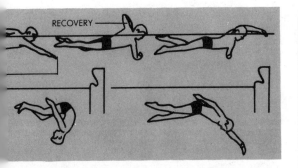

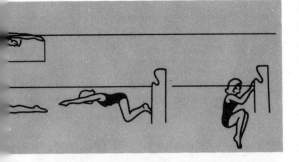

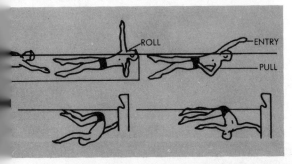

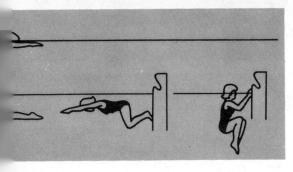

CRAWL/FRONT CRAWL

BACK CRAWL

BUTTERFLY

BREASTSTROKE

Table tennis is played by individuals or two-player teams. The object is to hit a hollow celluoid or plastic ball over a net so that it cannot be returned after one bounce by the receiver.

A player or team serves five times, then the opposition serves five times, and so on. A game is 21 points, unless tied 20-20, then the first player or team to gain a 2-point advantage wins.

Players also lose points for *volleying*, or striking the ball before it hits the table on their side, for touching the table with their free hand during a *rally* (the period the ball is in play), or for touching the ball before it goes out of bounds.

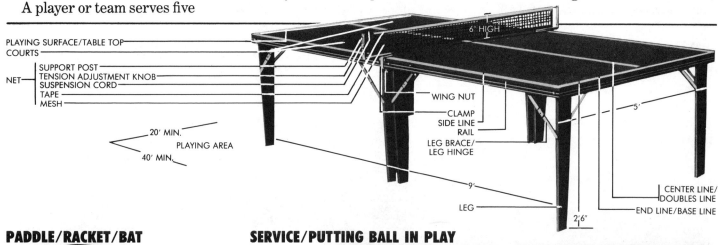

PLAYING SURFACE/TABLE TOP
COURTS
NET
SUPPORT POST
TENSION ADJUSTMENT KNOB
SUSPENSION CORD
TAPE
MESH
6" HIGH
WING NUT
CLAMP
SIDE LINE
RAIL
LEG BRACE/LEG HINGE
20' MIN.
PLAYING AREA
40' MIN.
5'
9'
LEG
2'6"
CENTER LINE/DOUBLES LINE
END LINE/BASE LINE

PADDLE/RACKET/BAT

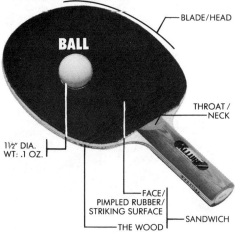

BLADE/HEAD
BALL
THROAT/NECK
1½" DIA. WT: .1 OZ.
FACE/PIMPLED RUBBER/STRIKING SURFACE
SANDWICH
THE WOOD

GRIPS

ORTHODOX/SHAKEHANDS

PENHOLDER/ORIENTAL

SERVICE/PUTTING BALL IN PLAY

SERVER
RACKET HAND
FOREHAND SERVE
FREE HAND
RECEIVER
GET-READY POSITION/NEUTRAL POSITION

After 15 minutes of play, the *Expedite System* is used. Under these rules each player or team serves once, then the opposition serves, and so on. If the receiver returns serve and 12 succeeding shots successfully, he or she wins the point.

A *let*, a rally in which no point is won, occurs when the serve touches the net but is otherwise playable, or if the serve is delivered when the receiver is not ready, or if an official interrupts play, or if an accident not caused by either player occurs and play is stopped.

The racket may be of any size, weight or shape.

DEFENDER/CHOPPER/RETRIEVER

PLAYING SHIRT

PLAYING SHORTS

TABLE TENNIS SHOES/PLAYING SHOES

RETURN

FOREHAND FOLLOW-THROUGH

SMASH/KILL SHOT/PUTAWAY

DEFENSIVE POSITION

TABLE NUMBER

COURT

Tennis, also called *lawn tennis*, is played by two individuals (*singles*) or pairs (*doubles*) on a grass, clay, asphalt or composition court divided by a low net. Players using rackets hit a ball over the net with the object of making a shot that lands within the boundaries of an opponent's court but that cannot be returned before it bounces twice.

Play is started by one player, standing behind the baseline, serving diagonally across the court into his opponent's service court. A serve that hits the net tape but falls into the appropriate court is a *let*, and is taken again. A serve into the net or out of the service court is a *fault*, and a second serve is taken. Although players serve alternate games, both serving and receiving

CENTER COURT/CENTRE COURT

SCOREBOARD
BALL BOY
LET JUDGE/NET JUDGE
UMPIRE/CHAIR UMPIRE

LINE JUDGE/
LINE UMPIRE

FAULT JUDGE
FAULT UMPIRE

FAULT JUDGE/
FAULT UMPIRE

LINE JUDGES/
LINE UMPIRES

sides can score points.

Zero, or no points is called *love*. The first point is 15, although it is also called 5. The second is 30, the third is 40, the fourth is *game*. However, when both sides score 40, it is called *deuce*. With the score tied at deuce a game may go on indefinitely, since a player or team must take a two-point lead to win.

The first player to win six games wins a *set*, unless each has won five. A two-game margin is then required to win the set. A *match* is best of three sets, except in men's championships which is best of five sets.

COURT

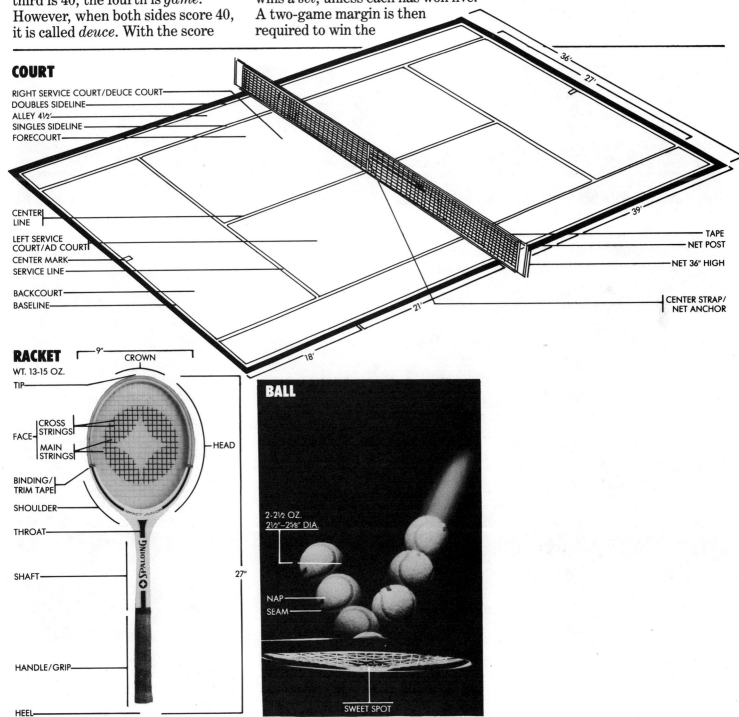

RIGHT SERVICE COURT/DEUCE COURT
DOUBLES SIDELINE
ALLEY 4½'
SINGLES SIDELINE
FORECOURT

CENTER LINE
LEFT SERVICE COURT/AD COURT
CENTER MARK
SERVICE LINE
BACKCOURT
BASELINE

36'
27'
39'
21'
18'

TAPE
NET POST
NET 36" HIGH
CENTER STRAP/ NET ANCHOR

RACKET

9"   CROWN
WT. 13-15 OZ.
TIP

CROSS STRINGS
FACE
MAIN STRINGS
HEAD

BINDING/ TRIM TAPE
SHOULDER
THROAT
SHAFT
27"
HANDLE/GRIP
HEEL

SPALDING

BALL

2-2½ OZ.
2½"–2⅝" DIA.

NAP
SEAM

SWEET SPOT

A server is generally considered to have an advantage in a game because he controls the beginning of each point and because the ball in a serve is not hit on the fly or on the run. If a player serves the ball so well that his opponent cannot even touch it, called an *ace*, he wins the point automatically. If, on the other hand, he fails to serve well and loses the game, he is said to have had his serve *broken*.

In serving, *ball placement* (deep in an opponent's service court corners) is most important. A serve can, in addition, be made more difficult to *return* if it is *angled* or *spun*, or hit flat with a great deal of speed, called a *cannonball*.

READY POSITION BACKSWING TOSS CONTACT FOLLOW-THROUGH

TYPES OF SERVE

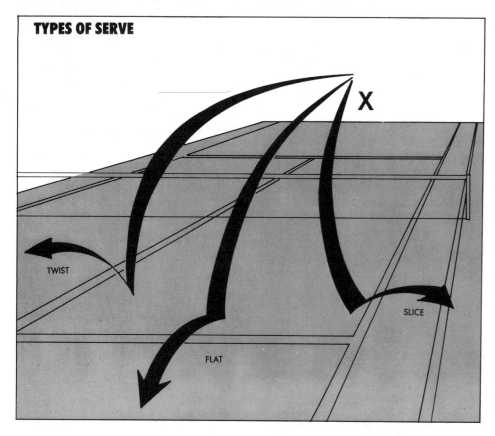

X

TWIST

SLICE

FLAT

All *shots* may be offensive or defensive in nature, depending on *court position*, skill and tactics.

Shots in which the ball is hit after bouncing are called *ground strokes* and consist of forehand and backhand. A *half-volley* is made immediately after the ball strikes the playing surface. A volley is hit near the net in mid-air with little or no *backswing*. An *overhead*, or *overhead smash*, is a stroke that resembles a serve but which may be hit anywhere within the court.

A *chop* is hit with a short, downward stroke which imparts backspin to reduce the ball's bounce and makes it *die*. A *chip* is an angled chop, aimed at an opponent's feet.

FOREHAND

VOLLEY

TWO-FISTED
BACKHAND

STROKES

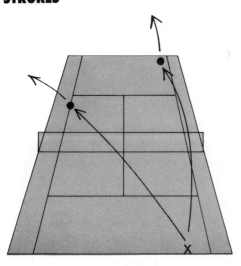

CROSS-COURT SHOT   DOWN-THE-LINE SHOT

PASSING SHOTS

X —— BASELINE POSITION

X —— NO-MAN'S LAND

X —— NET POSITION

X —— KNOCKOUT ZONE/
VOLLEY & OVERHEAD ZONE

X —— ATTACK ZONE/HALF-VOLLEY &
MID-COURT OVERHEAD ZONE

X —— UNBALANCING ZONE/
PRE-ATTACK ZONE

COURT ZONES

Tactics in tennis include mixing speed and spin in various shots, which makes the ball more difficult to return and puts an opponent on the defensive. In a flat shot, or *drive*, for example, the ball takes a level bounce. A ball hit with topspin travels faster and bounces higher after making contact with the court, whereas a backspin shot is intended to reduce the ball's momentum when it bounces.

There are two kinds of lob. A *defensive lob*, hit very high, gives a player time to get back into position. An *offensive lob* is hit over an opponent's head, out of reach.

A *putaway*, *kill*, or *winner*, is any hard hit shot that cannot be returned.

THE BOUNCE

LOBS

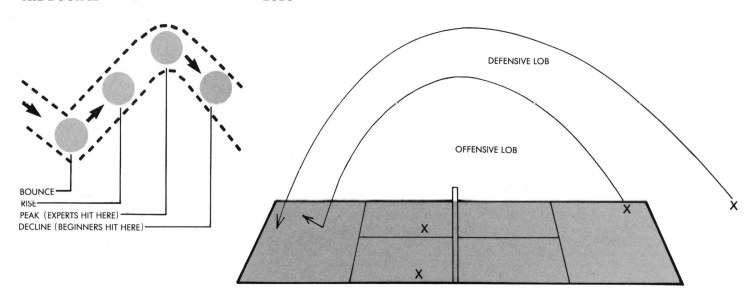

BOUNCE
RISE
PEAK (EXPERTS HIT HERE)
DECLINE (BEGINNERS HIT HERE)

DEFENSIVE LOB

OFFENSIVE LOB

BALL SPIN

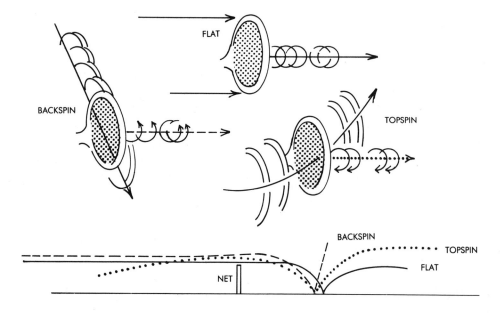

FLAT

BACKSPIN

TOPSPIN

BACKSPIN

TOPSPIN

FLAT

NET

Track and field is comprised of running, jumping and throwing events for men and women. *Track meets* are held both indoors and outdoors. In most events competitors wear lightweight shorts, T-shirts or *singlets*, and shoes designed especially for specific contests.

Both men and women compete in sprints and distance races, hurdle races and relays (at different distances), the shot put, discus, high jump and long jump.

Generally, only men compete in the steeplechase, race walking, hammer throw, pole vault and triple jump, although on occasion these events are held for women.

Track events take place on an oval track. Field events take place inside the track.

SCOREBOARD

TURN

FINISH LINE FOR ALL RACES

STRAIGHTAWAY

LANES

QUARTER-MILE (CIR.) TRACK

STAGGERED STARTING AREA

FIELD EVENTS AREA

STEEPLECHASE WATER JUMP

33½'

RELAY EXCHANGE ZONE

CHUTE/SPRINTS STARTING LINE

TUNNEL (MARATHON EXIT & ENTRY)

Sprints are run indoors and outdoors on oval tracks at distances of 100-, 200- and 400-meters. In races that make use of turns on the track, a *staggered start* is used to insure that all runners cover the same distance.

The first *sprinter* to break the vertical plane of the finish line with his or her torso wins.

Sprinters must stay in their lanes throughout the race. They cannot leave the track or obstruct other runners. Violators are disqualified.

Two *false starts*, or leaving the blocks before the starter fires his gun, also disqualify a competitor.

If there are numerous *entries*, qualifying races, or *heats*, are held to limit the final *field*.

STARTING BLOCKS

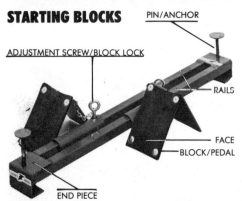

PIN/ANCHOR

ADJUSTMENT SCREW/BLOCK LOCK

RAILS

FACE

BLOCK/PEDAL

END PIECE

FINISH LINE

TAPE/FINISH TAPE

4'

2"

INSIDE LANE/POLE POSITION

STARTING TECHNIQUE

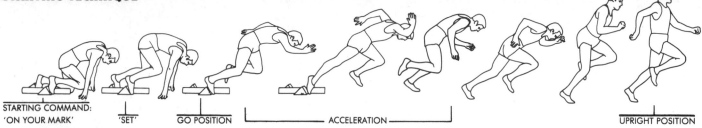

STARTING COMMAND: 'ON YOUR MARK'   'SET'   GO POSITION   —— ACCELERATION ——   UPRIGHT POSITION

In relay races, each of the four runners on a team covers the same distance consecutively. As each runner finishes, he or she passes a baton to the next runner.

Men and women's Olympic relays are run at 4x100- and 4x400-meters, but other meets include relays at most middle and long distances. *Medley races*, in which each runner covers a different distance, are also run on occasion.

The baton must be exchanged in the 22-yard-long passing zone. If dropped in the zone, either runner may retrieve it. If dropped outside the zone, the racer who dropped it must pick it up.

The first anchor man to cross the plane of the finish line wins.

BLIND PASS

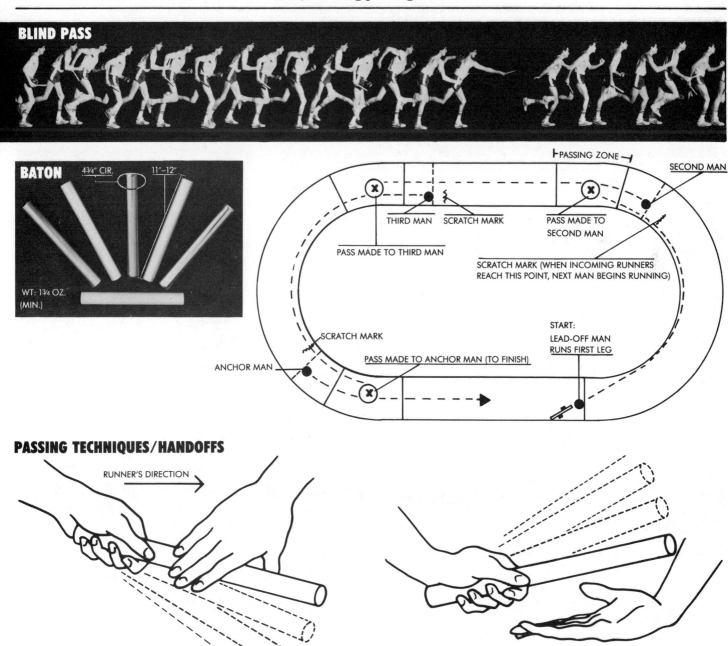

BATON

4¾" CIR.   11"–12"

WT: 1¾ OZ. (MIN.)

PASSING ZONE

SECOND MAN

THIRD MAN   SCRATCH MARK   PASS MADE TO SECOND MAN

PASS MADE TO THIRD MAN

SCRATCH MARK (WHEN INCOMING RUNNERS REACH THIS POINT, NEXT MAN BEGINS RUNNING)

SCRATCH MARK

ANCHOR MAN

PASS MADE TO ANCHOR MAN (TO FINISH)

START: LEAD-OFF MAN RUNS FIRST LEG

PASSING TECHNIQUES/HANDOFFS

RUNNER'S DIRECTION

UPWARD THRUST/UPSWEEP

DOWNWARD THRUST/DOWN PASS

The number of hurdles runners must pass over, the distance between them and their height varies according to race distance. *Indoor hurdlers* must clear four hurdles in the 50-yard dash, five in the 60 and six in the 70. In all outdoor races, including the decathlon and heptathlon events, runners must clear 10 hurdles.

Hurdlers must stay in their own lanes throughout the race. There is no penalty for accidentally knocking over a hurdle, but racers are disqualified for trailing a foot or leg alongside a hurdle, jumping a hurdle in the wrong lane or deliberately knocking over a hurdle with a hand or foot.

The first racer clearing all hurdles to cross the finish line wins.

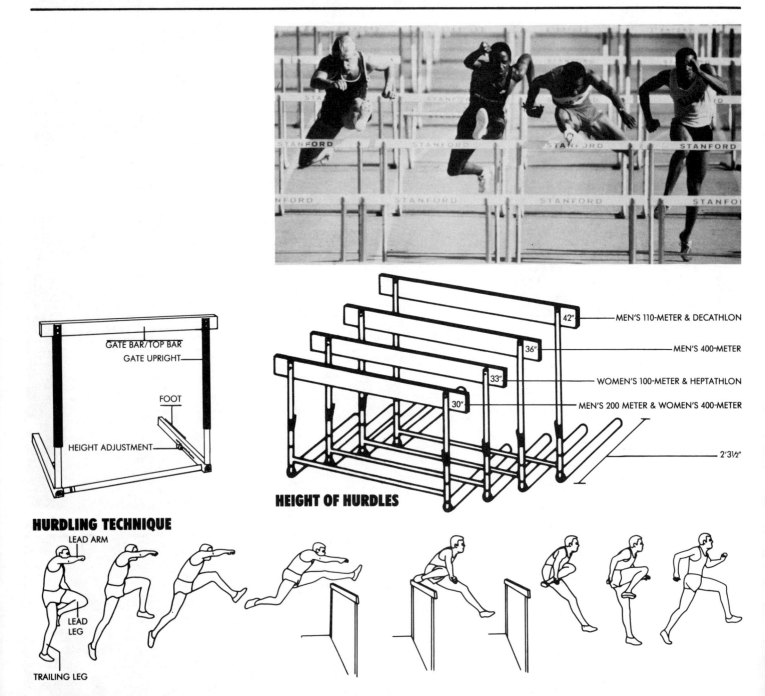

GATE BAR/TOP BAR
GATE UPRIGHT
FOOT
HEIGHT ADJUSTMENT

42" — MEN'S 110-METER & DECATHLON
36" — MEN'S 400-METER
33" — WOMEN'S 100-METER & HEPTATHLON
30" — MEN'S 200 METER & WOMEN'S 400-METER
2'3½"

HEIGHT OF HURDLES

HURDLING TECHNIQUE

LEAD ARM
LEAD LEG
TRAILING LEG

The steeplechase is a 3,000-meter (240 yds. less than two miles) race, consisting of seven laps around a track, during which runners go over 28 dry hurdles and seven water jumps.

Runners may clear hurdles by jumping over them, using one hand to vault over, or, as most runners do, landing on top of the bar with one foot and leaping off to land in the shallowest water.

Steeplers are disqualified for going around a jump, failing to go through or over the water, or trailing a foot or leg alongside any hurdle.

Racers wear shoes with perforations to allow drainage.

The first runner to cross the finish line with his torso wins.

DRY HURDLE

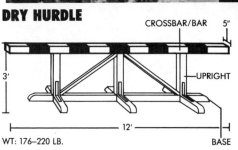

CROSSBAR/BAR   5"

3'

UPRIGHT

12'

WT: 176–220 LB.   BASE

WATER JUMP

TRAILING LEG

12'

12'

5"

3'

Men's and women's distance races cover 800 meters (half-mile), 1500 meters (metric mile) and the marathon distance. Women also run a 3000-meter race, while men compete at 5000 and 10,000 meters.

The 800-meter run begins from a staggered start and racers must stay in their lanes for the first two turns. All other races begin from a single starting line and runners may run wherever they choose. Many prefer the inside, or *pole lane*. In all running and walking races, the first competitor to break the vertical plane of the finish line with his or her torso wins.

The marathon covers 26 miles, 385 yards. Competitors may use any running or walking step to cover that distance. The taking of

RUNNING SHOE

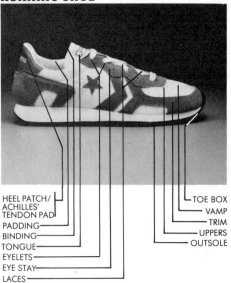

HEEL PATCH/
ACHILLES'
TENDON PAD
PADDING
BINDING
TONGUE
EYELETS
EYE STAY
LACES

TOE BOX
VAMP
TRIM
UPPERS
OUTSOLE

THE 'PACK' COMING AROUND A TURN

refreshments and sponging off are permitted at official stations. Special 'ultra-marathons', covering distances as long as 100 miles, are also run but are not generally part of any track and field meet.

Race walks are held at various distances, ranging from one mile to 75,000 meters, with men's olympic races held at 20 and 50 kilometers.

Race walkers must have part of one foot in contact with the ground at all times, i.e., the rear foot cannot leave the ground until the front foot has touched. The leg must also be momentarily straightened while the foot is on the ground. If three or more judges believe a walker is running, he is disqualified.

MARATHON START

RACE WALKING TECHNIQUE

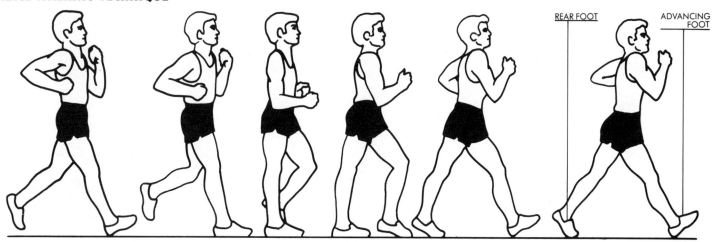

REAR FOOT ADVANCING FOOT

Javelin throwers are permitted six attempts, with the longest single throw winning. Ties are broken by comparing second best efforts.

The javelin must be thrown overhand. It cannot be hurled or slung. The thrower may go outside the runway lines during the approach, but must be between them and behind the arc when releasing the *jav*.

Crossing the arc before the javelin lands is a foul, nullifying the throw.

The point of the javelin must hit the ground first or the throw does not count, although the point does not have to stick in the ground. The throw is measured from the mark made by the point to the intersection of the sector lines.

Four judges officiate.

JAVELIN SHOES

HEEL SPIKES   HEEL WEDGE

JAVELIN

(MEN) 8'10¼"
WT: 1 LB. 12 OZ.

(WOMEN) · 7'6½"
WT: 1 LB. 5 OZ.

SHAFT

CORD
GRIP

THROWING SECTOR

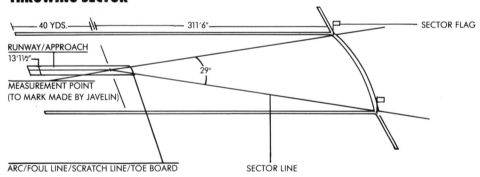

40 YDS.   311'6"   SECTOR FLAG

RUNWAY/APPROACH
13'1½"

29°

MEASUREMENT POINT
(TO MARK MADE BY JAVELIN)

ARC/FOUL LINE/SCRATCH LINE/TOE BOARD   SECTOR LINE

THROWING TECHNIQUE

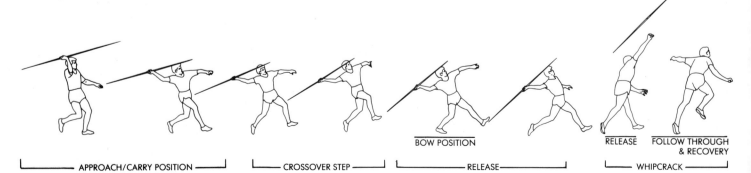

BOW POSITION   RELEASE   FOLLOW THROUGH
& RECOVERY

APPROACH/CARRY POSITION   CROSSOVER STEP   RELEASE   WHIPCRACK

Shot putters may use any body motion to put, or push, rather than throw the shot, so long as they start from a stationary position and the one hand used for putting never goes lower than it does at the starting position.

Competitors are permitted six attempts, with the longest single effort winning. Ties are broken by comparing second best puts. Distance is measured from the inner edge of the ring to the nearest mark made by the shot, and rounded off to the lowest quarter-inch.

Shot putters may touch the inside face of the raised toeboard, but if they touch its top, or the area beyond the ring, the attempt is nullified.

BUMPER

SHOT PUT SHOES

PHOTO BY WALTER IOOSS JR. FOR 'SHOOTING FOR THE GOLD' © 1984 FUJI PHOTO FILM USA

SHOTS

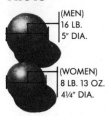

(MEN)
16 LB.
5" DIA.

(WOMEN)
8 LB. 13 OZ.
4¼" DIA.

SHOT PUTTING SECTOR

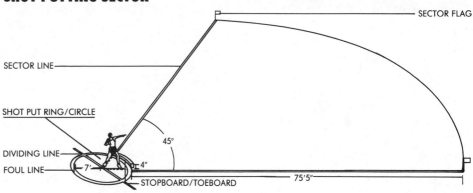

SECTOR FLAG

SECTOR LINE

SHOT PUT RING/CIRCLE

DIVIDING LINE

FOUL LINE

45°

7'   4"

STOPBOARD/TOEBOARD

75'5"

PUTTING TECHNIQUE

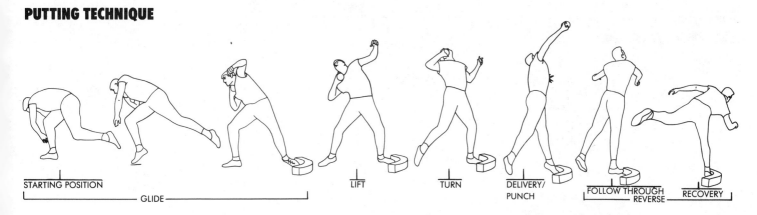

STARTING POSITION

GLIDE

LIFT

TURN

DELIVERY/
PUNCH

FOLLOW THROUGH
REVERSE

RECOVERY

Both discus and hammer throwers compete from inside a steel wire or fiber netting cage designed to catch errant throws.

Throwers in both events are given six attempts (although some competitors may be eliminated after three *qualifying throws*), with the longest single throw winning. Ties are broken by comparing second-best throws.

In both events throws are nullified if the competitor steps on or beyond the outer ring, leaves the ring before the discus or hammer has landed, fails to leave the ring from behind the dividing line, or if the throw lands outside the throwing sector.

Throws are measured from the inner edge of the ring to the nearest

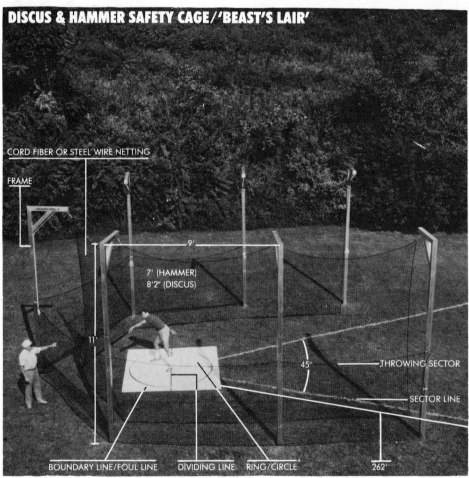

DISCUS & HAMMER SAFETY CAGE/''BEAST'S LAIR''

CORD FIBER OR STEEL WIRE NETTING

FRAME

9'

7' (HAMMER)
8'2" (DISCUS)

11'

45°

THROWING SECTOR

SECTOR LINE

262'

BOUNDARY LINE/FOUL LINE   DIVIDING LINE   RING/CIRCLE

DISCUS

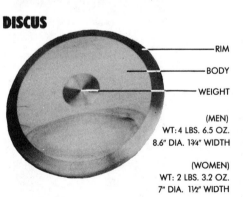

RIM

BODY

WEIGHT

(MEN)
WT: 4 LBS. 6.5 OZ.
8.6" DIA. 1¾" WIDTH

(WOMEN)
WT: 2 LBS. 3.2 OZ.
7" DIA. 1½" WIDTH

THROWING TECHNIQUE

PIVOT/TURN/SPIN/ROTATION

DELIVERY/RELEASE   FOLLOW THROUGH

REVERSE

mark made by the discus or the head of the hammer, and rounded off to the lowest inch.

Throwers must begin from a stationary position. The discus may be held and thrown by any method. The head of the hammer may touch the ground during preliminary swings.

Only men compete in the hammer throw. The entire hammer apparatus, including head, wire and handle is thrown. If the hammer breaks during a throw, that trial does not count against the competitor.

Five judges officiate, two watching for infringements within the ring, and three making sure the throw lands within the sector lines.

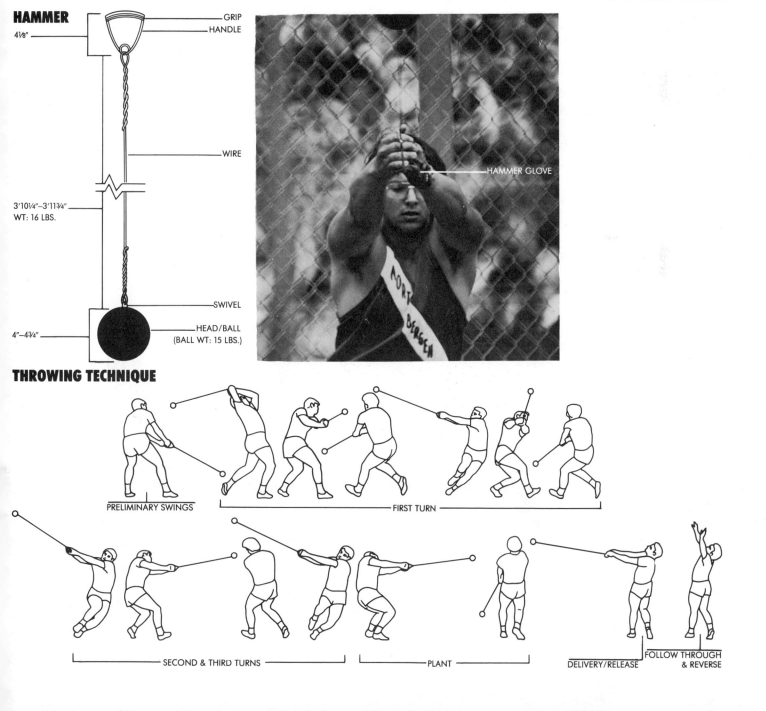

HAMMER

4⅛"

GRIP
HANDLE

WIRE

3'10¼"–3'11¾"
WT: 16 LBS.

SWIVEL

4"–4¾"

HEAD/BALL
(BALL WT: 15 LBS.)

HAMMER GLOVE

THROWING TECHNIQUE

PRELIMINARY SWINGS

FIRST TURN

SECOND & THIRD TURNS

PLANT

DELIVERY/RELEASE

FOLLOW THROUGH & REVERSE

Long jump and triple jump competitors may make as long a run-up as desired. If they touch the ground beyond the takeoff line it is a *foul*, and the jump is nullified.

Jumpers make six attempts, with the longest single jump winning.

Ties are broken by comparison of the second longest jumps.

Jumps are measured from the nearest mark, or *break*, made in the sand or sawdust by any part of the body to the takeoff line, and rounded off to the nearest quarter inch.

In the hop portion of the triple jump, jumpers must land on the same foot with which they hit the take-off board, and to complete the step must land on the other foot. The jump is nullified if they touch ground with the wrong foot.

JUMPING AREA

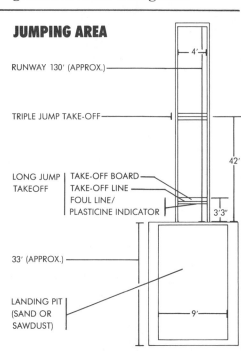

RUNWAY 130′ (APPROX.)

4′

TRIPLE JUMP TAKE-OFF

42′

LONG JUMP TAKEOFF | TAKE-OFF BOARD
TAKE-OFF LINE
FOUL LINE/
PLASTICINE INDICATOR

3′3″

33′ (APPROX.)

LANDING PIT (SAND OR SAWDUST)

9′

LONG JUMP/BROAD JUMP TECHNIQUE

FREE LEG

BOUNCE-OUT

RUN-UP — TAKE-OFF — HITCH KICK — FLIGHT — LANDING

HOP, STEP AND JUMP TECHNIQUE

'SLEEPING FOOT'

TAKE-OFF

TAKE-OFF

TAKE-OFF

HANG POSITION

LANDING POSITION

HOP — STEP — JUMP

High jumpers may begin competing at any height they choose above the minimum set by the judges, and then elect to pass at subsequent heights. A jumper is eliminated after three successive failures.

A jump is a failure if the jumper knocks the bar off its supports, steps into the landing area before clearing the bar, or takes off from both feet.

Final standings are determined by the greatest height cleared by a jumper. If jumpers tie, the jumper with the fewest misses wins.

Bar height is measured from take-off point to the lowest point on the upper side of the bar.

The main styles used are the flop, in which the jumper goes over the bar on his back, and the straddle.

PLASTIC HEEL CUP

PADDED COLLAR

HEEL SPIKES

HIGH JUMP (FLOP) SHOE

FLOP

Photo by Walter Iooss for Shooting For the Gold/© 1984 Fuji Photo Film U.S.A.

JUMPING AREA

LANDING AREA/LANDING PIT

UPRIGHT/STANDARD

8'4"

13'2"

CROSSBAR SUPPORT

RUN-UP/RUNWAY/FAN

16'4"

CROSSBAR/BAR

STRADDLE/ROLL

TRAIL LEG

LEAD LEG

RUN-UP/APPROACH

TAKE-OFF

CLEARANCE

LANDING

Pole vaulters use flexible poles to loft themselves over a crossbar. Vaulters may choose to jump or pass at any height, but if they elect to jump and fail on three attempts at a given height they are eliminated. The bar is raised after each vaulter has jumped or passed at a specific height. The winner is the vaulter who has cleared the greatest height. In case of ties, the vaulter with the fewest misses wins.

Poles may be of any length and diameter, and made of any material, although fiber glass 'sky poles' are favored.

If a vaulter knocks the crossbar off its *supports*, changes hands in mid-air, or touches the pit with the pole, the vault is a failure.

VAULTING TECHNIQUE

CARRY — SHIFT — PLANT

TAKE-OFF — SWING AND ROCK BACK — PULL — PUSH OFF AND CLEARANCE

FLIGHT

The 10-event decathlon, or *all around*, for men, and seven-event heptathlon for women, are tests of various track and field skills. Contested over two days, they require *decathletes* and *heptathletes* to demonstrate proficiency in running, jumping, endurance and strength sports.

Athletes compete against a predetermined standard in each event rather than against each other. Points are added or subtracted by comparing the athlete's effort to the set standard. In running, for example, points are deducted for each fraction of a second the competitor is slower than the set standard. Events do not carry equal value in the total score. Highest total points wins.

MEN'S EVENTS

WOMEN'S EVENTS

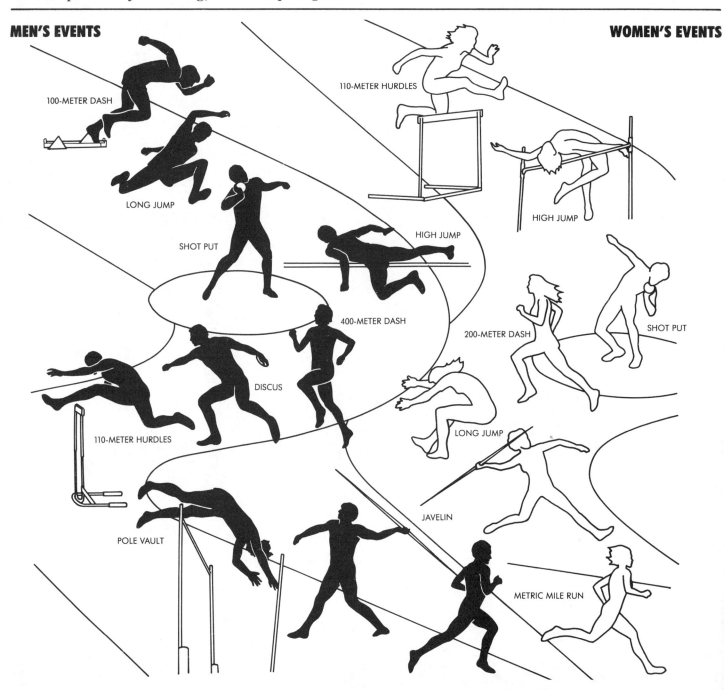

100-METER DASH

110-METER HURDLES

LONG JUMP

HIGH JUMP

SHOT PUT

HIGH JUMP

SHOT PUT

400-METER DASH

200-METER DASH

DISCUS

110-METER HURDLES

LONG JUMP

JAVELIN

POLE VAULT

METRIC MILE RUN

Numerous officials are necessary to run a track meet. Races are begun by a *starter* firing a gun. The starter also rings a bell at the beginning of the last, or *bell*, lap. A *recall starter* watches for premature movement. The *timer* clocks races, and *finish line judges* determine the order in which runners place.

In throwing events, two *judges* by the ring watch for violations, while two or more near the sector lines help measure distance and insure the throw lands within bounds.

Two *judges* control the high jump and three work the pole vault. Four oversee the long jump and a fifth is added for the triple jump.

The *clerk of the course* schedules races. The *scorer* tabulates results.

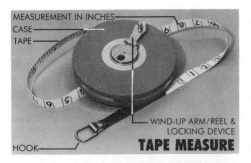

MEASUREMENT IN INCHES
CASE
TAPE
WIND-UP ARM/REEL & LOCKING DEVICE
HOOK
TAPE MEASURE

COMPUTERIZED PERFORMANCE INDICATOR
JAVELIN — EVENT
COMPETITOR ATTEMPT PLACE
354 2 1
PERFORMANCE
99.72
DISTANCE (METRIC & ARABIC)
STANDING AT TIME

STARTER'S PISTOL/GUN

WIND INDICATOR
WIND
+15
WIND TO COMPETITOR'S BACK
WIND SPEED (MPH)

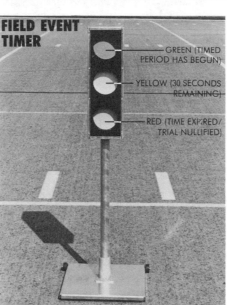

FIELD EVENT TIMER
GREEN (TIMED PERIOD HAS BEGUN)
YELLOW (30 SECONDS REMAINING)
RED (TIME EXPIRED/ TRIAL NULLIFIED)

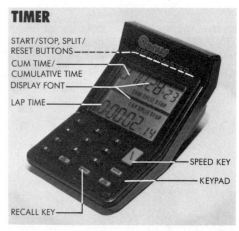

TIMER
START/STOP, SPLIT/ RESET BUTTONS
CUM TIME/ CUMULATIVE TIME
DISPLAY FONT
LAP TIME
SPEED KEY
KEYPAD
RECALL KEY

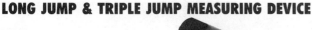

LONG JUMP & TRIPLE JUMP MEASURING DEVICE

SCOPE
DIGITAL READOUT
SLIDE
RAIL

STOPWATCH
BOW
CROWN/START & STOP BUTTON
RESET BUTTON
MINUTE HAND
SECOND HAND
SECOND BITS
BEZEL
SPORT CRAFT
1/10 TH
1/10 SECOND BITS

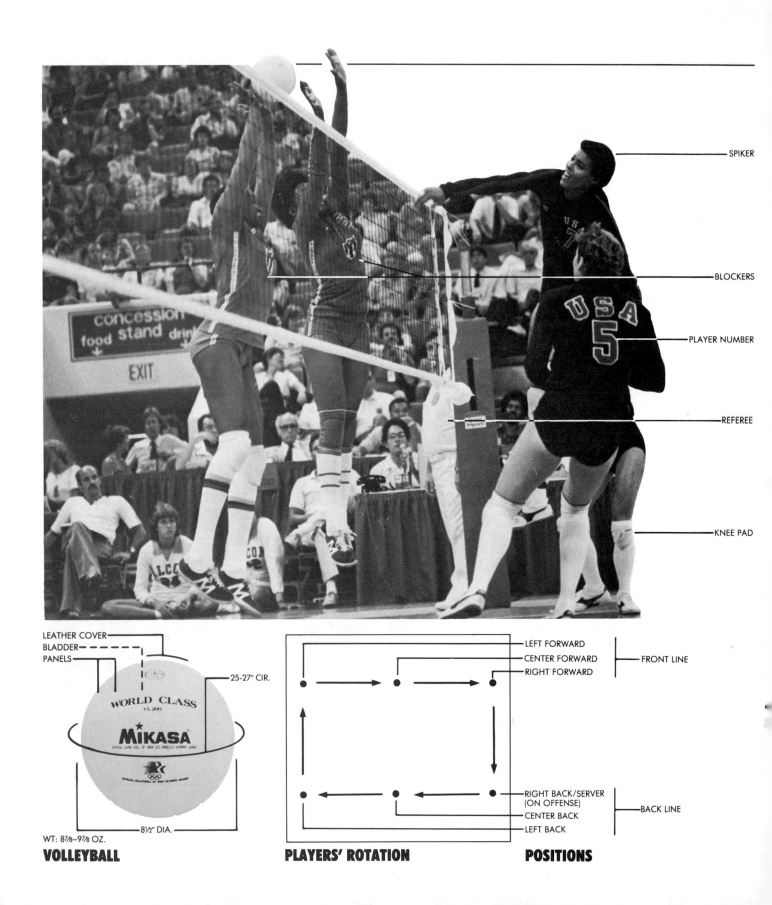

SPIKER

BLOCKERS

PLAYER NUMBER

REFEREE

KNEE PAD

LEATHER COVER
BLADDER
PANELS

25-27" CIR.

WORLD CLASS
VL 200

MIKASA

OFFICIAL GAME BALL OF 1984 LOS ANGELES OLYMPIC GAMES

OFFICIAL VOLLEYBALL OF 1984 OLYMPIC GAMES

8½" DIA.

WT: 8⅞–9⅞ OZ.

VOLLEYBALL

LEFT FORWARD
CENTER FORWARD — FRONT LINE
RIGHT FORWARD

RIGHT BACK/SERVER
(ON OFFENSE)
CENTER BACK — BACK LINE
LEFT BACK

PLAYERS' ROTATION

POSITIONS

Volleyball teams score by hitting the ball over the net, within the boundaries, so that the opposition is unable to return it. The team serving gains one point for doing this and continues serving. If the receiving team does it, it wins the right to serve. A game is 15 points, but it must be won by two points, thus a 14-14 tie continues until either team gains a two-point advantage.

When the serve changes hands, players rotate clockwise, so that each player gets to serve.

Three players may touch the ball before it goes over the net, so back line players *set-up* front line players with soft lobs so they can slam it downward, called *spiking*, or *killing*.

VOLLEYBALL COURT

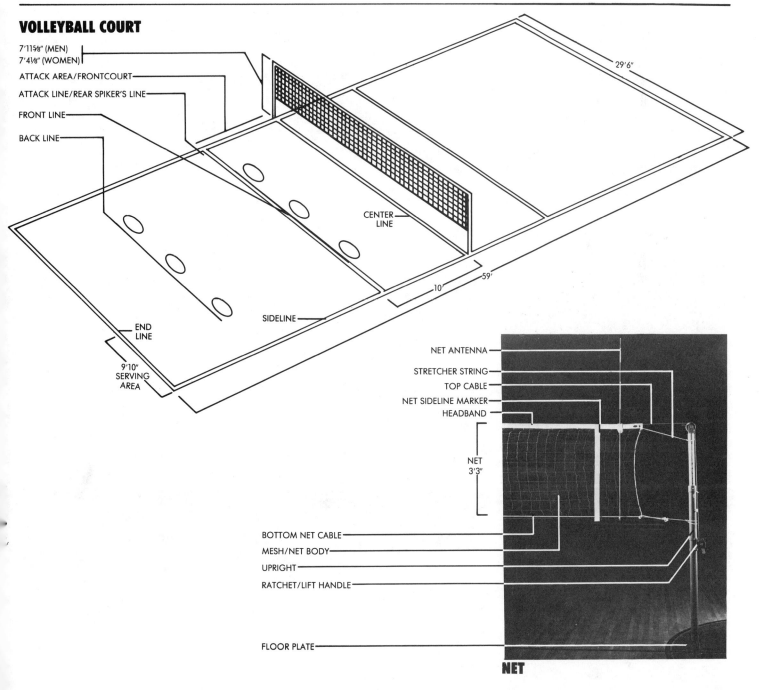

7'11⅝" (MEN)
7'4⅛" (WOMEN)
ATTACK AREA/FRONTCOURT
ATTACK LINE/REAR SPIKER'S LINE
FRONT LINE
BACK LINE
29'6"
CENTER LINE
10'
59'
SIDELINE
END LINE
9'10" SERVING AREA

NET ANTENNA
STRETCHER STRING
TOP CABLE
NET SIDELINE MARKER
HEADBAND
NET 3'3"
BOTTOM NET CABLE
MESH/NET BODY
UPRIGHT
RATCHET/LIFT HANDLE
FLOOR PLATE

NET

Water polo is played by two seven-player teams. The object is to throw the ball into the opponent's goal while preventing the opposition from scoring. The team scoring the most goals wins. A game is played in four seven-minute *periods* in a pool at least 5'11" deep. Only the goalie may touch bottom. A team has 35 seconds to shoot or it loses the ball.

The ball is advanced by striking it, passing or swimming with it. Only the goalie may touch the ball with both hands simultaneously.

Ordinary fouls, like *splashing* or *pushing*, are penalized by loss of possession. *Major fouls*, such as *kicking*, *clubbing* and *submerging*, may result in a 45-second ejection or a penalty shot.

FIELD OF PLAY/POOL/BATH

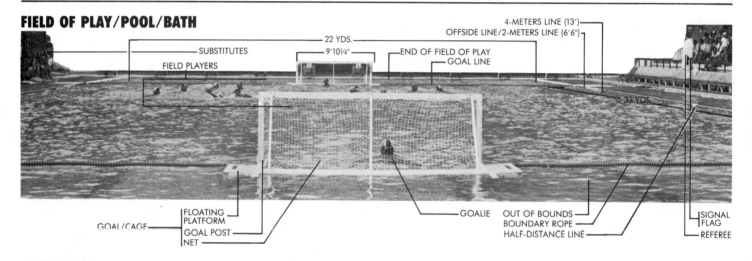

- 4-METERS LINE (13')
- OFFSIDE LINE/2-METERS LINE (6'6")
- SUBSTITUTES
- 22 YDS.
- 9'10¼"
- END OF FIELD OF PLAY
- GOAL LINE
- FIELD PLAYERS
- 33 YDS.
- FLOATING PLATFORM
- GOAL/CAGE
- GOAL POST
- NET
- GOALIE
- OUT OF BOUNDS
- BOUNDARY ROPE
- HALF-DISTANCE LINE
- SIGNAL FLAG
- REFEREE

EQUIPMENT

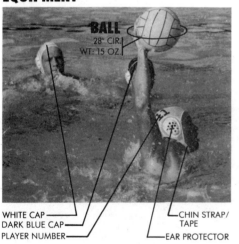

BALL
28" CIR.
WT: 15 OZ.

- WHITE CAP
- DARK BLUE CAP
- PLAYER NUMBER
- CHIN STRAP/TAPE
- EAR PROTECTOR

SHOT ON GOAL

- GOALKEEPER/GOALIE
- GOALIE'S RED CAP
- TWO-METER MAN/HOLE MAN/SETTER
- DEFENSIVE FIELD PLAYERS

Water skiers compete in *slalom*, *jumping* and figure, or *trick skiing*, events.

Slalom requires a skier on one ski to swing around a course of six buoys. The speed of the tow boat increases on each run until it reaches 36 mph; then the tow line is progressively shortened. The winner is the skier who completes the most runs without missing a buoy.

Jumping is judged on distance. Boats are limited to 35 mph, but skiers often attain speeds of 55 mph at the *takeoff point*.

Trick skiers make two passes of 20 seconds each on a 200-yard course, during which they perform as many maneuvers as possible. They are judged on form and the difficulty of their tricks.

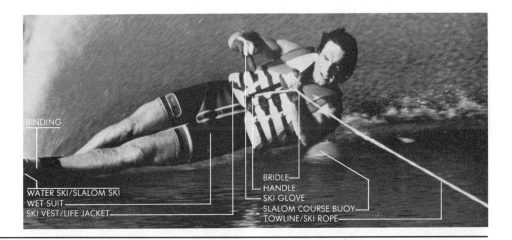

BINDING
WATER SKI/SLALOM SKI
WET SUIT
SKI VEST/LIFE JACKET
BRIDLE
HANDLE
SKI GLOVE
SLALOM COURSE BUOY
TOWLINE/SKI ROPE

SLALOM COURSE

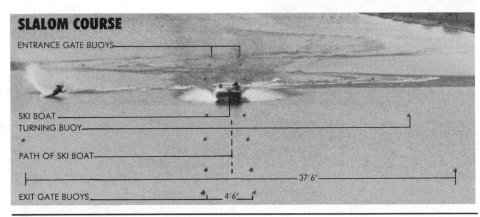

ENTRANCE GATE BUOYS
SKI BOAT
TURNING BUOY
PATH OF SKI BOAT
37'6"
EXIT GATE BUOYS
4'6"

SKI JUMP

HELMET
JUMP SURFACE
GUIDE BUOYS
RAMP
APRONS
14'
6'
25'

SLALOM SKI

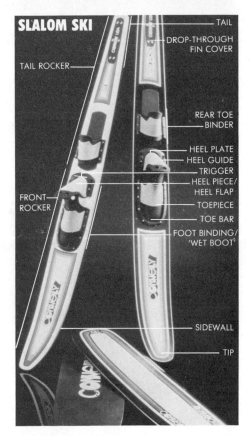

TAIL
DROP-THROUGH FIN COVER
TAIL ROCKER
REAR TOE BINDER
HEEL PLATE
HEEL GUIDE
TRIGGER
HEEL PIECE/HEEL FLAP
TOEPIECE
TOE BAR
FOOT BINDING/'WET BOOT'
FRONT ROCKER
SIDEWALL
TIP

Lifters compete in ten categories grouped by body weight. Once a barbell is *loaded*, or ready, a lifter has two minutes to begin. Timing stops when the barbell is raised above the knees. Competition consists of snatch and clean-and-jerk, with final placement determined by combined weight in both lifts. Each *lifter* pre-selects weights he will attempt to lift. He has three chances to perform a *'good lift.'* Two of the *referees* must approve a lift, signaling 'good lift' with a white light and 'no lift' with a red light. Discs are color-coded by weight for spectators' benefit.

The sequence at top and right is of the two-hand snatch. The bottom sequence shows the two-hand clean-and-jerk, which is performed last.

LIFT-OFF PHASE

LIFT-OFF PHASE

SHIFT PHASE

POWER POSITION/JUMP POSITION

PULLING UNDER PHASE/DROPPING UNDER PHASE

SQUAT SNATCH/LOCKED-OUT POSITION

RECOVERY PHASE

RECOVERY PHASE

RECOVERY PHASE

SHIFT AND POWER PHASE

PULLING-UNDER PHASE

SQUAT CLEAN/
RECEIVING PHASE

DIP

JERK

AFTER RECEIVING JUDGES
'DOWN' SIGNAL

COMPLETED/COMPLETION

COLLAR

OUTSIDE SLEEVE

INTERNATIONAL STANDARD BARBELL

WINGNUT UNIT

SPOKED ADJUSTMENT UNIT

MEASURE OF WEIGHT (KILOGRAMS)

ATTEMPT BOARD

LIFTER'S BODY WEIGHT CLASS

DISCS/PLATES

1¼ KG

2½ KG

BAR

25 KG/BUMPER PLATE

50 KG BUMPER PLATE

SNATCH AND CLEAN-
AND-JERK RECORD

EUROPEAN RECORD

WORLD RECORD

WEIGHTLIFTING COSTUME/SINGLET

COMPETITION PATCH

DISC STAND

PLATFORM/STAGE

LIFTER'S ATTEMPTS
IN THIS COMPETITION

LIFTER'S NAME

WEIGHT OF THIS ATTEMPT

MANUFACTURER'S LOGO

JUDGES' LIGHTS/REFEREE LIGHT SYSTEM

TIMING CLOCK/PLATFORM CLOCK

LIFTER'S NATIONALITY

WEIGHTLIFTING SHOE/BOOT

SNATCH 186 Kg

JERK 237.5 Kg

CATEGORIE 110 Kg TOTAL 417.5

WR Kg

ER Kg

ATTEMPT 3

WEIGHT 182.5 Kg

MIN SEC 0:59

LONGINES

NAME TARANENKO

NAT. URS

If a *wrestler* holds his opponent's shoulders to the *mat* for a designated *count*, it is a *pin* or *fall*, and ends the *match* or *bout*. Otherwise, a match lasts three *periods* and is decided by a *point system*. A *referee* awards two points for a *takedown* (a wrestler taking his opponent to the mat and gaining *control*), a point for an *escape* (gaining *neutral position* from an opponent's control), two points for a *reversal* of control, and two or three points for a *near fall* or *near pin* (three when held for five seconds). A wrestler may be penalized one or two points, or disqualified for violations. A point is awarded for *riding time* if a wrestler has been in control a minute more than his opponent.

NEUTRAL POSITION/ STANDING POSITION

EARGUARD/HEADGUARD

WRESTLING SHORTS/UNIFORM/COSTUME

WRESTLING TIGHTS/UNIFORM/COSTUME

WRESTLING MAT

WRESTLING BOOTS/SHOES
TOURNAMENT COLOR TAPE
SCHOOL INITIAL
CENTER CIRCLE/CONTEST AREA/BOUNDARY

REFEREE'S POSITION/ NEW PERIOD STARTING POSITION

'OFFENSIVE' WRESTLER

'DEFENSIVE' WRESTLER

TIE UP FROM STANDING POSITION

TIE UP FROM KNEELING POSITION

TAKEDOWN FROM NEUTRAL POSITION—TWO POINTS

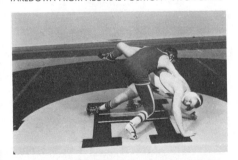

TAKEDOWN AFTER NEUTRAL POSITION—HIP THROW

Matches begin from a neutral position and wrestlers use *holds* and *counterholds*, which are set up by *feints*, *fakes*, *pushes* and *pulls* to gain advantage or control.

A takedown forces an opponent to support himself on his hands and knees. A *breakdown* flattens these supporting points until he is unable to free himself, or *escape*. 'Greco-Roman' wrestlers use only their legs for support and balance. In *freestyle*, or *catch-as-catch-can*, wrestlers may use a variety of holds and *trips*. Japanese *sumo wrestling* matches end when one huge wrestler drives his equally huge opponent out of a 15' diameter ring or throws him to the ground.

PREDICAMENT OR NEAR FALL—TWO POINTS

NEAR FALL, ONE SHOULDER TO MAT—THREE POINTS

NEAR FALL, DEFENSIVE WRESTLER BRIDGE POSITION

REVERSAL OF ADVANTAGE POSITION OR SWITCH—TWO POINTS

PINNING POSITION—3/4 NELSON

PINNING POSITION—WINGS/FIGURE FOUR ON HEAD

PINNING POSITION—CRADLE

Sailboats, ranging in size from small, one-man *dinghies* to crewed *offshore racers*, compete over distances varying from short 'around the buoys' courses to global circumnavigations. The standard Olympic course is a combination of triangles and *windward/leeward legs*, which are sailed zig-zag into the wind or off it.

In *one-design racing*, all boats in a *class* are identical, as in Olympic events. In *handicap racing*, dissimilar boats are assigned mathematically calculated time allowances. *Formula class racing* boats differ in appearance but comply to a formula which includes variables such as length, girth and sail area, and results in a number usually expressed in meters.

CREW

FOREDECK CREW
BOW MAN
MAST MAN
GRINDER
SAIL TRIMMER
AFTERGUARD | HELMSMAN
TACTICIAN

AMERICA'S CUP 1983 FINAL
DOWNWIND TACKING DUEL

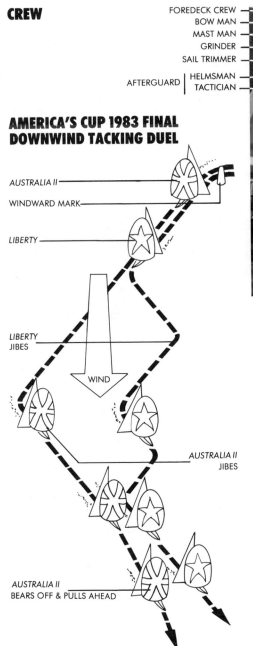

AUSTRALIA II
WINDWARD MARK

LIBERTY

LIBERTY
JIBES

WIND

AUSTRALIA II
JIBES

AUSTRALIA II
BEARS OFF & PULLS AHEAD

OLYMPIC COURSE

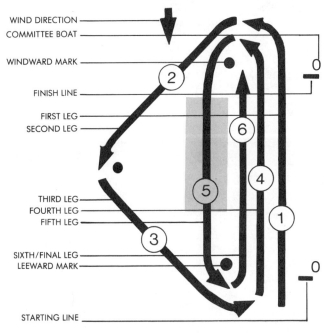

WIND DIRECTION
COMMITTEE BOAT
WINDWARD MARK
FINISH LINE
FIRST LEG
SECOND LEG
THIRD LEG
FOURTH LEG
FIFTH LEG
SIXTH/FINAL LEG
LEEWARD MARK
STARTING LINE

Each yacht has its own sail plan—one or more sails designed for sailing at different angles to the wind and under different conditions.

The most common rig consists of a mainsail, or *main*, and a *headsail*. Most headsails are used when the boat is *going to windward*, sailing into the wind at about a 45 degree angle. These sails vary in size, from small *storm jibs*, used in heavy wind, to larger *working jibs*, used in moderate weather, to big genoas, set to catch lesser winds.

A spinnaker is used when sailing *downwind*, with the wind behind the boat, pushing it. Sail materials range from light *dacron* and *nylon* to heavy *kevlar*.

SPINNAKER RUN

MAINSAIL

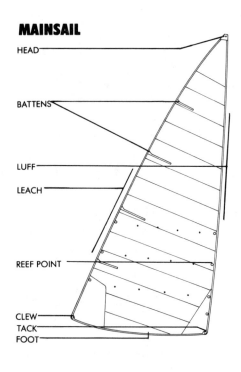

HEAD

BATTENS

LUFF

LEACH

REEF POINT

CLEW
TACK
FOOT

JIB/GENOA

HEAD

LEACH
LUFF

FOOT

SPINNAKER/TRI-RADIAL

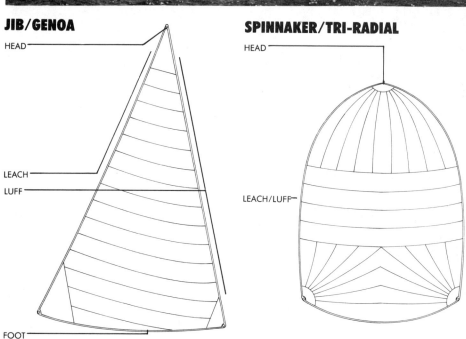

HEAD

LEACH/LUFF

Olympic sailing classes range from sailboards, the smallest at 12 feet, to *catamaran* and *centerboard* boats, to *keel designs*, the largest at 26¾ feet.

Course flags on the committee boat signal the order in which spe-cific *buoys* or markers are to be rounded. At the start, *skippers* maneuver to cross the starting line when the starting gun or *hooter* sounds. The first boat to cross the finish line wins. In Olympic scoring, the yacht receiving the fewest points in a race series wins. First place finishers get 0 points, second get 3, and so on.

The Windglider, the sailboard used in the Olympics, is basically a surfboard with a sail sleeved on a rotating mast.

SAILBOARD

SAIL

MAST

WINDOW

BOARD

UNIVERSAL JOINT

BOOM/WISHBONE

SAILING HARNESS

DAGGERBOARD

SKEG

FOOT STRAPS

RACE START

SIGNAL FLAGS/
COURSE FLAGS

STARTING LINE

RACE COMMITTEE BOAT

MARK

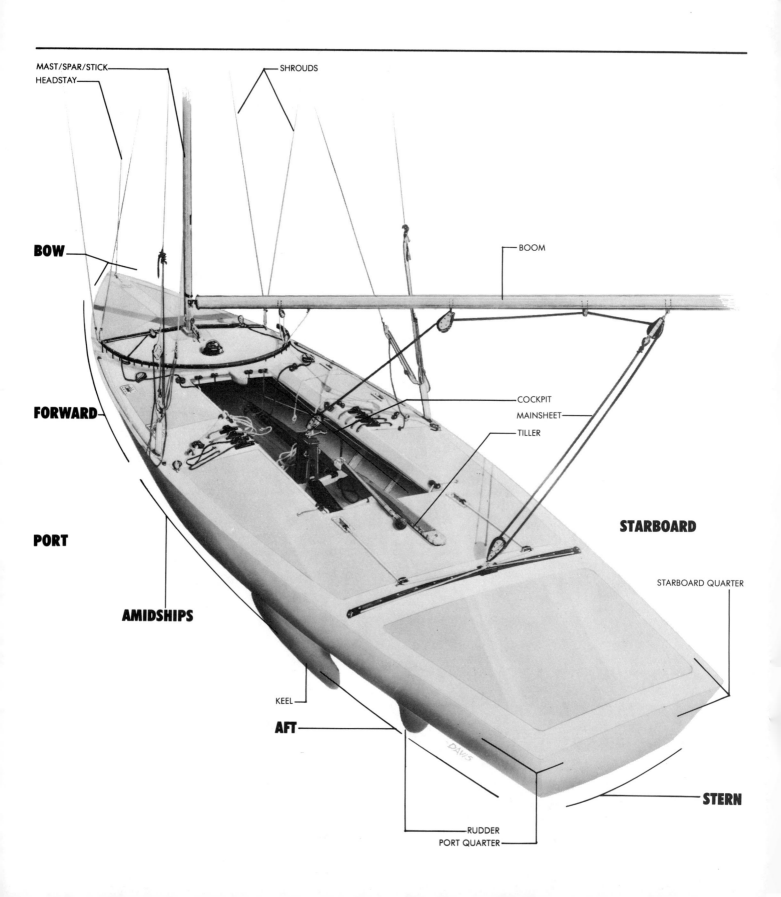

MAST/SPAR/STICK

HEADSTAY

SHROUDS

BOW

BOOM

FORWARD

COCKPIT

MAINSHEET

TILLER

PORT

STARBOARD

STARBOARD QUARTER

AMIDSHIPS

KEEL

AFT

DAVIS

STERN

RUDDER

PORT QUARTER

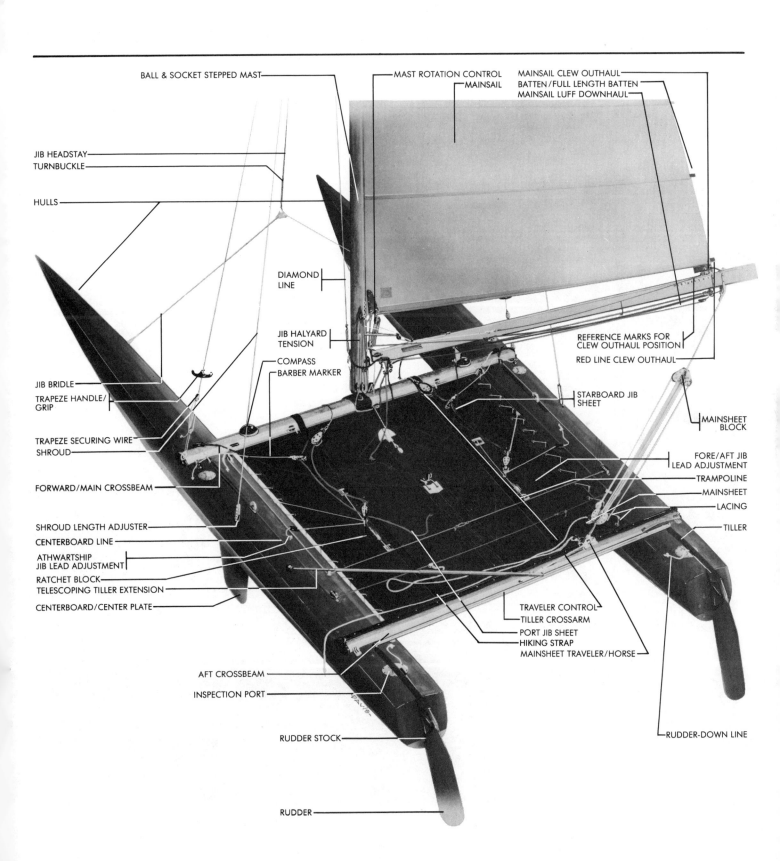

BALL & SOCKET STEPPED MAST

MAST ROTATION CONTROL

MAINSAIL

MAINSAIL CLEW OUTHAUL
BATTEN/FULL LENGTH BATTEN
MAINSAIL LUFF DOWNHAUL

JIB HEADSTAY

TURNBUCKLE

HULLS

DIAMOND LINE

JIB HALYARD TENSION

REFERENCE MARKS FOR CLEW OUTHAUL POSITION

RED LINE CLEW OUTHAUL

COMPASS
BARBER MARKER

STARBOARD JIB SHEET

JIB BRIDLE

TRAPEZE HANDLE/GRIP

MAINSHEET BLOCK

TRAPEZE SECURING WIRE
SHROUD

FORE/AFT JIB LEAD ADJUSTMENT

TRAMPOLINE

MAINSHEET

FORWARD/MAIN CROSSBEAM

LACING

SHROUD LENGTH ADJUSTER

CENTERBOARD LINE

TILLER

ATHWARTSHIP JIB LEAD ADJUSTMENT

RATCHET BLOCK

TELESCOPING TILLER EXTENSION

CENTERBOARD/CENTER PLATE

TRAVELER CONTROL

TILLER CROSSARM

PORT JIB SHEET

HIKING STRAP

MAINSHEET TRAVELER/HORSE

AFT CROSSBEAM

INSPECTION PORT

RUDDER STOCK

RUDDER-DOWN LINE

RUDDER

Powerboat racing is conducted on inland waters and offshore, in inboard or outboard motorboats or in inboard or outboard hydroplanes.

In offshore racing, boats in five classes compete at speeds of upwards of 170-mph over courses that vary in length from 80 to 160 miles. Boats range in size, from 17 to 50 feet in length; in power, ranging from 400-hp to 2,500-hp multi-engine configurations; and in design, either *catamaran hulls*, which are faster on smooth water, or *V-shaped* *monohulls*, which withstand heavy seas better.

Unlimited hydroplanes, or *thunderboats*, compete in their own race circuit.

OFFSHORE CREW

NAVIGATOR · DRIVER · THROTTLEMAN

Performer

UNLIMITED HYDROPLANE

'ROOSTER TAIL'

STABILIZER/WING

STRUT

ENGINE COMPARTMENT

COCKPIT

RAM WING

HULL

CENTER DECK

COMMAND CONSOLE

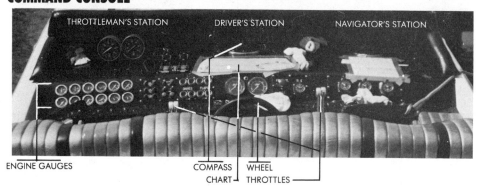

THROTTLEMAN'S STATION · DRIVER'S STATION · NAVIGATOR'S STATION

ENGINE GAUGES · COMPASS · CHART · WHEEL · THROTTLES

Non-racing powerboats are used to fish or dive from, or for *cruising* different *ports o'call* or stopping at various *anchorages*, called *gunkholing*.

Motorboats also engage in *rendezvous*, in which several power-boats congregate in one location for a series of events, including seminars on nautical subjects, and *predicted log contests*, in which skippers, relying on compass, engine tachometers and *charts* alone, power their boats over a course, passing prearranged *checkpoints* at exact times predicted before the start of the race. Errors, either fast or slow, are totaled by an on-board observer using a *timepiece*. The skipper with the smallest error wins.

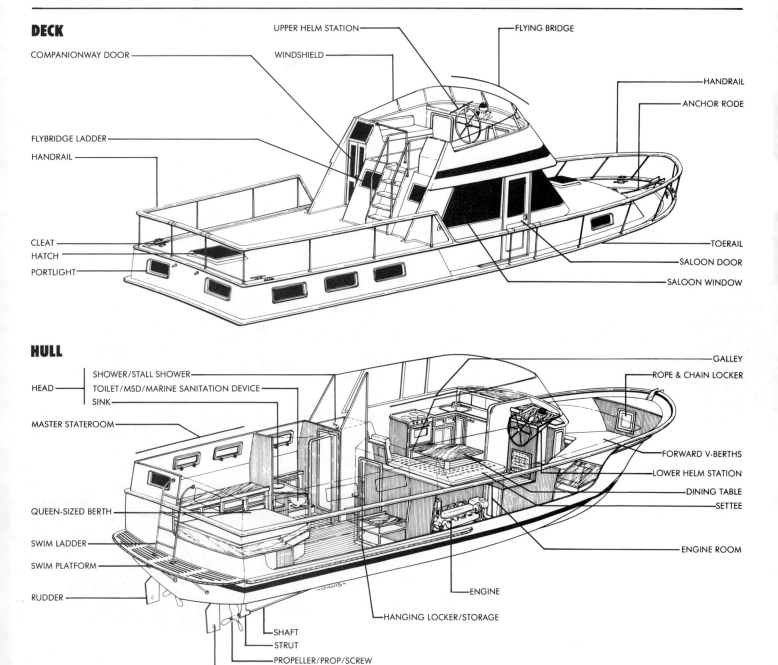

DECK

- COMPANIONWAY DOOR
- UPPER HELM STATION
- WINDSHIELD
- FLYING BRIDGE
- HANDRAIL
- ANCHOR RODE
- FLYBRIDGE LADDER
- HANDRAIL
- CLEAT
- HATCH
- PORTLIGHT
- TOERAIL
- SALOON DOOR
- SALOON WINDOW

HULL

- HEAD
  - SHOWER/STALL SHOWER
  - TOILET/MSD/MARINE SANITATION DEVICE
  - SINK
- MASTER STATEROOM
- QUEEN-SIZED BERTH
- SWIM LADDER
- SWIM PLATFORM
- RUDDER
- GALLEY
- ROPE & CHAIN LOCKER
- FORWARD V-BERTHS
- LOWER HELM STATION
- DINING TABLE
- SETTEE
- ENGINE ROOM
- ENGINE
- HANGING LOCKER/STORAGE
- SHAFT
- STRUT
- PROPELLER/PROP/SCREW
- ZINK

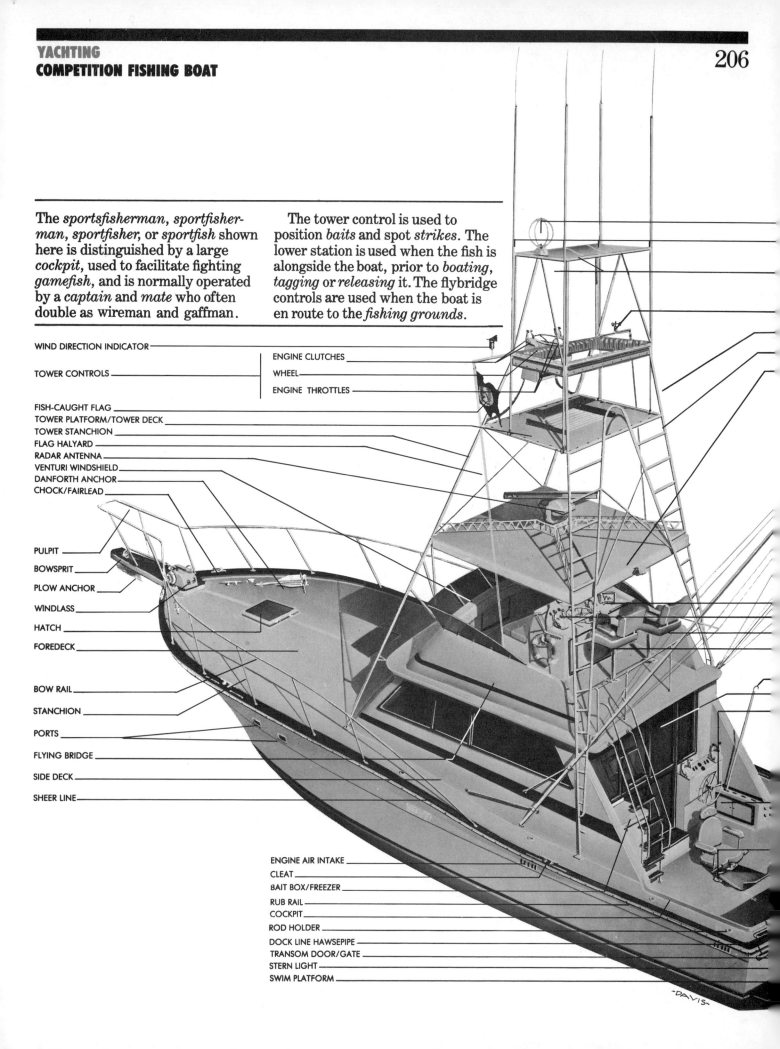

The *sportsfisherman, sportfisherman, sportfisher,* or *sportfish* shown here is distinguished by a large *cockpit*, used to facilitate fighting *gamefish*, and is normally operated by a *captain* and *mate* who often double as wireman and gaffman.

The tower control is used to position *baits* and spot *strikes*. The lower station is used when the fish is alongside the boat, prior to *boating, tagging* or *releasing* it. The flybridge controls are used when the boat is en route to the *fishing grounds*.

WIND DIRECTION INDICATOR

TOWER CONTROLS

ENGINE CLUTCHES
WHEEL
ENGINE THROTTLES

FISH-CAUGHT FLAG
TOWER PLATFORM/TOWER DECK
TOWER STANCHION
FLAG HALYARD
RADAR ANTENNA
VENTURI WINDSHIELD
DANFORTH ANCHOR
CHOCK/FAIRLEAD

PULPIT

BOWSPRIT

PLOW ANCHOR

WINDLASS

HATCH

FOREDECK

BOW RAIL

STANCHION

PORTS

FLYING BRIDGE

SIDE DECK

SHEER LINE

ENGINE AIR INTAKE
CLEAT
BAIT BOX/FREEZER
RUB RAIL
COCKPIT
ROD HOLDER
DOCK LINE HAWSEPIPE
TRANSOM DOOR/GATE
STERN LIGHT
SWIM PLATFORM

-DAVIS-

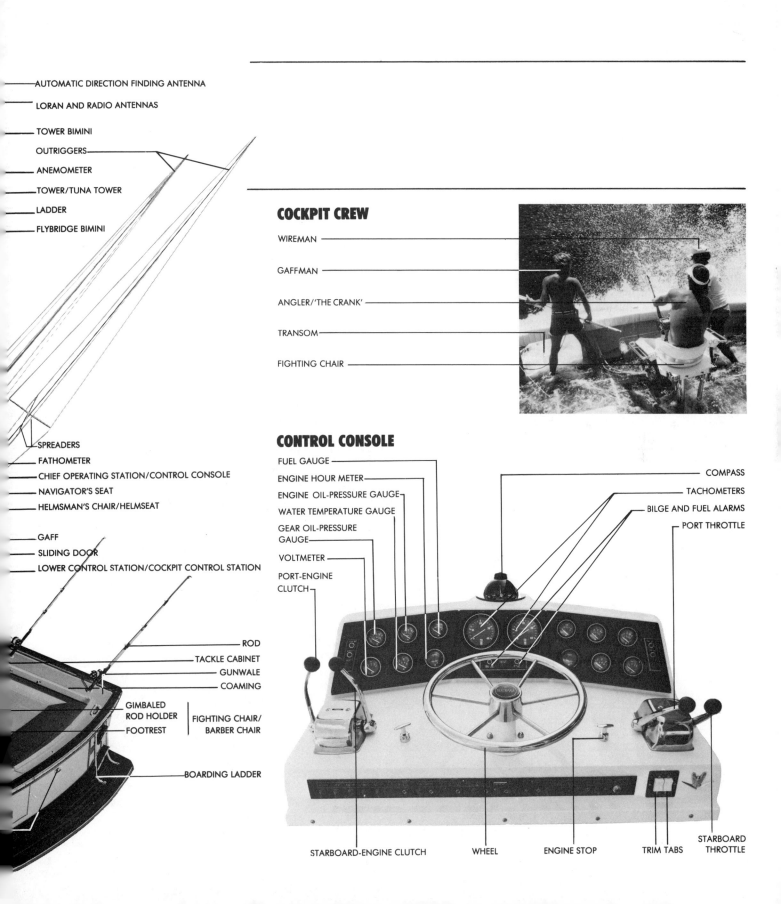

AUTOMATIC DIRECTION FINDING ANTENNA

LORAN AND RADIO ANTENNAS

TOWER BIMINI

OUTRIGGERS

ANEMOMETER

TOWER/TUNA TOWER

LADDER

FLYBRIDGE BIMINI

SPREADERS

FATHOMETER

CHIEF OPERATING STATION/CONTROL CONSOLE

NAVIGATOR'S SEAT

HELMSMAN'S CHAIR/HELMSEAT

GAFF

SLIDING DOOR

LOWER CONTROL STATION/COCKPIT CONTROL STATION

ROD

TACKLE CABINET

GUNWALE

COAMING

GIMBALED ROD HOLDER

FOOTREST

FIGHTING CHAIR/ BARBER CHAIR

BOARDING LADDER

COCKPIT CREW

WIREMAN

GAFFMAN

ANGLER/'THE CRANK'

TRANSOM

FIGHTING CHAIR

CONTROL CONSOLE

FUEL GAUGE

ENGINE HOUR METER

ENGINE OIL-PRESSURE GAUGE

WATER TEMPERATURE GAUGE

GEAR OIL-PRESSURE GAUGE

VOLTMETER

PORT-ENGINE CLUTCH

COMPASS

TACHOMETERS

BILGE AND FUEL ALARMS

PORT THROTTLE

STARBOARD-ENGINE CLUTCH

WHEEL

ENGINE STOP

TRIM TABS

STARBOARD THROTTLE

Cruising sailboats are designed to accommodate skipper and crew on *offshore passages* and on *coastal cruises*, called *coasting*. Although most yachts over 20 feet in length are equipped with mechanical propulsion, called *auxiliary power*, crews rely on a selection of sails cut to particular specifications for different wind conditions.

A sailboat moving before, or in front of , the wind is said to be *running*; when moving across the wind it is *reaching*; when sailing into the wind it is *tacking*.

Shifting sails from one side of the boat to the other is called a *tack* when sailing into the wind, a *jibe* when sailing off the wind.

DECK

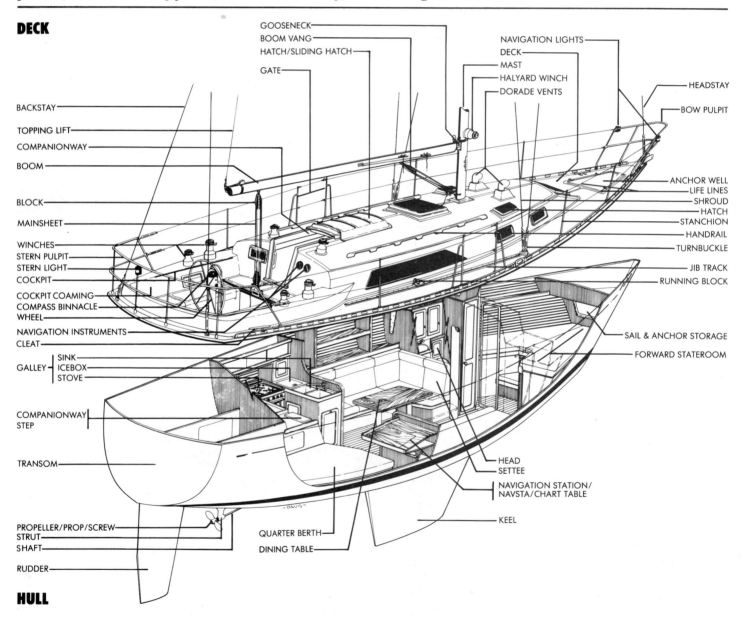

HULL

Labels (clockwise/left side):
BACKSTAY
TOPPING LIFT
COMPANIONWAY
BOOM
BLOCK
MAINSHEET
WINCHES
STERN PULPIT
STERN LIGHT
COCKPIT
COCKPIT COAMING
COMPASS BINNACLE
WHEEL
NAVIGATION INSTRUMENTS
CLEAT
GALLEY — SINK / ICEBOX / STOVE
COMPANIONWAY STEP
TRANSOM
PROPELLER/PROP/SCREW
STRUT
SHAFT
RUDDER

Top labels:
GOOSENECK
BOOM VANG
HATCH/SLIDING HATCH
GATE
NAVIGATION LIGHTS
DECK
MAST
HALYARD WINCH
DORADE VENTS

Right labels:
HEADSTAY
BOW PULPIT
ANCHOR WELL
LIFE LINES
SHROUD
HATCH
STANCHION
HANDRAIL
TURNBUCKLE
JIB TRACK
RUNNING BLOCK
SAIL & ANCHOR STORAGE
FORWARD STATEROOM

Lower/interior labels:
HEAD
SETTEE
NAVIGATION STATION/NAVSTA/CHART TABLE
KEEL
QUARTER BERTH
DINING TABLE

COMMISSIONER'S TROPHY— BASEBALL

STANLEY CUP— HOCKEY

OLYMPIC MEDAL

LOMBARDI TROPHY— PRO FOOTBALL

DAVIS CUP— TENNIS

O'BRIEN TROPHY— PRO BASKETBALL

**U.S. OPEN TROPHY—
GOLF**

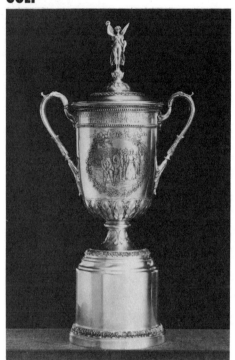

**AMERICA'S CUP—
YACHTING**

**INDIANAPOLIS 500 TROPHY—
AUTO RACING**

**CHAMPIONSHIP BELT—
BOXING**

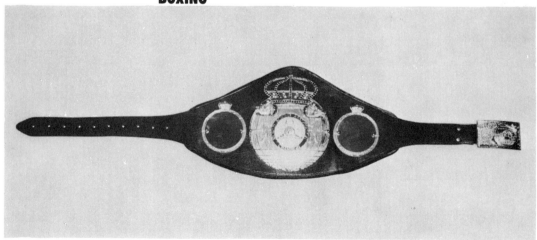

INDEX

Abdomen, martial arts striking point 126
abdomen/abdominal muscles/abdominal wall/'abdominals,' bodybuilder 36
abdominals pose, bodybuilding 36
able zone, football 77
absence of blade, fencing 66
acceleration, sprints (track and field) 174
acceleration contest, drag racing 20
access door, Formula One aircraft (air racing) 4
ace, tennis 170
ace/hole-in-one, golf scorecard 86
Achilles' tendon, martial arts striking point 126
acrobatic movement, balance beam (gymnastics) 98
'action,' fishing rod 10
action bolt/king pin/truck bolt, roller skate 140
action nut/lock nut, roller skate 140
ad court/left service court, platform tennis 133
ad court/left service court, tennis 169
Adam's apple, martial arts striking point 126
adjustable back rest/steering handle, fighting chair (angling) 15
adjustable foot rest, fighting chair (angling) 15
adjustable front gimbal/gusseted main gimbal, fighting chair (angling) 15
adjustable primary wing part, sports car 22
adjustable rear wing/spoiler/tail, sports car 22
adjustable seat, kayak 45
adjustable secondary wing part, sports car 22
adjustment screw/block lock, starting blocks (track and field) 174
advance lead foot, fencing 67
advancing foot, race walking technique (track and field) 179
aerial sports 1–7
aerobatic box, aerial sports 1
aerobatics 1
aerobatics, aerial sports 1–3
aerofoil/airfoil, race car 22
aft, yachting 202
aft crossbeam, yachting 203
aft deck, kayak 45
afterdeck, rowing shell 142
afterguard, yacht-racing crew 199
age, past performance chart (horse racing) 103
aglet, ice hockey skate 108
aid line, orienteering compass 132
aikido, martial arts 124
aikidoists, aikido (martial arts) 124
aileron, biplane (aerial sports–aerobatics) 2
aileron slave tube, biplane (aerial sports–aerobatics) 2
ailerons, glider (aerial sports) 6
aim, spinning cast (angling) 12
aim off, orienteering 132
air blower, dragster 21
air chuck, automobile racing pit 19
air filter, motocross bike 129
air flight position/air foil position, ski jumping 153
air foil/front wing/spoiler, dragster 21
air foil/main wing, dragster 21

air hose/regulator hose, scuba diver 58
air intake/cooling duct, race car 17
air intake/radiator, race car 17
air racing, aerial sports 4
air resistance, luge 118
air rifle, shooting 144
air scoop, motocross bike 129
air scoop/intake valves, dragster 21
air scoops, Nordic skiing 153
air speed indicator, glider cockpit (aerial sports) 6
air spring, bobsled 34
air starts, air racing 4
air vents, ski helmet 152
aircraft name, biplane (aerial sports–aerobatics) 2
aligner, canoeing & kayaking 44
all around/decathlon, track and field 188
all-around gymnast, gymnastics 87
all fives, clockface game (darts) 53
alley, platform tennis court 133
alley, tennis court 169
alley (for defensive lineman), football 77
alley line, platform tennis court 133
alleys/lanes, bowling 38, 39
allowance races, horse racing 102
Alpine skiing 150
alternate, football officials 80
altimeter, ballooning basket 5
altimeter, Formula One aircraft cockpit (air racing) 4
altimeter, glider cockpit (aerial sports) 6
altimeter setting knob, Formula One aircraft cockpit (air racing) 4
altimeter setting knob, glider cockpit (aerial sports) 6
aluminum rim, dragster front wheel 21
amateur boxers, boxing 41
amber/yellow pre-starting lights, drag racing Christmas tree 21
ambulance, automobile racetrack 18
amidships, yachting 202
'ammo'/shotgun shells/cartridges, marksman (shooting) 147
ammo pouch/shell bag, skeet shooter 147
amplitude, gymnastics 88
anal fin, fish 9
anatomy of a wave, surfing 161
anchor man, relays (track and field) 175
anchor/pin, starting blocks (track and field) 174
anchor point, archery 16
anchor rode, motoryacht deck 205
anchor well, cruising sailboat (yachting) 208
anchorages, yachting 205
anemometer, competition fishing boat 207
angled, tennis 170
angler, angling 8
angling 8-15
ankle extension, baseball catcher's equipment 26
antenna, race car 17
anti-friction pad, ski binding 152
anti-reverse lever, big game reel (angling) 15
anti-reverse lever, trolling reel (angling) 13
anti-reverse lever/anti-reverse lock, spinning reel (angling) 12
anti-submarine belt/crotch strap, drag racing 20

'antireverse,' fly reel (angling) 11
apex, ballooning 5
apparatus, gymnastics 87
apparel & accessory pockets, golf bag 84
'apple'/horsehide/baseball 26
approach/carry position, javelin throwing technique (track and field) 180
approach/runway, bowling lane 38
approach/run-up, high-jump straddle (track and field) 185
approach/runway, javelin throwing sector (track and field) 180
apron, boxing ring 41
apron/fringe/collar/froghair, golf course green 82
apron/paved shoulder, automobile racetrack 18
apron/tare, kendo (martial arts) 128
aprons, ski jump (water skiing) 193
arabesque, gymnastics 88
arabesque spin/parallel spin/camel spin, freestye figure skating 73
arc/foul line/scratch line/toe board, javelin throwing sector (track and field) 180
arc/'rocker,' luge 118
arch, football equipment 79
archer/bowman in hold position, archery 16
archery 16
areas of play, football 77
arena, dressage (equestrian events) 63
arm, fighting chair (angling) 15
arm cushion, fighting chair (angling) 15
arm extension, fencing 66, 67
arm guard/bracer, archery 16
arm-leg developmental harmony, bodybuilder 37
armpit, martial arts striking point 126
armstand dive 57
aro/frame, jai alai cesta 113
around the buoys, yachting 199
arrow, archery 16
arrow rest, archery bow 16
arrowhead/point/pile/head, target arrow (archery) 16
articulation, bobsled 34
artificial bait, angling 8
artificial court, bocce 35
artificial flies, angling 10, 11
artificially raised curve, luge 118
artistic impression, freestyle figure skating 72
ascot, dressage turnout (equestrian events) 63
aspirin/rising fastball/bullet, pitch movement (baseball) 29
assault/match/bout, fencing 65
assigned weight to be carried/handicap, horse-racing program entry 103
association football/soccer 155-157
asymmetrical bars/uneven parallel bars, gymnastics 97
at bat/batters/hitters, baseball scoreboard 27
athletic shoe, field hockey goalie 69
athwartship, yachting 203
attachment loops, basketball hoop 30
attack area/front court, volleyball court 191
attack by male, karate kumite (martial arts) 120

attack line/rear spiker's line, volleyball court 191
attack points, orienteering 132
attack zone/half-volley & mid-court overhead zone, tennis 171
attacker, soccer 155
attackers, field hockey pitch 68
attackmen, lacrosse field 115
attempt board, weightlifting 195
attic/upstairs/belfry, boxing slang 42
auto inflation hose, scuba diver (diving/spear fishing) 58
automatic direction finding antenna, competition fishing boat 207
automatic scoreboard, Olympic swimming pool 163
automatic scorer/console, bowling 39
automobile racing 17-22
auxiliary power, yachting 208
avoidable hinders, racquetball 136
axel jump, freestyle figure skating 73
axel lift, freestyle figure skating 72
axis, figure skating 71
axle, roller skate 140
axle nut, roller skate 140

Back, wave (surfing) 161
back alley/doubles service area, badminton court 23
back arch/cantle, polo saddle 134
back/belly side, archery bow 16
back boundary line/singles long service line, badminton court 23
back crawl, swimming 164, 165
back double biceps pose, bodybuilding 36
back extension roll, gymnastics 88
back fist, martial arts fighting 126
back hand, martial arts fighting 127
back handspring, gymnastics 88
back judge, football officials 80
back layout, synchronized swimming position 162
back line, volleyball court 190, 191
back outside spin/death spiral, freestyle figure skating 72
back pike, synchronized swimming position 162
back score line, curling 50
back screen/back wall, platform tennis court 133
back sideplate/tail plate, fly reel (angling) 11
back sizer, football helmet 79
back-stance knife hand, karate kata (martial arts) 121
back walkover, gymnastics 89
back walkover split, gymnastics 89
back wall, court handball 99
back wall, racquetball court 136
back wall, squash racquets court 160
backboard, basketball court 30
backboard, field hockey goal 69
backboards, ice hockey rink 108
backcourt, platform tennis court 133
backcourt, tennis court 169
backcourt area, squash racquets court 160
backcourt players/halfbacks, team handball 100
backfield line, football 77
backhand/two-fisted backhand, tennis stroke 171
backlash, angling 12

backroll protector, ice hockey glove 110
backs, football formation 76
backs, polo ground 134
backs, rugby scrummage formation 143
backs, soccer formations 156
backs, volleyball 190
back's stripe, polo 135
backspin, tennis 172
backstay, cruising sailboat (yachting) 208
backstop, shuffleboard court 148
backstretch, dog racetrack 59
backstretch, horse-racing track 101
backstretch/crossover straight/crossing
    zone, speed skating rink 159
backstroke, swimming 164
backstroke start handgrip, Olympic
    swimming pool 163
backstroke turning line/flag line,
    Olympic swimming pool 163
backswing, golf stroke 83
backswing, tennis serve 170
backswing and stride, batting (baseball)
    27
backswing/exposition, softball pitcher's
    delivery 158
backup ball/reverse curve, bowling 39
backward roll, gymnastics 88
backward short-leg, cricket position 48
backwards dive 56
badminton 23
bag/envelope, ballooning 5
bag holder, golf cart 84
bag retaining line, sky diving parachute
    (aerial sports) 7
bag/sack, baseball slang 25
bag well, golf cart 84
bail/pickup arm, spinning reel (angling)
    12
bait, angling 8–15
bait, basic fishing rig 9
bait, competition fishing boat 206
bait/bottom-feeder bait, double-level
    fishfinder rig (angling) 14
bait box/freezer, competition fishing
    boat 206
bait cage, angling 9
bait casting, angling 12
bait fish, angling 14
bait leader, live minnow rig (angling) 14
baitfish/minnow, angling 14
baker zone, football 77
balance, bodybuilding 36
balance, figure skating 71
balance beam, gymnastics 98
bale/butt/matt/boss, archery target 16
balkline, croquet 49
ball, baseball 26
ball, basketball 30, 31
ball, bocce 35
ball, bowling 38
ball, croquet 49
ball, field hockey 68
ball, golf 84
ball, hurling 106
ball, lacrosse 115, 116
ball, platform tennis 133
ball, polo 135
ball, rugby 143
ball, soccer 155
ball, softball 158
ball, squash racquets 160
ball, table tennis 166
ball, team handball 100

ball, tennis 169
ball, water polo 192
ball, women's rhythmic exercise
    (gymnastics) 91
ball bearings, roller skate 140
ball boys, tennis 168
ball carriers, football formation 76
ball/football/Gaelic football 81
ball/head, hammer (track and field) 183
ball identification, golf 84
ball of foot, martial arts fighting 127
ball/pelota, jai alai 113
ball placement, tennis 170
ball pocket, golf bag 84
ball return, bowling lane 38
ball return capping/'subway ball return,'
    bowling lane 38
ball socket stepped mast, yachting 203
ballast, ballooning 5
ballast, bobsledding 34
ballet leg, synchronized swimming
    position 162
ballet leg double position, synchronized
    swimming position 162
ballooners, ballooning 5
ballooning, aerial sports 5
balustrade/fence, cycling velodrome 52
bamboo sword/shinai, kendo (martial
    arts) 128
bandage, eventing (equestrian events) 64
bandage, harness horse racing 103
bandages, racehorse 102
bandages/wrapper, boxing slang 42
bank, stock car racing 22
banked, cycling velodrome 52
bantamweights, boxing 43
bar, hurdle (track and field) 176
bar, weightlifting 195
bar/crossbar, high-jumping area (track
    and field) 185
bar/crossbar, steeplechase dry hurdle
    (track and field) 177
barb, fishhook 9
barber chair/fighting chair, competition
    fishing boat 207
barber marker, yachting 203
bareback bronc rider, rodeo 137
bareback rigging & pad, rodeo 137
barrage, fencing 67
barrel, baseball bat 26
barrel, dart 53
barrel, rifle (shooting) 144
barrel, shotgun (skeet and trapshooting)
    146
barrel, softball bat 158
barrel, target pistol 145
barrel racer, rodeo 138
barrel roll, aerobatics (aerial sports) 3
barrel stock, spear gun (spear fishing) 58
barrels, rodeo cowgirls barrel racing 138
barrier, mobile starting gate (harness
    horse racing) 104
barrier/railing/traffic line, speed (roller)
    skating 140
bars, equestrian show jumping fences 62
bars, parallel (gymnastics) 96
base, bowling pin 39
base, downrigger (angling) 13
base, drag racing Christmas tree 21
base, horizontal bar (gymnastics) 95
base, steeplechase dry hurdle (track and
    field) 177

base, vaulting horse (gymnastics) 92
base chord, skeet shooting range 147
base line, shuffleboard court 148
base line/end line, basketball court 30
base line/end line, table tennis 166
base locking, downrigger (angling) 13
base of cerebellum, martial arts striking
    point 126
base on balls, baseball 25
base path, baseball field 25
base runners, baseball 26
base spot circles, roller hockey rink 140
base spots, roller hockey rink 140
base/support, bowling console 39
baseball, clockface game (darts) 53
baseball field 25
baseball/horsehide/'apple,' 26
baseball mitt 26
baseball slang, ball 25
baseball 24–28
baseline, platform tennis court 133
baseline, tennis court 169
baseline position, tennis 171
basic attack formation, team handball
    100
basic competitive figures & maneuvers,
    aerobatics (aerial sports) 2
basic defenses, basketball 33
basic fishing rig, angling 9
basic formations, football 77
basic formations, soccer 156
basic movements, gymnastics 88, 89
basic plays, ice hockey 111
basket, on basketball court 30
basket/cesta, jai alai 113
basket/field goal, basketball 30
basket/gondola, ballooning 5
basket/hoop/goal, basketball 30
basket/snow ring, Alpine ski pole 150
basket/snow ring, cross country skier
    154
basketball court 30
basketball 30–33
basketball 32
bass boat/bass rig, angling 13
bat, baseball 26
bat, cricket 47
bat, softball 158
bat/paddle/racket, table tennis 166
bat/whip/crop/stick, horse racing 102
bath/pool, water polo field 192
baton, relays (track and field) 175
batsman, cricket pitch 48
batsman, cricketer 47
batsman's gloves, cricket 47
batten, iceboat 107
battens, hang glider (aerial sports) 6
battens, mainsail (yachting) 200
battens/full-length battens, yachting 203
batter's box, baseball field dimensions 25
batter's defensive position, baseball
    scoreboard 27
batter's equipment, baseball 28
batter's uniform number, baseball
    scoreboard 27
batting average, baseball scoreboard 27
batting glove, baseball 26
batting helmet/hard hat, baseball 26
batting/hitting/swinging, baseball 27
batting order, baseball scoreboard 27
batting practice shirt/pre-game jersey,
    baseball 26
batting stance, baseball 27

base, vaulting horse (gymnastics)
BC inflator mouthpiece, scuba diver
    (diving/spear fishing) 58
beach, angling 14
beam, balance beam (gymnastics) 98
bear hand, martial arts fighting 127
'bear trap' binding/cable binding, ski
    jumping 153
bearing cover, spinning reel (angling) 12
bearings, skateboard 149
'beast's lair'/discus & hammer safety
    cage, 182
beat board/springboard/ruether board,
    gymnastics 92
belfry/attic/upstairs, boxing slang 42
bell, boxing 41
bell, track and field 189
bell bead, spinner (angling) 12
bell boot, harness horse racing 103
bell plug/guard socket, electric foil
    fencing 66
bell sinker, deep trolling rig (angling) 13
belly, bowling pin 39
belly, surfboard 161
belly/venter, fish 9
belt, boxing slang 42
belt, football uniform 79
bench, basketball court 30
bench rest, rifle shooting position 144
bend, curling 50
bend, fishhook 9
bent knee, synchronized swimming
    position 162
'berm'/bullet barricade/richochet
    fencing, shooting range 145
bertillion card/identity card, dog racing
    59, 60
betting board, jai alai 112
betting odds for next game, jai alai 112
betting payoffs, jai alai
    scoreboard/betting board 112
betting pool, horse-racing tote board 102
betting ticket/parimutuel ticket, horse
    racing 103
bettors, horse racing 103
bezel, stopwatch (track and field) 189
biathlon targets 154
bib, fencing mask 65
bib, lacrosse 116
bib/entry number, ski jumper 153
biceps brachialis, bodybuilder 37
biceps brachii, bodybuilding 37
biceps femoris, bodybuilder 36
biceps muscle, bodybuilder 36
big game fish, deep sea fishing 15
big game reel, deep sea fishing 15
big game rod, deep sea fishing 15
bigbore, rifle shooting 144
bike, motorcycling 129
bilge and fuel alarms, competition
    fishing boat 207
bill, fish 9
bill/lip, plug (angling) 12
binding, running shoe (track and field)
    178
binding, ski jumping boot 153
binding, water skier 193
binding/laces, baseball glove 26
binding/trim tape, tennis racket 169
bindings, water ski 193
binnacle, cruising sailboat (yachting) 208
biplane (aerial sports–aerobatics) 2
bird/shuttlecock/shuttle, badminton 23

birdcage/cage/face mask, football helmet 79
birdie, golf 86
birds/pigeons/targets/clays, skeet and trapshooting 147
bit, dressage bridle (equestrian events) 63
bit, polo pony 134
bit, racehorse 102
bit, rodeo horse 138
bitches, female racing dogs 59
bits, harness horse racing 103
'black,' pistol shooting target 145
bladder, volleyball 190
blade, canoe paddle 44
blade, fencing sword 65
blade, ice hockey goalie stick 110
blade, oar & scull 142
blade, scuba diver (diving/spear fishing) 58
blade, spinner (angling) 12
blade decal, spinner (angling) 12
blade/head, table tennis paddle 166
blade positions, figure skating 71
blade/rod tip, spinning rod (angling) 12
blade/runner, ice hockey skate 108, 110
blades, kayak paddle 45
blank, big game rod (angling) 15
blanket, dog racing 59, 60
blanket, rodeo horse 138
blanket/jacket, dog racing 59
blanket/pad, rifle shooting 144
bleachers, baseball field 25
blind pass, relays (track and field) 175
blinker hood, racehorse bridle 102
blinkers/blinders/rogue's badge, horse racing 102
block, cruising sailboat (yachting) 208
block/pedal, starting blocks (track and field) 174
blockers, football formation 76
blockers, volleyball 190
blocking, basketball officials' signal 32
blocking, football 79
blocking a kick, karate (martial arts) 122
blocking a punch, karate (martial arts) 122
blocking back, football formation 76
blocks lock/adjustment screw, starting blocks (track and field) 174
blood knot, angling 10
bloodline, horse-racing program entry 103
blouse, baseball uniform 26
blow/open/miss, bowling 39
blue line/zone marking, ice hockey rink 108
blue tees/championship tees/professional tees, golf 82
board, sailboard (yachting) 201
board/surfboard, surfing 161
board/telltale/tin, squash racquets court 160
boarding, ice hockey officials' signal 111
boarding ladder, competition fishing boat 207
boards, bowling lane 38
boards, ice hockey 109
boat name, iceboat 107
boat number, iceboat 107
boated, angling 8
bobber/float, basic fishing rig 9
'boblets,' bobsledding 34

bobrun/course, bobsledding 34
bobs, bobsledding 34
bobsled suit 34
bobsledders 35
bobsledding 34
bocce ball 35
bocce 35
body, discus (track and field) 182
body, downrigger (angling) 13
body, dragster 21
body, dry fly (angling) 11
body, plug (angling) 12
body balance/on-guard position, fencing 67
body-checks, ice hockey 109
body cord, fencing strip 66
body pad/chest protector, ice hockey goalkeeper 110
body panel, race car 17
bodybuilding/physique 36
bogey, golf 86
boinger/rear shock absorber, motorcycle 130
bolt, rifle (shooting) 144
bolt-on pedal, track racing bicycle 52
bomb/fly, football pass pattern 78
boom, cruising sailboat (yachting) 208
boom, downrigger (angling) 13
boom, iceboating 107
boom, yachting 202
boom vang, cruising sailboat (yachting) 208
boom/wishbone, sailboard (yachting) 201
boot, boxing 41
boot, cricket 47
boot, cross country skier 154
boot, dressage turnout (equestrian events) 63
boot, field hockey goalie 69
boot, figure skate 71
boot, ice hockey skate 108, 110
boot, jockey (horse racing) 102
boot, racehorse 102
boot, roller skate 140
boot, rugby 143
boot, ski jumping 153
boot, sky diving (aerial sports) 7
boot, weightlifting 195
boot/bootie, scuba diver (diving/spear fishing) 58
boot/rubber cleats, field hockey 69
boot/shoe, soccer 155
booties/boots/shoes, luge 118
boots (see also shoes)
boots, equestrian events 62
boots, harness horse racing 103
boots, motocross rider 131
boots, wrestling 196
bore, shooting 144
bore, shotgun (skeet and trapshooting) 146
boss, hurling hurley 106
bottom cuff, golf bag 84
bottom feeders, angling 14
bottom fish, angling 14
bottom fist, martial arts fighting 126
bottom girdle, ballooning 5
bottom net cable, volleyball net 191
bottom of the order, baseball scoreboard 27
bottom trolling, angling 13
bounce, tennis 172

bounce-out, long-jumping technique (track and field) 184
boundary, cricket ground 48
boundary line, gymnastics 91
boundary line/foul line, discus & hammer cage (track and field) 182
boundary ropes, water polo field 192
boundary/contest center/area circle, wrestling 196
bout, title (boxing) 41
bout, wrestling 196
bout/match/assault, fencing 65
bout/match/fight, boxing 41
bouting, fencing 67
bow, canoe 44
bow, kayak 45
bow, stopwatch (track and field) 189
bow, yacht-racing crew 199
bow, yachting 202
bow arm, archery 16
bow ball, sculling heat (rowing) 141
bow coaming, canoe 44
bow control panel, bass boat 13
bow grab loop, slalom kayaking 46
bow marker, sculling heat (rowing) 141
bow-mounted depth sounder, bass boat 13
bow oar, rowing crew 142
bow position, javelin throwing technique (track and field) 180
bow pulpit, cruising sailboat (yachting) 208
bow rail, competition fishing boat 206
bow sight, archery bow 16
bowl-riding event, skateboarding 149
bowl/wood, lawn bowling 117
bowler, bowling 38
bowler, cricket ground & pitch 48
bowler, cricketer 47
bowler mid-on, cricket position 48
bowlers, lawn bowling 117
bowling 38
bowling crease, cricket pitch 48
bowling green/green, lawn bowling 117
bowls, cricket 47
bowls, lawn bowling 117
bowsprit, competition fishing boat 206
bowstring, archery bow 16
box, baseball slang 25
'box,' luge 118
box man, football officials 80
box/planting box/vault box, pole vault (track and field) 186
boxer/fighter, boxing scorecard 41
boxes/starting traps, dog racing 59
boxing glove 41
boxing mask, sparring equipment (boxing) 42
boxing/prize fighting 40
boxing ring/prize ring, 41
boxing shoe/boot 41
boxing slang 42
brace member, basketball backboard 30
bracer/arm guard, archery 16
brachioradialis, bodybuilder 36
bracket, figure skating 71
braided mane, dressage turnout (equestrian events) 63
braided tail, polo pony 134
brake, luge 118
brake, motocross bike 129
brake, ski binding 152

brake/brake screw, spinning reel (angling) 12
brake cooling air intake scoop, race car 17
brake cooling duct, sports car 22
brake fluid reservoir, race car 17
brake handle, bobsled 34
brake lever, road racing bicycle 51
brake line, motocross bike 129
brake pedal, kart 114
brakeman, bobsledding 34
brakeman's seat, bobsled 34
branch/knuckle bow, sabre (fencing) 65
brassie/number two wood, golf club 84, 85
bread head, curling broom 50
breadbasket/labonza/lunch box, boxing slang 42
break, long and triple jump (track and field) 184
breakaway coupling, angling 13
breakdown, wrestling 198
breast collar, harness horse racing 103
breast collar, rodeo horse 138
breast plate, polo pony 134
breast protector, fencing 65
breastplate, eventing (equestrian events) 64
breastplate/do, kendo (martial arts) 128
breaststroke, swimming 164, 165
breath, swimming 164
breathhold diving, competitive diving 58
breechblock, shotgun (skeet and trapshooting) 146
breeches, equestrian events 61, 64
breeches, polo 134, 135
breeder, past performance chart (horse racing) 103
bridge, bowling ball 38
bridge, wrestling 198
bridge of nose, martial arts striking point 126
bridle, dressage turnout (equestrian events) 63
bridle, equestrian events 62
bridle, harness horse racing 103
bridle, polo pony 134
bridle, racehorse 102
bridle, water skier 193
broad jump/long jump, track and field 184
brogues/wading shoes, flyfisherman 10
broken, tennis 170
bronc/bucking bronco, rodeo 137
Brooklyn pocket/Jersey side/left-handed pocket, bowling 39
brought to wire, deep sea fishing 15
browband, dressage bridle (equestrian events) 63
bucket harness/sea harness, fighting chair harness (angling) 15
bucking rein/bronc rein/buck rein, rodeo saddle bronc riding 138
buckle, harness horse racing 103
buckles ski boot 152
bucktail lure, deep trolling rig (angling) 13
bucktails, angling 10
'builders,' bodybuilding 36
bulb/magnifying lens, orienteering compass 132
bulge, figure skating 71
bull, rodeo 138

...l riding, rodeo 138
...ldogging/steer wrestling, rodeo 138
...llet barricade/richochet
...ncing/'berm,' shooting range 144
...llet/rising fastball/aspirin, pitch movement (baseball) 29
...llet/slug/head, cartridge (shooting) 145
...lpens,' stock car racing 22
...llings,' karting 114
...llseye/gold/10, archery target 16
...llseye, pistol shooting target 145
...llseye/25-point ring, dart board 53
...lly,' field hockey 68
...mper, shot put shoes 181
...mper cowl, bobsled 34
...mper plate, weightlifting 195
...nker/sand trap, golf course 82
...nils'/rear bumper, bobsled 34
...bum area, baseball slang 25
...buoyancy compensator/flotation device, scuba diver 58
...buoy, water skiing 193
...buoys, yachting 201
...burner, ballooning basket 5
...burner assembly, ballooning 5
...burnout director, drag strip 20
...butt, big game rod (angling) 15
...butt, fly rod (angling) 11
...butt, racquetball racquet 136
...butt, spear gun (spear fishing) 58
...butt/butt end/knob, lacrosse stick 115
...butt cap, spinning reel (angling) 12
...butt end/cap, badminton racket 23
...butt guide, spinning reel (angling) 12
...butt guide/ring guide, fly rod (angling) 11
...butt plate, shotgun (skeet and trap shooting) 146
...butt section, spinning rod (angling) 12
...butt stock, spear gun (spear fishing) 58
...butterfly, swimming 164, 165
...butting, boxing foul 43
...button, badminton shuttlecock 23
...button, boxing slang 42
...button/tip/point/end, fencing sword 65
...buttonhook/curl-in, football pass pattern 78

Cable binding/ "bear trap" binding, ski jumping 153
cable wheel assembly, downrigger (angling) 13
caddy cart/golf cart 84
cage, baseball catcher's equipment 26
cage/face mask/birdcage, football helmet 79
cage/goal, water polo 192
calf, bodybuilder 36
calf, martial arts striking point 126
calf, rodeo 138
calf roping, rodeo 138
calf-roping rope/lariat, rodeo 138
calibers, shooting 144
calibrated tape/tape, lawn bowling 117
caliente/safety helmet, eventing (equestrian events) 64
calipers, lawn bowling 117
camel back ramp, motocross track 129
camel spin, roller skating 139
camel spin/parallel spin/arabesque spin, freestyle figure skating 73
camera position, automobile racetrack 18
campo, bocce court 35
cancha/jai alai court 113

candlepins, bowling 38
cane fencing, field hockey goalie's leg guard 69
cannonball, tennis 170
canoeing and kayaking 44–46
canoeists 44
canopy, biplane (aerial sports–aerobatics) 2
canopy, sky diving parachute (aerial sports) 7
canter, dressage (equestrian events) 63
cantle/back arch, polo saddle 134
cantle/hind bow, western saddle (rodeo) 137
canvas, boxing ring 41
cap, football equipment 79
cap, swimming 163
cap, water polo equipment 192
cap/butt end, badminton racket 23
cap/polo helmet 134
captain, yachting 206
carburetor, motocross bike 129
carburetor, motorcycle 130
carburetor heat control, Formula One aircraft cockpit (air racing) 4
card, golf 86
card/scorecard, boxing 41
career money run, past performance chart (horse racing) 103
carpet, baseball slang 25
carpet cover, gymnastics 91
carpet/putting surface, golf course green 82
carriage, bodybuilding 36
carry, pole vaulting technique (track and field) 186
carry position/approach, javelin throwing technique (track and field) 180
carrying handle, ballooning basket 5
carrying sling/shoulder sling, golf bag 84
cartridge block, rifle shooting bench 144
cartridge/bullet, shooting 145
cartwheel, gymnastics 89, 98
cartwheel/tumbling movement, balance beam (gymnastics) 98
case, cartridge (shooting) 145
case, tape measure (track and field) 189
case head, cartridge (shooting) 145
cast, flycasting technique (angling) 11
cast, spinning cast (angling) 12
cast wrap, uneven parallell bars (gymnastics) 97
casting decks/casting platforms, bass boat 13
castle, synchronized swimming position 162
catamaran, yachting 201
catamaran hulls, powerboat racing (yachting) 204
catch, sculling (rowing) 141
catch a crab, sweep rowing 142
catch-as-catch-can, freestyle wrestling 198
catch fencing, sports car racing 22
catch glove, ice hockey goalkeeper 110
catcher, baseball player position 25
catcher's box, baseball field dimensions 25
catcher's equipment/'tools of ignorance,' baseball 26
catcher's mitt, baseball catcher's equipment 26

catches, angling 8
catching features, orienteering 132
caudal fin/tail fin, fish 9
caudal keels, fish 9
caudal peduncle, fish 9
cauliflower ear, boxing slang 42
CB radio, hang glider (aerial sports) 6
ceiling, court handball 99
ceiling, racquetball court 136
cells, sky diving parachute (aerial sports) 7
'cement snake'/cement tube, luge 118
cement chin, boxing slang 42
center, ice hockey 110
center, polo ground 134
center back/center fullback, soccer formations 156
center back/center fullback, soccer formations 156
center back/stopper, soccer formations 156
center back/sweeper/libero, soccer formations 156
center circle, basketball court 30
center circle, ice hockey rink 108
center circle, roller hockey rink 140
center circle, soccer field 156
center circle/contest area/boundary, wrestling 196
center court/centre court, tennis 168
center deck, unlimited hydroplane (yachting) 204
center fielder, baseball player position 25
center flag, field hockey pitch 68
center flag, soccer field 156
center forward, field hockey pitch 68
center forward, soccer formations 156
center halfback, field hockey pitch 68
center letters, equestrian events dressage arena 63
center line, badminton court 23
center line, fencing strip 66
center line, field hockey pitch 68
center line, roller hockey rink 140
center line, team handball 100
center line, tennis court 169
center line, volleyball court 191
center line/doubles line, table tennis 166
center line/halfway line/midway line, soccer field 156
center line/red line, ice hockey rink 108
center mark, platform tennis court 133
center mark, tennis court 169
center of court, squash racquets court 160
center of rink marker, lawn bowling 117
center players, lacrosse 115
center service line/half-court line, squash racquets court 160
center/'snapper,' football formation 76
center spot/center field mark, soccer field 156
center strap/net anchor, tennis court 169
centerboard boats, yachting 201
centerboard/center plate, yachting 203
centerboard line, yachting 203
centerline divider, drag strip 20
centers, Gaelic football 81
centers, hurling 106
centers, ice hockey 110
centers, rugby scrummage formation 143
cesta/basket, jai alai 113
chain, kart 114

chain, motocross bike 129
chain drive, kart 114
chain gang, football officials 80
chain ring, road racing bicycle 51
chain stay, road racing bicycle 51
chair locking handle, fighting chair (angling) 15
chalked, gymnastics 95, 96
champagne bottle, ballooning basket 5
championship tees/blue tees/professional tees, golf 82
Chandelle, aerobatics (aerial sports) 3
change of direction/'stutz,' parallel bars routine (gymnastics) 96
channel/gutter, bowling lane 38
chaps, rodeo 137
charging, ice hockey officials' signal 111
charging, soccer foul 157
charging/offensive foul, basketball officials' signal 32
'charity stripe'/goal line/free throw line, basketball court 30
charlie zone, football 77
chart, powerboat command console (yachting) 204
charts, yachting 205
chassis, drag racing funny car 20
check, orienteering 132
check bit, harness horse racing 103
check rein, harness horse racing 103
check runner, pitcher's stretch position (baseball) 28
checkered flag, automobile racing 17
checkering, shotgun (skeet and trapshooting) 146
checkpoint, yachting 205
cheek, bowling pin 39
cheek piece, biathalon 154
cheekstrap, dressage bridle (equestrian events) 63
chest & stomach pad, lacrosse 116
chest-high waders/'stocking-foot waders'/ 'stocking wader,' flyfisherman 10
chest protector, baseball catcher's equipment 26
chest protector/body pad, ice hockey goalkeeper 110
chest raphe/chest depression/pectoral separation, bodybuilder 37
chest strap, sky diving parachute (aerial sports) 7
chicanes, automobile racing 17
chief of take-off, ski jumping 153
chief operating station/control, competition fishing boat 207
chief timekeeper, speed skating 159
chin, martial arts striking point 126
chin pad, lacrosse 116
chin piece, ski helmet 152
chin strap, cycling 51
chin strap, eventing (equestrian events) 64
chin strap, football helmet 79
chin strap, ice hockey player 110
chin strap, lacrosse 116
chin strap, polo player 134
chin strap, ski helmet 152
chin strap/tape, water polo cap 192
china chin/glass jaw/cement chin, boxing slang 42
chip, tennis 171

chock/fairlead, competition fishing boat 206
chop, tennis 171
chopper/defender/retriever, table tennis 167
choreography, bodybuilding 36
Christmas tree/starting lights, drag racing 20, 21
chuck, spinning reel (angling) 12
chukker, polo 134
chute, bobsledding 34
chute, horse-racing track 101
chute/bucking chute, rodeo plant 138
chute/sprints starting line, track and field 173
cinch, western saddle (rodeo) 137
cinta, jai alai cesta 113
circle, dressage figure (equestrian events) 63
circle/goal area, team handball 100
circle/ring, discus & hammer cage (track and field) 182
circle runner/pivot player, team handball 100
circle/shotput ring, track and field 181
circles, basketball court 30
circuit, motorcycling 129
claiming price, horse racing 102
claiming race, horse racing 102
clamp, downrigger (angling) 13
clamp, table tennis net 166
class, yacht racing 199
class symbol, iceboat 107
classes, boxing 43
clavicle, martial arts striking point 126
clay court, bocce 35
clays/targets/birds/pigeons, skeet and trapshooting 147
clean-and-jerk, weightlifting 194
'clean-up hitter,' baseball scoreboard 27
clearance, high-jump straddle (track and field) 185
cleat, competition fishing boat 206
cleat, cruising sailboat (yachting) 208
cleat, cycle racing shoe 51
cleat, motoryacht deck 205
cleats/spikes, baseball 26
clerk of the course, track and field 189
clevis, spinner (angling) 12
clew, mainsail (yachting) 200
climbs, aerobatics (aerial sports) 2
clinch, boxing strategy 43
clip/marker, croquet wicket 49
clip/pin/loop, basic fishing rig 9
clipped mane, polo pony 134
clippers/line clipper, flyfishing vest 10
clipping, football 80
clock, basketball court 30
clockface games, darts 53
'closed circuit' road race course, speed (roller) skating 140
closed-circuit road racing, automobile racing 17
closed-fist methods, martial arts fighting 126
closed gates, Alpine skiing 150
'closes out,' surfing 161
closure, golf glove 84
closure, ski boot 152
club symbol, iceboat 107
clubbing, water polo foul 192
clubhouse turn, horse-racing track 101

clubs, gymnastics 90
clutch, motocross bike 129
clutch, motorcycle 130
clutch cable, motocross bike 129
clutch cover, motocross bike 129
clutch shaft & bearing, downrigger (angling) 13
coach's box, baseball field 25
coach's diagram, football passing play 78
coach's diagram, football running play 77
coaming, competition fishing boat 207
coaming/cockpit rim/splash guard, kayak 45
coastal cruises, yachting 208
coasting, yachting 208
coat, equestrian show jumping 62
cobwebs, boxing slang 42
coccyx, martial arts striking point 126
cock feather, target arrow (archery) 16
cockpit, competition fishing boat 206
cockpit, competition fishing boat 206
cockpit, cruising sailboat (yachting) 208
cockpit, Formula One aircraft (air racing) 4
cockpit, glider (aerial sports) 6
cockpit, kayak 45
cockpit, unlimited hydroplane (yachting) 204
cockpit, yachting 202
cockpit canopy, glider (aerial sports) 6
cockpit coaming, cruising sailboat (yachting) 208
cockpit/driver's compartment, race car 19
cockpit fire-extinguisher activator button, race car 19
cocoon harness, hang glider (aerial sports) 6
coffin corner, football field 76
collar, Gaelic football sweater 81
collar, horizontal bar (gymnastics) 95
collar, hurling sweater 106
collar, ice hockey skate 108
collar, oar & scull 141
collar, weightlifting international standard barbell 195
collar/apron/fringe/froghair, golf course green 82
color, dog racing 60
color, horse-racing program entry 103
color, past performance chart (horse racing) 103
color of trunks, boxing scorecard 41
coloration and markings, dog racing bertillion card 60
colors/order of play, croquet 49
colors/silks, driver (harness horse racing) 103
colors/silks, jockey (horse racing) 102
column/upright/stanchion, basketball 30
comb/forecomb, shotgun (skeet and trap shooting) 146
combination jump/in and out, equestrian show jumping fence 62
combination shoe/round and swedge shoe, harness horse racing 103
command console, powerboat racing (yatching) 204
committee boat, Olympic yacht-racing course 199
companionway, cruising sailboat (yachting) 208

companionway door, motoryacht deck 205
companionway step, cruising sailboat (yachting) 208
comparison posing, bodybuilding 37
compass, competition fishing boat 207
compass, cruising sailboat (yachting) 208
compass, glider cockpit (aerial sports) 6
compass, orienteering 132
compass, powerboat command console (yachting) 204
compass, scuba diver (diving/spear fishing) 58
compass, yachting 203
compensator, archery bow 16
competition fishing boat 206
competition patch, weightlifter's singlet 195
competition suit/regulation suit/posing outfit, bodybuilding 37
competitive area, gymnastics 91
completed/completion, weightlifting two-hand snatch 195
components of a dive & judging points 54
compulsory dances, ice dancing (figure skating) 74
compulsory figures, roller skating 139
compulsory figures, synchronized swimming 162
compulsory routines, gymnastics 87
computer code/anti-counterfeiting code, parimutuel ticket (horse racing) 103
concrete retaining wall, sports car racing 22
concrete track, cycling velodrome 52
connector link, sky diving parachute (aerial sports) 7
console/automatic scorer, bowling 39
contact, batting (baseball) 27
contact, tennis serve 170
contest area/shiago, judo mat (martial arts) 123
contestant bib & number, cross country skier 154
contestant number, speed (roller) skating 140
contour, orienteering 132
control, figure skating 71
control, wrestling 196
control bar, hang glider (aerial sports) 6
control clipper/needle punch, orienteering 132
control console/chief operating station, competition fishing boat 207
control gates, whitewater canoe races 46
control marker, orienteering 132
control point card, orienteering 132
control point/check point/control, orienteering 132
control stick, Formula One aircraft cockpit (air racing) 4
control stick, glider cockpit (aerial sports) 6
control tower, automobile racetrack 18
control tower, rifle range (shooting) 144
conversion lines, football field 76
cooling duct/air intake, race car 17
cord grip, javelin (track and field) 180
corner, boxing ring 41
corner, squash racquets court 160
corner cushion/turnbuckle padding, boxing ring 41
corner flag, field hockey pitch 68

corner flag, soccer field 156
corner kick, soccer 156
corner kick area, soccer field 156
corner markers/pylons, speed (roller) skating 140
cornerbacks, football formation 76
cornermen/handlers/seconds, fighter's corner (boxing) 42
corners, baseball strike zone 26
costilla/ribs, jai alai cesta 113
costume, wrestling 196
costume (see also suit, uniform)
count, bowling 39
count, wrestling 196
count on batter, baseball scoreboard 27
counter, figure skating 71
counterbalance, trolling reel (angling) 13
counterholds, wrestling 198
course, equestrian show jumping 62
course, Formula One air racing 4
course, golf 82
course, iceboating 107
course, luge 118
course, rodeo cowgirls barrel racing 138
course, slalom (water skiing) 193
course/bobrun, bobsledding 34
course flags/signal flags, sailboarding race (yachting) 201
course planners, orienteering 132
course setters, orienteering 132
course starts, dog racetrack 59
course/track, dog racing 59
course vetters, orienteering 132
courses, Alpine skiing 150
courses, automobile racing 17–22
courses, luge 118
coursing greyhounds, dog racing 59
court, badminton 23
court, basketball 30
court, croquet 49
court, jai alai 113
court, platform tennis 133
court, racquetball 136
court, shuffleboard 148
court, squash racquets 160
court, team handball 100
court, tennis 168, 169
court handball 99
court hinders, racquetball 136
court position, tennis 171
court zones, tennis 171
courts, table tennis 166, 167
cover, baseball 26
cover, softball 158
cover plate, spinning reel (angling) 12
cover point, cricket position 48
cowboy boot, rodeo 137
cowboy hat, rodeo 137
cowboy skills, rodeo 137
cowgirls barrel racing, rodeo 138
cowling, race car 17
coxswain/cox, rowing crew 142
cradle, wrestling 198
crampit/hack, curling 50
crane, synchronized swimming position 162
crank, spinning reel (angling) 12
crank assembly, downrigger (angling) 13
crank bait/deep-diving plug, fishing tackle box 9

crank/crewman, competition fishing boat 207
crank handle, downrigger (angling) 13
crank handle, fly reel (angling) 11
crash helmet, automobile racing 17
crash helmet, karting 114
crash helmet, luge 118
crash helmet/safety helmet, iceboating 107
crash helmet/'skull cap', jockey (horse racing) 102
crawl/front crawl, swimming 164, 165
crease, cricket wicket 47
crease, roller hockey rink 140
creases, cricket pitch 48
creel, flyfisherman 10
creepers/spikes, iceboating 107
crest, wave (surfing) 161
crest/cresting, target arrow (archery) 16
crew, competition fishing boat 207
crews, sculling (rowing) 141
cricket 47, 48
cricket, clockface game (darts) 53
cricket grounds & fielding positions 48
cricket square 48
cricketers, cricket 47
crimp, cartridge (shooting) 145
critical point, ski jumping 153
crop/whip, eventing (equestrian events) 64
crop/whip/bat/stick, horse racing 102
croquet 49
cross, boxing punch 43
cross bar/top tube, track racing bicycle 52
cross beam/cross bar, soccer goal 155
cross-checking, ice hockey officials' signal 111
cross country, equestrian events 64
cross country ski 154
cross-court shot, tennis 171
cross-step, karate kata (martial arts) 121
cross strings, tennis racket 169
crossbar, field hockey goal 68
crossbar, football goal 75
crossbar, hurling net 106
crossbar, rugby goal 143
crossbar/bar, high-jumping area (track and field) 185
crossbar/bar, pole vault (track and field) 186
crossbar/bar, steeplechase dry hurdle (track and field) 177
crossbar, ice hockey goal 110
crossbar support, high-jumping area (track and field) 185
crossbars/spread, equestrian show jumping fence 62
crossing controller/flagman, speed skating rink 159
crossover step, javelin throwing technique (track and field) 180
crossover straight/crossing zone/backstretch, speed skating rink 159
crotch, court handball 99
crotch strap/anti submarine belt, drag racing 20
croup, pommel horse (gymnastics) 93
crown, croquet wicket 49
crown, golf wood 85
crown, tennis racket 169
crown stabilizer, football helmet 79

crown/start & stop button, stopwatch (track and field) 189
crownpiece, racehorse bridle 102
cruising, yachting 205
cruising sailboat, yachting 208
crupper, harness horse racing 103
Cuban Eight, aerobatics (aerial sports) 3
cue, shuffleboard 148
cue/pallino/jack/object ball, bocce 35
cuff, handball glove 99
cuff, ice hockey goalkeeper 110
cuff, ski boot 152
cuff padding, ski boot 152
cuissard, fencer 65
cum time/cumulative time, timer (track and field) 189
cup, curling stone 50
cup, eventing (equestrian events) 64
cup and ball holder, golf cart 84
cup/flyer, spinning reel (angling) 12
cup/hole, golf course green 82
cup/hole, golf putting 86
curl, curling 50
curling 50
curve, speed skating rink 159
curve ball, bowling 38
curve ball, pitch movement (baseball) 29
cushion/fault line, jai alai cancha 113
cushion swivel kit, downrigger (angling) 13
cushions, roller skate 140
cut bait, angling 14
cut man, fighter's corner (boxing) 42
cut/undercut, pommel horse routine (gymnastics) 93
cycling 51, 52
cylinder head, Formula One aircraft cockpit (air racing) 4
cylinder heads, race car 17

Dacron, yachting 200
daggerboard, sailboard (yachting) 201
dam/mother, dog racing 60
dam/mother, horse-racing program entry 103
dance skating, roller skating 139
danforth anchor, competition fishing boat 206
danger area, judo mat (martial arts) 123
dangerous hitting, field hockey 69
dangerous play, soccer foul 157
dark blue cap, water polo equipment
dart board/English clock, darts 53
dart 53
darting, 53
darts 53
darts, clockface games 53
dash/instrument panel, race car 19
dashes/sprints, track and field 174
date of birth/whelping date, dog racing 60
daylight/gap, football 77
DD/degree of difficulty, diving 54
dead bait, angling 14
dead ball line, rugby field 143
dead lines, shuffleboard court 148
dead targets/hit pair, skeet shooting 147
'deadened' tennis ball, paddle tennis 133
death spiral/back outside spin, freestyle figure skating 72
decal, Formula One aircraft (air racing) 4
decathletes, track and field 188
decathlon, track and field 188
decision, boxing match 41, 42

decisions, boxing match 41
deck, canoe 44
deck, cruising sailboat (yachting) 208
deck, scull (rowing) 141
deck, skateboard 149
deck, surfboard 161
deck plate/deck mount, fighting chair (angling) 15
deck/shelf, bowling console 39
declination correcting tip, orienteering compass 132
declination dialing-out scales, orienteering compass 132
dee ring, western saddle (rodeo) 137
deep-diving plug/crank bait, fishing tackle box 9
deep left zone/able zone, football 77
deep mid-wicket, cricket position 48
deep right zone/charlie zone, football 77
deep sea fishing 15
deep trolling, angling 13
deep trolling rigs, angling 13
defender/chopper/retriever, table tennis 167
defense, football formation 76
defense, football 75
defenseman, ice hockey 110
defensemen, lacrosse field 115
defensemen, roller hockey rink 140
defensemen, soccer 155
defensive backs, football formation 76
defensive field players, shot on water polo goal 192
defensive formation/'4-3-4,' football 76
defensive lob, tennis 172
defensive players, soccer formations 156
defensive position, table tennis 167
defensive positions, baseball scoreboard 27
defensive rebound, basketball 31
defensive secondary/defensive backfield, football 77
defensive tackles, football formation 76
defensive wrestler 196
deflecting (parrying), fencing 66
deflector, shooting range 145
delay of game, excess time out, football officials' signal 80
delayed calling of penalty, ice hockey officials' signal 111
delivering, curling 50
delivery/punch, shot putting technique (track and field) 181
delivery/release, discus throwing technique (track and field) 182
delivery/release, hammer throwing technique (track and field) 183
delta-form hull, canoe 44
deltoid muscle segments, bodybuilder 36
deployment bag, sky diving parachute (aerial sports) 7
depth-control fishing 13
depth gauge, scuba diver (diving/spear fishing) 58
depth-meter assembly, downrigger (angling) 13
depth-meter reading, downrigger (angling) 13
depth sounder, bass boat 13
designated hitter/DH/batting for pitcher, baseball scoreboard 27
deuce, tennis 169

deuce court/right service court, platform tennis 133
deuce court/right service court, tennis 169
dial and bearing ring, orienteering compass 132
dial gradation, orienteering compass 132
diamond/infield, baseball field 25
diamond line, yachting 203
die, tennis 171
difficulty, gymnastics vaults 92
difficulty, gymnastics 88
difficulty coefficient, aerobatics (aerial sports) 2
dig, volleyball 191
digital readout, long- & triple-jump measuring device (track and field) 189
dimple, plastic polo ball 135
dimples, golf ball 84
dinghies, yachting 199
dip, weightlifting clean-and jerk 194
direct free kick, soccer 157
direction of play, basketball officials' signal 32
direction-of-travel arrow, orienteering compass 132
dirt court, bocce 35
dirt/skin, baseball slang 25
dirt track, motorcycling 129
disassembly notch, target pistol 145
disc brake, kart 114
disc brake, motocross bike 129
disc brake, race car 17
disc brakes, motorcycle 130
disc stand, weightlifting 195
discs, swimming wave control 163
discs/plates, weightlifting 195
discus, decathlon (track and field) 188
discus & hammer safety cage/'beast's lair,' track and field 181
discus, track and field 181
discus throw, track and field 182
discus throwing technique, track and field 182
dish, baseball slang 25
disk, shuffleboard 148
dismount/double back salto, parallel bars routine (gymnastics) 96
dismounting, rings trick (gymnastics) 94
display font, timer (track and field) 189
disqualification, boxing match 41
distance, Nordic skiing 153
distance, on computerized performance indicator (track and field) 189
distance 'away' from pallino, bocce 35
distance in yards, range & loft of golf clubs 85
distance of race, past performance chart (horse racing) 103
distance races, canoeing & kayaking 44
distance races, speed (roller) skating 140
distance running, track and field 178
ditch/wall, lawn bowling 117
dive plane/front wing/spoiler, race car 17
divers' elevator, diving pool 54
diver's watch/submersible watch/dive timer, scuba diver 58
dives, aerobatics (aerial sports) 2
divided skirt/hakama, kendo 128
divider line, automobile racetrack 18
dividing line, discus & hammer cage (track and field) 182

dividing line, shot putting sector (track and field) 181
diving 54–58
diving pool/tank 54
diving/spear fishing 58
diving tank, Olympic swimming pool 163
diving tank 54
do/breastplate, kendo (martial arts) 128
dock line hawsepippe, competition fishing boat 206
doctor, fighter's corner (boxing) 42
dog & ratchet shaft assembly, downrigger (angling) 13
dog racing 59, 60
dog/trip, spinning reel (angling) 12
dog zone/short zone, football 77
dogleg, golf 85
dogs, male racing dogs 59
dojo/school, judo (martial arts) 123
dolphin kick/fishtail kick, swimming 164
dome, skeet and trapshooting target 147
door, court handball 99
dorade vents, cruising sailboat (yachting) 208
dorsal fin/spiny dorsal fin, fish 9
double, baseball 25
double, bet (horse racing) 103
double ball-bearing stanchion, fighting chair (angling) 15
double barb tip, spear gun (spear fishing) 58
double-bladed paddle, kayaking 45
double bogey, golf 86
double bullseye/50-point ring, dart board 53
double leg circles, pommel horse routine (gymnastics) 93
double-level fish-finder rig, angling 14
double middle quarter block in horse stance, martial arts move 119
double seat, polo breeches 135
double-seaters, luge 118
doubles, platform tennis 133
doubles, tennis 168
doubles box/service box, court handball 99
doubles court, platform tennis 133
doubles line/center line, table tennis 166
doubles long service line, badminton court 23
doubles ring/double-score ring, dart board 53
doubles service area, badminton court 23
doubles service box, racquetball court 136
doubles side line, badminton court 23
doubles sideline, tennis court 169
'doughnut'/on-deck bat weight, baseball 26
down, football 75
down-the-line shot, tennis 171
downfield, football 77
downhill Alpine skiing 150
downrigger, angling 13
downstairs/south of the border, boxing slang 42
downswing, golf stroke 83
downtube, track racing bicycle 52
downward thrust/down pass, relays baton handoff (track and field) 175
downwind, yachting 200
drafts, karting 114

drag-adjustment knob/drag knob/drag, spinning reel (angling) 12
drag/drag control knob/drag hub, fly reel (angling) 11
drag rope, ballooning 5
drag strip/dragway/rack, drag racing 20
drag systems & anti-reverse spool lock, fly reel (angling) 11
dragster/rail, drag racing 21
drain port/inspection port, scull (rowing) 141
draw, soccer 155
draw/hook, golf drive 85
drawing hand, archery 16
dressage arena, equestrian events 63
dressage figures, equestrian events 63
dressage/schooling, equestrian events 63
dribble, team handball 100
dribbling, basketball 31
drinking bottle, fighter's corner (boxing) 42
drive, tennis 172
drive chain, road racing bicycle 51
drive/pull through, sculling (rowing) 142
drive/pull through, sweep-rowing 142
driver, bobsledding 34
driver, dragster 21
driver, mobile starting gate (harness horse racing) 104
driver, powerboat offshore crew (yachting) 204
driver/number one wood, golf club 84, 85
driver's compartment/cockpit, race car 19
driver's fire suit, drag racing 20
driver's push bar, bobsled 34
driver's safety net, stock car 22
driver's seat, bobsled 34
driver's station, powerboat command console (yachting) 204
driving bit, harness horse racing 103
driving glove, drag racing fire suit 20
driving suit, drag racing 20
driving track, luge 118
drop-through fin cover, water ski 193
dropkick, rugby 143
dropped goal, rugby 143
dropped handlebar, road racing bicycle 51
dropping fastball, pitch movement (baseball) 29
dropping-under phase/pulling-under, weightlifting two-hand snatch 194
dropping zone, sport parachuting (aerial sports) 7
dry fly, angling 11
dry hurdle, steeplechase (track and field) 177
dry matches/non-electric matches, fencing 67
drying rib, fishing tackle box 9
dual pneumatic line system, football helmet 79
duckpins, bowling 38
duffers, golf 86
dugout, baseball field 25
duke/knuckle sandwich, boxing slang 42
dummy button, race car 19
dunk/jam/slam/stuff, basketball 30

Eagle, golf 86
ear muffs/silencers, shooting 145
ear protector, water polo cap 192
earguard/headguard, wrestling 196

earhole, football helmet 79
earthworks, shooting range 145
easy zone/short zone, football 77
eddy, whitewater canoe races 46
egg position, Alpine skiing 150
eight-pin, bowling 39
ejection port, target pistol 145
elapsed time/ET (in seconds), drag strip 20
elastic band, skier 150
elbow, martial arts fighting 127
elbow guard, luge 118
elbow pad, bobsledder 34
elbow pad, ice hockey center/wing/defenseman 110
elbow pad, lacrosse 115
elbow pad, skateboarder 149
elbow protector, fencing equipment 65
elbowing, ice hockey officials' signal 111
electric foil, fencing 66
electric trolling motor, bass boat 13
electrical switch for variometer, glider cockpit (aerial sports) 6
electrical system kill switch, race car 19
electrically operated lure, (dog racing) 59
electrically scored matches, fencing 67
electronic ignition chassis box, ballooning burner assembly 5
electronic point cover, motorcycle 130
electronic starting system, drag strip 20
electronic timing equipment, Olympic swimming pool 163
elevator, diving pool 54
elevator, glider (aerial sports) 6
eliminator, drag racing 20
emblem/engraving, lawn bowling bowl 117
employed foot/skating foot, figure skating 71
empty-handed fighting, karate (martial arts) 120
empty shells/hulls to reload, marksman (shooting) 147
end, archery 16
end, lawn bowling 117
end board/end wall, bocce 35
end/button/tip/point, fencing sword 65
end covers, fishing bait cage 9
end/inning, curling 50
end line, court handball 99
end line, lacrosse field 115
end line, volleyball court 191
end line/base line, basketball court 30
end line/base line, table tennis 166
end line/goal line, polo ground 134
end line/rear limit line, fencing strip 66
end/nose, football 75
end of field of play, water polo 192
end piece, starting blocks (track and field) 174
end plate/side plate, race car 17
end ring/top ring, spinning rod (angling) 12
end wall, Olympic swimming pool 163
end wall/end board, bocce 35
end zone/safety zone/retreat zone, fencing strip 66
ends, football formation 76
endurance, eventing (equestrian events) 64
enduro kart/roadracing kart, karting 114
enduro races, karting 114

engagement, fencing 66
engine, dragster 21
engine, motoryacht hull 205
engine, race car 17
engine air intake, competition fishing boat 206
engine clutches, competition fishing boat 206
engine compartment, unlimited hydroplane (yachting) 204
engine cover, race car 17
engine cowling, biplane (aerial sports–aerobatics) 2
engine cowling, Formula One aircraft (air racing) 4
engine gauges, powerboat command console (yachting) 204
engine hour, competition fishing boat 207
engine oil-pressure gauge, competition fishing boat 207
engine room, motoryacht hull 205
engine stop, competition fishing boat 207
engine throttles, competition fishing boat 206
engines, karting 114
English clock/dart board, darts 53
English saddle, equestrian events 62
English saddle, polo 134
entrance, equestrian events dressage arena 63
entrance gate buoys, slalom course (water skiing) 193
entries, sprints (track and field) 174
entry, diving 55
entry, swimming 164
entry number, eventing (equestrian events) 64
envelope/bag, ballooning 5
epaulet, football equipment 79
épée target area, fencing 68
equestrian events 61–64
equestrianism 61
equipment, football 79
errors, baseball 26
escape, wrestling 198
escape road, automobile racetrack 18
Ess-turns, karting 114
Esses, automobile racing 17
established racing weight, dog racing 60
'ET'/elapsed time, drag racing 20
European record, on weightlifting attempt board 195
event, drag racing 20
event, on computerized performance indicator (track and field) 189
eventers, rodeo 137
eventing dressage, equestrian events 64
events & entry board, Olympic swimming pool 163
execution, diving 55
exhaust header/valve cover & head, dragster 21
exhaust pipe, motocross bike 129
exhaust pipe, motorcycle 130
exhaust system/pipes, kart 114
exhaust systems, race car 17
exit gate buoys, slalom course (water skiing) 193
exotic bets, horse racing 103
Expedite System, table tennis 167
exposition/backswing, softball pitcher's delivery 158
extension, fencing 66, 67

extension scoring lights, fencing strip 66
extension/spire, croquet 49
extra cover, cricket position 48
extra innings, baseball 24
extra reel spool, flyfishing vest 10
extractor, shotgun (skeet and trapshooting) 146
eye, fish 9
eye, fishhook 9
eye, jig (angling) 12
eye, plug (angling) 12
eye, spinner (angling) 12
eye stay, running shoe (track and field) 178
eyelet, ice hockey skate 108
eyelet, skate 159
eyelet facing, cycle racing shoe 51
eyelet facing, ice hockey skate 108
eyelets, running shoe (track and field) 178
eyeshade, biathlon 154

Face, croquet mallet 49
face, golf wood 85
face, ice hockey stick 110
face, lacrosse field 115
face, starting blocks (track and field) 174
face, tennis racket 169
face, wave (surfing) 161
face insert, golf wood 85
face mask, baseball catcher's equipment 26
face mask, field hockey goalie 69
face mask/cage/birdcage, football helmet 79
face mask, ice hockey goalkeeper 110
face mask/mask, lacrosse 116
face mask, scuba diver (diving/spear fishing) 58
face-off, lacrosse referee signal 115
face-off, lacrosse 115
face-off circle, ice hockey rink 108
face/pimpled rubber/striking surface, table tennis paddle 166
face shield/visor, luge 118
face side, archery bow 16
factory challenges, sports car racing 22
fade/slice, golf drive 85
fair ball, baseball umpire's signal 29
fair territory, baseball field 25
fairlead/chock, competition fishing boat 206
fairway, golf course 82
faja/sash, jai alai 113
fakes, wrestling 198
fall, wrestling 196
fall line, Alpine skiing 150
fallbacks, field hockey 68
false start, illegal shift, illegal procedure, football officials' signal 80
false starts, sprints (track and field) 174
false starts, swimming 163
fan assembly quick release clamps, ballooning burner assembly 5
fan/run-up/runway, high-jumping area (track and field) 185
fancy diving 54
far turn, horse-racing track 101
fast pitch, softball 158
fasteners, football helmet 79
fastest qualifying swimmers, Olympic swimming pool 163
father/sire, dog racing 60
fathometer, competition fishing boat 207

fault, badminton 23
fault, tennis 168
fault judges/fault umpires, tennis–center court 168
fault line/cushion, jai alai cancha 113
fault line/underserve line, jai alai cancha 113
faults, show jumping (equestrian events) 61
feathering, angling 12
feathers, target arrow (archery) 16
feeding pattern, angling 8
'feeds,' deep sea fishing 15
feints, wrestling 198
felt, wading shoes (fishing) 10
female ferrule, spinning rod (angling) 12
fence/ballustrade, cycling velodrome 52
fence-off, fencing 67
fence/wall, baseball field 25
fencing 65–67
fencing equipment 65
fencing precedence, fencing 66
fencing shoe, fencing 65
fender, motocross bike 129
fender, western saddle (rodeo) 137
ferrule, badminton racket 23
ferrule, fly rod (angling) 11
ferrule, golf iron 85
field, softball 158
field, baseball 25
field, horse racing 102
field, lacrosse 115
field, sprints (track and field) 174
field, water polo 192
field archers, archery 16
field event timer, track and field 189
field events area, track and field 173
field goal, football 78
field goal/basket, basketball 30
field-goal team, football 76
field handball 100
field hockey 68, 69
field judge, football officials 80
field/pitch, field hockey 68
field/pitch, Gaelic football 81
field/pitch, hurling 106
field/pitch, rugby 143
field/pitch, soccer 156
field player, water polo field 192
field/polo ground 134
field/race cars, automobile racetrack 18
fields, archery 16
fieldsmen, cricket 47
fight/match/bout, boxing 41
fighter's corner, boxing 42
fighting arts/martial arts 119
fighting belt brackets, big game reel (angling) 15
fighting chair, competition fishing boat 207
fighting chair, deep sea fishing 15
fighting chair harness, deep sea fishing 15
fighting chairs/pedestal seats, bass boat 13
figure eight, dressage figure (equestrian events) 63
figure four on head, wrestling 198
figure skating 71
figure skating, roller skating 139
figures, aerobatics (aerial sports) 2, 3
figures dressage (equestrian events) 63
fill, bowling 39

fin/skeg, surfboard 161
fin/swim fin/flipper, scuba diver 58
fine leg/long leg, cricket position 48
finger hole, bowling ball 38
finger sling, archery bow 16
fingers, baseball glove 26
fingers, lacrosse glove 115
finish, bobsled course 34
finish, drag racing 20
finish, equestrian show jumping course 62
finish & recovery, sculling (rowing) 141
finish line, dog racetrack 59
finish line, Formula One racecourse (air racing) 4
finish line, iceboating course 107
finish line, kayaking racecourse 45
finish line, Olympic yacht-racing course 199
finish line, sprints (track and field) 174
finish line, track and field 173
finish line judge, speed skating 159
finish line judges, track and field 189
finish line photo/photo finish, horse racing 104
finish line/start line, cycling velodrome 52
finish line/'the wire,' horse-racing track 101
finish straight, speed skating 159
finish wire, horse-racing photo finish 104
finishes, past performance chart (horse racing) 103
finishes, speed skating rink 159
fire crewman, automobile racing pit crew 19
fire extinguisher, automobile racing pit 19
fire extinguisher, dragster 21
fire extinguisher on-off switch, race car 19
fire suit, drag racing 20
fire truck, automobile racetrack 18
fireproof gloves, automobile racing pit crew 19
fireproof uniform, automobile racing pit crew 19
firewall, stock car 22
firing line, pistol shooting 145
firing lock, target pistol 145
firing point number, biathlon 154
firing station, pistol shooting 145
firing stations, skeet and trapshooting ranges 146, 147
first base, baseball field 25
first baseman, baseball player position 25
first down, football officials' signal 80
first down, football 75
first flight/pre-flight, vaulting (gymnastics) 92
first position, fencing salute 65
first string, football 76
first turns, hammer throwing technique (track and field) 183
fish, 9
fish-caught flag, competition fishing boat 206
fish-finder rig, angling 14
fisherman/angler 8
fishhook, 9
fishing, spear fishing 58
fishing equipment, tackle box 9

fishing grounds, traveling to 206
fishing license, flyfishing vest 10
fishing line, angling 9
fishing net, flyfisherman 10
fishing tournaments, angling 8
fishing, angling 8–15
fishtail, synchronized swimming position 162
fishtail kick/dolphin kick, swimming 164
fisting, Gaelic football 81
five-meter platform, diving pool 54
five pin/kingpin, bowling 39
flag, football 80
flag halyard, competition fishing boat 206
flag line/backstroke turning line, Olympic swimming pool 163
flagman, automobile racetrack 18
flagman/crossing controller, speed skating rink 159
flags, automobile racing 17
flags, field hockey pitch 68
flags, sailboarding race (yachting) 201
flags, soccer field 156
flagstick/stick/pin golf course green 82
'flak jacket'/rib protector, football equipment 79
flamingo, synchronized swimming position 162
flange, spinning reel (angling) 12
flank billet, western saddle (rodeo) 137
flank strap/bucking strap, rodeo bareback bronc riding 137
flank strap/bucking strap, rodeo bull riding 138
flanker/wide out/halfback, football formation 76
flanks, rugby scrum positions 143
flap, polo saddle 134
flap control knob, glider cockpit (aerial sports) 6
flap control mechanism, glider cockpit (aerial sports) 6
flap handle, Formula One aircraft cockpit (air racing) 4
flat, football 77
flat, tennis serve 170
flat, tennis 172
flat edge, ice hockey skate 108
flat-freestyle event, skateboarding 149
flat green bowls, lawn bowling 117
flat racing (Thoroughbred, Quarter horse) 101, 102
flat side/left hand side, field hockey goalie 69
flat water courses, canoeing & kayaking 44
flatting, figure skating imperfection 71
fléche/running attack, fencing 66
fletching/vanes/feathers, target arrow (archery) 16
flex adjuster, ski boot 152
fliers, aerobatics (aerial sports) 2
flies, flyfishing vest 10
flight, dart (darts) 53
flight, pole vaulting technique (track and field) 186
flight, vaulting (gymnastics) 92
flight/hitch kick, long-jumping technique (track and field) 184
flight instruments, hang glider (aerial sports) 6
float, fishfinder rig (angling) 14

float/bobber, basic fishing rig 9
floating cuff, lacrosse 116
floating platforms, water polo field 192
'floor,' basketball court 30
floor cable, fencing strip 66
floor exercises, gymnastics 90
floor plate, volleyball net 191
flop, high-jump (track and field) 185
flop shoe/high-jump shoe (track and field) 185
flotation device/buoyancy compensator, scuba diver 58
'flow in the ice groove,' luge 118
flow roof overlay, sports car 22
fluorescent bead, spinner (angling) 12
flush nut & bolt, platform tennis paddle 133
flutter kick, swimming 164
fly dressings, flyfishing vest 10
fly half/stand off half, rugby scrummage formation 143
fly reel, angling 11
fly rod, angling 11
flybridge bimini, competition fishing boat 207
flybridge ladder, motoryacht deck 205
flycasting, angling 10, 11
flycasting technique, angling 11
flyer/cup, spinning reel (angling) 12
flyfisherman, angling 10
flyfishing vest, angling 10
flying bridge, competition fishing boat 206
flying bridge, motoryacht deck 205
flying gaff, deep sea fishing 15
flying start, luge 118
flyline leader sink, flyfishing vest 10
flyweights, boxing 43
foible, fencing sword 65
foil & épée electric scoring machine/recording machine, fencing strip 66
foil target area, fencing 68
foil warning line, fencing strip 66
foils, fencing swords 67
follow-through, batting (baseball) 27
follow-through, discus throwing technique (track and field) 182
follow-through, golf stroke 83
follow-through, karate kumite (martial arts) 121
follow-through, pitcher's full wind-up (baseball) 28
follow-through, pitcher's stretch position (baseball) 28
follow through & recovery, javelin throwing technique (track and field) 180
follow-through & recovery, karate kumite (martial arts) 121
follow-through & reverse, hammer throwing technique (track and field) 183
follow-through, shot putting technique (track and field) 181
follow-through, softball pitcher's delivery 158
follow-through, table tennis 167
follow-through, tennis serve 170
fondo, jai alai 113
'foot, hurdle (track and field) 176
foot, sail plans (yachting) 200
foot, shuffleboard 148

foot binding/'wet boot,' water ski 193
foot brace, canoe 44
foot-controlled rudder, kayaking 45
foot edge, martial arts fighting 127
foot launch, hang gliding (aerial sports) 6
foot methods, martial arts fighting 127
foot placement, fencing 67
foot pocket, scuba diver (diving/spear fishing) 58
foot rest legs, fighting chair (angling) 15
foot/rod mount, spinning reel (angling) 12
foot straps, sailboard (yachting) 201
football equipment 79
football field/gridiron 76
football formation 76
football/Gaelic football/ball 81
football/pigskin 75
football shoe/cleat 79
football uniform 79
football 75–80
footballer, soccer 155
footer/mat, lawn bowling 117
footing, sports car racing 22
footrest, competition fishing boat 207
footrest, motorcycle 130
footwork, roller skating 139
force, baseball 26
fore/aft jib, yachting 203
fore fist, martial arts fighting 126
forearm/fore-end/slide handle, shotgun (skeet and trapshooting) 146
forearm pad, football equipment 79
forecomb/comb, shotgun (skeet and trapshooting) 146
forecourt, platform tennis court 133
forecourt, tennis court 169
forecourt area, squash racquets court 160
foredeck, competition fishing boat 206
foredeck, kayak 45
foredeck, rowing shell 142
foredeck, yacht-racing crew 199
foregrip/forward grip, spinning reel (angling) 12
forehand, tennis stroke 171
forehand follow-through, table tennis 167
forehand serve, table tennis 166
foreknuckle fist, martial arts fighting 126
foreleg bandage/polo & exercise bandage, polo pony 134
forestay, iceboating 107
fork, shuffleboard cue 148
fork, track racing bicycle 52
fork/fork blade, road racing bicycle 51
fork/swell, western saddle (rodeo) 137
fork tube, motocross bike 129
forkball, pitch movement (baseball) 29
form and execution, gymnastics vaults 92
formal jacket/swallowtail jacket, dressage turnout (equestrian events) 63
formations, football 76–78
formations, soccer 156
formations, team handball 100
Formula-class racing, yachting 199
Formula One aircraft, air racing (aerial sports) 4
Formula race car 17–19
Formulas, sports car racing 22
forte, fencing sword 65

forward, field hockey 68
forward, yachting 202
forward bulkhead, race car 17
forward dive 56
forward 4½ somersault, diving 54
forward gate, whitewater slalom (canoeing & kayaking) 46
forward/main crossbeam, yachting 203
forward pirouette, parallel bars routine (gymnastics) 96
forward roll/front pike roll, gymnastics 88
forward short-leg, cricket position 48
forward stateroom, cruising sailboat (yachting) 208
forward V-berth, motoryacht hull 205
forwards, Gaelic football 81
forwards, hurling 106
forwards, polo ground 134
forwards, roller hockey rink 140
forwards, rugby scrum positions 143
forwards, soccer formations 156
forwards, volleyball 190
foul, boxing 43
foul, long and triple jump (track and field) 184
foul light, drag racing Christmas tree 21
foul light/foul detector, bowling lane 38
foul line, baseball field 25
foul line, basketball court 30
foul line, bocce 35
foul line, bowling lane 38
foul line, shot putting sector (track and field) 181
foul line/arc/scratch line/toe board, javelin throwing sector (track and field) 180
foul line/boundary line, discus & hammer cage (track and field) 182
foul line/free throws line/'charity' stripe, basketball court 30
foul line/plasticine indicators, jumping area (track and field) 184
foul lines, horseshoes 105
foul pole, baseball field 25
foul shots, basketball 30
foul start, drag racing 20
foul territory, baseball field 25
foul throw, soccer officials' signal 157
foul/time out, baseball umpire's signal 29
foul tip, baseball umpire's signal 29
foul weather gear, iceboating 107
fouling out, basketball 32
fouls, water polo 192
four-hundred meter dash, decathlon (track and field) 188
four pin, bowling 39
four runs, cricket umpire signal 48
fourth down, football 76
foxtrot hold, ice dancing (figure skating) 74
fractional times of race leader, past performance chart (horse racing) 103
frame, bocce 35
frame, bowling 39
frame, discus & hammer cage (track and field) 182
frame, racquetball racquet 136
frame/aro, jai alai cesta 113
frame/head, badminton racket 23
frame/tree, polo saddle 134
frames, cycling 51
free diving, competitive diving 58

free fall, sky diving (aerial sports) 7
free flight skirt, ballooning burner assembly 5
free hand, rodeo bareback bronc riding 137
free hand, table tennis 166
free hit, field hockey 69
free hit, roller hockey 140
free leg, long-jumping technique (track and field) 184
free leg/unemployed leg, figure skating 71
free pass, baseball 25
free pistol, shooting 145
free posing, bodybuilding 36
free position, diving 56
free safety, football formation 76
free skating, ice dancing (figure skating) 74
free skating, roller skating 139
free throw lane/key/3-second lane/'paint,' basketball court 30
free throw line, team handball 100
free-throw circle, basketball court 30
freestyle, swimming 164
freestyle/free skating, figure skating 72
freestyle/individual posing, bodybuilding 37
freestyle medley, swimming 164
freestyle wrestling 198
freezer/bait box, competition fishing boat 206
freshwater tackle, angling 8
fringe/apron/collar/froghair, golf course green 82
frog kick, swimming 164
front, synchronized swimming position 162
front and rear articulation mechanism, bobsled 34
front axle/suspension, dragster 21
front brake, road racing bicycle 51
front brake cable, road racing bicycle 51
front bridge, luge 118
front bumper shoe, bobsled 34
front court/attack area, volleyball court 191
front crawl/crawl, swimming 164, 165
front double biceps pose, bodybuilding 37
front double-disc brakes, motorcycle 130
front fender, motorcycle 130
front gimbal bracket, fighting chair (angling) 15
front hub, road racing bicycle 51
front jockey, western saddle (rodeo) 137
front kick, karate kata (martial arts) 121
front kick, karate (martial arts) 122
front line, volleyball court 190, 191
front line/service line, court handball 99
front pike, synchronized swimming position 162
front porch & bumper, kart 114
front rocker, water ski 193
front scissors/leg work, pommel horse routine (gymnastics) 93
front shock absorber, bobsled 34
front sideplate/head plate, fly reel (angling) 11
front sight, .22 rifle (biathlon) 154
front sight, target pistol 145
front sizer, football helmet 79
front spoiler, stock car 22

front thwart, canoe 44
front wall, court handball 99
front wall, racquetball court 136
front wall, squash racquets court 160
front wheel, dragster 21
front wheel quick release, road racing bicycle 51
front wing/air foil/spoiler, dragster 21
front wing/spoiler/dive plane, race car 17
frontis/front wall, jai alai cancha 113
fronton, jai alai 112
fuel filler, sports car 22
fuel gauge, competition fishing boat 207
fuel gauge, motorcycle 130
fuel hose, automobile racing pit 19
fuel hoses, ballooning basket 5
fuel intake valve, race car 17
fuel line, ballooning basket 5
fuel overflow hose, automobile racing pit 19
fuel overflow man, automobile racing pit crew 19
fuel tank, ballooning basket 5
fuel tank, dragster 21
fuel tank, Formula One aircraft cockpit (air racing) 4
fuel tank, kart 114
fuel tank, motocross bike 129
fuel tank, motorcycle 130
fuel tank lock, motorcycle 130
fuel tank straps, ballooning basket 5
fuel valve, race car 17
full-pipe event, skateboarding 149
full-posing routine, bodybuilding 37
full wind-up, pitching (baseball) 28
fullbacks, Gaelic football 81
fullbacks, hurling 106
fullbacks, soccer formations 156
fullface helmet, automobile racing pit crew 19
funny cars, drag racing 20
fuselage, Formula One aircraft (air racing) 4
fuselage, race car 17
fuselage/hull, iceboat 107

'G' meter, Formula One aircraft cockpit (air racing) 4
'G' meter, glider cockpit (aerial sports) 6
Gaelic football/football/ball 81
Gaelic football 81
gaff, angling 14
gaff, competition fishing boat 207
gaff, deep sea fishing 15
gaffman, competition fishing boat 206, 207
gainer/Mohlberg, diving 57
gaits, harness horses 104
galley, cruising sailboat (yachting) 208
galley, motoryacht hull 205
game, bowling 38
game, football 75
game, tennis 169
game birds, skeet shooting 147
game fish/fish 9
game number, jai alai scoreboard/betting board 112
gamefish 8, 206
gap, fishhook 9
gap/daylight, football 77
gas pedal/throttle kart 114
gastrocnemius muscle, bodybuilder 36
gate, cruising sailboat (yachting) 208
gate, horse-racing 101

gate, slalom kayaking 46
gate bar/bar, hurdle (track and field) 176
gate judges, whitewater slalom (canoeing & kayaking) 46
gate number, (flat) horse-racing 101
gate/transom door, competition fishing boat 206
gate/upright, equestrian show jumping fence 62
gate upright, hurdle (track and field) 176
gauntlet/handguard/kote, kendo (martial arts) 128
gear housing, spinning reel (angling) 12
gear oil-pressure gauge, competition fishing boat 207
gear/tackle/fishing equipment, tackle box 9
genoa/jib, yachting 200
get-ready position/neutral position, table tennis 166
giant, rings trick (gymnastics) 94
giant slalom Alpine skiing 150
giant swing grip change, horizontal bar (gymnastics) 95
gill cover/operculum/opercule preopercle, fish 9
gill opening, fish 9
gimbal, big game rod (angling) 15
gimbaled rod holder, competition fishing boat 207
gimbals, fighting chair (angling) 15
girdle pad/hip pad, football equipment 79
girth, harness horse racing 103
girth & surcingle, polo pony 134
girth & surcingle, racehorse 102
girth pad, racehorse 102
gladiator, boxing slang 42
glass, basketball backboard 30
glass, court handball 99
glass, ice hockey rink 108
glass jaw/china chin/cement chin, boxing slang 42
glassless window, stock car 22
glide, shot putting technique (track and field) 181
glide, swimming 164
glide kip, uneven parallel bars (gymnastics) 97
glide/runner, shuffleboard cue 148
glider, aerial sports 6
glider cockpit, aerial sports 6
glove, fencing 65
glove, field hockey goalie 69
glove, jai alai 113
glove, lacrosse 115, 116
glove, luge 118
glove, scuba diver (diving/spear fishing) 58
glove, ski jumper 153
glove, skier 150
glove, soccer goalie 155
glove/gloved hand/handhold, rodeo bareback bronc riding 137
glove/mitt, baseball 26
glove model, baseball glove 26
glove racquetball 136
glove studs, luge 118
gloves, bobsledder 34
gloves, ice hockey 110
gloves, riding (equestrian events) 63
GO-light, on drag racing Christmas tree 20, 21

go position, sprints (track and field) 174
goal, field hockey 68, 69
goal, Gaelic football 81
goal, hurling 106
goal, ice hockey 108
goal, lacrosse 116
goal, roller hockey rink 140
goal, rugby field 143
goal, rugby 143
goal, soccer field 156
goal, soccer 155
goal, team handball 100
goal area, lacrosse field 115
goal area, soccer field 156
goal area/circle, team handball 100
goal area line, team handball 100
goal/cage, water polo 192
goal crease, ice hockey rink 108
goal/goalpost/uprights, football 75
goal/head/house, curling 50
goal/hoop/basket, basketball 30
goal judge box, ice hockey rink 108
goal kick, soccer 156
goal line, field hockey 68, 69
goal line, ice hockey rink 108, 109
goal line, polo ground 134
goal line, soccer field 156
goal line, team handball 100
goal line, water polo 192
goal-line defensive team, football 76
goal line/try line, rugby field 143
goal net, ice hockey rink 108
goal pad, ice hockey goalkeeper 110
goal post, field hockey 69
goal post, ice hockey goal 110
goal post, polo ground 134
goal post, water polo field 192
goal post/upright, soccer 155
goal posts, rugby 143
goal tending, basketball officials' signal 32
goalie, roller hockey rink 140
goalie, water polo field 192
goalie equipment, field hockey 69
goalie glove, soccer 155
goalie/goaltender, lacrosse field 115
goalie stick, ice hockey 110
goalie's red cap, water polo field 192
goalkeeper/goalie, field hockey pitch 68
goalkeeper/goalie/goaler, ice hockey 110
goalkeeper/goalie, water polo goal 192
goalkeeper/goalie, soccer 155
goalkeeper/goalie, team handball 100
goalkeeper, soccer formations 156
goalkeeper's penalty line, roller hockey rink 140
goalpost, hurling net 106
goaltender, Gaelic football 81
goaltenders, hurling 106
goggles, bobsledder 34
goggles, court handball 99
goggles, iceboating 107
goggles, jockey (horse racing) 102
goggles, motocross rider 131
goggles, racquetball 136
goggles, ski jumper 153
goggles, skier 150
goggles, swimming 163
gold/bullseye/10, archery target 16
golf bag & club set 84
golf ball 84

golf cart/caddy cart 84
golf cart path, golf course 82
golf club/wood 82
golf clubs 84, 85
golf course/links 82
golf green 82
golf shoes 84
golf swing 83
golf tee 82, 84
golf 82–86
golfer 82
gondola/basket, ballooning 5
good lift, weightlifting 194
'goofy foots,' surfing 161
gooseneck, cruising sailboat (yachting) 208
gooseneck, iceboat 107
gooseneck/main standard, football goal 75
gore seams, ballooning 5
grace, bodybuilding 36
grace, figure skating 71
Grand Touring (GT), sports car racing 22
grandstand, baseball field 25
grandstand and clubhouse area horse-racing track 101
grandstands, automobile racetrack 18
grandstands, cycling velodrome 52
grass court, bocce 35
gravity waves, swimming 163
Greco-Roman wrestling 198
green/bowling green, lawn bowling 117
green flag, automobile racing 17
green (timed period has begun), on field event timer (track and field) 189
greyhound performance rating (dog racing) 59
greyhound racing 59
gridiron/football field 76
grinder, yacht-racing crew 199
grip, Alpine ski pole 150
grip, badminton racket 23
grip, big game rod (angling) 15
grip, canoe paddle 44
grip, golf clubs 85
grip, hammer (track and field) 183
grip, hurling hurley 106
grip, softball bat 158
grip, spear gun (spear fishing) 58
grip ball, pitcher's set position (baseball) 28
grip/handguard/palm protector, horizontal bar (gymnastics) 95
grip/handle, croquet mallet 49
grip/handle, racquetball racquet 136
grip/handle, squash racket 160
grip/handle, tennis racket 169
grip safety, target pistol 145
grip tape, skateboard 149
grip/trapeze handle, yachting 203
grips, table tennis 166
groin, boxing slang 42
groin, martial arts striking point 126
groin strap, fencer 65
grommets, fighting chair harness (angling) 15
grooming, bodybuilding 36
groove, automobile racing 17
'groove,' luge 118
grooves/tracking, ski jumping 153
ground cloth/pad/blanket, rifle shooting 144
ground strokes, tennis 171

group, archery target 16
Group, sports car racing 22
group facing, bodybuilding 37
groups, diving 56
guante/glove, jai alai cesta 113
guard, racquetball racquet 136
guard socket/bell plug, electric foil fencing 66
guards, football formation 76
guide, big game rod (angling) 15
guide, spinning rod (angling) 12
guide buoys, ski jump (water skiing) 193
guides, bowling lane 38
guillotine, wave (surfing) 161
gullet, western saddle (rodeo) 137
gully, cricket position 48
gum guard/mouthpiece, boxer 41
gun, spear fishing 58
gun, track and field equipment 189
gunkholing, yachting 205
gunwale, canoe 44
gunwale, competition fishing boat 207
gunwale/washboard, scull (rowing) 141
gutter, shuffleboard court 148
gutter/channel, bowling lane 38
guy, horizontal bar (gymnastics) 95
guy brace, uneven parallel bars (gymnastics) 97
guy wire, uneven parallel bars (gymnastics) 97
gymnastics 87–98

H ack/crampit, curling 50
hackers, golf 86
hacking/illegal use of hands, basketball officials' signal 32
hackle, dry fly (angling) 11
hairpin-curve, luge 118
hakama/gauntlet/kendo (martial arts) 128
half backs, rugby scrummage formation 143
half court marker, bocce 35
half-distance line, water polo field 192
half-jacket/jacket, fencer 65
half-jacket sleeve, fencer 65
half-pipe event, skateboarding 149
half-volley & mid-court overhead zone/attack zone, tennis 171
half-volley, tennis 171
half-way line, rugby field 143
halfback flare, football pass pattern 78
halfbacks, field hockey 68
halfbacks, football formation 76
halfbacks, Gaelic football 81
halfbacks, hurling 106
halfbacks/backcourt players, team handball 100
halfway line, soccer field 156
halter & horse's champion title, rodeo 138
halts, equestrian events 63
halves, rugby game 143
halyard winch, cruising sailboat (yachting) 208
hammer, target pistol 145
hammer glove, hammer throw (track and field) 183
hammer throw, track and field 182, 183
hammer throwing technique, track and field 183
hand grip, fly rod (angling) 11
hand stop, race car 19

handball, soccer officials' signal 157
handball/court handball 99
handball glove 99
handball/team handball 100
handbrake, motorcycle 130
handgrip, Olympic swimming pool 163
handguard/gauntlet/kote, (martial arts) 128
handguard/grip/palm protector, horizontal bar (gymnastics) 95
handhold, rodeo bareback bronc riding 137
handholds, harness horse racing 103
handicap, horse-racing program entry 103
handicap, polo 135
handicap distance markers, trapshooting range 146
handicap race, motorcycling 129
handicap races, air racing 4
handicap racing, yachting 199
handicap weight, racehorse 102
handicaps, horse racing 102
handle, badminton racket 23
handle, ballooning basket 5
handle, baseball bat 26
handle, big game reel (angling) 15
handle, curling broom 50
handle, curling stone 50
handle, hammer (track and field) 183
handle, hurling hurley 106
handle, oar & scull 141
handle, platform tennis paddle 133
handle, spear gun (spear fishing) 58
handle, spinning reel (angling) 12
handle, trolling reel (angling) 13
handle, water skier 193
handle/butt grip, spinning reel (angling) 12
handle/grip, croquet mallet 49
handle/grip, racquetball racquet 136
handle/grip, tennis racket 169
handle riser, archery bow 16
handlebars, road racing bicycle 51
handlebars, track racing bicycle 52
handlers/seconds/cornermen, fighter's corner (boxing) 42
handoffs/passing techniques, relays (track and field) 175
handrail, bass boat 13
handrail, cruising sailboat (yachting) 208
handrail, motoryacht deck 205
handstand, gymnastics floor exercises 90
handstand, gymnastics vault 92
handstand, gymnastics 88
handstand/swinging part, rings (gymnastics) 94
hang glider, aerial sports 6
hang gliding/self soaring/sky surfing, aerial sports 6
hang position, hop, step and jump technique (track and field) 184
hanging locker/storage, motoryacht hull 205
hard hat/batting helmet, baseball 26
hard hat/hunt cap, equestrian show jumping 62
hard rubber, handball 99
hardwater sailing, iceboating 107
hardwood base, ballooning basket 5
harmony, bodybuilding 36
harness, .22 rifle (biathlon) 154
harness, fighting chair (angling) 15

harness, sky diving parachute (aerial sports) 7
harness horse racing 103, 104
hash marks/inbound lines, football field 76
hatch, competition fishing boat 206
hatch, cruising sailboat (yachting) 208
hatch, motoryacht deck 205
hatch/sliding hatch, cruising sailboat (yachting) 208
haystacks, whitewater canoe races 46
hazard lights, motorcycle 130
hazards, golf 82
hazer, rodeo steer wrestling 138
head, bowling pin 39
head, croquet mallet 49
head, cruising sailboat (yachting) 208
head, dry fly (angling) 11
head, field hockey goalie 69
head, fish 9
head, javelin (track and field) 180
head, jig (angling) 12
head, lacrosse stick 115
head, motoryacht hull 205
head, platform tennis paddle 133
head, polo mallet 134
head, racquetball racquet 136
head, sail plans (yachting) 200
head, shuffleboard 148
head, squash racquets 160
head, tennis racket 169
head/arrowhead/point/pile, target arrow (archery) 16
head/ball, hammer (track and field) 183
head/blade, table tennis paddle 166
head catch/horn catch, rodeo team roping 138
head covers, golf bag & club set 84
head/frame, badminton racket 23
head/house/goal, curling 50
head linesman/chain gang supervisor, football officials 80
head number, harness horse racing 103
head of the river races, sculling (rowing) 141
head plate/front sideplate, fly reel (angling) 11
head/pommel/saddlebow, polo saddle 134
head referee, sculling heat (rowing) 141
head roper, rodeo team roping 138
head tube, track racing bicycle 52
headband, cross country skier 154
headband, volleyball net 191
headband/sweatband, court handball player 99
headband/sweatband, racquetball 136
headboard, iceboat 107
headcloth/hachimaki, kendo (martial arts) 128
headers/zoomies, dragster 21
headgear/headguard, sparring equipment (boxing) 42
headguard/earguard, wrestling 196
heading a soccer ball 157
headlight, motorcycle 130
headlight box, sports car 22
headpiece, dressage bridle (equestrian events) 63
headpiece, racehorse bridle 102
headpin, bowling 39
headsail, yachting 200
headstall, rodeo horse 138

headstay, cruising sailboat (yachting) 208
headstay, yachting 202
heats, bobsledding 34
heats, drag racing 20
heats, karting 114
heats, sculling (rowing) 141
heats, speed skating 159
heats, sprints (track and field) 174
heats, surfing 161
heavy-duty suspensions, stock car racing 22
heavyweights, boxing 43
heel, baseball glove 26
heel, golf iron 85
heel, ice hockey stick 110
heel, martial arts fighting 127
heel, roller skate 140
heel, shotgun (skeet and trap shooting) 146
heel, ski binding 152
heel, tennis racket 169
heel and toe/race walking, track and field 178
heel calks, horseshoes 105
heel cap, ice hockey skate 108
heel cup, skate 159
heel front kick, karate kata (martial arts) 120–121
heel guide, water ski 193
heel height adjustment screw, ski binding 152
heel patch/Achilles' tendon pad, running shoe (track and field) 178
heel piece, ski binding 152
heel piece/heel flap, slalom water ski 193
heel plate, figure skate 71
heel plate, skate 159
heel plate, water ski 193
heel release setting indicator, ski binding 152
heel spikes, javelin shoes (track and field) 180
heel spikes, long and triple jump (track and field) 184
heel strap, scuba diver (diving/spear fishing) 58
heel wedge, javelin shoes (track and field) 180
height adjustment, hurdle (track and field) 176
helmet, baseball 26
helmet, bobsled 34
helmet, drag racing 20
helmet, equestrian events 64
helmet, hang gliding (aerial sports) 6
helmet, harness horse racing 103
helmet, ice hockey center/wing/defenseman 110
helmet, ice hockey skate 110
helmet, iceboating 107
helmet, jai alai 113
helmet, jockey (horse racing) 102
helmet, karting 114
helmet, lacrosse 116
helmet, luge 118
helmet, motocross rider 131
helmet, skateboarder 149
helmet, ski jumper 153
helmet, sky diving (aerial sports) 7
helmet, slalom kayaking 46
helmet, water ski 193
helmet/mask, fencer 65

helmet/shell, track cycle racing 52
helmet skirt, drag racing fire suit 20
helmsman, yacht-racing crew 199
helmsman's chair/helmseat, competition fishing boat 207
hen feathers, target arrow (archery) 16
heptathletes, track and field 188
heptathlon, track and field 188
high, baseball strike zone 26
high bar/horizontal bar, gymnastics 95
high house/trap house, skeet shooting range 147
high inside line, fencing 66
high jump, decathlon (track and field) 188
high jump, heptathlon (track and field) 188
high-jump, track and field 185
high-jump shoe/flop shoe (track and field) 185
high outside line, fencing 66
high position, Alpine skiing 150
high score, clockface game (darts) 53
high-sticking, ice hockey officials' signal 111
highboard, diving pool 54
hiking, football 75
hiking straps, yachting 203
hill/box, baseball slang 25
hill climbing, motorcycling 129
hind legs catch, rodeo team roping 138
hind-legs roper, rodeo team roping 138
hind scalpers, harness horse racing 103
hinder, racquetball 136
hinge, ski boot 152
hip pad, ice hockey center/wing/defenseman 110
hip pad/girdle pad, football equipment 79
hip throw, wrestling 197
hit pair/dead targets, skeet shooting 147
hit/touch, fencing 67
hitch and go, football pass pattern 78
hitch kick/flight, long-jumping technique (track and field) 184
hitter at bat, baseball scoreboard 27
hitting, baseball 27
hitting a man who is down, boxing foul 43
hitting below the belt, boxing foul 43
hitting on back of head or shoulder, or wrestling, boxing foul 43
hitting on back of neck/rabbit punch, boxing foul 43
hitting on the back/kidney punch, boxing foul 43
hitting surface, amateur boxing glove 41
hitting with open glove, boxing foul 43
hobber/leaner, horseshoes 105
hobble hangers, harness horse racing 103
hobble strap, western saddle (rodeo) 137
hobbles, harness horse racing 103
hockey boot, roller hockey 140
hockey line/throwing line/toe line, darts 53
hockey skate, ice hockey 108, 110
hog score line, curling 50
hold/handstand, parallel bars routine (gymnastics) 96
hold position, rings (gymnastics) 94
hold/set, pitcher's stretch position (baseball) 28
holding, basketball officials' signal 32
holding, football officials' signal 80

holding, ice hockey officials' signal 111
holding, lacrosse referee signal 115
holding, soccer foul 157
holds, wrestling 197, 198
hole, baseball slang 25
hole, golf 82
hole/cup, golf course green 82
hole/cup, golf putting 86
hole (for running back), football 77
hole-in-one/ace, golf scorecard 86
hole man/two-meter man/setter, water polo 192
holes, platform tennis paddle 133
hollow of knee, martial arts striking point 126
home plate, baseball field dimensions 25
home plate area, baseball field 25
home run, baseball 25
home runs, baseball scoreboard 27
home team, baseball scoreboard 27
homestretch, horse-racing track 101
hood, speed skater 159
hood, spinning reel (angling) 12
hood pin, race cars 22
hook, basic fishing rig 9
hook, bowling 39
hook, boxing punch 43
hook, jig (angling) 9
hook, spinner (angling) 12
hook, tape measure (track and field) 189
hook, umbrella rig (angling) 13
hook/draw, golf drive 85
hook eye, dry fly (angling) 11
hook hanger, plug (angling) 12
hook sharpener, flyfishing vest 10
hook-up, sky diving (aerial sports) 7
hooker, rugby scrum positions 143
hooking, ice hockey officials' signal 111
hooks, surf fishing 14
hoop, women's rhythmic exercise (gymnastics) 91
hoop/basket/goal, basketball 30
hoop/steel band, hurling hurley 106
hoop/wicket, croquet 49
hooter, yachting 201
hop, step and jump technique (track and field) 184
horizontal, gymnastics vault 92
horizontal bar/high bar, gymnastics 95
horizontal eight/layout, aerobatics (aerial sports) 3
horizontal slow roll, aerobatics (aerial sports) 3
horizontal stabilizer, biplane (aerial sports–aerobatics) 2
horizontal stabilizers, glider (aerial sports) 6
horizontal target trajectory, skeet shooting 147
horn, western saddle (rodeo) 137
horn cap, western saddle (rodeo) 137
horn neck, western saddle (rodeo) 137
horse, vaulting (gymnastics) 92
horse/mainsheet traveler, yachting 203
horse/mount/polo pony 134
horse number/post position, horse-racing tote board 102
horse racing 101–103
horse trials, equestrian events 61
horsehide/baseball/'apple' 26
horses, rodeo 137, 138

horse's name, horse-racing program entry 103
horse's owner, horse-racing program entry 103
horseshoes/horseshoe pitching 105
hosel, golf iron 85
hot air balloon/montgolfier 5
hot corner, baseball slang 25
hours, automobile racing 17
house/target area, curling 50
housing, ice hockey skate 108
hub, motocross bike 129
huddles, football 75
hull, cruising sailboat (yachting) 208
hull, unlimited hydroplane (yachting) 204
hull/fuselage, iceboating 107
hulls, drag racing funny car 20
hulls, yachting 203
hulls to reload/empty shells, marksman (shooting) 147
Humpty Bumps, aerobatics (aerial sports) 3
hunter-class horses, show jumping (equestrian events) 61
hurdle, diving 55
hurdles, track and field 176
hurdling technique, track and field 176
hurley, hurling 106
hurling 106
hydraulic brake line, motorcycle 130

Ice, bobsledding 34
ice, fighter's corner (boxing) 42
ice chest/storage compartment, bass boat 13
ice dancing 74
'ice groove,' luge 118
ice hockey 108
ice sheet, luge 118
iceboat, iceboating 107
iceboating 107
icebox, cruising sailboat (yachting) 208
icing, ice hockey officials' signal 111
identity card/bertillion card, dog racing 59, 60
ignition, motorcycle 130
illegal cut, blocking below the waist, football officials' signal 80
illegal dribble/double dribble, basketball officials' signal 32
illegal formation, kickoff out of bounds, football officials' signal 80
illegal use of hands, arms, body, football officials' signal 80
Immelmann, aerobatics (aerial sports) 3
improved clinch knot, angling 10
in and out/combination jump, equestrian show jumping fence 62
in-bounds lines, bocce 35
in-dash depth sounder, bass boat 13
in-line sinker, deep trolling rig (angling) 13
in-run, ski jumping 153
in-run position, ski jumping 153
'in the marbles,' automobile racetrack 17, 18
inch rule, orienteering compass 132
incoming runners, relays (track and field) 175
index pointer, orienteering compass 132
Indianapolis-type race car 17–19
indirect free kick, soccer officials' signal 157

individual medley, swimming 164
individual posing/freestyle, bodybuilding 37
individual pursuit & time trial flat, cycling velodrome 52
individual races, speed skating 159
indoor hurdlers, track and field 176
Indy car, automobile racing 17–19
ineligible receiver, ineligible member of kicking team downfield, football officials' signal 80
infield, dog racetrack 59
infield, horse-racing track 101
infield cover/tarp, baseball field 25
infield/diamond, baseball field 25
infield/warm-up area, cycling velodrome 52
inflation hose, scuba diver (diving/spear fishing) 58
infraction, football 80
injector, dragster 21
inner forearm, martial arts striking point 126
inner lane, speed skating rink 159
inner wrist, martial arts striking point 126
inners, field hockey 68
inning, badminton 23
inning, horseshoes 105
inning/end, curling 50
innings, baseball scoreboard 27
inside, baseball strike zone 26
inside & outside elbow, martial arts striking point 126
inside corner, baseball strike zone 26
inside edge, figure skating 71
inside lane/pole position, sprints (track and field) 174
inside lure track, dog racing 59
inside rail, horse-racing track 101
inside track retaining wall, automobile racetrack 18
inspection port, yachting 203
inspection port/drain port, scull (rowing) 141
instep, martial arts fighting 127
instep, martial arts striking point 126
instrument cluster, motorcycle 130
instrument panel, motorcycle 130
instrument panel/dash, race car 19
intake valves/air scoop, dragster 21
intentional grounding of pass, football officials' signal 80
interchangeable spool, fly reel (angling) 11
intercom, bowling console 39
interference, ice hockey officials' signal 111
interference with forward pass, fair catch, football officials' signal 80
international foul lane, basketball court 30
international standard barbell, weightlifting 195
interplane strut 2
invalid light/off-target light (white/white), fencing strip 66
inverted position, balance beam (gymnastics) 98
inward dive 56
ippon, karate (martial arts) 121
ippon seoinage/one-point shoulder throw, judo (martial arts) 123

iron cross, rings (gymnastics) 94
irons, golf clubs 84, 85
Izaak Walton/angler 8

J stroke, canoeing 45
jab, boxing punch 43
jack/cue/pallino/object ball, bocce 35
jack/kitty, lawn bowling 117
jack-point indicator, stock car 22
jacket, cartridge (shooting) 145
jacket, curling broom 50
jacket, dressage turnout (equestrian events) 63
jacket/blanket, dog racing 59
jacket/half-jacket, fencer 65
jacking air hose, automobile racing pit 19
jackknife, diving 57
jai alai/pelota 112, 113
jam/dunk/slam/stuff, basketball 30
jav, javelin (track and field) 180
javelin, decathlon (track and field) 188
javelin, heptathlon (track and field) 188
javelin, track and field 180
javelin shoes (track and field) 180
jaw, martial arts striking point 126
jaw pad, football helmet 79
jaws, croquet wicket 49
jerk, weightlifting clean-and-jerk 194
jersey, baseball 26
jersey, basketball player 30
jersey, lacrosse 116
jersey, motocross rider 131
jersey, rugby 143
jersey/shirt, soccer 155
Jersey side/left-handed pocket/Brooklyn pocket, bowling 39
jersey/sweater, Gaelic football 81
jersey/sweater, hurling 106
jib adjustment, yachting 203
jib bridle, yachting 203
jib/genoa, yachting 200
jib halyard tension, yachting 203
jib headstay, yachting 203
jib track, cruising sailboat (yachting) 208
jibe, yachting 208
jibes, tacking duel (yacht racing) 199
jig, lure (angling) 12
jockey, horse-racing program entry 103
jockey, past performance chart (horse racing) 103
jockey & racehorse 102
jockeys, western saddle (rodeo) 137
joint/middle, fly rod (angling) 11
judge, jai alai cancha 113
judge, speed skating 159
judges, bodybuilding 36
judges, boxing 42
judges, diving pool 54
judges, equestrian events dressage arena 63
judges, football 80
judges, rodeo 137
judges, track and field 189
judges, vaulting (gymnastics) 92
judges, whitewater slalom 46
judges' down signal, weightlifting clean-and-jerk 194
judges' lights/referee light system, weightlifting 195
judges signature, boxing scorecard 41
judges' stand, skeet shooting range 147
judges' tower, cycling velodrome
judge's tower, ski jumping 153

judges/umpires, tennis–center court 168
judging points, bodybuilding 36
judging points, diving 55
judo, martial arts 123
judo mat, martial arts 123
judoka, martial arts 123
juggling a soccer ball 157
jujutsu, martial arts 123
jump, motocross race 129
jump position/power/position, weightlifting two-hand snatch 194
jump shot, basketball 30
jump surface, water skiing 193
jumper, ski jumping 153
jumping, water skiing 193
jumping area, high-jump (track and field) 185
jumping area, long and triple jump (track and field) 184
jumping boot, ski jumping 153
jumping hill, ski jumping 153
jumping ski 153
jumpmasters, sky diving (aerial sports) 7
jumps, motocross track 131
jumps, roller skating 139
jumps, freestyle figure skating 72, 73
jungle/rough, golf course 82
jury, fencing 65

Karate, martial arts 120–122
karters, karting 114
karting 114
karts, karting 114
kata, karate match (martial arts) 120
kayaking 45
keel, cruising sailboat (yachting) 208
keel, yachting 202
keel designs, yachting 201
keeper, polo saddle 134
keeper ring, fly rod (angling) 11
keeper/wrist strap, platform tennis paddle 133
kegler, bowling 38
kempo/kung fu/wu shu, martial arts 125
kendo, martial arts 128
kendo jacket/shirt/keikogi, (martial arts) 128
kendoka, kendo (martial arts) 128
kenjutsu, kendo (martial arts) 128
kennel, dog racing 60
kevlar, yachting 200
key/free throw lane/3-second lane/'paint,' basketball court 30
keyboard, bowling console 39
keypad, timer (track and field) 189
keys, bowling console 39
keystone sack, baseball slang 25
kiai, kendo (martial arts) 128
kick, pitcher's stretch position (baseball) 28
kick areas, soccer field 156
kick off, football 75
kick-off return team, football 76
kick plate, ice hockey rink 108
kick starter, motocross bike 129
kick/swivel, pitcher's full wind-up (baseball) 28
kicking, water polo foul 192
kicking boot/kicker, field hockey goalie 69
kickoff team, football 76
kicks, rodeo 137
kicktail/tail, skateboard 149
kickturn arabesque/scale, gymnastics 89

kidney, martial arts striking point 126
kidney protection belt, luge 118
kidney punch, boxing foul 43
kilian hold, ice dancing (figure skating) 74
kill, tennis 172
kill shot/smash/putaway, table tennis 167
killer, clockface game (darts) 53
killing 191
kilt/skirt, field hockey uniform 69
kiltie, golf shoes 84
king pin/ action bolt/truck bolt, roller skate 140
king post, hang glider (aerial sports) 6
kingpin, bobsled 34
kingpin, bowling 39
kisser, archer 16
kitty/jack, lawn bowling 117
knee, martial arts fighting 127
knee boot, harness horse racing 103
knee-boot suspenders, harness horse racing 103
knee cups, motocross rider 131
knee guards, polo player 134
knee hose/socks/stockings, fencer 65
knee pad, canoe 44
knee pad, football equipment 79
knee pad, ice hockey center/wing/defenseman 110
knee pad, roller hockey 140
knee pad, skateboarder 149
knee pad, volleyball 190
knee protector, luge 118
knee roll, eventing (equestrian events) 64
knee roll/sweat flap, polo saddle 134
knee sock, cross country skier 154
knee sock, field hockey 69
kneeling, rifle shooting position 144
kneeling pad, rifle shooting 144
kneeling position, wrestling 197
knickers, cross country skier 154
knickers/pantaloons/trousers, fencer 65
knicks/togs, Gaelic football 81
knife, scuba diver (diving/spear fishing) 58
knife hand, karate kata (martial arts) 121
knife hand, martial arts fighting 127
knife hand to back of neck, karate kumite (martial arts) 121
knight/castle, synchronized swimming position 162
knob, baseball bat 26
knob, softball bat 158
knob/butt end/butt, lacrosse stick 115
knockdown, boxing match 43
knockout/KO, boxing match 41, 42
knockout zone/volley & overhead zone, tennis 171
knoll, ski jumping 153
knots, angling 10
knuckle bow/branch, sabre (fencing) 65
knuckle sandwich/duke, boxing slang 42
knuckleball, pitch movement (baseball) 29
kote/gauntlet/kendo (martial arts) 128
kumite, karate match (martial arts) 120
kung fu, martial arts 125

Label, curling broom 50
label/trademark, baseball bat 26
labonza/lunch box/breadbasket, boxing slang 42
labyrinth, luge 118

lace, ice hockey skate 108
laces, ice hockey player 110
laces, running shoe (track and field) 178
laces/binding, baseball glove 26
laces/stitches, baseball 26
lacing, football 75
lacing, ice hockey goalkeeper's catch glove 110
lacing, yachting 203
lacing gap, figure skate 71
lacing ropes, boxing ring 41
lacrosse 115, 116
ladder, competition fishing boat 207
ladies' tees/red tees, golf 82
lambswool patch, flyfishing vest 10
land and stick on-target, fencing 67
landed, angling 8
landing, high-jump straddle (track and field) 185
landing, horizontal bar (gymnastics) 95
landing, long-jumping technique (track and field) 184
landing, vaulting (gymnastics) 92
landing area/landing pit, high-jumping area (track and field) 185
landing gear strut, biplane (aerial sports–aerobatics) 2
landing hill, ski jumping 153
landing mat, vaulting (gymnastics) 92
landing pit, jumping area (track and field) 184
landing pit, pole vault (track and field) 186
landing position, hop, step and jump technique (track and field) 184
lane line, Olympic swimming pool 163
lane marker, Olympic swimming pool 163
lane marker, sculling heat (rowing) 141
lane marker discs, Olympic swimming pool 163
lane markers/snow ridges, speed skating rink 159
lane one, drag strip 20
lane space marks, basketball court 30
lane two, drag strip 20
lanes, basketball court 30
lanes, track and field 173
lanes/alleys, bowling 38,39
lanyard, orienteering compass 132
lap, speed skating 159
lap belt, drag racing fire suit 20
lap scorer, speed skating 159
lap time, timer (track and field) 189
laps, automobile racing 17
lariat, rodeo 138
last race, past performance chart (horse racing) 103
lateral line, fish 9
lateral side wall, jai alai cancha 113
latissimus dorsi muscle, bodybuilder 36
launch site, hang gliding (aerial sports) 6
lawn bowling 117
lawn tennis 168
lay up, basketball 33
'laydown position,' karting 114
layout, diving 57
layout eight/horizontal eight, aerobatics (aerial sports) 3
leach, sail plans (yachting) 200
lead adjustment, yachting 203
lead arm, hurdling technique (track and field) 176

lead cars scoring lights, automobile racetrack 18
lead-core line, angling 13
lead leg, high-jump straddle (track and field) 185
lead leg, hurdling technique (track and field) 176
'lead off hitter,' baseball scoreboard 27
lead-off man, relays (track and field) 175
lead weight, scuba diver (diving/spear fishing) 58
lead weights, horse racing 102
leader, umbrella rig (angling) 13
leader dressing, flyfishing vest 10
leaders, angling rip 14
leaders, fishing tackle box 9
leading edge, hang glider (aerial sports) 6
leadweight, racehorse 102
leaner/hobber, horseshoes 105
leather cover, football 75
leather cover, volleyball 190
leathers/webs, racehorse 102
leeward mark, iceboating course 107
leeward mark, Olympic yacht-racing course 199
left back/left fullback, soccer formations 156
left-center, slang baseball field 25
left cornerback/left corner, football formation 76
left-curve, luge 118
left defensemen, ice hockey 110
left defensive end, football formation 76
left fullback, field hockey pitch 68
left guard/weak side guard/quick guard, football formation 76
left halfback, field hockey pitch 68
left halfback, soccer formations 156
left-handed hitter's power alley/right-center, baseball slang 25
left-handed pocket, bowling 39
left hook, boxing punch 43
left inner, field hockey pitch 68
left jab, boxing punch 43
left linebacker/outside linebacker/strong side linebacker, football formation 76
left rail, surfboard 161
left safety/strong safety/monster/rover, football formation 76
left service court/ad court, platform tennis 133
left service court/ad court, tennis 169
left tackle/weak side tackle/quick tackle, football formation 76
left-turns, karting 114
left wing, field hockey pitch 68
left wing, soccer formations 156
left wings, ice hockey 110
leg, darts 53
leg brace/leg hinge, table tennis 166
leg bye, cricket umpire signal 48
leg development, bodybuilder 37
leg guard, field hockey goalie 69
leg guards, cricket 47
leg/stem, spinning reel (angling) 12
leg strap, sky diving parachute (aerial sports) 7
leg guard, cricket 47
legs, cricket positions 48
legs, Olympic yacht-racing course 199

legs, relays (track and field) 175
lens, scuba diver (diving/spear fishing) 58
let, table tennis 167
let, tennis 168
let judge, tennis–center court 168
lever, toe clamp binding (cross country skiing) 154
librero/center back/sweeper, soccer formations 156
lie, golf 85
lie, ice hockey stick 108
life jacket/ski vest, water skier 193
life lines, cruising sailboat (yachting) 208
life ring, competition fishing boat 206
life vest, slalom kayaking 46
lift, flycasting technique (angling) 11
lift, shot putting technique (track and field) 181
lift, weightlifting 194
lift-off phase, weightlifting two-hand snatch 194
lift/one-arm reverse Kennedy, roller skating 139
lifter/weightlifter 194, 195
lifter's attempts, on weightlifting attempt board 195
lifter's body weight class, on weightlifting attempt board 195
lifter's name, on weightlifting attempt board 195
lifter's nationality, on weightlifting attempt board 195
lifting handle, scull (rowing) 141
lifts, freestyle figure skating 72, 73
light beam, drag racing 20
light-heavyweights, boxing 43
light switch, motorcycle 130
lightweights, boxing 43
lightweights, sweep rowing 142
limb, archery bow 16
limb tip, archery bow 16
line, Alpine skiing 150
line, angling 8–15
line, basic fishing rig 9
line, bowling 38
line, golf 85
line dressing, flyfishing vest 10
line-guide posts, fly reel (angling) 11
line guides, fly reel (angling) 11
line judge/official timer, football officials 80
line judges/line umpires, tennis–center court 168
line of scrimmage/neutral zone, football 77
line orienteering 132
line roller/line guide, spinning reel (angling) 12
linebackers, football formation 76
lineman's hand pad, football equipment 79
lineman's stance/three-point stance, football 75
linemen, football formation 76
lines, basketball court 30
lines, bocce court 35
lines, court handball 99
lines, discus & hammer cage (track and field) 182
lines, fencing strip 66
lines, field hockey field 68
lines, football field 76, 77

lines, Olympic swimming pool 163
lines, platform tennis court 133
lines, polo ground 134
lines, rugby field 143
lines, shuffleboard court 148
lines, soccer field 156
lines, table tennis 167
lines, team handball 100
lines, water polo field 192
lines of attack&defense, fencing 66
'lineup,' surfing 161
lining, ice hockey skate 108
lining, western saddle (rodeo) 137
links/golf course 82
linksmen/midfielders, soccer formations 156
lip, wave (surfing) 161
lip/bill, plug (angling) 12
lip/extended toe, cross country skier's racing boot 154
lip/overhang, golf course 82
lip/rim, golf putting 86
lip/take-off point, ski jumping 153
live bait, angling 8
live bait cage, angling 9
live (bait) well, bass boat 13
live minnow rig, angling 14
load cords, ballooning 5
loaded, weightlifting 194
loading gate, shotgun (skeet and trapshooting) 146
lobe, figure skating 71
lobs, tennis 172
locating spigot, lawn bowling 117
lock, horizontal bar (gymnastics) 95
lock, parallel bars (gymnastics) 96
lock forwards, rugby scrum positions 143
lock nut/action nut, roller skate 140
lock ring, spinning reel (angling) 12
locked-out position/squat snatch, weightlifting two hand-snatch 194
locking nut, trolling reel (angling) 13
loft, golf clubs 85
logo/sponsor name, race car 17
long axis, figure skating 71
long hose/uniform sock, football uniform 79
long jump, decathlon (track and field) 188
long jump, heptathlon (track and field) 188
long jump & triple jump measuring device, track and field 189
long jump/broad jump, track and field 183
long-jump takeoff, jumping area (track and field) 184
long-jumping technique, track and field 184
long leader, double-level fishfinder rig (angling) 14
long leg/fine leg, cricket position 48
long-off, cricket position 48
long-on, cricket position 48
long program, freestyle figure skating 72
loop, figure skating 71
loop/clip/pin, basic fishing rig 9
loops, aerobatics (aerial sports) 2
loran and radio antennas, competition fishing boat 207
love, tennis 169
low, baseball strike zone 26
low bar rail, uneven parallel bars (gymnastics) 97

low house, skeet shooting range 147
low inside line, fencing 66
low outside line, fencing 66
lower body development/leg development, bodybuilder 37
lower control station/cockpit control, competition fishing boat 207
lower helm station, motoryacht hull 205
lower jaw/mandible, fish 9
lower limb, archery bow 16
lower panel, ice hockey skate 108
lower wing, biplane (aerial sports–aerobatics) 2
luff, sail plans (yachting) 200
luge toboggan sled/luge/rodel 118
luge 118
luger/luge tobogganist/luge racer 118
luminous point, orienteering compass 132
lumps, rodeo 137
lunge, fencing 67
lunge punch by male, karate kumite (martial arts) 120
lure, surfcasting rig (angling) 14
lure/rabbit/mechanical hare, dog racing 59
lures, angling 12
lures, fishing tackle box 9

M/Maiden, greyhound performance rating (dog racing) 59
machines, motorcycling 130
magazine cap, shotgun (skeet and trapshooting) 146
magazine catch, target pistol 145
magazine floor plate, rifle (shooting) 144
magazine pouch belt, biathlon contestant 154
magazine tube, shotgun (skeet and trapshooting) 146
magneto switch, Formula One aircraft cockpit (air racing) 4
magnifying lens/bulb, orienteering compass 132
maiden races, horse racing 102
main, sail plans (yachting) 200
main backstop, shooting range 145
main crossbeam/forward, yachting 203
main riser, sky diving parachute (aerial sports) 7
main sheet, iceboating 107
main standard/gooseneck, football goal 75
main steering arms/steering post, bobsled 34
main strings, tennis racket 169
main wing/air foil, dragster 21
mainsail, yachting 203
mainsail clew outhhaul, yachting 203
mainsail luff downhaul, yachting 203
mainsheet, cruising sailboat (yachting) 208
mainsheet, yachting 202
mainsheet block, iceboating 107
mainsheet block reference marks for clew outhaul position, yachting 203
mainsheet traveler/horse, yachting 203
major fouls, water polo 192
male ferrule, spinning rod (angling) 12
mallet, croquet 49
mallet/stick, polo 134
man-to-man defenses, basketball 33
manager, fighter's corner (boxing) 42
mandatory poses, bodybuilding 36

mandible/lower jaw, fish 9
manifold pressure gauge, race car 19
manual release, ski binding 152
manufacturer plate/spec plate, big game reel (angling) 15
manufacturer plate/spec plate, trolling reel (angling) 13
manufacturer's logo, ice hockey skate 108
map scales, orienteering compass 132
maple/bowling pin 39
marathon, track and field 178
mark, rodeo 137
mark, sailboarding race (yachting) 201
mark/spare, bowling 39
mark/strike, bowling 39
marker/clip, croquet wicket 49
marker for distance from ditch, lawn bowling 117
markers/spots/target arrows, bowling lane 38
marksman, shooting 147
martial arts striking points 126
martial arts 119–128
martingale, eventing (equestrian events) 64
mask/face mask, lacrosse 116
mask/face mask, scuba diver (diving/spear fishing) 58
mask/helmet, fencer 65
mask/men, kendo (martial arts) 128
mast, cruising sailboat (yachting) 208
mast, iceboat 107
mast, sailboard (yachting) 201
mast, yacht-racing crew 199
mast rotation control, yachting 203
mast/spar/stick, yachting 202
master brake cylinder, kart 114
master stateroom, motoryacht hull 205
maststep, iceboat 107
mat, gymnastics 91
mat, judo (martial arts) 123
mat, lawn bowling 117
mat, wrestling 196
mat/footer, lawn bowling 117
mat/strip/piste, fencing 66
match, court handball 99
match, Gaelic football 81
match, shuffleboard 148
match, soccer 155
match, tennis 169
match, wrestling 196
match/bout/assault, fencing 65
match/bout/fight, boxing 41
match play, golf 82
match race, motorcycling 130
mate, deep sea fishing 15
mate, yachting 206
materiality, fencing 67
matt/bale/butt/boss, archery target 16
maxilla, fish 9
measure, lawn bowling 117
measurement, tape measure (track and field) 189
measurement points, javelin throwing sector (track and field) 180
'meat'/sweet spot, baseball bat 26
mechanical hare/rabbit/lure, dog racing 59
mechanical surface agitation, diving pool 54
medal play, golf 82
medals 209
medley races, relays (track and field) 175

medley relay, swimming 164
meet winner, bodybuilding 37
meets, gymnastics 87
men's archery field 16
men's vault, gymnastics 92
mesh, lacrosse stick 115
mesh, table tennis net 166
mesh/net body, volleyball net 191
mesh screen, jai alai fronton 112
mesh top, cycle racing shoe 51
metal bat, softball 158
metallic jacket/lamé vest, electric foil fencing 66
meter markers, ski jumping 153
metric mile run, heptathlon (track and field) 188
mid-off, cricket position 48
mid-section shaft, spinning rod (angling) 12
mid-wicket, cricket position 48
midcourt area, squash racquets court 160
midcourt line/division line, basketball court 30
midcourt/substitute box area, basketball court 30
middle, baseball strike zone 26
middle deep zone/baker zone, football 77
middle-finger one-knuckle fist, martial arts fighting 126
middle/joint, fly rod (angling) 11
middle linebacker/inside linebacker, football formation 76
middleweights, boxing 43
midfielder, lacrosse field 115
midfielders/linksmen, soccer formations 156
midsection, fencing sword 65
midway line, soccer field 156
miles, automobile racing 17
minus square/ten-off square, shuffleboard court 148
minute hand, stopwatch (track and field) 189
mirror, freestyle figure skating 72
mirror, motorcycle 130
mis-hit drives, golf 85
misconduct, ice hockey officials' signal 111
misfires, trapshooting 146
miss/open/blow, bowling 39
mitt/glove, baseball 26
mitten, cross country skier 154
mobile starting gate, harness horse racing 104
Mohlberg/gainer, diving 57
money bet, horse-racing tote board 102
money bet, parimutuel ticket (horse racing) 103
monohull, yachting 202
monster, football formation 76
montgolfier/hot air balloon 5
mother/dam, dog racing 60
mother-in-law/seven pin, bowling 39
motion sickness pills, fishing tackle box 9
motocross bike, motorcycling 129
motor, kart 114
motorcycling 129–131
motoryacht 205
motos/heats, motorcycling motocross races 130
mounds, motocross track 129
mount, dog racing rabbit 59
mount, horizontal bar (gymnastics) 95

mount, parallel bars routine (gymnastics) 96
mount/polo pony/horse, polo 134
mount/racehorse 102
mounts, equestrian events 61
mounts, rodeo 137
mouse/shiner, boxing slang 42
mouth, ballooning 5
mouth, fish 9
movement of pitches, baseball 29
movements, gymnastics 87–98
mud mark/how horse runs in poor weather, past performance chart (horse racing) 103
muffler, motocross bike 129
Mulligan, clockface game (darts) 53
mulligan, golf 86
multihull/catamaran, yachting 203
muscle definition, bodybuilding 36
muscle development, bodybuilding 36
muscle hardness, bodybuilding 36
muscle size, bodybuilding 36
muscularity, bodybuilding 36
muzzle, dog racing 59
MX/motorcross, motorcycling 129

'N' number, ballooning 5
nap, tennis ball 169
national match target pistol, shooting 145
natural gaits, dressage (equestrian events) 63
navigation instruments, cruising sailboat (yachting) 208
navigation lights, cruising sailboat (yachting) 208
navigation station/navsta/chart table, cruising sailboat (yachting) 208
navigator, powerboat offshore crew (yachting) 204
navigator's seat, competition fishing boat 207
navigator's station, powerboat command console (yachting) 204
near falls, wrestling 196, 197
near pin/near fall, wrestling 196, 198
nearest ball/bocce ball 35
necessary yards, football 80
neck, curling stone 50
neck, golf 85
neck, pommel horse (gymnastics) 93
neck roll, football equipment 79
neck sock, drag racing fire suit 20
neck/throat, table tennis paddle 166
neckpiece, racehorse bridle 102
needle capsule, orienteering compass 132
needle punch/control clipper, orienteering 132
nelson, wrestling 198
nerf bar, kart 114
net, angling 14
net, badminton court 23
net, field hockey goal 69
net, Gaelic football 81
net, ice hockey goal 110
net, lacrosse 116
net, platform tennis court 133
net, soccer goal 155
net, table tennis 166
net, tennis court 169
net, volleyball 191
net, water polo goal 192

net anchor/center strap, tennis court 169
net antenna, volleyball 191
net body/mesh, volleyball net 191
net/cords, basketball hoop 30
net/goal, ice hockey rink 108
net position, tennis 171
net post, tennis court 169
net sideline marker, volleyball 191
netting, discus & hammer cage (track and field) 182
neutral corner, boxing ring 41
neutral position, wrestling 196
neutral position/get-ready position, table tennis 166
neutral zone, ice hockey rink 108
neutral zone, shuffleboard court 148
neutral zone/line of scrimmage, football 77
next shooter up, skeet shooting range 147
nine pin, bowling 39
ninin dori, aikido (martial arts) 124
no ball, cricket umpire signal 48
no basket/play does not count, basketball officials' signal 32
'no bird,' trapshooting 146
'no lift,' weightlifting 194
no-man's land, tennis 171
no score, karate (martial arts) 122
no scoring ring, dart board 53
no time out, time in with whistle, football officials' signal 80
nobby tire, motocross bike 129
nock, archery bow 16
nock, target arrow (archery) 16
non-striker, cricket 47
non-transparent jersey, speed (roller) skating 140
Nordic combined, skiing 153
Nordic skiing 153
norm point, ski jumping 153
north balkline, croquet 49
nose, cartridge (shooting) 145
nose, race car 17
nose, skateboard 149
nose, surfboard 161
nose bumper, football helmet 79
nose/end, football 75
nose plate, hang glider (aerial sports) 6
nose shroud & breathing filter, drag racing fire suit 20
noseband, dressage bridle (equestrian events) 63
nostril, fish 9
notches, spear gun (spear fishing) 58
number, basketball jersey 30
number cloth, racehorse 102
number four wood, golf club 85
number of points awarded, boxing scorecard 41
number one wood/driver, golf club 84, 85
number panels, kart 114
number plate, motocross bike 129
number three wood/spoon, golf club 84, 85
number two wood/brassie, golf club 84, 85
number 2 man, bobsledding 34
nursery course, horse-racing track 101
nylon, yachting 200
nylon webbing/anti-rope chafe strip, fighting chair harness (angling) 15
nymphs, angling 10

O-offense, team handball 100
O-ring, fighting chair harness (angling) 15
oar numbers, rowing crew 142
oar (rowing)/scull (sculling) 142
oarlock, rowing shell 142
oarsmen, sculling (rowing) 141
object ball/cue/jack/pallino, bocce 35
obstacles, show jumping (equestrian events) 61
obstruction, field hockey 69
obstructions, golf 85
octave position, fencing 66
odds, horse racing 103
odds, jai alai 112
odds, past performance chart (horse racing) 103
odds board/tote board, horse racing 102
odds on winning, horse-racing tote board 102
off-hand/standing, rifle shooting position 144
offense, football formation 76
offense, football 75
offensive backfield, football 77
offensive formation/T formation, football 76
offensive foul/charging, basketball officials' signal 32
offensive lob, tennis 172
offensive players, soccer formations 156
offensive rebound, basketball 31
offensive wrestler 196
officials, track and field 189
official's equipment, track and field 189
official's observation deck, automobile racetrack 18
officials' positioning, football 80
officials' signals, basketball 32
officials' signals, football 80
officials' signals, ice hockey 111
officials' signals, soccer 157
official's stand, motocross race 129
offshore crew, powerboat racing, yachting 204
offshore passages, yachting 208
offshore racers, yachting 199
offside, encroaching, football officials' signal 80
offside, soccer officials' signal 157
offside line, water polo 192
offsides, football 80
offsides, lacrosse referee signal 115
oil cooler, race car 17
oil cooler, sports car 22
oil filler, sports car 22
oil pressure gauge, race car 19
oil pressure gauge throttle, Formula One aircraft cockpit (air racing) 4
oil temperature, Formula One aircraft cockpit (air racing) 4
on-deck bat weight/'doughnut,' baseball 26
on-deck circle, baseball field 25
on-guard line, fencing strip 66
on-guard position/body balance, fencing 67
on-guard positions, fencing 66
on-off switch, ballooning basket 5
'on your mark,' sprints (track and field) 174
one-arm reverse Kennedy/lift, roller skating 139

one-design racing, yachting 199
one-hundred-and-ten meter hurdles, decathlon (track and field) 188
one-hundred-and-ten-meter hurdles, heptathlon (track and field) 188
one-hundred-meter dash, decathlon (track and field) 188
one-knuckle fist, martial arts fighting 126
one-meter springboard, diving pool 54
one-piece jump suit, ski jumping 153
one-piece suit/tank suit, swimming 163
one pin/headpin, bowling 39
one short, cricket umpire signal 48
one-tenth-of-a-second bits, stopwatch (track and field) 189
open/blow/miss, bowling 39
open class, hang gliding (aerial sports) 6
open-cockpit, open-wheel, single-seat race cars, 17–19
open-faced spinning reels, angling 12
open gates, Alpine skiing 150
open-hand methods, martial arts fighting 127
Open Jumpers, show jumping (equestrian events) 61
'open' road race course, speed (roller) skating 140
opening score, darts 53
opercule/operculum/gill cover/preopercle, fish 9
optional routines, gymnastics 87
order of play/colors, croquet 49
ordinary fouls, water polo 192
Oriental/penholder, table tennis 166
orienteering arrow, compass 132
orienteering map/'O' map 132
orienteering 132
orienteers 132
orienting lines, orienteering compass 132
orthodox/shakehands, table tennis 166
out, cricket umpire signal 48
out of bounds, basketball officials' signal 32
out of bounds, football 77
out-of-bounds, golf course 82
out of bounds, water polo field 192
out of bounds area, jai alai cancha 113
out-run, ski jumping 153
out-run position, ski jumping 153
out/strike, baseball umpire's signal 29
outboard engine, bass boat 13
outer lane, speed skating rink 159
outer markers, equestrian events dressage arena 63
outfield, baseball field 25
outfielders (left fielder, center fielder, right fielder), baseball 25
outline, skeet and trapshooting target 147
outrigger, scull (rowing) 141
outriggers, competition fishing boat 207
outside, baseball strike zone 26
outside backs, soccer formations 156
outside corner, baseball strike zone 26
outside edge, figure skating 71
outside rail, horse-racing track 101
outside retaining wall, automobile racetrack 18
outside sleeve, weightlifting international standard barbell 195
outsole, running shoe (track and field) 178

oval, speed skating 159
oval bead, spinner (angling) 12
over, cricket 47
over & under shotgun, skeet and trapshooting 147
overflow gutter, Olympic swimming pool 163
overhand/roundhouse, boxing punch 43
overhang header, firing range station (pistol shooting) 145
overhang/lip, golf course 82
overhead, tennis 171
overhead cam, motorcycle 130
overhead smash, tennis 171
overhead spinning cast, angling 12
overlapping grip, golf putting 86
overserve line/pass line, jai alai cancha 113
overshoot area, sport parachuting (aerial sports) 7
owner, dog racing 60
owner, past performance chart (horse racing) 103
owner's plaque, ballooning basket 5
ox-jaw hand, martial arts fighting 127
oxer/spread, equestrian show jumping fence 62

Pace, dressage (equestrian events) 63
pace, orienteering 132
pace car, automobile racetrack 17, 18
pace counter, orienteering compass 132
pacers, horse racing 104
'pack,' distance running (track and field) 178
pack, sky diving (aerial sports) 7
pack rod, spinning travel set (angling) 12
pad/blanket, rodeo horse 138
pad/blanket/rifle rest, shooting 144
pad/ground cloth/blanket, rifle shooting 144
pad pocket, football uniform 79
padded base, basketball column 30
padded case, spinning travel set (angling) 12
padded collar, high-jump shoe (track and field) 185
padded fan motor guard 18
padded glove, luge 118
padded glove, roller hockey 140
padded gloves, motocross rider 131
padded helmet, cycling 51
padded palm/dress palm, handball glove 99
padded pants, motocross rider 131
padding, ballooning basket 5
padding, baseball catcher's equipment 26
padding, fencing shoe 65
padding, running shoe (track and field) 178
paddle, canoeing 44
paddle, kayaking 45
paddle, platform tennis 133
paddle/racket/bat, table tennis 166
paddle tennis 133
paddlers, canoeing 45
paddock judges, dog racing 59
'paint'/free throw lane/3-second lane, basketball court 30
pairs, freestyle figure skating 72
palle, bocce ball 35
pallino/jack/cue/object ball, bocce 35
palm, baseball glove 26

palm, ice hockey goalkeeper's catch glove 110
palm, lacrosse glove 115
palm heel, martial arts fighting 127
palm protector/handguard/grip, horizontal bar (gymnastics) 95
palomar knot, angling 10
panel, Gaelic football 81
panel, polo saddle 134
panel seams, ballooning 5
panels, ballooning 5
panels, football 75
panels, volleyball 190
pantaloons/knickers/trousers, fencer 65
pants, baseball 26
pants, football uniform 79
pants, ice hockey player 110
pants/trunks/shorts, lacrosse 116
par for hole, golf scorecard 86
parachute, hang glider (aerial sports) 6
parachute, sky diving (aerial sports) 7
parachute pack, dragster 21
parachute valve/parachute vent, ballooning 5
paragraph, figure skating 71
parallel bars, gymnastics 96
parallel poles/spread, equestrian show jumping fences 62
parallel spin/camel spin/arabesque spin, freestyle figure skating 73
parallelogram, Gaelic football 81
parallelogram, hurling 106
parimutuel betting, horse racing 103
parimutuel betting, jai alai 112
parimutuel ticket/betting ticket, horse racing 103
parry, fencing 67
parry 4, fencing 66
parry 6, fencing 66
parry 7, on guard positions, fencing 66
parry 8, fencing 66
parts, gymnastics 88
pass line/overserve line, jai alai cancha 113
pass patterns/pass routes, football 78
passage, dressage (equestrian events) 63
passes, relay race (track and field) 175
passing, football 75
passing from the pocket, football 78
passing pocket, football 77
passing shots, tennis 171
passing techniques/handoffs, relays (track and field) 175
past performance chart, dog racing 60
past performance chart, horse racing 103
PAT, football 78
paved shoulder/apron, automobile racetrack 18
payoff, horse racing 103
peak, tennis 172
pectoral fin, fish 9
pectoral muscles, bodybuilder 36
pectoral separation/chest raphe/chest depression, bodybuilder 37
pedal, road racing bicycle 51
pedal/block, starting blocks (track and field) 174
pedestal seats/fighting chairs, bass boat 13
pedigree, past performance chart (horse racing) 103
peg/stake, croquet 49
pelota/ball, jai alai 113

pelvic fins/ventral fins, fish 9
penalties, football 80
penalties, ice hockey 108
penalty area, roller hockey rink 140
penalty area, soccer field 156
penalty area arc, soccer field 156
penalty box/'sin bin,' ice hockey rink 108
penalty bully, field hockey 69
penalty corner, field hockey 69
penalty kick, soccer 155
penalty kick mark/penalty spot, soccer field 156
penalty mark, team handball 100
penalty spot, field hockey pitch 68
penalty spot, roller hockey rink 140
penalty spot/40-yd mark, polo ground 134
penalty stroke, field hockey 69
penalty strokes, golf 86
penholder/Oriental, table tennis 166
periods, ice hockey 108
periods, water polo 192
periods, wrestling 196
personal foul, basketball officials' signal 32
personal foul, clipping, roughing, football officials' signals 80
personal fouls, basketball 32
petticoat, archery target 16
philtrum, martial arts striking point 126
photo finish/finish line photo, horse racing 104
phrase d'armes, fencing 67
physique contest, bodybuilding 36
piaffe, dressage (equestrian events) 63
pickup arm/bail, spinning reel (angling) 12
'pig farm'/running boar range, rifle shooting 144
pigeons/birds/clays/targets, skeet and trapshooting 147
piggin' string, rodeo calf roping 138
pigskin/football 75
pike position, diving 56
pike position, vaulting (gymnastics) 92
pimpled, table tennis paddle 166
pin, wrestling 196
pin/anchor, starting blocks (track and field) 174
pin/clip/loop, basic fishing rig 9
pin deck, bowling 39
pin-finder, bowling lane 38
pin/flagstick/stick, golf course green 82
pin hole, archery target 16
pin-setter, bowling lane 38
pinch-hitters, baseball 28
ping pong/table tennis 166, 167
pinning positions, wrestling 198
pins, bowling 38, 39
pipeline/tube, wave (surfing) 161
pipes/exhaust system, kart 114
piping, baseball pants 26
piping vent, handball glove 99
pips/pimples/pebbles, table tennis paddle 166
pirouettes, equestrian events 63
piste/strip/mat, fencing 66
pistol grip/small of stock, shotgun (skeet and trapshooting) 146
pistol range, shooting 145
piston, horizontal bar (gymnastics) 95
piston, horse (gymnastics) 92
piston, parallel bars (gymnastics) 96

pit, bocce court 35
pit, bowling 39
pit, motocross track 131
pit crew, automobile racing 19
pit headset, automobile racing pit crew 19
pit line, automobile racetrack 18
pit runway, automobile racetrack 18
pit steward/sanctioning-body official, autombile racing pit 19
pit (track and field), high-jump 185, long jump and triple jump 184, pole vault 186
pit/trenches/the line, football 77
pitboard area 17
pitch, cricket 48
pitch, field hockey field 68
pitch & trim adjustment, Formula One aircraft cockpit (air racing) 4
pitch/field, Gaelic football 81
pitch/field, hurling 106
pitch/field, rugby 143
pitch/field, soccer field 156
pitcher, baseball player position 25
pitcher's delivery/windmill, softball 158
pitchers' grips, baseball 28
pitcher's mound, baseball field 25
pitching, baseball 28
pitching box/pitcher's box, horseshoes 105
pitching wedge, golf 85
pitchng court, horseshoes 105
pitot tube, glider (aerial sports) 6
pits, automobile racetrack 18
pivot, roller skate 140
pivot player/circle runner, team handball 100
pivot point, sweep rowing 142
pivot/turn/spin/rotation, discus throwing technique (track and field) 182
place, horse racing 103
placekick, rugby 143
plant, pole vaulting technique (track and field) 186
planting box/vault box/box, pole vault (track and field) 186
plastic-coated racing suit, luge 118
plastic disc, harness horse racing 103
plastic heel cup, high-jump shoe (track and field) 185
plastic spool, trolling reel (angling) 13
plasticine indicator/foul line, jumping area (track and field) 184
plate, downrigger (angling) 13
plate, golf shoes 84
plates/discs, weightlifting 195
platform, platform tennis 133
platform/stage, weightlifting 195
platform tennis 133
platform tennis ball 133
platform tennis court 133
platform tennis paddle 133
platforms, diving pool 54
player, bocce 35
player, shuffleboard 148
player benches, ice hockey rink 108
player number, football uniform 79
player number, soccer jersey 155
player number, volleyball 190
player number, water polo cap 192
player number committing foul, basketball officials' signal 32

players, karate (martial arts) 120
player's cage, jai alai cancha 113
players' rotation, volleyball 190
player's surname, basketball jersey 30
playing area/face, platform tennis paddle 133
playing zone, shuffleboard court 148
plays, football 75
plow anchor, competition fishing boat 206
plug, lure (angling) 12
'plug casting,' angling 12
pocket, baseball glove 26
pocket, ice hockey goalkeeper's catch glove 110
pocket, lacrosse stick 115
pocket, scuba diver (diving/spear fishing) 58
pocket, spinning travel set (angling) 12
pocket/strike pocket, bowling 39
pockets, polo breeches 135
point, dart (darts) 53
point, fishhook 9
point, Gaelic football 81
point, ice hockey skate 108
point-after-touchdown, football 78
point/button/tip/end, fencing sword 65
point orienteering 132
point/pile/arrowhead/head, target arrow (archery) 16
point system, wrestling 196
point value, pistol shooting target 145
points, boxing scorecard 41
points, jai alai scoreboard/betting board 112
points, wrestling 196–198
pole, drag racing Christmas tree 21
pole exit socket, ski binding 152
pole lane, distance running & race walking (track and field) 178
pole position, (flat) horse-racing 101
pole position/inside lane, sprints (track and field) 174
pole vault, decathlon (track and field) 188
pole/vaulting pole, track and field 186
poles, harness horse racing 101
poll, hurling hurley 106
polo 134, 135
polo & exercise bandage/foreleg bandage, polo pony 134
polo ground/polo field 134
polo helmet/cap, polo player 134
polo pony 134, 135
polo shirt, eventing (equestrian events) 64
polo spurs, polo player 134
pommel, western saddle (rodeo) 137
pommel/handle, pommel horse (gymnastics) 93
pommel horse/side horse, gymnastics 93
pommel/saddlebows/head, polo saddle 134
pool, diving 54
pool/bath, water polo field 192
pool deck, Olympic swimming pool 163
popoff valve, race car 17
popping crease, cricket pitch 48
port, yachting 202
port-engine clutch, competition fishing boat 207
port jib sheet, yachting 203
port quarter, yachting 202
port tack position, iceboating 107

port throttle, competition fishing boat 207
portlight, motoryacht deck 205
ports, competition fishing boat 206
ports o'call, 205
posedown, bodybuilding 37
posing ability, bodybuilding 36
posing outfit, bodybuilding 37
posing platform, bodybuilding 36
position, fencing 66
position and odds, jai alai 112
position at finish, past performance chart (horse racing) 103
position during race, past performance chart (horse racing) 103
position lines, jai alai cancha 113
position number, polo 135
position of fingers, figure skating 71
position of hands, figure skating 71
position of non-skating foot, figure skating 71
positions, baseball 25
positions, biathlon rifle shooting 154
positions, cricket 48
positions, diving 56
positions, fencing 65–67
positions, field hockey 68
positions, hurling 106
positions, iceboating 107
positions, rifle shooting 144
positions, rugby 143
positions, skeet and trapshooting 147, 148
positions, ski jumping 153
positions, soccer 156
positions, synchronized swimming 162
positions, tennis court 171
positions, volleyball 190
positions, wrestling 197, 198
post, badminton court 23
post, football pass pattern 78
post, platform tennis court 133
post-flight/second flight, vaulting (gymnastics) 92
post position, dog racing program 60
post position/starting gate, horse-racing program entry 103
post position/team number, jai alai 113
'post'/starting gate, (flat) horse-racing 101
posture, bodybuilding 36
posture, figure skating 71
power alleys, slang baseball field 25
power cord, drag racing Christmas tree 21
power hook-up, trapshooting range 146
power I, football formation 77
power play, ice hockey 108, 111
power position/jump position, weightlifting two-hand snatch 194
powerboat racing (yachting) 204
practice boards/warm-up boards, diving pool 54
pre-flight/first flight, vaulting (gymnastics) 92
pre-game jersey/batting practice shirt, baseball 26
predicament, wrestling 198
predicted log contests, yachting 205
preliminary contests, diving 54
preliminary swings, hammer throwing technique (track and field) 183

preopercle/gill cover/operculum/opercule, fish 9
presentation, bodybuilding 36
presenting the ball, softball pitcher's delivery 158
press box, automobile racetrack 18
press to handstand/strength part, parallel bars (gymnastics) 96
pressure fan assembly, ballooning burner assembly 5
pressure gauge, ballooning burner assembly 5
pressure gauge, scuba diver (diving/spear fishing) 58
pressure gauge hose, scuba diver (diving/spear fishing) 58
pressure skirt, ballooning 5
prestart, speed skating rink 159
primer, cartridge (shooting) 145
prize fighters/professional boxers, boxing 42
prize ring/boxing ring, boxing 41
probable morning odds/pre-race betting odds, horse-racing program entry 103
Production, sports car racing 22
production roof, sports car 22
professional boxers/prize fighters, boxing 42
professional tees/championship tees/blue tees, golf 82
program number/starting gate number, horse racing 101
projection, bodybuilding 36
prone, rifle shooting position 144
prone position, biathlon rifle shooting 154
prop forwards, rugby scrum positions 143
propeller, biplane (aerial sports–aerobatics) 2
propeller/prop/screw, motoryacht hull 205
protective caps, .22 rifle (biathlon) 154
protective cone, pommel horse (gymnastics) 93
protective padding, under football uniform 79
protector/protective cup, sparring equipment (boxing) 42
protractor-type compass, orienteering 132
puck, ice hockey 108
pug nose, boxing slang 42
pugilist/pug/palooka/gladiator, boxing slang 42
pull, flycasting technique (angling) 11
pull, pole vaulting technique (track and field) 186
pull, swimming 164
'pull,' trapshooting 146
puller, skeet and trapshooting 147
pulling-under phase, weightlifting clean-and-jerk, two-hand snatch 194
pullout/strength maneuver, rings (gymnastics) 94
pulls, wrestling 198
pulls leather, rodeo 137
pulpit, competition fishing boat 206
pump, pitcher's full wind-up (baseball) 28
pump, pitcher's stretch position (baseball) 28
pump, using a fighting chair (angling) 15
'pump up,' bodybuilding 36

punch/delivery, shot putting technique (track and field) 181
punches & strategies, boxing 43
punt, football 76
punt return team, football 76
punta/point, jai alai cesta 113
punting, football 76
purse, horse racing 102
pursuit races, speed skating 159
pursuits, cycling 51
push bar retraction assembly, bobsled 34
push-off and clearance, pole vaulting technique (track and field) 186
pusher handle, bobsled 34
pushes, wrestling 198
pushing, basketball officials' signal 32
pushing, lacrosse referee signal 115
pushing, soccer officials' signal 157
pushing, water polo foul 192
put down rubber, automobile racing 17
putaway, tennis 172
putaway/smash/kill shot, table tennis 167
putter, golf club 85
putting, golf 86
putting surface/carpet, golf course green 82
pylons, Formula One racecourse (air racing) 4
pylons/corner markers, speed (roller) skating 140
pyramid sinkers, angling 14
pyrometer, ballooning basket 5

Qualifying throws, discus (track and field) 182
quantity gauge, ballooning basket 5
quarte position, fencing 66
quarter berth, cruising sailboat (yachting) 208
quarter circles/serving box, squash racquets court 160
Quarter horse racing 101, 102
Quarter horses, rodeo 138, 139
quarter-mile track, track and field 173
quarter-mile/440 yard course, drag strip 20
quarter-turns, bodybuilding 37
quarterback/field general, football formation 76
quarters, football 75
quarters, lacrosse 115
queen-sized berth, motoryacht hull 205
quick-disconnect refueling safety valve, automobile racing pit 19
quick drop, using a fighting chair (angling) 15
quinella, bet (horse racing) 103
quiver, archery 16
quiver belt, archery 16

Rabbit/lure/mechanical hare, dog racing 59
rabbit punch, boxing foul 43
race committee boat, sailboarding race (yachting) 201
race course, Olympic kayaking 45
race lane, swimming 163
race number, betting ticket (horse racing) 103
race number, Formula One aircraft (air racing) 4
race start, sailboarding (yachting) 201
race walking, track and field, 178, 179

race walking/heel and toe, track and field 178
race-walking technique, track and field 179
racehorse/mount 102
racehorse starts, air racing 4
racetrack, automobile 18, 20, 22
racetrack, dog racing 59
racetrack/raceway/racecourse, horse racing 101
raceway, karting 114
racing, automobile 17–22
racing, swimming 163
racing bib & entry number, slalom kayaking 46
racing boot, cross country skier 154
racing cap, swimming 163
racing program, dog racing 60
racing program, horse racing 103
racing shells, sculling (rowing) 141
racing shoe, cycling 51
racing shoe, drag racing fire suit 20
racing shorts, cycling 51
racing slick/tire, dragster 21
racing slick/tire, kart 114
racing suit, luge 118
racing tire, race car 17
racing track/velodrome, cycling 52
rack & pinion steering and suspension systems, race car 17
rack/set-up, bowling 38, 39
racket, squash racquets 160
racket, tennis lines 169
racket hand, table tennis 166
racket/paddle/bat, table tennis 166
racquet, racquetball 136
racquetball glove 136
racquetball 136
radar antenna, competition fishing boat 206
radiator, motocross bike 129
radiator/air intake, race car 17
radio antenna, race car 17
radio antenna, stock car 22
radio push-to-talk switch, race car 19
radio wiring, race car 19
rail, long- & triple-jump measuring device (track and field) 189
rail, surfboard 161
rail, table tennis 166
rail/dragster, drag racing 21
rail grabs, skateboard 149
rail/low bar, uneven parallel bars (gymnastics) 97
rail/top bar, uneven parallel bars (gymnastics) 97
railing/barrier/traffic line, speed (roller) skating 140
rails, horse-racing track 101
raised boards, equestrian events dressage arena 63
rally, badminton 23
rally, table tennis 166
ram wing, unlimited hydroplane (yachting) 204
ramp, motocross track 131
ramp, ski jump (water skiing) 193
range & loft of clubs, golf 85
range, pistol shooting 145
range, running game target shooting 144
range, skeet shooting 147
range, trapshooting 146
range officer, shooting 144

rapid-fire pistol, shooting 145
ratchet block, yachting 203
ratchet/lift handle, volleyball net 191
rating in strokes, golf scorecard 86
RBI/runs batted in, baseball scoreboard 27
reach, flycasting technique (angling) 11
reaching, yachting 208
'Ready,' shooting 145
ready position, tennis serve 170
rear arm, fencing 67
rear bearing, spinning reel (angling) 12
rear body panel, race car 17
rear brake, road racing bicycle 51
rear brake cable, road racing bicycle 51
rear brake lever, motocross bike 129
rear brake lever, motorcycle 130
rear bumper/'bunks,' bobsled 34
rear cinch/flank billet/flank cinch, western saddle (rodeo) 137
rear deck overlay, sports car 22
rear derailleur, road racing bicycle 51
rear foot, race walking technique (track and field) 179
rear hood and butt cap, fly rod (angling) 11
rear hood/rear seat ring, spinning reel (angling) 12
rear jockey/back housing, western saddle (rodeo) 137
rear limit line/end line, fencing strip 66
rear rigging ring/dee ring, western saddle (rodeo) 137
rear shock absorber/boinger, motorcycling 130
rear sight, biathalon 154
rear sight, target pistol 145
rear single-disc brake, motorcycle 130
rear spiker's line/attack line, volleyball court 191
rear spoiler, stock car 22
rear spoiler/wing, race car 17
rear suspension system, race car 17
rear toe binder, water ski 193
rearview mirror, race car 17
rebote/back wall, jai alai cancha 113
rebounding, basketball 31
recall key, timer (track and field) 189
recall rope, Olympic swimming pool 163
recall starter, track and field 189
receiver, football formation 76
receiver, shotgun (skeet and trapshooting) 146
receiver, table tennis 166
receiver restraining line, court handball 99
receiving line, court handball 99
receiving line/5-foot line, racquetball court 136
receiving phase/squat clean, weightlifting 194
recoil spring plug, target pistol 145
record alignments system, photo finish (horse racing) 104
recording machine, electric fencing 66
records, on weightlifting attempt board 195
recovery, shot putting technique (track and field) 181
recovery, swimming 164
recovery phase, weightlifting two-hand snatch 194
rectangle, basketball backboard 30

rectus abdomins, bodybuilder 36
recurve, archery bow 16
red flag, automobile racing 17
red light, ice hockey goal judge's box 108
red-lighting, drag racing 20
red line/center line, ice hockey rink 108
red line clew outhaul, yachting 203
red tees/ladies' tees, golf 82
red (time expired/trial nullified) on field event timer (track and field) 189
reduce drag and wait, using a fighting chair (angling) 15
reef points, mainsail (yachting) 200
reel, fencing strip 66
reel, spinning (angling) 12
reel, tape measure (track and field) 189
reel attachment, fencing strip 66
reel foot, big game reel (angling) 15
reel foot, fly reel (angling) 11
reel foot, trolling reel (angling) 13
reel-foot posts, fly reel (angling) 11
reel frame/rim, fly reel (angling) 11
reel housing/sideplate assembly, big game reel (angling) 15
reel housing/sideplate assembly, trolling reel (angling) 13
reel reinforcement, big game reel (angling) 15
reel seat, fly rod (angling) 11
reel seat, spinning reel (angling) 12
reel seat/machined-hood reel seat, big game rod (angling) 15
reel-seat washer, fly rod (angling) 11
referee, Olympic swimming pool 163
referee, polo 135
referee, sculling heat (rowing) 141
referee, volleyball 190
referee, water polo field 192
referee, wrestling 196
referee light system/judges lights, weightlifting 195
referee/ref, boxing ring 41
referee signals, lacrosse 115
referees, basketball 32
referees, weightlifting 194
referee's crease, ice hockey rink 108
refrigerated luge track 118
refueler, automobile racing pit crew 19
registration number, biplane (aerial sports–aerobatics) 2
registration number, Formula One aircraft (air racing) 4
registration number/'N' number, ballooning 5
'regular foot,' surfing 161
regulation play, ice hockey 108
regulation play tees/white tees, golf 82
regulator hose/air hose, scuba diver 58
regulator mouthpiece, scuba diver (diving/spear fishing) 58
rein, racehorse 102
reinforcing, skate 159
reining, rodeo 137
reins, dressage turnout (equestrian events) 63
reins, harness horse racing 103
reins, luge 118
reins, rodeo cowgirls barrel racing 138
reins/steering cables, bobsled 34
relative work, team sky diving (aerial sports) 7
relay exchange zone, track and field 173
relay orienteering 132

relays/relays races, track and field 175
release, javelin throwing technique (track and field) 180
release, pitcher's full wind-up (baseball) 28
release, spinning cast (angling) 12
release adjustment, ski binding 152
release adjustment screw, ski binding 152
release cable, skeet shooting range 147
release/delivery, discus throwing technique (track and field) 182
release/delivery, hammer throwing technique (track and field) 183
release/flight, parallel bars routine (gymnastics) 96
release lever/release button, fly reel (angling) 11
release point, pitcher's stretch position (baseball) 28
release/snap, softball pitcher's delivery 158
released, angling 8
releasing a fish 8, 206
relief pitchers, baseball 28
relief valve, race car 17
remote cameras, automobile racetrack 18
remote electronic blast valve controls, ballooning basket 5
rendezvous, yachting 205
repechage, sculling (rowing) 141
repulsion, vaulting (gymnastics) 92
reserve chute, sky diving (aerial sports) 7
reset button, motorcycle 130
reset button, stopwatch (track and field) 189
resin, fighter's corner (boxing) 42
rest, fighting chair (angling) 15
rest position, figure skating 71
restraining circle, basketball court 30
retirement, weightlifting 195
retractable lifting handle, bobsled 34
retreat zone/safety zone/end zone, fencing strip 66
retrieved, angling 12
retriever/defender/chopper, table tennis 167
return, table tennis 167
return, tennis 170
return crease, cricket pitch 48
returned, platform tennis 133
reversal of advantage, wrestling 196, 198
reverse, discus throwing technique (track and field) 182
reverse, hammer throwing technique (track and field) 183
reverse, shot putting technique (track and field) 181
reverse curve/backup ball, bowling 39
reverse dive 57
reverse gate, whitewater slalom (canoeing & kayaking) 46
reverse left-hand punch, karate kata (martial arts) 120
reverse punch by female, karate kumite (martial arts) 120–121
reverse right-hand punch, karate kata (martial arts) 120
rhythmic exercises, gymnastics 90
rib, hurling hurley 106
rib, scuba diver (diving/spear fishing) 58
rib cage, bodybuilder 36

rib protector/'flak jacket,' football equipment 79
ribbon, gymnastics 90
ribs, badminton shuttlecock 23
ribs, martial arts striking point 126
ribs, sky diving parachute (aerial sports) 7
ribs/costilla, jai alai cesta 113
richochet fencing/bullet barricade/'berm,' shooting range 145
ride, rodeo 137
ride off, polo 135
rider, cycling 51
rider number, motocross helmet 131
riders, show jumping (equestrian events) 61
ridge hand, martial arts fighting, 127
riding boot, polo 134, 135
riding glove, polo player 134
riding gloves, dressage turnout (equestrian events) 63
riding shirt/'rat catcher,' equestrian show jumping 62
riding time, wrestling 196
rifle, biathlon 154
rifle, shooting 144
rifle rest/pad/blanket, rifle shooting 144
rigger, rowing shell 142
rigging, hang glider (aerial sports) 6
rigging handle/handhold, rodeo bareback bronc riding 137
right-angle flex, fencing 67
right back/right fullback, soccer formations 156
right-center, slang baseball field 25
right cornerback/right corner, football formation 76
right cross, boxing punch 43
right-curve, luge 118
right defensemen, ice hockey 110
right defensive end, football formation 76
right defensive tackle, football formation 76
right fielder, baseball player position 25
right fullback, field hockey pitch 68
right guard/strong side guard/tight guard, football formation 76
right halfback, soccer formations 156
right-handed hitter's power alley/left-center, baseball slang 25
right inner, field hockey pitch 68
right linebacker/outside linebacker/weak side linebacker, football formation 76
right of way, fencing 66
right of way, polo 135
right rail, surfboard 161
right safety/free safety, football formation 76
right service court/deuce court, platform tennis 133
right service court/deuce court, tennis 169
right side cover, motorcycle 130
right tackle/strong side tackle/tight tackle, football formation 76
right-turns, karting 114
right wing, field hockey pitch 68
right wing, soccer formations 156
right wings, ice hockey 110
rigs, angling 9, 14
rim, cartridge (shooting) 145

rim, discus (track and field) 182
rim, skeet and trapshooting target 147
rim, track racing bicycle 52
rim/hoop/ring/iron, basketball hoop 30
rim/lip, golf putting 86
rim/metal rim, platform tennis paddle 133
rim/reel frame, fly reel (angling) 11
ring/circle, discus & hammer cage (track and field) 182
ring guide/butt guide, fly rod (angling) 11
ring post, boxing ring 41
ringer, horseshoes 105
rings, gymnastics 94
ringside, boxing ring 41
rink, ice hockey 108
rink, speed skating 159
rink barrier, roller hockey rink 140
rink/curling team 50
rink number, lawn bowling 117
rinks, lawn bowling 117
rip entry, diving 57
rip panel, ballooning 5
riposte, fencing 66
rise, tennis 172
rising fastball/aspirin/bullet, pitch movement (baseball) 29
rising target trajectory, skeet shooting 147
road, golf course 82
road and track, eventing (equestrian events) 64
road holder, competition fishing boat 206
road race course, speed (roller) skating 140
road racing bike, cycling 51
roadracing bike/street bike, motorcycling 130
roadracing kart/enduro kart, karting 114
rock back, pole vaulting technique (track and field) 186
rock/stone, curling 50
rocker, figure skating 71
rocker, surfboard 161
'rocker'/arc, luge 118
rod, competition fishing boat 207
rod, spinning (angling) 12
rod holder/rod butt holder, flyfisherman 10
rod man, football officials 80
rod mount/foot, spinning reel (angling) 12
rod/pack rod, spinning travel set (angling) 12
rod/pole, basic fishing rig 9
rod tip/blade, spinning rod (angling) 12
rod-winding thread, fishing rod 15
rodel/luge toboggan sled/luge 118
rodeo 137, 138
rodeo clown, rodeo 137
rodeo plant/rodeo arena 138
rodholder, downrigger (angling) 13
rogue's badge/blinkers/blinder's, horse racing 102
roll, rifle shooting 144
roll, swimming 164
roll bar, race car 17
rollcage, dragster 21
roll line, bocce foul line 35
roll/straddle, high-jump (track and field) 185
rollcage, sports car 22
rollcage, stock car 22

roller, big game rod (angling) 15
roller skate, roller hockey 140
roller skating 139–140
roller tip, big game rod (angling) 15
rolling circle with four horizontal rolls,
    aerobatics (aerial sports) 3
rolls, aerobatics (aerial sports) 2
rolls, bowling 38
rooster tail, unlimited hydroplane
    (yachting) 204
rope & chain locker, motoryacht hull 205
rope, women's rhythmic exercise
    (gymnastics) 91
rope connector/reel connector, fighting
    chair harness (angling) 15
rope strap, western saddle (rodeo) 137
ropes, boxing ring 41
roquet, croquet 49
rotating bait lid, fishing bait cage 9
rotation, volleyball 190
rotation/pivot/turn/spin, discus
    throwing technique (track and field)
    182
rough/jungle, golf course 82
roughing, ice hockey officials' signal 111
round, golf 82
round, skeet shooting 147
round heel, boxing slang 42
round judged even, boxing scorecard 41
round-the-clock, darts 53
rounded seat front, fighting chair
    (angling) 15
rounded side/right hand side, field
    hockey goalie 69
roundhouse kick, karate kata (martial
    arts) 121
roundhouse/overhand right, boxing
    punch 43
rounds, archery 16
rounds, boxing 41
routines, gymnastics 87–98
routines, synchronized swimming 162
rover, football formation 76
rover, softball 158
rowel/spur wheel, rodeo 137
rowing technique 141, 142
rowing 141, 142
rub rail, competition fishing boat 206
rubber bands, spear gun (spear fishing)
    58
rubber grip, softball bat 158
rubber/slab, baseball slang 25
rubber-soled shoes, court handball 99
rubber-soled shoes, jai alai 113
ruck, rugby 143
rudder, biplane (aerial
    sports–aerobatics) 2
rudder, cruising sailboat (yachting) 208
rudder, glider (aerial sports) 6
rudder, motoryacht hull 205
rudder, rowing shell 142
rudder, yachting 202
rudder cable, glider cockpit (aerial
    sports) 6
rudder-down line, yachting 203
rudder stock, yachting 203
ruether board/springboard/beat board,
    gymnastics 92
rugby league 143
rugby union 143
rugby 143
run, baseball 24
run, cricket 47

run, deep sea fishing 15
run, diving 55, 56
run, drag racing 20
run-up, long-jumping technique (track
    and field) 184
run-up/approach, high-jump straddle
    (track and field) 185
run-up/runway/fan, high-jumping area
    (track and field) 185
runner, baseball 25
runner, iceboating 107
runner, luge 118
runner/blade, ice hockey skate 108, 110
runner/blade, skate 159
runner/blade/'steels,' luge 118
runner chock, iceboating 107
runner/glide, shuffleboard cue 148
runner plank, iceboating 107
runner shoe, bobsled 34
runner tip, bobsled 34
runner's direction, relays baton handoff
    (track and field) 175
running, football 75
running, yachting 208
running block, cruising sailboat
    (yachting) 208
running boar range/'pig farm' rifle
    shooting 144
running dives, diving 56
running edge, curling stone 50
running game target shooting 144
running (see track 173–179)
running shoe, track and field 178
runs, hits, errors/totals, baseball
    scoreboard 27
runs, luge 118
runs batted in, baseball scoreboard 27
runs in inning, baseball scoreboard 27
runs scored, baseball scoreboard 27
runway, Formula One racecourse (air
    racing) 4
runway, long-jumping technique (track
    and field) 184
runway, vaulting (gymnastics) 92
runway/approach, bowling lane 38
runway/approach, javelin throwing
    sector (track and field) 180
runway markings, Formula One aircraft
    (air racing) 4

S-curve, luge 118
sabre/saber, fencing equipment 65
sabre target area, fencing 68
sack/bag, baseball slang 25
saddle, dressage turnout (equestrian
    events) 63
saddle, harness horse racing 103
saddle, polo 134
saddle, pommel horse (gymnastics) 93
saddle, racehorse 102
saddle blanket, polo pony 134
saddle bronc riding, rodeo 138
saddle pad, dressage turnout
    (equestrian events) 63
saddle pad, equestrian events 62
saddle string/tie, western saddle (rodeo)
    137
saddlebow/pommel/head, polo saddle 134
saddlecloth, harness horse racing 103
safe, baseball umpire's signal 29
safe, baseball 26
safe-point wire fence, automobile
    racetrack 18

safe start, automobile racing 17
safety, football officials' signal 80
safety, football 78
safety, shotgun (skeet and trapshooting)
    146
safety, spear gun (spear fishing) 58
safety area, judo mat (martial arts) 123
safety barrier, automobile racetrack 18
safety goggles, iceboating 107
safety helmet/crash helmet, iceboating
    107
safety line, automobile racetrack 18
safety line, cycling velodrome 52
safety padding, football goal 75
safety snap, fighting chair harness
    (angling) 15
safety zone, archery fields 16
safety zone, Formula One racecourse (air
    racing) 4
safety zone, polo ground 134
safety zone/end zone/retreat zone,
    fencing strip 66
safety, football formation 76
sail & anchor storage, cruising sailboat
    (yachting) 208
sail, hang glider (aerial sports) 6
sail, iceboating 107
sail, sailboard (yachting) 201
sail panel, iceboat 107
sail plans, yachting 200
sail trimmer, yacht-racing crew 199
sailboarding, yachting 201
sailboats, yachting 199
sailing harness, sailboard (yachting) 201
sailmaker's logo, iceboat 107
sailplanes, soaring (aerial sports) 6
saloon door, motoryacht deck 205
saloon window, motoryacht deck 205
saltwater tackle, angling 8
salute, fencing 65
sanctioning bodies' inspection stickers,
    race car 17
sand, landing pit (track and field) 184
sand trap/bunker, golf course 82
sand wedge, golf 85
sand whoops, motocross race 129
sand worm/surf bait, angling 14
sandwich, table tennis paddle 166
sanitary hose, baseball uniform 26
sanitary hose, football uniform 79
sash/faja, jai alai 113
save, ice hockey 108
sawdust, landing pit (track and field) 184
scale, gymnastics 89
scend, wave (surfing) 161
school figures/compulsory figures, figure
    skating 71
school initial, wrestling mat 196
schooling/dressage, equestrian events 63
scissors, flyfishing vest 10
scoop, lacrosse stick 115
scope, long- & triple-jump measuring
    device (track and field) 189
scope/telescopic scope, rifle (shooting)
    144
score, bowling 39
score counts & number of free throws,
    basketball officials' signal 32
scoreboard, baseball 25, 27
scoreboard, bocce 35
scoreboard, darts 53
scoreboard, drag strip 20
scoreboard, jai alai 112

scoreboard, tennis–center court 168
scoreboard, track and field 173
scorecard/card, boxing 41
scorecard/card, golf 86
scorer, archery 16
scorer, lawn bowling 117
scorer, rifle shooting 144
scorer, skeet and trapshooting 146
scorer, track and field 189
scorer's table, basketball court 30
scoring, bowling 39
scoring an ippon, karate (martial arts)
    122
scoring areas, shuffleboard 148
scoring blows, boxing 43
scoring box, pistol shooting target 145
scoring diagram/scoring triangle,
    shuffleboard court 148
scoring format, bowling console 39
scoring pylon, automobile racetrack 18
scoring/scoring lines, golf wood 85
scoring triangle/scoring diagram,
    shuffleboard court 148
scoring zones point value, archery 16
scramble, motorcycling 129
scratch line/arc/foul line/toe board,
    javelin throwing sector (track and
    field) 180
scratch marks, relays (track and field)
    175
scratch race, motorcycling 130
screen, bowling console 39
screen, ice hockey 108
screen play, ice hockey 111
screen-wire cover, stock car 22
screw-locking nut and hood, fly rod
    (angling) 11
screw/propeller/prop, motoryacht hull
    205
screwball, pitch movement (baseball) 29
scrubbers, clockface game (darts) 53
scrum, rugby 143
scrum half, rugby scrummage formation
    143
scrum positions, rugby 143
scrummage formation, rugby 143
scuba/self-contained underwater
    breathing apparatus 58
scuff pad, ballooning basket 5
scull (sculling) oar 142
scullers, rowing 141
sculling technique 141
sea floor/sea bottom, surf fishing 14
seam, football 75
seam, handball glove 99
seam, tennis ball 169
seat, bobsled 34
seat, fighting chair (angling) 15
seat, harness horse racing 103
seat, kart 114
seat, luge 118
seat, motorcycle 130
seat, polo breeches 135
seat, race car 17
seat, track racing bicycle 52
seat, western saddle (rodeo) 137
seat bolt, luge 118
seat fastening/clasps, luge 118
seat/rider's posture, dressage
    (equestrian events) 63
seat/sliding seat, scull (rowing) 141
seat stay, track racing bicycle 52
seat tube, track racing bicycle 52

seatback, fighting chair (angling) 15
second, hammer throwing technique (track and field) 183
second base, baseball field 25
second baseman, baseball player position 25
second bits, stopwatch (track and field) 189
second flight/post-flight, vaulting (gymnastics) 92
second hand, stopwatch (track and field) 189
second man, relays (track and field) 175
second position, fencing salute 65
seconds/handlers/cornermen, fighter's corner (boxing) 42
sector flag, shot putting sector (track and field) 181
sector line, discus & hammer cage (track and field) 182
sector line, javelin throwing sector (track and field) 180
sector line, shot putting sector (track and field) 181
sectors/single-score ring, dart board 53
Sedan, sports car racing 22
segmented thumb, lacrosse glove 115
self launch open class, hang gliding (aerial sports) 6
self soaring/hang gliding/sky surfing, aerial sports 6
sensei, martial arts 119
separation triangle, shuffleboard court 148
septime position, fencing 66
series, shooting 145
serpentine, dressage figure (equestrian events) 63
serratus anterior, bodybuilder 36
serve, tennis 170
server, table tennis 166
service area, jai alai cancha 113
service box/doubles box 99
service courts, badminton court 23
service line, jai alai cancha 113
service line, platform tennis court 133
service line, racquetball court 136
service line, squash racquets court 160
service line, tennis court 169
service line/front line, court handball 99
service/putting ball in play, table tennis 167
service side line, platform tennis court 133
service zone, court handball 99
service zone, racquetball court 136
serving area, volleyball court 191
serving box/quarter circle, squash racquets court 160
serving player's line, jai alai cancha 113
set, badminton 23
set, tennis 169
set dance, ice dancing (figure skating) 74
set/hold, pitcher's stretch position (baseball) 28
set the hook, angling 8
set up, volleyball 191
set-up/rack, bowling lane 38, 39
settee, cruising sailboat (yachting) 208
settee, motoryacht hull 205
setter/two-meter man/hole man, water polo 192

seven-and-a-half meter platform, diving pool 54
seven pin/mother-in-law, bowling 39
sewing, Gaelic football 81
sex, dog racing bertillion card 60
sex, past performance chart (horse racing) 103
shadow roll, racehorse 102
shadowed, freestyle figure skating 72
shaft, Alpine ski pole 150
shaft, badminton racket 23
shaft, canoe paddle 44
shaft, croquet mallet 49
shaft, dart (darts) 53
shaft, field hockey stick 69
shaft, golf clubs 85
shaft, harness horse racing 103
shaft, ice hockey goalie stick 110
shaft, javelin (track and field) 180
shaft, kayak paddle 45
shaft, lacrosse stick 115
shaft, motoryacht hull 205
shaft, oar & scull 142
shaft, polo mallet 134
shaft, shuffleboard cue 148
shaft, spear gun (spear fishing) 58
shaft, squash racquets 160
shaft, target arrow (archery) 16
shaft, tennis racket 169
shaft carrier, harness horse racing 103
shakehands/orthodox, table tennis 166
Shanghai, clockface game (darts) 53
shank, fishhook 9
shank, golf drive 85
sheath, scuba diver (diving/spear fishing) 58
sheer, competition fishing boat 206
sheet, curling rink 50
shelf/deck, bowling console 39
shell, baseball catcher's equipment 26
shell, football helmet 79
shell, rowing 142
shell, ski boot 152
shell bag/ammo pouch, skeet shooter 147
shell/helmet, track cycle racing 52
shiaigo/contest area, judo mat (martial arts) 123
shift, pole vaulting technique (track and field) 186
shift and power phase, weightlifting clean-and-jerk 194
shift phase, weightlifting two-hand snatch 194
shifters, road racing bicycle 51
shin & ankle boot, harness horse racing 103
shin, martial arts striking point 126
shin guard, roller hockey 140
shin guards, football equipment 79
shin pad, soccer 155
shin pad/shin guard, ice hockey center/wing/defenseman 110
shinai/bamboo sword, kendo (martial arts) 128
shiner/mouse, boxing slang 42
shinguard, baseball catcher's equipment 26
shinguard, rodeo cowgirls barrel racing 138
shinpad, field hockey equipment 69
shirt, baseball 26

shirt, roller hockey 140
shirt, table tennis 167
shirt/jersey, soccer 155
shirt/kendo jacket/keikogi, kendo (martial arts) 128
shock absorber, bobsled 34
shock cord, spear gun (spear fishing) 58
shock cord release finger, spear gun (spear fishing) 58
shoe, baseball 26
shoe, bobsledding 34
shoe, cycling 51
shoe, fencing 65
shoe, football 79
shoe, harness horse racing 103
shoe, high-jump (track and field) 185
shoe, horseshoe pitching 105
shoe, running (track and field) 178
shoe, weightlifting 195
shoe/boot, soccer 155
shoes (see also boots)
shoes, automobile racing 20
shoes, basketball sneakers 30
shoes, court handball 99
shoes, fishing 10
shoes, golf 84
shoes, jai alai 113
shoes, javelin (track and field) 180
shoes, sculling (rowing) 141
shoes, table tennis 167
shoes, wading (fishing) 10
shoes, wrestling 196
shoot, flycasting technique (angling) 11
shooter, team handball 100
shooters' running boards/targets, running game target shooting 144
shooters' scoring & timing clocks, running game target shooting 144
shooting 144–147
shooting bench 144
shooting circle/striking circle, field hockey pitch 68
shooting glasses, rifle shooting 144
shooting lines, archery fields 16
shooting position, rifle 144
shooting position, skeet range 147
shootout, soccer officials' signal 157
shootout, soccer 155
short axis, figure skating 71
short double-level fishfinder rig (angling) 14
short fielder, softball 145
short-handed, ice hockey 108
short line, court handball 99
short program, freestyle figure skating 72
short service line, badminton court 23
short service line, racquetball court 136
short track speed skating 159
short zone/dog zone, football 77
short zone/easy zone, football 77
shorts, basketball player 30
shorts, court handball player 99
shorts, roller hockey 140
shorts, rugby 143
shorts, soccer player 155
shorts, table tennis 167
shorts/trunks/pants, lacrosse 116
shortstop, baseball player position 25
shot, bowling 38
shot, golf 86
shot, ice hockey 108

shot clock/24-second clock, basketball 30
shot on goal, water polo 192
shot put, decathlon (track and field) 188
shot put, heptathlon (track and field) 188
shot put, track and field 181
shot put ring/circle, track and field 181
shot put shoe, track and field 181
shot putters, track and field 181
shot putting sector, track and field 181
shot putting technique, track and field 181
shotgun, football formation 77
shotgun, skeet and trapshooting 146
shotgun shell/cartridges/'ammo,' marksman (shooting) 147
shots, shot put (track and field) 181
shots, tennis 171
shoulder, curling stone 50
shoulder, ski 152
shoulder, tennis racket 169
shoulder and arm protection, ice hockey goalkeeper 110
shoulder carrying cord, fishing bait cage 9
shoulder harness, drag racing 20
shoulder harness, race car 17
shoulder pad, lacrosse 116
shoulder pads, football equipment 79
shoulder pads, ice hockey center/wing/defenseman 110
shoulder sling/carrying sling, golf bag 84
shoulder strap, fishing creel 10
shoulder/wall, wave (surfing) 161
shoulder-width stance, karate kata (martial arts) 120
shovel, ski 152
show, horse racing 103
show jumping, equestrian events 62
shower/stall shower, motoryacht hull 205
shroud, cruising sailboat (yachting) 208
shroud length adjuster, yachting 203
shroud/sidestay, iceboating 107
shrouds, yachting 202
shuffleboard 148
shuttlecock/shuttle/bird, badminton 23
side, synchronized swimming position 162
side aerial, gymnastics 89
side alley, badminton court 23
side boards/side line/touch line, polo ground 134
side-chest pose, bodybuilding 36
side deck, competition fishing boat 206
side gimbal/gimballed socket, fighting chair (angling) 15
side horse/pommel horse, gymnastics 93
side judge, football officials 80
side kick, karate kata (martial arts) 121
side kick, karate (martial arts) 122
side line, platform tennis court 133
side line, table tennis 166
side lines, badminton court 23
side mirrror, sports car 22
side of knee, martial arts striking point 126
side of neck, martial arts striking point 126
side plate, sports car 22
side plate/end plate, race car 17
side push handle, bobsled 34
side rail, scuba diver (diving/spear fishing) 58
side rail cover, ballooning basket 5

side screen, platform tennis court 133
side skirt/aerofoil, sports car 22
side triceps pose, bodybuilding 36
side wall, bocce 35
side wall, court handball 99
side wall, racquetball court 136
side wall, squash racquets court 160
sideboard, bocce court 35
sideboard, field hockey goal 69
sideboards/boards, ice hockey rink 108
sidecars, motorcycling motocross races 130
sideline, basketball court 30
sideline, fencing strip 66
sideline, field hockey pitch 68
sideline, football 77
sideline, lacrosse field 115
sideline, volleyball court 191
sideline/touchline, soccer field 156
sideplate, big game reel (angling) 15
sideplate, trolling reel (angling) 13
sideplate assembly/reel housing, big game reel (angling) 15
sideplate assembly/reel housing, trolling reel (angling) 13
sideplates, fly reel (angling) 11
sidepod, race car 17
sidewall, lacrosse stick 115
sidewall, ski 152
sidewall, water ski 193
sight, spear gun (spear fishing) 58
sight gauge, Formula One aircraft cockpit (air racing) 4
signal flag, water polo field 192
signature/autograph, baseball bat 26
silencers/ear muffs, shooting 145
silent anti-reverse housing, spinning reel (angling) 12
silhouette, shooting 145
silks/colors, driver (harness horse racing) 103
silks/colors, jockey (horse racing) 102
silly mid-off, cricket position 48
silly mid-on, cricket position 48
'sin bin'/penalty box, ice hockey rink 108
single handhold, rodeo 137
single-seat, open wheel, open cockpit race cars 17–19
single wing, football formation 77
singles, freestyle figure skating 72, 73
singles, platform tennis 133
singles, racquetball 136
singles, tennis 168
singles court, platform tennis 133
singles side line, badminton court 23
singles sideline, tennis court 169
singlet/weightlifting costume 195
singlets, track and field 173
sink, cruising sailboat (yachting) 208
sink, motoryacht hull 205
sinker leader, live minnow rig (angling) 14
sinker/weight/split shot, basic fishing rig 9
sinkers, surf fishing rigs 14
sire/father, dog racing 60
sire/father, horse-racing program entry 103
sire of dam, horse-racing program entry 103
sissy bar, motorcycling 130
sitting, rifle shooting position 144
six, freestyle figure skating 72

six pin, bowling 39
six runs, cricket umpire signal 48
sixte position, fencing 66
skate, speed skating 159
skateboarding 149
skating dress, figure skating 71
skating foot/employed foot, figure skating 71
skating surface/track, speed (roller) skating 140
skeet & trap machine/trap, shooting 147
skeet range, shooting 147
skeet vest/trap vest, marksman (shooting) 147
skeg, sailboard (yachting) 201
skeg/fin, surfboard 161
ski, cross country 154
ski, water skiing 193
ski boat, water skiing 193
ski brake, ski binding 152
ski glove, water skier 193
ski jump, water skiing 193
ski jumping 153
ski pole, Alpine skiing 150
ski pole, cross country skier 154
ski rope/towline, water skier 193
ski vest/life jacket, water skier 193
skiing 150–154
skin/dirt, baseball slang 25
skip/curling captain 50
skipper, iceboating 107
skippers, yachting 201
skirt, badminton shuttlecock 23
skirt, ballooning 5
skirt, curling broom 50
skirt, jig (angling) 12
skirt, polo saddle 134
skirt, scuba diver (diving/spear fishing) 58
skirt, slalom kayaking 46
skirt, spinning reel (angling) 12
skirt, western saddle (rodeo) 137
skirt band, ballooning 5
skirt/kilt, field hockey uniform 69
skirt/tail, spinner (angling) 12
skis, Alpine 150, 152; Nordic 153, cross country and biathlon 154
skull, martial arts striking point 126
'skull cap'/crash helmet, horse racing 102
sky, golf drive 85
sky diving, aerial sports 7
sky diving/hang gliding/sky surfing, aerial sports 6
sky surfing/hang gliding/sky surfing, aerial sports 6
'sky poles,' pole vault (track and field) 186
slab/rubber, baseball slang 25
slack line, deep sea fishing 15
slalom, skateboarding 149
slalom, water skiing 193
slalom Alpine skiing 150
slalom course, water skiing 193
slalom course buoy, water skiing 193
slalom kayak, 46
slalom ski/water ski 193
slalom sweater, skier 150
slam/stuff/dunk/slam, basketball 30
slant/slant-in, football pass pattern 78
slanted front pockets, polo breeches 135
slash, spare in bowling 38, 39
slashing, ice hockey officials' signal 111
slashing, lacrosse referee signal 115
sleds, bobsledding 34

sleds runners, luge 118
'sleeping foot,' hop, step and jump technique (track and field) 184
sleeve, Gaelic football sweater 81
sleeved jersey, cycling 51
slice, tennis serve 170
slice/fade, golf drive 85
slick, automobile racing track condition 17
slide, long- & triple-jump measuring device (track and field) 189
slide handle, shotgun (shooting) 146
slide lock safety, target pistol 145
slide lock safety notch, target pistol 145
slide notch, target pistol 145
slide spring, spear gun (spear fishing) 58
slide stop, target pistol 145
slider, pitch movement (baseball) 29
slider, sky diving parachute (aerial sports) 7
slides, target pistol 145
sliding door, competition fishing boat 207
sliding pyramid sinker, double-level fishfinder rig (angling) 14
sling, .22 rifle (biathlon) 154
sling, rifle (shooting) 144
slingshot dragsters, drag racing 20
slippers, gymnast 93
slips, cricket position 48
'slips' the punch, boxing defense 43
slipstreams, karting 114
slot, football 77
slot, ice hockey rink 108
slow pitch, softball 145
slug/bullet/head, cartridge (shooting) 145
small of stock/pistol grip, shotgun (skeet and trap shooting) 146
small of the back, martial arts striking point 126
smallbore, rifle shooting 144
smallbore sport pistol, shooting 145
smash/kill shot/putaway, table tennis 167
smoothness, figure skating 71
snake guard, fly rod (angling) 11
snap, live minnow rig (angling) 14
snap, sky diving parachute (aerial sports) 7
snap/release, softball pitcher's delivery 158
snapped, football 80
'snapper'/center, football formation 76
snatch/two-hand snatch, weightlifting 194, 195
sneakers, basketball player 30
snorkel, scuba diver (diving/spear fishing) 58
snout, fish 9
snow board, platform tennis 133
snow ridges/lane markers, speed skating rink 159
snow ring/basket, cross country skier 154
soaring, aerial sports 6
soccer/association football 155–157
sock, baseball 26
sock, cross country skier 154
sock, field hockey 69
sock, ice hockey center/wing/defenseman 110
sock, roller hockey 140
sock/stocking, soccer 155
socks, basketball player 30

socks (see also stockings)
socks/stockings, Gaelic football 81
socks/stockings, hurling 106
socks/stockings/knee hose, fencer 65
softball bat 158
softball field 158
softball 158
solar plexus, martial arts striking point 126
sole, cycle racing shoe 51
sole, golf iron 85
sole, ice hockey skate 108
sole, martial arts fighting 127
sole cup, skate 159
sole plate, roller skate 140
sole plate, skate 159
soleus muscle, bodybuilder 36
somersault, diving 54, 57
soup/swash, wave (surfing) 161
south balkline, croquet 49
south of the border/downstairs, boxing slang 42
spacer bead, spinner (angling) 12
span, bowling ball 38
spar/mast/stick, yachting 202
spare/mark, bowling 39
sparring, kung fu (martial arts) 125
sparring equipment, boxing 42
spear fishing 58
spear gun, spear fishing 58
spear hand, martial arts fighting 127
spearfishermen/spear fishers 58
spearing, ice hockey officials' signal 111
special substitution area, lacrosse field 115
special team, football 76
spectator interference, baseball umpire's signal 29
spectator section, court handball 99
speed, eventing (equestrian events) 64
speed at finish, drag strip 20
speed key, timer (track and field) 189
speed skating 159
speedometer, motorcycle 130
speedway, automobile racing track 17
speedway, motorcycling 130
speedway karters, karting 114
spike, golf shoes 84
spike-proof floor mat, golf cart 84
spiked shoe, bobsledding 34
spiker, volleyball 190
spikes/cleats, baseball 26
spikes/creepers, iceboating 107
spiking, volleyball 191
spin, aerobatics (aerial sports) 2
spin casting, angling 12
spin/pivot/turn/rotation, discus throwing technique (track and field) 182
spindle, dragster 21
spindle, fly reel (angling) 11
spinnaker run, yachting 200
spinnaker/tri-radial, yachting 200
spinner, biplane (aerial sports–aerobatics) 2
spinner, lure (angling) 12
spinner, in spinning travel set (angling) 12
spinning rod, angling 12
spinning travel set, angling 12
spins, aerobatics (aerial sports) 2
spins, freestyle figure skating 72, 73
spins, roller skating 139

spiny dorsal fin/dorsal fin, fish 9
spiny rays, fish 9
spire/extension, croquet 49
splash guard/coaming/cockpit rim, kayak 45
splashing, water polo foul 192
split, bowling 38
split, synchronized swimming position 162
split converted, bowling 38
split decision, boxing match 41
split end, football formation 76
split end/wide receiver/wide out, football formation 76
split side/weak side, football 77
splitter, sports car 22
spock, bocce 35
spock line, bocce foul line 35
spoiler/air foil/front wing, dragster 21
spoiler/dive plane/front wing, race car 17
spoiler/wing/tail, race car 22
spoked adjustment unit, weightlifting international standard barbell collar 195
spokes, harness horse racing 103
spokes, motocross bike 129
spokes, track racing bicycle 52
sponges, fighter's corner (boxing) 42
sponson, unlimited hydroplane (yachting) 204
sponsor name/logo, race car 17
sponsor's decals, motocross rider 131
'spook,' angling 13
spool, spinning reel (angling) 12
spool cap, fly reel (angling) 11
spool centering & tension knob, big game reel (angling) 15
spool centering & tension knob, trolling reel (angling) 13
spoon, surfboard 161
spoon/number three wood, golf club 84, 85
spoons, angling 12
spoons, fishing tackle box 9
sport parachuting, aerial sports 7
sport shoelaces, skate 159
sportfish/competition fishing boat 206
sportfisherman/angler 8
sports car 22
sportsfisherman/competition fishing boat 206
spot weld, skate 159
spots/target arrows/markers, bowling lane 38
spotter, shooting 144
spotting scope, shooting 144
spray bottle, fighter's corner (boxing) 42
spreader, uneven parallel bars (gymnastics) 97
spreaders, competition fishing boat 207
spreads, equestrian show jumping fences 62
spring board, iceboat 107
spring-loaded retriever button, flyfishing vest 10
spring point, electric foil fencing 66
spring races, canoeing & kayaking 44
springboard, diving pool 54
springboard/ruether board/beat board, gymnastics 92
sprint draw pass football passing play 78
sprint kart, karting 114
sprint karters, karting 114

sprint/regatta, sculling (rowing) 141
sprinter, track and field 174
sprints, cycling 51
sprints, speed (roller) skating 140
sprints/dashes, (track and field) 174
sprints starting line/chute, track and field 173
sprocket, motocross bike 129
spun, tennis 170
spur, jockey (horse racing) 102
spurring, rodeo 137
spurring out area, rodeo bareback bronc riding 137
spurs, equestrian show jumping 62
square-in, football pass pattern 78
square leg, cricket position 48
square-out, football pass pattern 78
squash racquets/squash 160
squash tennis 160
squat clean/receiving phase, weightlifting clean-and-jerk 194
squat snatch/locked-out position, weightlifting two-hand snatch 194
stabilizer, luge 118
stabilizer blocks, football helmet 79
stabilizer rod, archery bow 16
stabilizer/wing, unlimited hydroplane (yachting) 204
stabilizers, glider (aerial sports) 6
stage/platform, weightlifting 195
stages, cycling 51
staggered start, speed skating 159
staggered start, sprints (track and field) 174
staggered starting area, track and field 173
stainless steel spool, big game reel (angling) 15
staircase/triple bars, equestrian show jumping fence 62
stake, horseshoes
stake/peg, croquet 49
stall gate, sports car 22
stall turn/hammerhead, aerobatics (aerial sports) 3
stanchion, competition fishing boat 206
stanchion, cruising sailboat (yachting) 208
stanchion, fighting chair (angling) 15
stanchion/brace, figure skate 71
stanchion/column/upright, basketball 30
stand, archery target 16
stand off half/fly half, rugby scrummage formation 143
standard blast valve, ballooning basket 5
standard bottom fishing rig, angling 14
standard/upright, high-jumping area (track and field) 185
standard/upright, pole vault (track and field) 186
standing at time, on computerized performance indicator (track and field) 189
standing dives 56
standing/off-hand, rifle shooting position 144
standing position, biathlon rifle shooting 154
stands, drag strip 20
star class monohull, (yachting) 203
star drag, big game reel (angling) 15
star drag, trolling reel (angling) 13
starboard, yachting 202

starboard-engine clutch, competition fishing boat 207
starboard quarter, yachting 202
starboard sheet, yachting 203
starboard tack position, iceboating 107
starboard throttle, competition fishing boat 207
start, bobsled course 34
start, dog racing 59
start, equestrian show jumping course 62
start, relays (track and field) 175
start, swimming meet 163
start/finish line, cycling velodrome 52
start gate, motocross track 131
start handle, luge 118
start/stop, split/reset buttons, timer (track and field) 189
starter, drag strip 20
starter, (flat) horse-racing 101
starter, mobile starting gate (harness horse racing) 104
starter, Olympic swimming pool 163
starter, speed skating rink 159
starter, track and field 189
starter's pistol/gun, track and field 189
starter's stand, (flat) horse-racing 101
starting, sailboarding race (yachting) 201
starting blocks, luge 118
starting blocks, sprints (trade and field) 174
starting blocks, swimming 163
starting boxes, dog racing 59
starting field, automobile racing 17
starting gate, ski jumping 153
starting gate crewmen, (flat) horse-racing 101
starting gate mover, (flat) horse-racing 101
starting gate number/program number, horse racing 101
starting gate/post position, horse-racing program entry 103
starting grooves, bobsledding 34
starting lights/Christmas tree, drag racing 20, 21.
starting line, drag racing 20
starting line, Formula One racecourse (air racing) 4
starting line, luge 118
starting line, Olympic yacht-racing course 199
starting pontoon, kayaking racecourse 45
starting position, shot putting technique (track and field) 181
starting positions, diving 55
starting technique, sprints (track and field) 174
starting traps/boxes, dog racing 59
starts, dog racing program 60
starts, speed skating rink 159
static port tube rudder cable, glider cockpit (aerial sports) 6
stationary rear foot, fencing 67
statistics for season, baseball scoreboard 27
steal, baseball 26
steel band/hoop, hurling hurley 106
steel compression spring, springboard (gymastics) 92
steel toe, field hockey goalie 69
'steels'/runner/ blade, luge 118

steeplechase, eventing (equestrian events) 64
steeplechase, track and field 177
steeplechase course, horse-racing track 101
steeplechase water jump, track and field 173
steer, luge 118
steer, rodeo steer wrestling 138
steer wrestling/bulldogging, rodeo 138
steering cables, rowing shell 142
steering controls, golf cart 84
steering handle/adjustable back 15
steering hub/wheel hub, race car 19
steering ratio adjustment, bobsled 34
steering rings, bobsled 34
steering runner, iceboat 107
steering shaft, kart 114
steering toggle, sky diving parachute (aerial sports) 7
steering wheel, kart 114
steering wheel, race car 19
stem, road racing bicycle 51
stem/leg, spinning reel (angling) 12
step & ridge hand to throat, karate kumite (martial arts) 121
stern, canoe 44
stern, kayak 45
stern, yachting 202
stern light, competition fishing boat 206
stern light, cruising sailboat (yachting) 208
stern pulpit, cruising sailboat (yachting) 208
stern thwart, canoe 44
'stevie'/throat protector, baseball catcher's equipment 26
stick, field hockey 69
stick, ice hockey 110
stick, lacrosse 115, 116
stick, roller hockey 140
stick-checking, ice hockey 109
stick/flagstick/pin, golf course green 82
stick-glove backpad, ice hockey goalkeeper 110
stick/whip/bat/crop, horse racing 102
still positions, balance beam (gymnastics) 98
stirrup, harness horse racing 103
stirrup, poloist and mount 134
stirrup, rodeo cowgirls barrel racing 138
stirrup, speed skater 159
stirrup, western saddle (rodeo) 137
stirrup iron, racehorse 102
stirrup leather bar, polo saddle 134
stirrup sock, baseball uniform 26
stirrup strap, western saddle (rodeo) 137
stirrups, dressage turnout (equestrian events) 63
stirrups, gymnast 93
stitches, softball 158
stitches/laces, baseball 26
stock, rifle (shooting) 144
stock, rodeo 137
stock, target pistol 145
stock/buttstock, shotgun (skeet and trap shooting) 146
stock car 22
stock grip cap, shotgun (skeet and trapshooting) 146
stock performance, rodeo 137
stock saddle/western saddle, rodeo 137
stockings (see also socks)

stocking/sock, rugby 143
stockings, football uniform 79
stone court, bocce 35
stone/rock, curling 50
stone/upright, equestrian show jumping fence 62
stool, fighter's corner (boxing) 42
stop, flycasting technique (angling) 11
stop, lacrosse stick 115
stop, spinning cast (angling) 12
stopboard/toeboard, shot putting sector (track and field) 181
stopper/center back, soccer formations 156
stops, parallel bars (gymnastics) 96
stopwatch, eventing (equestrian events) 64
stopwatch, track and field 189
storage compartment/ice chest, bass boat 13
storage/hanging locker, motoryacht hull 205
storm jibs, yachting 200
stove, cruising sailboat (yachting) 208
straddle/roll, high-jump (track and field) 185
straight ball, bowling 38
straight left, boxing punch 43
straight-line course, drag racing 20
straight position, diving 56
straightaway, luge 118
straightaway, track and field 173
straightaways, Formula One racecourse (air racing) 4
stranglehold, judo (martial arts) 123
strap, scuba diver (diving/spear fishing) 58
strap rings, gymnastics 94
strap/wrist thong, racquetball racquet 136
straps, baseball catcher's equipment 26
straps, western saddle (rodeo) 137
strategies & punches, boxing 43
streamer/wet fly, angling 11
street tire, motorcycle 130
strength maneuver/pullout, rings (gymnastics) 94
strength start/press to handstand, parallel bars (gymnastics) 96
stretch calf, polo breeches 135
stretch-knit back, handball glove 99
stretch position/set position, pitching (baseball) 28
stretch trousers, gymnast 93
stretcher, rowing shell 142
stretcher, scull (rowing) 141
stretcher string, volleyball net 191
stride, pitcher's full wind-up (baseball) 28
stride, pitcher's stretch position (baseball) 28
stride, softball pitcher's delivery 158
strike, baseball 24
strike, bowling 38
strike/mark, bowling 39
strike/out, baseball umpire's signal 29
strike pocket/pocket, bowling 39
strike zone, baseball 25, 26
striker, croquet 49
strikers, cricket 47
strikers, soccer formations 156
strikes, in fishing 8, 206
striking arms, fighting chair (angling) 15

striking band, curling stone 50
striking points, martial arts 126
striking the fish, angling 8
striking zone, angling 14
string, polo 135
strings, badminton racket 23
strings, racquetball racquet 136
strings, squash racquets 160
strings, tennis racket 169
strip bait, angling 14
strip/piste/mat, fencing 66
stripe/band, Gaelic football sweater 81
stripe/band, hurling sweater 106
stroke, golf 82
stroke, rowing crew 142
strokes, tennis 171
strong side, football formation 76
strong side/tight side, football 77
strut, race car suspension 17
strut, unlimited hydroplane (yachting) 204
struts, motoryacht hull 205
stud book, dog racing 59
'stutz'/change of direction, parallel bars routine (gymnastics) 96
style judges, Nordic skiing 153
submerging, water polo foul 192
submersible watch/diver's watch/diver timer, scuba diver 58
substitute box area/midcourt, basketball court 30
substitutes, water polo field 192
'subway ball return'/ball return capping, bowling lane 38
sudden-death chukker, polo 134
sudden-death overtime, ice hockey 108
suicide squads, football 76
suit (see also costume, uniform)
suit, automobile racing 20
suit, bobsled 34
suit, bodybuilding 37
suit, luge 118
suit, ski jumper 153
suit, swimming 163
sumo wrestling 198
sun visor, motocross rider 131
sunken seat, luge 118
supercharger, dragster 21
superkarts, karting 114
support bar/wing strut, dragster 21
support belt/kidney protection belt, luge 118
support position, parallel bars routine (gymnastics) 96
support post, table tennis net 166
support unit, basketball column 30
support/wing strut, race car 17
supports, pole vault (track and field) 186
supports/support beams, luge track 118
surf fishing/surfcasting 14
surf leash/shock cord, surfing 161
surface anatomy, bodybuilder 37
surface tension waves, swimming 163
surface trolling, angling 13
surfboard/board, surfing 161
surfcasting rig, angling 14
surfing 161
surgeon's knot, angling 10
surgical tubing, deep trolling rig (angling) 13
suspenders, gymnast 93
suspenders, harness horse racing 103
suspension air tank, motocross bike 129

suspension cord/tension cord, table tennis net 166
suspension/front axle, dragster 21
suspension line/shroud line, sky diving parachute (aerial sports) 7
suspension rope, ballooning 5
suspension strut, race car 17
swallowtail jacket/formal jacket, dressage turnout (equestrian events) 63
swan dive, diving 57
sweat pants, sparring equipment (boxing) 42
sweat sock, boxer 41
sweatband/headband, court handball player 99
sweatband/headband, racquetball 136
sweater, cricket 47
sweater/jersey, Gaelic football 81
sweater/jersey, hurling 106
sweatshirt, sparring equipment (boxing) 42
sweep, sweep rowing 142
sweep-rowing technique 142
sweeper, curling broom 50
sweeper/center back/librero, soccer formations 156
sweepers, curling 50
sweeping score line, curling 50
sweeps/sweepstakes, horse racing 102
sweet spot, golf wood 85
sweet spot, tennis racket 169
'sweet spot'/head center, table tennis paddle 166
sweet spot/'meat,' baseball bat 26
swim ladder, motoryacht hull 205
swim platform, competition fishing boat 206
swim platform, motoryacht hull 205
swimming 162–164
swing, batting (baseball) 27
swing, golf 82
swing and rock back, pole vaulting technique (track and field) 186
swing arm, motocross bike 129
swing arm bolt, motorcycle 130
swinging/batting/hitting, baseball 27
swinging part/drop to underbar somersault, parallel bars routine (gymnastics) 96
swinging part/handstand, rings (gymnastics) 94
switch, wrestling 198
swivel, hammer (track and field) 183
swivel head assembly & sideplate, downrigger (angling) 13
swivel-head pulley wheel, downrigger (angling) 13
swivel/kick, pitcher's full wind-up (baseball) 28
swivel mount, pistol-shooting range 145
swivels, angling rigs 14
symmetry, bodybuilding 36
synchro, synchronized swimming 162

T-handle/lock, horse (gymnastics) 92
T-piece, badminton racket 23
tab closure, handball glove 99
table point, ski jumping 153
table tennis/ping pong 166, 167
tachometer, Formula One aircraft cockpit (air racing) 4
tachometer, motorcycle 130
tachometer, race car 19

tachometers, competition fishing boat 207
tack, mainsail (yachting) 200
tacking, yachting 208
tackle box, angling 9
tackle cabinet, competition fishing boat 207
tackle/gear/fishing equipment, tackle box 9
tackled, rugby 143
tackles, football formation 76
tackling, soccer officials' signal 157
taco, jai alai cesta 113
tactician, yacht-racing crew 199
tag/tinsel body, wet fly/streamer (angling) 11
tagged, angling 8
tagging a fish 8, 206
tail, dry fly (angling) 11
tail, fish 9
tail, polo pony 134
tail, race car 22
tail, ski 152
tail, surfboard 161
tail, water ski 193
tail fin/caudal fin, fish 9
tail/kicktail, skateboard 149
tail light, motorcycle 130
tail plate/back sideplate, fly reel (angling) 11
tail rocker, water ski 193
tail side/whip stall, aerobatics (aerial sports) 3
tail/skirt, spinner (angling) 12
take off, diving 55
take-off, high-jump straddle (track and field) 185
take-off, long-jumping technique (track and field) 184
take-off, pole vaulting technique (track and field) 186
take-off, vaulting (gymnastics) 92
take-off board, jumping area (track and field) 184
take-off line, jumping area (track and field) 184
take-off point/lip, ski jumping 153
take-off point, water skiing 193
take-off position, ski jumping 153
take signal from catcher, pitcher's full wind-up (baseball) 28
take signal from catcher, pitcher's stretch position (baseball) 28
takedown, wrestling 196, 197
taken, angling 8
takes the bait, angling 8
tango hold, ice dancing (figure skating) 74
tank/diving pool 54
tank suit/one-piece swimming 163
tank top/T-shirt, amateur boxer 41
tanto randori, aikido (martial arts) 124
tape, baseball bat 26
tape, ice hockey stick 110
tape, table tennis 166
tape, tape measure (track and field) 189
tape, tennis court 169
tape, tennis racket 169
tape/calibrated tape, lawn bowling 117
tape/finish tape, sprints finish line (track and field) 174
tape handling, lawn bowling 117
tape measure, track and field 189

taped handle, field hockey stick 69
taper, fishing rod 10
tapping out, judo (martial arts) 123
tare/apron, kendo (martial arts) 128
target, archery 16
target, pistol shooting 145
target, shooting range 145
target area, sky diving (aerial sports) 7
target area/house, curling 50
target areas/valid hit areas, fencing 67
target arrow, archery 16
target arrows/spots/markers, bowling lane 38
target board/prone targets, biathlon 154
target circle, sky diving (aerial sports) 7
target crossing point, skeet shooting 144
target disk, sky diving (aerial sports) 7
target face, archery 16
target frames, pistol-shooting range 145
target line, swimming 163
target number, pistol-shooting range 145
target pistol, shooting 145
target trajectory, trapshooting range 146
target turner, firing station (pistol shooting) 145
targets, biathlon rifle shooting 154
targets/clays/birds/pigeons, skeet and trapshooting 146
tarp/infield cover, baseball field 25
tattoo numbers, dog racing bertillion card 60
TD, football 78
team challenges, sports car racing 22
team/club insignia, soccer jersey 155
team handball 100
team handicap, polo 135
team logo, baseball batting helmet 26
team number/post position, jai alai 113
team relay races, speed skating 159
team roping, rodeo 138
team roping rope, rodeo 138
team shirt, polo player 134
technical foul, basketball officials' signal 32
technical knockout/TKO, boxing match 41, 42
technical merit, freestyle figure skating 72
tee, curling 50
tee, golf 82, 84
tee markers, golf 82
tee-shirt, court handball player 99
teeing area 82
teeth/toepicks/notches, figure skate 71
telemark landing position, ski jumping 153
telescopic sights, rifle shooting 144
telescoping tiller extension, yachting 203
telltale/tin/board, squash racquets court 160
temperature gauge, Formula One aircraft cockpit (air racing) 4
temperature select knob, Formula One aircraft cockpit (air racing) 4
temple, martial arts striking point 126
ten-meter platforms/highboards, diving pool 54
ten-off square/minus square, shuffleboard court 148
ten-pin/widow, bowling 39
tendon guard, ice hockey skate 108
tennis 168–172
tennis, types of serve 170

tennis ball 169
tennis court 168, 169
tennis racket 169
tension adjustment knob, table tennis net 166
tension bar, motocross bike 129
terminal tackle, angling 14
test, dressage (equestrian events) 63
tether block, ballooning basket 5
tether lines, ballooning 5
Texas Leaguer/bloop hit area, baseball slang 25
thermals, gliding (aerial sports) 6
thigh, bodybuilder 36
thigh pad, football equipment 79
thigh protector, cricket 47
thimble, harness horse racing 103
third base, baseball field 25
third baseman, baseball player position 25
third man, cricket position 48
third man, relays (track and field) 175
thirty three banked turns, cycling velodrome 52
Thoroughbred and Quarter horse racing 101, 102
Thoroughbred and Quarter horse starting gate/'post' 101
three, figure skating 71
three-day event, equestrian events 61
three-meter platform, diving pool 54
three-meter springboard, diving pool 54
three pin, bowling 39
three-point field goal attempts, basketball officials' signal 32
three-point line, basketball court 30
three-point stance/lineman's stance, football 75
three-quarter backs, rugby scrummage formation 143
three-quarter nelson, wrestling 198
three-second lane/free throw lane/key/'paint,' basketball court 30
three-way swivel, surf fishing rig (angling) 13
throat, canoe paddle 44
throat, fishhook 9
throat, lacrosse stick 115
throat, tennis racket 169
throat lash, dressage bridle (equestrian events) 63
throat protector/'stevie,' baseball catcher's equipment 26
throat, squash racquets 160
throatneck, table tennis paddle 66
throttle, motocross bike 129
throttle, motorcycle 130
throttle cable, motocross bike 129
throttle/gas pedal, kart 114
throttleman, powerboat offshore crew (yachting) 204
throttleman's station, powerboat command console (yachting) 204
throttles, powerboat command console (yachting) 204
throw, darts 53
throw in, soccer 156
throwing sector, discus & hammer cage (track and field) 182
throwing sector, javelin (track and field) 180
throwing technique, discus (track and field) 182

throwing technique, hammer (track and field) 183
throwing technique, javelin (track and field) 180
'throws in the towel,' boxing match 41
thrust, fencing 67
thrust/extension of weapon arm, fencing 67
thumb, baseball glove 26
thumb hole, bowling ball 38
thunderboats, powerboat racing (yachting) 204
tie, western saddle (rodeo) 137
tie-breaker, court handball 99
tie-down, rodeo horse 138
tie rod, kart 114
tie up/clinch, boxing strategy 43
tie ups, wrestling 197
tiger-mouth hand, martial arts fighting 127
tight side/strong side, football 77
tights, figure skating 71
tiller, iceboating 107
tiller, yachting 202
tiller crossarm, yachting 203
time out, basketball officials' signal 32
time out, football officials' signal 80
time out/foul, baseball umpire's signal 29
time remaining on shot clock, basketball officials' signal 32
time trials, cycling 51
timekeeper, boxing 41
timekeeper, speed skating 159
timekeeper and scorer's box, ice hockey rink 108
timepiece, yachting 205
timer, sculling heat (rowing) 141
timer, track and field equipment 189
timing clock/platform clock, weightlifting 195
tinsel body/tag, wet fly/streamer (angling) 11
tip, Alpine ski pole 150
tip, fly rod (angling) 11
tip, ski 152
tip, water ski 193
tip/button/point/end, fencing sword 65
tip guard, spear gun (spear fishing) 58
tip in, basketball 31
tip-top, fly rod (angling) 11
tip-top, spinning rod (angling) 12
tire, (flat) horse-racing starting gate 101
tire, harness horse racing 103
tire, track racing bicycle 52
tire changer/wheel changer, automobile racing pit crew 19
tire/racing slick, dragster 21
tire/racing slick, kart 114
tire/wheel, biplane (aerial sports–aerobatics) 2
title bouts, boxing 41
toe, golf wood 85
toe, shotgun (skeet and trapshooting) 146
toe bar, water ski 193
toe board/arc/foul line/scratch line, javelin throwing sector (track and field) 180
toe box, running shoe (track and field) 178
toe calk, horseshoes 105
toe cap, ice hockey skate 108
toe clamp, cross country skiing 154

toe clip, road racing bicycle 51
toe cup, ski binding 152
toe cup/toe box, roller skate 140
toe piece, ski binding 152
toe-piece release setting indicator, ski binding 152
toe pin holes, cross country skier's racing boot 154
toe stanchion, skate 159
toe stop, roller skate 140
toe strap, road racing bicycle 51
toenail color, dog racing bertillion card 60
toepicks/teeth/notches, figure skate 71
toepiece, water ski 193
toerail, motoryacht deck 205
togs, hurling 106
togs/knicks, Gaelic football 81
toilet/MSD/marine sanitation device, motoryacht hull 205
tongue, fencing mask 65
tongue, ice hockey skate 108
tongue, roller skate 140
tongue, running shoe (track and field) 178
tongue, skate 159
tongue, ski boot 152
tongue attachment, ice hockey skate 108
tools, fishing tackle box 9
top bar, horizontal bar (gymnastics) 95
top bar/gate bar, hurdle (track and field) 176
top bar rail, uneven parallel bars (gymnastics) 97
top cable, volleyball net 191
top cuff, golf bag 84
top hat, dressage turnout (equestrian events) 63
top lip, lacrosse 115
top ring/end ring, spinning rod (angling) 12
top tube/cross bar, track racing bicycle 52
topping lift, cruising sailboat (yachting) 208
topspin, tennis 172
tori, aikido (martial arts) 124
tornada class, catamaran (yachting) 203
toss, tennis serve 170
totals/runs, hits, errors for game, baseball scoreboard 27
tote board/betting board, horse-racing track 101
tote board/odds board, horse racing 102
touch line, rugby field 143
touch line, team handball 100
touch line/side boards/side line, polo ground 134
touchdown, football 78
touchers, lawn bowling 117
touches, fencing 67
touchline/sideline, soccer field 156
tournament color tape, wrestling mat 196
tournament darts 53
tow hook release spring, glider cockpit (aerial sports) 6
tow pin, dragster 21
tow release knob, glider cockpit (aerial sports) 6
towel, sparring equipment (boxing) 42
tower, diving pool 54
tower, ski jumping 153

tower bimini, competition fishing boat 207
tower controls, competition fishing boat 206
tower platform/tower deck, competition fishing boat 206
tower stanchion, competition fishing boat 206
tower/tuna tower, competition fishing boat 207
towline/ski rope, water skier 193
traces/tracing, figure skating 71
track, automobile racing 18, 20, 22
track, cycling velodrome 52
track, luge 118
track, rabbit (dog racing) 59
track, scull (rowing) 141
track, ski jumping 153
track, speed skating 159
track and field 173–189
track bike, cycling 52
track condition, past performance chart (horse racing) 103
track/course, dog racing 59
track/drag strip/dragway, drag racing 20
track meets, track and field 173
track secretary, horse racing 102
track shoes, scull (rowing) 141
track/skating surface, speed (roller) skating 140
track/trail, cross country skiing 154
tracking/grooves, ski jumping 153
trademark/label, baseball bat 26
traffic line/barrier/railing, speed (roller) skating 140
trail leg, high-jump straddle (track and field) 185
trail rope, ballooning 5
trailing leg, hurdling technique (track and field) 176
trailing leg, steeplechase (track and field) 177
trainer, dog racing 60
trainer, fighter's corner (boxing) 42
trainer, horse-racing program entry 103
trainer, past performance chart (horse racing) 103
trajectories, skeet and trapshooting ranges 147, 148
trampoline, yachting 203
transition curve, ski jumping 153
transitions, dressage (equestrian events) 63
transom, cruising sailboat (yachting) 208
transom door/gate, competition fishing boat 206
trap, trap and skeet shooting range 147
trap house/low house, skeet shooting range 147
trap number, dog racing 59
trap release/pulling mechanism, trapshooting 146
trap/skeet & trap machine, shooting 147
trap window, skeet shooting range 147
trapeze handle/grip, yachting 203
trapeze securing wire, yachting 203
trapezius muscle, bodybuilder 36
traphouse, trapshooting 146
trapping a soccer ball 157
trapshooting 146
trapshooting range, shooting 146
trapshooting range 146

travel set, angling 12
traveler control, yachting 203
traveling, basketball officials' signal 32
travels, gymnastics 93
treble hook, plug (angling) 12
tree/frame, polo saddle 134
trench shooting/trapshooting 146
trenches, football 77
tri-radial/spinnaker, yachting 200
triceps muscle, bodybuilder 36
trick skiing, water skiing 193
tricks, gymnastics 88
trifecta, bet (horse racing) 103
trigger, shotgun (skeet and trapshooting) 146
trigger, target pistol 145
trigger, water ski 193
trigger guard, shotgun (skeet and trapshooting) 146
trigger mechanisms, spear gun (spear fishing) 58
trigger stop, target pistol 145
trim, baseball pants 26
trim, fencing mask 65
trim, running shoe (track and field) 178
trim tabs, competition fishing boat 207
trim tape/binding, tennis racket 169
triple, baseball 25
triple bars/staircase, equestrian show jumping fence 62
triple bogey, golf 86
triple jump/hop, step and jump, track and field 184
triple jump takeoff, jumping area (track and field) 184
triple ring/triple-score ring, dart board 53
tripping, field hockey 69
tripping, football officials' signal 80
tripping, ice hockey officials' signal 111
tripping, soccer foul 157
trips, wrestling 198
trolling, angling 13
trolling motor, bass boat 13
trolling reel, angling 13
trophies 209
trot, dressage (equestrian events) 63
trotters, horse racing 104
trotting and pacing gaits, harness horse racing 104
trough, wave (surfing) 161
trousers, jai alai 113
trousers/knickers/pantaloons, fencer 65
truck, roller skate 140
truck, skateboard 149
truck bolt/king pin/action bolt, roller skate 140
true drive, golf 85
trunk, fish 9
trunk development/upper body development, bodybuilder 37
trunks, boxer 41
trunks, speed (roller) skating 140
trunks/shorts/pants, lacrosse 116
try, rugby 143
try line/goal line, rugby field 143
tube, skate 159
tube lure, umbrella rig (angling) 13
tube/pipeline, wave (surfing) 161
'tubing,' surfing 161
tuck, synchronized swimming position 162

tuck position, diving 56
tuck position, parallel bars routine (gymnastics) 96
tug, gliding (aerial sports) 6
tumbling, gymnastics 88, 89
tumbling movement/cartwheel, balance beam (gymnastics) 98
tunnel, track and field 173
tunnel entrance, cycling velodrome 52
turbocharger, race car 17
turbocharger popoff valve, race car 17
turbocharger wastegate, race car 17
turf, baseball slang 25
turf course & steeplechase course, horse-racing track 101
turf/field, polo 134
turn, shot putting technique (track and field) 181
turn, swimming 163
turn, track and field 173
turn and slip indicator, glider cockpit (aerial sports) 6
turn/pivot/spin/rotation, discus throwing technique (track and field) 182
turn signal, motorcycle 130
turnbuckle, boxing ring 41
turnbuckle, cruising sailboat (yachting) 208
turnbuckle, yachting 203
turning buoys, kayaking racecourse 45
turning buoys, slalom course (water skiing) 193
turning light, motorcycle 130
turnout, horse and rider in dressage (equestrian events) 63
turns, freestyle figure skating 72, 73
twenty-four-second clock/shot clock, basketball 30
twenty-point must system, amateur boxing 42
twist, tennis serve 170
twist dive 57
two-finger spear hand, martial arts fighting 127
two-hand snatch/snatch, weightlifting 194, 195
two-hundred-meter, heptathlon (track and field) 188
two-meter man/hole man/setter, shot on water polo goal 192
two pin, bowling 39
two-point conversion, football 78
two-way swivel, surf fishing rigs 14

Uke, aikido (martial arts) 124
umbrella, golf bag & club set 84
umbrella rig, angling 13
umpire, baseball 29
umpire, cricket ground & pitch 48
umpire, football officials 80
umpire/chair umpire, tennis–center court 168
umpire signals, cricket 48
umpires, polo 134, 135
umpires/judges, tennis–center court 168
unanimous decision, boxing match 41
unavoidable hinders, racquetball 136
unbalancing zone/pre-attack zone 168
underarm protector, fencing equipment 65
undercut/cut, pommel horse routine (gymnastics) 93

underserve line/fault line, jai alai cancha 113
undershirt, baseball 26
underwater hockey, breathhold diving game 58
unemployed leg/free leg, figure skating 71
uneven parallel bars/asymmetrical bars, gymnastics 97
unfair tackle from behind, soccer officials' signal 157
uniform (see also costume, suit)
uniform, automobile racing pit crew 19
uniform, football 79
uniform, Gaelic football 81
uniform, wrestling 196
uniform jersey, football uniform 79
uniform shirt/blouse, baseball player 26
uniforms, baseball 26
universal joint, sailboard (yachting) 201
unlimited-class races, motorcycling 130
unlimited hydroplane, powerboat racing (yachting) 204
unsportsmanlike conduct, ice hockey officials' signal 111
upfield, football 77
upper back, martial arts striking point 126
upper body development, bodybuilder 37
upper deck, automobile racetrack 18
upper helm station, motoryacht deck 205
upper jaw, fish 9
upper limb, archery bow 16
upper panel, ice hockey skate 108
upper stitching, curling broom 50
upper wing, biplane (aerial sports–aerobatics) 2
uppercut, boxing punch 43
uppers, running shoe (track and field) 178
upright, croquet wicket 49
upright, football goal 75
upright, horizontal bar (gymnastics) 95
upright, parallel bars (gymnastics) 96
upright, steeplechase dry hurdle (track and field) 177
upright, vaulting horse (gymnastics) 92
upright, volleyball net 191
upright/column/stanchion, basketball 30
upright/goal post, soccer 155
upright handlebars, track racing bicycle 52
upright position, balance beam (gymnastics) 98
upright position, sprints (track and field) 174
upright/standard, high-jumping area (track and field) 185
upright/standard, pole vault (track and field) 186
uprights, equestrian show jumping fences 62
uprights/goal/goalposts, football 75
upshot, archery 16
upstairs/attic/belfry, boxing slang 42
upstream gate, whitewater slalom (canoeing & kayaking) 46
upward thrust/upsweep, relays baton handoff (track and field) 175
using a fighting chair, angling 15

V-shaped monohulls, powerboat racing (yachting) 204

valid hits, fencing 67
valid light (green/red), fencing strip 66
valve, football 75
valve, Gaelic football 81
valve cover & head/exhaust header, dragster 21
valve line, ballooning 5
vamp, running shoe (track and field) 178
vanes/fletching/featherrs, target arrow (archery) 16
variometer, glider cockpit (aerial sports) 6
variweight, archery bow 16
vastus externas, martial arts striking point 126
vault box/planting box/box, pole vault (track and field) 186
vaulting, gymnastics 92
vaulting board, gymnastics springboard 92
vaulting pole, track and field 186
vaulting technique, pole vault (track and field) 186
vaults with turns, gymnastics 92
velcro fastener/adjustable tab closure, handball glove 99
velodrome/racing track, cycling 52
vent, scuba diver (diving/spear fishing) 58
vent closure, ballooning 5
vent port, drag racing fire suit 20
venter/belly, fish 9
ventilation holes, cycle racing shoe 51
ventilation holes, golf glove 84
ventilation holes, handball glove 99
ventral fins/pelvic fins, fish 9
venturi windshield, competition fishing boat 206
vertical, synchronized swimming position 162
vertical eight, aerobatics (aerial sports) 2
vertical event, skateboarding 149
vertical half roll, aerobatics (aerial sports) 2
vertical speed indicator, glider cockpit (aerial sports) 6
vertical stabilizer, biplane (aerial sports–aerobatics) 2
vertical stabilizer, glider (aerial sports) 6
vest pockets, flyfisherman 10
vetters, orienteering 132
video display screen/screen, bowling console 39
visiting team, baseball scoreboard 27
visor/face shield, luge 118
volley, court handball 99
volley & overhead zone/knockout zone, tennis 171
volley, tennis stroke 171
volleyball 190, 191
volleying, table tennis 166
volte, dressage figure (equestrian events) 63
voltmeter, competition fishing boat 207
vorlage position, ski jumping 153

Waders, flyfisherman 10
wading shoes/brogues, flyfisherman 10
waist, ski 152
waiting line, archery fields 16
walk, baseball 25
walk, dressage (equestrian events) 63

walkway, horseshoes 105
wall/ditch, lawn bowling 117
wall/fence, baseball field 25
wall/shoulder, wave (surfing) 161
walls, court handball 99
walls, jai alai cancha 113
walls, racquetball court 136
walls, squash racquets court 160
waltz hold, ice dancing (figure skating) 74
warm-up area/infield, cycling velodrome 52
warm-up boards/practice boards, diving pool 54
warm-up room, bodybuilding 37
warming rooms, ski jumping 153
warning track, baseball field 25
wash hanging, canoeing maneuver 45
wash lane, Olympic swimming pool 163
wash-out, ice hockey officials' signal 111
washboard/gunwale, scull (rowing) 141
water barrel, drag strip 20
water bottle holder, road racing bicycle 51
water buckets, fighter's corner (boxing) 42
water hazard, golf course 82
water hook, harness horse racing 103
water jump, equestrian show jumping fences 62
water jump, steeplechase (track and field) 177
water polo 192
water ski helmet 193
water ski/slalom ski, water skiing 193
water skiing 193
water surface/surf, angling 14
water temperature gauge, competition fishing boat 207
water temperature gauge, race car 19
water vents, dragster 21
waves, swimming 163
waza ari, karate (martial arts) 121
weak side, football formation 76
weak side/split side, football 77
weapon hand, fencing 67
webbing, baseball glove 26
webbing, fighting chair harness (angling) 15
webbing, football equipment 79
webs/leathers, racehorse 102
wedge, golf club 85
weight, curling 50
weight, on weightlifting attempt board 195
weight, spinner (angling) 12
weight belt, scuba diver (diving/spear fishing) 58
weight carried, past performance chart (horse racing) 103
weight divisions, boxing 43
weight/sinker/split shot, basic fishing rig 9
weightlifter/lifter 194, 195
weightlifting belt 195
weightlifting costume/singlet 195
weightlifting shoe/boot 195
weightlifting 194, 195
well/fork, western saddle (rodeo) 137
welping date, dog racing 60
welterweights, boxing 43
welting, baseball glove 26
western saddle/stock saddle, rodeo 137

'wet boot'/foot binding, water ski 193
wet fly/streamer, angling 11
wet suit, water skier 193
wet-suit jacket, scuba diver (diving/spear fishing) 58
wet-suit pants, scuba diver (diving/spear fishing) 58
wetsuit, surfer 161
wheel, competition fishing boat 206, 207
wheel, cruising sailboat (yachting) 208
wheel, kart 114
wheel, powerboat command console (yachting) 204
wheel, roller skate 140
wheel, skateboard 149
wheel cover, race car 17
wheel fence, automobile racetrack 18
wheel hub/steering hub, race car 19
wheel pants, biplane (aerial sports–aerobatics) 2
wheel/tire, biplane (aerial sports–aerobatics) 2
wheelchanger, automobile racing pit crew 19
wheeled carriage, dog racing rabbit 59
whelping date/date of birth, dog racing 60
whiff, golf 86
whip, harness horse racing 103
whip/bat/crop/stick, horse racing 102
whip/crop, eventing (equestrian events) 64
whip stall/tail side, aerobatics (aerial sports) 3
whipcrack, javelin (track and field) 180
whipping, golf wood 85
white cap, water polo equipment 192
white flannels, cricket 47
white tees/regulation play tees, golf 82
whitewater canoe races 46
whoops, motocross track 131
wicket, cricket 47, 48
wicket/hoop, croquet 49
wicket keeper, cricket pitch 48
wicketkeeper, cricket 47
wicketkeeper's gloves, cricket 47
wide out/wide receiver/split end, football formation 76
wide receiver/split end/wide out, football formation 76
widow/ten pin, bowling 39
wild-cow milking, rodeo 137
wild-horse racing, rodeo 137
win, place, show (horse racing) 103
win, place and show payoff prices, jai alai scoreboard/betting board 112
winches, cruising sailboat (yachting) 208
wind, Olympic yacht-racing course 199
wind direction, iceboating course 107
wind direction indicator, competition fishing boat 206
wind indicator, track and field 189
wind speed, wind indicator (track and field) 189
wind to competitor's back, wind indicator (track and field) 189
wind-up, pitcher (baseball) 28
wind-up arm/reel & locking device, tape measure (track and field) 189
winding check, fly rod (angling) 11
winding/wind, spinning rod (angling) 12
windlass, competition fishing boat 206

windmill, softball pitcher's delivery 158
window, ballooning basket 5
window, iceboating 107
window, sailboard (yachting) 201
windpipe, martial arts striking point 126
windscreen, race car 17
windshield, motoryacht deck 205
windshield wipers, sports car 22
windsock, automobile racetrack 18
windsock pole, automobile racetrack 18
windward-leeward courses, iceboating 107
windward/leeward legs, yachting 199
windward mark, iceboating course 107
windward mark, Olympic yacht-racing course 199
wing, baseball catcher's equipment 26
wing, dry fly (angling) 11
wing, field hockey 68
wing, ice hockey 110
wing area, lacrosse field 115
wing/rear spoiler, race car 17
wing/spoiler, race car 22
wing/stabilizer, unlimited hydroplane (yachting) 204
wing strut/support, race car 17
wing strut/support bar, dragster 21
wingnut unit, weightlifting international standard barbell collar 195
Wingover, aerobatics (aerial sports) 2
wings, rugby scrummage formation 143
wings, soccer formations 156
wings, team handball 100
wings, wrestling 198
wingspan, air racing 4
winner of round, boxing scorecard 41
wire, hammer (track and field) 183
wire eye bolt, fishing bait cage 9
'wire'/finish line, horse-racing track 101
wire leader, surfcasting rig (angling) 14
wire line, angling 13
wire mesh, fencing mask 65
wire-mesh screen, platform tennis 133
wire run down, curling broom 50
wire shaft, spinner (angling) 12
wireman, competition fishing boat 206, 207
wishbone, spear gun (spear fishing) 58
wishbone/boom, sailboard (yachting) 201
women's archery field 16
wood, jai alai cancha 113
wood, table tennis paddle 166
wood/bowl, lawn bowling 117
woods, golf clubs 84, 85
working jibs yachting 200
working surface, balance beam gymnastics 98
world record, on weightlifting attempt board 195
world record catches, angling 8
wrapper/bandages, boxing slang 42
wrestling 196–198
wrestling boots/shoes 196
wrestling mat 196
wrestling shorts/uniform/costume 196
wrestling tights/uniform/costume 196
wrist flex, bodybuilder 36
wrist flex, fencing 67
wrist pad, ice hockey goalkeeper's catch glove 110
wrist strap/keeper, platform tennis paddle 133

wrist thong/strap, racquetball racquet
    136
wrist wrap, rings (gymnastics) 94
wrist wraps, weightlifting 194
wristband, racquetball 136
wristband, soccer player 155
wristpad, lacrosse glove 115
wu shu/kempo/kung fu, martial arts 125

X, strike in bowling 38, 39
X-defense, team handball 100

Yachting 199–208
yard lines, archery fields 16
yard lines, field hockey pitch 68
yard lines, football field 76
yard lines, Gaelic football 81
yard lines, hurling 106
yard lines, polo ground 134
yard lines, pool (swimming) 163
yard lines, rugby field 143
yard lines, soccer field 156
year of birth, horse-racing program
    entry 103
yellow flag, automobile racing 17
yellow (30 seconds remaining), on field
    event timer (track and field) 189

Zanshin, karate (martial arts) 122
zink, motoryacht hull 205
zipper, speed skater 159
zone defenses, basketball 33
zone marking/blue line, ice hockey rink
    108
zones, court handball 99
zones, fencing strip 66
zones, football field 76, 77
zones, relays (track and field) 175
zones, tennis 171
zoomies/headers, dragster 21

ACKNOWLEDGEMENTS

1–2, Christen Industries, Inc.; 5, Raven Industries; 9, Oberlin Canteen Company, Wisconsin Division of Tourism; 11, Orvis Company, Martin Reel Company, Don Zahner, A.J. McClaine; 12, Martin Reel Company; 13, Shakespeare Company, S&K Products, Inc.; 15, Murray Brothers, Rosemary Murray; 16, National Archery Association, Easton Aluminum, Inc., Kathy O'Brien; 17, Deke Holgate Enterprises, Penzoil Products Company; 18–19, Indianapolis Motor Speedway; 20–21, Les Lovett, National Hot Rod Association, Deke Houlgate Enterprises, Ron McQueen; 22, Wayne Baker; 23, U.S. Badminton Association, Carlton Corporation; 26, Rawlings, Adirondack; 27, Tony Ferrara; 34, Tip Sempliner, Chelsea Designs; 35, International Bocce Association; 36–37, Kerri Keenan; 38, Brunswick Corporation, Murray Lanes; 40–43, Caesars Palace, Tuf-Wear Company, U.S.A. Amateur Boxing Federation, Madison Square Garden; 50, Air Canada; 53, Sportcraft, Larry Gazley, The Dart Store; 58, The A.B. Biller Company; 59–60, American Greyhound Track Association; 63-64, American Horse Shows Association; 68, Sportcraft, India Press Information Bureau; 75, 79, James Ramey; New York Jets; 82, Professional Golfer's Association, Kathy Gallagher; 84, Champion, Colombia, Titalist; 86, Professional Golfer's Association; 88, Brenda Bernhardt Frasca, Manhattan Gymnastic Center, NYC; 90, A.B. Fredericks; 91–95, Nissen; 98, Fuji Film, Dave Black; 99, U.S. Handball Association, Saranac Gloves; 100, Peter Bruehning, U.S. Handball Team Association; 101, Churchill Downs, Ruidoso Downs; 102, Meadowlands Racetrack, Ruidoso Sunland, Dick Alwan; 104, Meadowlands Racetrack; 105, Sportcraft; 106, Irish Press; 112, Dania Jai Alai; 113, Milford Jai Alai; 114, International Kart Federation, Doug Stokes, Cartman Company; 115, STX Company; 117, Henselite Company, Australian Tourist Bureau; 119–128, World Taekwondo Academy, Loren Lalli, Japan National Tourist Organization, Japan Air Lines, Noburu Kataoka, Linda Sakariasen, John Antonellis, Vincent De Martino, Bobby Troka, Harlan Cary Poe, Andy Nichols; 129–130, Kawasaki; 132, Silva Company, Johnson Camping, Precise International, U.S. Orienteering Federation, Al Smith; 133, U.S. Platform Tennis Association, Jim McNerney, ACE; 134, Polo Magazine, Saddle Shop, Fifth Avenue Polo Imports; 136, Sportcraft; 138, International Professional Rodeo Association; 139–140, U.S. Amateur Confederation of Roller Skating; 148, Susan Koenig; 153–154, Austrian Travel Bureau, Saranac; 155, Chicago Sting, Sgt. Frank Karcher; 158, U.S. Softball Association, Kathy Aronson, DeBeer; 160, AMF/Voit; 161, Surfing Magazine; 166–167, U.S. Table Tennis Association, Malcolm Anderson, Martin Kilpatrick, Table Tennis Company, Michigan Ladder Company; 168, British Tourist Authority; 171–172, Virginia Slims; 174, Cramer Moore; 178, Converse, Northwestern University; 180–181, Adidas; 182, AAE; 185, Adidas; 186, 188, Beth Goodman; Portapit; 189, AAE, Sportcraft, Cronus; 190, Mikasa, U.S. Olympic Volleyball Team; 191, Sports Imports; 192, Porter Equipment Company, U.S. Water Polo Incorporated, Gregory Kincheloe; 193, Connelly; 194–195, U.S. Weightlifting Federation, Harvey Newton; 196–198, Housatonic Valley Regional High School, Michael Thompson, Thomas Breuler; 204, Budweiser.

In addition, the editors would like to acknowledge the contributions of the staff at Hammond, Inc., without whom this book could not possibly have been done. These include, but are certainly not limited to Publisher Hugh Johnson, a friend in difficult times, copy editors extraordinaire Dorothy Bacheller and Sherry Wheaton Wert, and the Mark Resnick Express. We also appreciate the support of Richard Curtis, Richard Curtis Literary Agency.

PHOTO CREDITS

Page 4 Jim Vliet; 6 (bottom) George Uveges, Santa Monica, Calif.; 7 (top left, right) Cos Colgrove, (bottom left) M. Anderson Jenkins, Wittier, Calif.; 8 Burton McNeely; 17 (top) Ron McQueeney; 18 John Gray, Indianapolis Motor Speedway; 19 (top) Ron McQueeney, (bottom) Tom Lucas; 20 Les Lovett; 22 (top) Sheila Hill, (bottom) Rusty Jarett; 23 (bottom) Martin Hoke; 24 Joe DiMaggio, Centerport, NY; 25 (bottom) Al Messerschmidt, Miami Beach, Fla.; 27 (sequential) Globus Brothers/Steve Borowski, New York City, NY, (middle) Betty Suyker, NYC, NY, (bottom) Al Messerschmidt; 28–29 Globus Brothers/Steve Borowski, NYC, NY; 30 (bottom right) Brent Nicastro, Madison, Wis.; 31 (left) Betty Suyker, (right) © Estate of Ben Rose/Courtesy Sol Shamilzadeh, New York City, NY, (bottom right) Brent Nicastro; 32 (left) Brent Nicastro, (right) Betty Suyker; 34 Nancie Battaglia, Lake Placid, New York; 35 Dennis Floss; 36–37 Phillip Stark, New York City, NY; 40 Joe DiMaggio; 41 (top) Al Messerschmidt, (bottom) Bob Davis, Reno, Nevada; 42 (left) Ben Rose, (top right) Al Messerschmidt, (bottom right) Bob Davis; 45 Frank Dallas; 46 James Thresher; 49 (top right) Cliff Johnson, Loxahtchee, Fla.; 50 (lower right) Michael Burns; 51 Brent Nicastro; 52 (right) Robert George/Velo-News, Brattleboro, Vt., (left) Long Photography, Los Angeles, Calif.; 54 (bottom) Joe DiMaggio; 58 (lower right) Reg Bragonier; 62 David Fisher; 63 Bodo Hangan; 65 Globus Brothers/Steve Borowski; 66 (top) Jeff Bukantz, (bottom) Globus Brothers/Steve Borowski; 67 Globus Brothers/Steve Borowski; 69, 70 Eduardo Patino, New York City, NY; 74 Eduardo Patino; 78 Richard Dubin, Tampa, Fla.; 79 (top) David Fisher, (bottom) Richard Dubin; 83 Ben Rose; 87 Ben Rose; 88–89 Globus Brothers/Steve Borowski; 92 Roman Leos, Los Angeles, Calif.; 94 Roman Leos; 96 Roman Leos; 97 Ben Rose; 98 (top) Ben Rose, (bottom left) Roman Leos; 107 Sharon Green; 112 (top) Ben Rose; 114 Doug Stokes; 118 Nancie Battaglia; 119 Ben Rose; 120–121 Globus Brothers/Steve Borowski; 122 Phillip Stark; 123 (top right) Phillip Stark; 124-125 Phillip Stark; 128 (bottom) Globus Brothers/Steve Borowski; 129 (right) Guy Gurney, New York City, NY; 131 Guy Gurney; 132 (top) Al Smith, US Orienteering Federation; 135 (right) Al Messerschmidt; 137 Ginny Southworth, Aiken, South Carolina; 138 (top left) Brent Nicastro, (top center, top right) Ginny Southworth; 139 Ted Kirk; 142 (right) Joe DiMaggio; 143 Brent Nicastro; 145–148 Joe DiMaggio; 149 Bruce Walker, Melbourne, Fla.; 154 (bottom center, bottom right) Nancie Battaglia; 157 (top) Globus Brothers/Steve Borowski; 158 (top) Globus Brothers/Steve Borowski; 160 (right) Robert H. Lehman, New York City, NY; 161 Aaron Chang; 162 Nancy Hines, Santa Clara, Calif.; 163 (top three) Brent Nicastro; 165 (bottom left, top right) Brent Nicastro; 166–167 Malcolm Anderson; 169 (bottom right) Globus Brothers/Steve Borowski; 174 (top) Globus Brothers/Steve Borowski, (middle, right) Brent Nicastro; 177 Rich Clarkson, Denver, Colorado; 178–179 (top) Globus Brothers/Steve Borowski; 180 Al Messerschmidt; 181 Joe DiMaggio; 182 (top left) Joe DiMaggio; 183 Al Messerschmidt; 184 Joe DiMaggio; 186 (bottom) Rich Clarkson; 187 Rich Clarkson; 192 Bud Symes; 194–195 Bruce Klemens, Clifton, New Jersey; 196–198 John Thompson; 199 Guy Gurney; 200 Guy Gurney; 201 Guy Gurney; 204 (top left) Guy Gurney

AFTERWORD

WHAT'S WHAT™ books are designed to provide visual and verbal access to the physical world. At the conclusion of the first volume in this series we invited readers to correspond with us, letting us know where the book proved useful and suggesting improvements and corrections. We were extremely pleased to have received replies from around the world and have attempted to incorporate many of the suggestions into this book. To ensure that WHAT'S WHAT™ IN SPORTS, as well as future volumes in the WHAT'S WHAT™ series, continues to provide accurate information in an entertaining manner, we invite readers of this volume to write us. We would like to know how successfully this book fulfilled your needs and expectations. We would also like to know in what subject areas future volumes in the WHAT'S WHAT™ information series would be most helpful to you. Please correspond with us at:

David Fisher
Reginald Bragonier Jr.
WHAT'S WHAT™ BOOKS
357 West 19th Street
New York, New York
10019